ALICE WALKER

ALSO BY EVELYN C. WHITE

Chain Chain Change:
  For Black Women in Abusive Relationships

The Black Women's Health Book:
  Speaking for Ourselves

ALICE WALKER

A Life

EVELYN C. WHITE

W. W. NORTON & COMPANY

New York • London

For information about permission to reproduce selections from this book, write to
Permissions, W. W. Norton & Company, Inc.
500 Fifth Avenue, New York, NY 10110

Since this page cannot legibly accommodate all the copyright notices, pages
520–521 constitute an extension of the copyright page.

Manufacturing by Maple-Vail Book Manufacturing Group
Book design by Brooke Koven
Production manager: Julia Druskin

Library of Congress Cataloging-in-Publication Data
White, Evelyn C., 1954–
Alice Walker : a life / by Evelyn C. White.— 1st ed.
p. cm.
Includes bibliographical references and index.
ISBN 0-393-05891-3 (hardcover)
1. Walker, Alice, 1944– 2. Authors, American—20th century—Biography.
3. African American authors—Biography. I. Title.
PS3573.A425Z93 2004
813'.54—dc22
2004011513

ISBN 0-393-32826-0 pbk.

W. W. Norton & Company, Inc.
500 Fifth Avenue, New York, N.Y. 10110
www.wwnorton.com

W. W. Norton & Company Ltd.
Castle House, 75/76 Wells Street, London W1T 3QT

2 3 4 5 6 7 8 9 0

For the ancestors

"Ye shall know them by their fruits."
—MATTHEW 7:16

Contents

Part Three / LIFE IS THE AWARD

Prologue

In Service

THE SETTING WAS an elite college near Boston in the early 1990s. Alice Walker was being honored for her literary achievements and, as part of the festivities, was to deliver a luncheon address. By chance, I was in the area and attended the event.

Alice read from and then spoke briefly about her then-just-released novel, *Possessing the Secret of Joy*. She said that the crafting of the saga—which centers on female genital mutilation (FGM)—had taxed her emotionally and drained her creative energy. But ever hopeful, she said, that "one girl born somewhere on the planet" might be spared the circumciser's knife because of her work, Alice allowed that she'd pressed on. Confiding that whenever she read from the novel someone in the audience, inevitably, collapsed, Alice said she was heartened that *Possessing* appeared to have touched a universal pain in humanity.

After the speech, there was a reception at which Alice agreed to take a few questions. The first query came from a middle-aged white woman who identified herself as a college official. As she put it to Alice, "I'm one of the people responsible for bringing you here." The woman went on to say that many of the luncheon guests had been unsettled, if not irreparably offended, by remarks in which Alice made mention (by way of explaining FGM) of the words *vagina* and *clitoris*. Clearly agitated, the woman insisted that her office was soon to receive a deluge of complaints. Galled by Alice's address, some guests, the woman ventured, might refuse to contribute to the college's coffers or, even worse, rescind financial pledges already made. "Just how am I supposed to deal," the woman sniped at Alice, "with all the people who are going to call and complain about your speech?"

With tension having mounted steadily, the air was now sucked out of the room. In Alice's visage, I detected the weariness of generations of black women whose flesh-and-blood vulnerabilities have never been acknowledged; the fatigue of sisters consistently called on to bring moral clarity to whites and to soothe, placate, and otherwise nurture them through myriad calamities.

After several moments of fraught silence, Alice took a deep breath and began to speak. In a voice clear and methodic, she challenged the woman to use her clout to inform the putative complaint callers that most people in the world are not wealthy or white. As impoverished women of color ravaged by imperialism, racism, sexism, and inadequate shelter, education, and health care, the better portion of the earth's inhabitants, Alice schooled her critic, mirrored Tashi, the protagonist of *Possessing the Secret of Joy*. Alice told Miss "I Brought You Here" that people upset by her remarks would be well advised to read her *entire* novel because, in her speech, she'd only touched on a few of the issues necessary for their twenty-first century enlightenment. Then making plain her familiarity with women like the college official and her ilk, Alice noted that, in her experience, many rich people were often tight with their money. As for those who might not want to spend cash on her book, Alice urged the woman to apprise her peers that *Possessing* could be borrowed from any public library. And with that, dear reader, the reception was over.

As a reporter for the *San Francisco Chronicle*, I'd tracked (though never covered) the controversy surrounding *The Color Purple*, the novel for which Alice Walker, in 1983, became the first black woman to win a Pulitzer Prize in fiction. After bearing witness to the exchange at the reception, I understood, immediately, that my task was to chronicle the life of the woman who'd instantly transformed an insult (and a wholly unoriginal one at that) into an impassioned paean to the dispossessed. What was it, I wondered, about Alice and her work that always seemed to generate such intense emotion?

While Alice cooperated fully in my investigation, agreeing to numerous interviews and providing unrestricted access to her papers and files, she did not request manuscript approval. An undiluted champion of artistic freedom, she simply stood steady as a proposed four-year project stretched into nearly a decade. And why the "delay"? I soon realized that in writing about Alice Walker, I was in service to spiritual forces that guided me to people, places, and things that would have otherwise eluded me, no matter how diligent my effort. How else to explain the photo of the menacing Mississippi cops (Alice had once lived in the state) that just happened to be hanging on the wall of an acquaintance I had not seen in twenty years? Or a chance introduction to a woman who, in passing, revealed that she'd attended college with Alice? Or the Yoko Ono poem (relevant beyond measure) that the ancestors delivered one evening as I idly thumbed through a book while waiting for tea water to boil?

And then there were the spirit voices. So many of the ancestors communed with me about Alice. Most profound was the voice that, one day, exhorted me to "tell Lorraine." That would be Lorraine Hansberry. The voice (I've come to believe it was that of James Baldwin) said that the pioneering playwright, dead in 1965 at age thirty-four, would have *enjoyed* Alice Walker. I heartily agree.

I also know that I am a better person for having examined the life of an artist who, as evidenced at the reception, has lived in full possession of herself.

Alice Walker's Family Tree

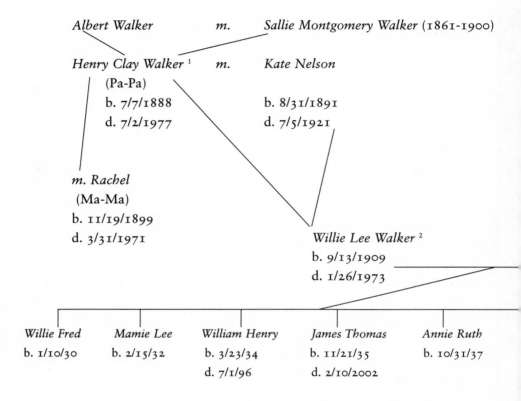

Albert Walker   m.   Sallie Montgomery Walker (1861-1900)

Henry Clay Walker [1]   m.   Kate Nelson
  (Pa-Pa)
  b. 7/7/1888   b. 8/31/1891
  d. 7/2/1977   d. 7/5/1921

m. Rachel
  (Ma-Ma)
  b. 11/19/1899
  d. 3/31/1971   Willie Lee Walker [2]
                                 b. 9/13/1909
                                 d. 1/26/1973

Willie Fred   Mamie Lee   William Henry   James Thomas   Annie Ruth
b. 1/10/30   b. 2/15/32   b. 3/23/34   b. 11/21/35   b. 10/31/37
                                  d. 7/1/96   d. 2/10/2002

1. Henry Walker also had two children, Willa Mae and Annie Julia, by Estella "Shug" Perry

2. Willie Lee's siblings: Sally, Henry, Addie Mae, James

3. Minnie Lou's siblings: Malsenior, Mildred, Willie, Thomas, Ulysses, Nettie, Ruth, Hattie, Essie, Annie Mae, Alice

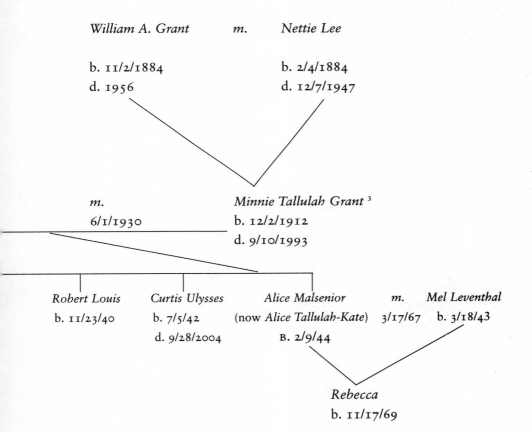

William A. Grant   *m.*   *Nettie Lee*

b. 11/2/1884   b. 2/4/1884
d. 1956   d. 12/7/1947

m.   *Minnie Tallulah Grant* [3]
6/1/1930   b. 12/2/1912
                        d. 9/10/1993

Robert Louis   *Curtis Ulysses*   *Alice Malsenior*   *m.*   *Mel Leventhal*
b. 11/23/40   b. 7/5/42   (now *Alice Tallulah-Kate*)   3/17/67   b. 3/18/43
               d. 9/28/2004   B. 2/9/44

Rebecca
b. 11/17/69

Sisters,
where there is cold silence—
no hallelujahs, no hurrahs at all, no handshakes,
no neon red or blue, no smiling faces—
prevail.
Prevail across the editors of the world!
Who are obsessed, self-honeying and self-crowned
In the seduced arena.

      It has been a
hard trudge, with fainting, bandaging and death.
There have been startling confrontations.
There have been tramplings. Tramplings
of monarchs and of other men.

But there remain large countries in your eyes.
Shrewd sun.
The civil balance.
The listening secrets.

And you create and train your flowers still.

        —"To Black Women" by GWENDOLYN BROOKS

Purple is black blooming.
      —CHRISTOPHER SMART (1722–1771)

PART ONE

Kudzu

1

Georgia, the Whole Day Through

"WHY YOU wanna waste $250 getting your sister's eye fixed? She's just gonna end up marrying a no-good nigger like you."

While the words cut through the revving of engines and the cacophonous thuds, bangs, clinks, and clangs in the mechanic's shop, Bill Walker was not surprised in the least by Dickie Stribling's response to his request for a loan. After all, Dickie, owner of Eatonton, Georgia's premier auto repair shop, had a reputation for bad-mouthing black people that was second only to his ability for putting the hum back in busted transmissions. In fact, the only reason Bill had even considered working for Dickie—a short, ruddy-faced man who kept a pocket full of half-dollars that he shifted from hand to hand—was to learn how to build car engines. At nineteen, Bill had his sights on becoming a mechanic and maybe starting his own business one day. And Stribling's garage was the only shop in Putnam County where a black man was allowed to do more than pump gas, patch tires, or wash cars.

Ignoring Dickie's comment, Bill pulled a rag from the back pocket of his green coveralls and wiped oil from his hands. He had stood up before to Dickie and other whites like him, but he was in no mood for arguments today. Bill's baby sister Alice, a smart, sassy eight-year-old, had suffered a blow to her eye from a BB gun pellet while playing in the yard with two of her other brothers, Curtis and Bobby. A white doctor in nearby Macon had told the family that he could treat the little girl and repair the damage to her eye for about $250—up front.

For Bill's parents, the former Minnie Tallulah Grant and Willie Lee Walker, struggling tenant farmers who were barely getting by, the sum might as well have been $250 million. Given all the ways landlords had for cheating poor, black sharecroppers out of their pay, the Walkers were lucky if their labor brought them $250 a year. Seeing as Dickie was the only person Bill knew who had a ready stash of cash, he turned to him for help. He couldn't stand to see Alice—who was writhing in pain and feverish from a mounting infection—in anguish anymore.

"Are you gonna loan me the money or not?" Bill recalled saying, as he calmly stuffed the rag back into his pocket. "Yeah," Dickie grunted, adding, "Damn these niggers . . ." as he walked out of the garage. Bill picked up a wrench and went back to work. It was late summer 1952.

"NIGGERS" and their woes. That is exactly what English statesman James Edward Oglethorpe had been trying to avoid when, in 1732, the British monarchy granted him the royal charter for Georgia. As founding father, he decreed an absolute prohibition of slavery in the colony. Slave trade had begun, in what was to become the United States of America, in 1619 when twenty Africans were put ashore in Jamestown, Virginia—and had quickly expanded. Oglethorpe's mandate made Georgia the first (and only) British outpost in the New World where ownership of blacks was forbidden.

But it was neither outrage, disgust, nor a sense of the immorality of trafficking in human beings that had prompted Oglethorpe to outlaw slavery in the colony he hoped to transform into a silk-producing paradise for the British crown. He was against slave trade in Georgia because he didn't want the province to become another South Carolina, a colony Oglethorpe viewed as nearly ungovernable because of its constant slave revolts. And when enslaved blacks in South Carolina weren't taking up arms against their masters, they were plotting schemes to "steal away" from bondage. The way Oglethorpe saw it, Georgia would be much more peaceful and productive without the "bother" of blacks constantly clamoring for freedom.

Besides, there were economic matters to consider. Promoting their enterprise under the banner "England will grow rich by sending her poor abroad," Georgia's founders planned to develop the colony by using the labor of indigent whites who would have their passage to the New World paid in full. Thus, Oglethorpe also disdained slavery because the purchase of blacks would drain the coffers needed to support the whites who were being relocated to Georgia. "The first cost of a Negro is about thirty pounds," wrote the colony's leaders by way of explanation for their antislavery stance. "Such a sum would pay the passage over, provide tools and other necessaries, and defray the charge of subsistence of a white man for a year."

Eager to expand their holdings, officials in England gave their blessing to Oglethorpe's unorthodox plan. And so, slavery was against Georgia law when 114 passengers in "reduced circumstances" set sail from England to Georgia aboard the frigate *Ann* in November 1732.

On a brisk afternoon in early February 1733, Georgia's first colonists set foot on a site near present-day Savannah that was to become their home. The rugged, steep-bluffed landscape was somewhat different from the lush paradise Oglethorpe had described in a promotional booklet he had published in England to drum up interest in his new enterprise. "Georgia's soil is impregnated with such a fertile mixture that they use no manure. . . . ," Oglethorpe had declared, with aplomb. "Georgia's oranges, lemons, apples, pears, peaches and apricots are so dilicious [*sic*] that whoever tastes them will despise the insipid watery taste of those we have in

England. . . . A person who doesn't want to raise his own cattle and fowls or to shoot them in the woods may purchase meat from Indians at ridiculous prices."

As for the Native Americans, working with an interpreter shortly after his arrival in Georgia, Oglethorpe drafted a treaty by which chiefs from the indigenous Creek, Cherokee, and Yamacraw nations "freely gave up their right to all the land they did not use themselves"—roughly one million acres. In exchange for their largesse, Oglethorpe gave Georgia's native people, among other treasures, "laced coats, Irish linen and cags of rum to carry home to their respective towns." Confident that the tribal leaders would now pose no threat, Georgia's new residents set about the task of bringing the colony to its purported splendor.

In his pitch to both prospective settlers and the colony's financial underwriters in England, Oglethorpe had projected that Georgia would be self-sufficient by the end of 1733 and prosperous enough to begin exporting its lucrative bounty (cotton, silk, and rice) shortly thereafter. Instead, he found his enterprise bogged down by an array of calamities ranging from unskilled workers to a scarcity of food (the "discount" trade with Indians did not come to pass and the colonists did not know how to hunt). Far from the bonanza Oglethorpe had vowed to ship back to England, the colony's primary output, a decade after it was settled, included "112 barrels of tar, eight pounds of raw silk, and the bark of a tree, thought useful for the dyers."

As time passed and Georgia's soil still refused to blossom at the hands of the white settlers, many of them began to complain bitterly about the law that prohibited them from owning slaves. One influential Oglethorpe detractor lamented, "Nothing but Negroes will do to make this colony like Carolina."

He would tolerate desultory attitudes and poor work habits, but on the question of slavery, Oglethorpe held fast to his founding principle for the colony: "No Blacks, now or ever." But as Georgia continued to decline, the malcontents found, in England, a growing receptivity to their demands to abolish Oglethorpe's law. Persuaded that only slavery could save the colony from collapse, British officials, in 1750, revoked the decree and announced that "Negroes would be introduced" to the region. Among the blacks enslaved in Georgia after the repeal of Oglethorpe's law were the forebears of Alice Walker.

AS HE RECALLED the racial slur uttered by Dickie Stribling, James (Jimmy) Walker said that his brother Bill might not have had to subject himself to such invectives had another white man the Walker family encountered been more charitable on the day the copper BB pellet shattered Alice's right eye. Trapped in an inhumane sharecropping system that forced poor blacks to take jobs wherever white landowners would hire them, the Walkers found themselves, in the summer of 1952, working a farm off Highway 441 in a rural, isolated stretch of Milledgeville, Georgia. Because Bill used the family's only car to drive the twenty miles back and forth between the Walkers' rustic shack and his job at Dickie's in Eatonton, there was no vehicle available to rush Alice to medical aid on the day she was injured.

"So me and Daddy was going up there to the big highway trying to find somebody with a car that could take us to get help for Alice," Jimmy remembered.

"We were walking up the hill when we saw a car coming and Daddy flagged it down. It was this white man, and Daddy said, 'My little girl's been hurt and I need to take her to the doctor.' The man gave Daddy a dirty look and just drove off. He didn't ask what was wrong with this little girl, how serious it was, nothing. So we commenced walking on down the road."

ON A COOL, crisp Saturday evening, thirty-four years after the man refused Willie Lee Walker's plea for a ride, that same highway would be packed with motorists, many of them white, en route to a special premiere of *The Color Purple,* the film adaptation of Alice Walker's Pulitzer Prize–winning novel.

As they arrived at the event—held January 18, 1986, at the Pex

Theater on the purple-swathed Eatonton town square—guests were bathed in an arc of Hollywood floodlights that lit up the Georgia sky for miles in every direction. The community of five thousand about seventy miles southeast of Atlanta had been transformed! Indeed, city officials, their oratory usually limited to crowning dairy queens at the county fair, stopped midsentence each time a sleek limousine pulled up to deliver the author, her friends, and family members to the red carpet that had been rolled out by a troop of fresh-scrubbed Boy Scouts. It was just as well. The steady clicking and whirring of the photographers' cameras were drowning out their high-flown proclamations anyway.

As people rushed past a wall of jostling reporters to secure their seats for the most spectacular event in Eatonton's history (news groups from *Entertainment Tonight* to the British Broadcasting Corporation had dispatched crews), they passed under a billowing, hand-lettered sign that stretched across Jefferson Street, the town's main thoroughfare. It read, "Welcome Home, Alice Walker." The irony of the message was not lost on the woman it honored.

"When I was a child, on the same street where that banner was hung, black people had to step off the sidewalk to allow white people to go by," Alice later said. "It is love that makes me look at what I can't stand. When you love deeply, you can stand to see a lot more."

2

Babies and Stumps

ALICE'S TRIUMPHANT return to Eatonton seemed to her and her family nothing less than a miracle. After all, the Jim Crow laws, a system of rigid racial segregation adopted by most Southern states in the 1880s, were designed specifically to prevent blacks from achieving the kind of freedom, respect, and economic success Alice had attained as an internationally acclaimed author. Derived from the name of a grinning, wild-eyed blackface minstrel character popular among Southern white audiences, the term *Jim Crow* itself was an affront to the dignity of black people. And whether they cared to admit it, segregation also debased whites, making them appear barbaric and willfully inhuman.

"Few blacks spent much time discussing hatred of white people," Alice would later write, recalling her youth in Georgia. "It was understood that they were—generally—vicious and unfair, like floods, earthquakes, or other natural catastrophes. Your job, if you were black, was to live with that knowledge. . . . You had as good a time (and life) as you could, under the circumstances."

. . .

SEGREGATION WAS an absurd obsession with keeping the races apart— laughable if not for its devastating impact on every facet of black life. For within the Jim Crow system that required blacks to use separate (and always unequal) public facilities, officials spared no detail in degrading the people who had actually *built* the South with their slave labor and been promised freedom and equality after the Civil War.

Under Jim Crow laws, it was common for courts in Georgia to provide one Bible for the swearing in of white witnesses and another for blacks. Blacks used separate water fountains, elevators, taxicabs, and telephone booths. Making plain not only the inhumanity but also the wastefulness of segregation, Lucy Montgomery, a white woman raised under Jim Crow, described its impact this way: "White people were so fixated on maintaining two of everything, that we didn't have one good anything. The result has been an affliction of ignorance, mediocrity and backwardness that is still crippling the South today."

And having been denounced by segregationists for his 1958 children's book about a marriage between a white rabbit and a black rabbit in an enchanted forest, white writer Garth Williams issued a statement that, perhaps better than any, summed up the Southern psychosis about race. "I was completely unaware," declared Williams, author of *The Rabbits' Wedding,* "that animals with white fur, such as white polar bears and white dogs and white rabbits, were considered blood relatives of white human beings."

Annie Ruth Walker Hood, who had organized the festive Eatonton premiere, was mindful of the many obstacles her baby sister had overcome as she watched Alice make her way down the red carpet into the thunderous standing ovation that greeted her inside the Pex Theater. This was the movie house where Alice had been restricted to watching her beloved Tom Mix and Hopalong Cassidy films from a broken seat in the balcony, the section white people called "nigger heaven." Now John Peck, the owner of the theater, was running up and down the aisles, trying to make sure that Alice and her guests were happy. Laborers in the auto repair industry and highway construction, Alice's brothers Fred, Bill, Jimmy, and Bobby also attended the premiere. A college administrator and nightclub owner, respectively, siblings Mamie and Curtis were unable to join the celebration.

Taking in the scene as the audience got settled, waiting excitedly for *The Color Purple* to begin, Ruth (as she was called by her family) found her thoughts drifting back more than forty years to another time when she had felt such elation. As the lights dimmed and the opening shot of two black girls skipping through a field of flowers appeared on the screen, she remembered the warmth that filled her family's tiny sharecropper's shack on February 9, 1944, when Alice, her parents' eighth and last child, was born in the community of Eatonton's Wards Chapel.

Ruth said that for her, Alice's birth was a landmark event for two reasons. Then age six, Ruth was ecstatic that her prayers for a baby sister had been answered. And the arrival of the bright-eyed infant with the thick black curls brought an end to her belief in a time-honored Southern folk myth—that babies came from stumps.

"That's what Mama and the old folks told us; that babies came from stumps," explained Ruth, a stout, deep-voiced former beautician. "One day, I just about drowned searching for a baby in a tree stump that was stuck in the creek.

"So, when Mama got ready to have Alice, I was determined to find out how the stump fit in. I hid in the bedroom closet and pressed my nose up against the plank. Mama was in bed with her hands on her stomach just moanin' and groanin.' Daddy had gone to get Miss Fannie, who was the midwife. I must have made a noise because the next thing I knew, my sister Mamie had snatched me out of the closet and sent me to bed. The next morning we had this beautiful, smiling baby, Alice.

"When I first saw her, somehow my little brain started working and I figured out that Miss Fannie had made Alice come out of Mama's belly. This was kind of confusing to me because Mama's stomach didn't have any holes in it. All I know is that after Alice was born, I was through with looking for babies in stumps. And as far as I was concerned, she was mine. It was as if Mama had had Alice just for me because I'd prayed so hard for a baby sister."

Alice had actually entered the world before the midwife's arrival. According to the story she later heard, Mrs. Walker, mute and nearly unconscious from the pain of her labor, signaled to her mother-in-law, with her eyes, that she'd given birth. Stunned, Alice's grandmother threw back the bed covers and announced, "Lord have mercy, Minnie Lou done gone and had this child!"

With the most strenuous part of her task already successfully completed, Miss Fannie had little to do other than clean and swaddle baby Alice, whom she then placed in the arms of her weary, but joyful mother. As an adult, Alice would find merit in a horoscope for those born, like her, under the sign of Aquarius: "These colorful individuals are attracted by exciting happenings and at the same time generate a good bit of energy themselves. They are most often highly spontaneous and somewhat unrestrained. . . . They are fighters—aggressive, explosive and unpredictable."

LOCATED A few miles outside of Eatonton proper, Alice's birthplace, Wards Chapel, takes its name from a Methodist church that was donated to local blacks by Mrs. Sarah H. Ward, a member of a prominent plantation family, after the end of slavery. Eatonton was founded in 1808 and was named after William Eaton, a military hero hailed by President Thomas Jefferson. Over time, the town would become known as the birthplace of Joel Chandler Harris (1848–1908), a white writer celebrated for the *Uncle Remus* stories, his interpretation of black folktales he had heard recounted by slaves during his youth.

The Walker family traces its beginnings in the area to the early 1800s when Mary Poole, the enslaved great-great-great-great-grandmother of Alice Walker, was sold on the auction block in Virginia and then walked to Eatonton with a baby straddled on each hip. More than a century later, still in Putnam County, Alice's parents were determined to raise their children close to the earth, in a place they could at least run freely in nature. Their hopes were realized in the bucolic landscape of Wards Chapel, where Miss Birda Reynolds, the local primary-school teacher, saw Alice

Malsenior Walker (named after two of her mother's sisters) a few hours after she was born.

"Mr. Willie Lee came by and told me that he and Miss Minnie Lou had a new little baby daughter," recalled Reynolds, who lived down the road from the Walkers. "I went to see the baby and brought her a little outfit. Alice was a very alert baby, and we could all tell, by the way her eyes took in everything, that she was going to be special."

Indeed, although her parents still endured grinding poverty as exploited tenant farmers, Alice's birth marked the first time that Mr. and Mrs. Walker were able to pay the midwife for her assistance. Alice would later commemorate the special circumstances of her birth in the poem "Three Dollars Cash":

> *Three dollars cash*
> *For a pair of catalog shoes*
> *Was what the midwife charged*
> *My mama*
> *For bringing me.*
> *"We wasn't so country then," says Mom,*
> *"You being the last one—*
> *And we couldn't, like*
> *We done*
> *When she brought your*
> *Brother,*
> *Send her out to the*
> *Pen*
> *And let her pick*
> *Out*
> *A pig."*

It was unheard of for a sharecropper's wife to "convalesce" after the birth of a child. So Mrs. Walker, shortly after Alice's arrival, returned to her job working the cotton fields beside her husband on a sprawling six-hundred-acre farm. But still determined to experience the joys of her infant daughter, Mrs. Walker would sometimes settle Alice under the cooling, natural umbrella of a tree while she planted seeds or pulled weeds. Other days, Alice was left in the care of Ruth, who would barrel home from school to dote on her sister and serenade her with sweet lullabies.

Coddled and adored, Alice stole the show at a baby contest in Wards Chapel before she was even a year old. Her first-place prize? A framed copy of the Lord's Prayer, still in Alice's possession sixty years later. "The community would raise funds by people offering donations in the name of the cutest baby," Alice explained. "With my family making such a fuss over me and showing me off every minute, well, naturally, I won."

But when it came to real bragging rights, it was hard for Alice's parents not to crow about a child who, once she started to crawl, would back herself up against a wall and pretend to read the Sears and Roebuck catalog. Deemed the "wish book" by rural blacks who could rarely afford any of its offerings, the catalog, along with the Bible, could be found in nearly every sharecropper's home. And when a new catalog appeared, the pages of the old would be put to immediate use as insulation for the rickety shacks and as toilet paper in the outhouses.

"In addition to 'reading' the catalog, I'd pick up twigs and 'scribble' in the margins," Alice later remembered with a gleeful laugh.

Alice responded to the loving affection she received by blossoming into an open, sweet-natured child with intense curiosity. As much as Mrs. Walker took pride in her daughter's independent spirit, she worried about Alice's tendency, as she got older, to wander off for a better look at a spider's web or stand of cattails that had caught her eye. Unable to keep a close watch on Alice because of the endless hours she and her husband toiled to support their family, Mrs. Walker asked Miss Reynolds if her daughter could join the teacher's first-grade class at age four, a year ahead of schedule. Also weighing heavily on Mrs. Walker's mind were her past struggles with landlords who expected the children of black sharecroppers to work the fields as soon as their tiny fingers could grasp a cotton boll and drop it into a croker sack. Mrs. Walker had already had to fight, with varying degrees of success, to keep her other children in school. Indeed, she was known throughout Putnam County for her bold reply to a white plantation owner who, asserting that blacks had "no need for education," had once tried to bully her into sending her children to the fields.

"You might *have* some black children somewhere," Mrs. Walker told the man as she stood, steely eyed, on her front porch, "but they don't live in this house. Don't you ever come around here again talking about how *my children* don't need to learn how to read and write."

Eager to help the Walkers stop the landowners from stealing Alice's future, and knowing how much they valued education, Miss Reynolds welcomed the four-year-old into her class. "Alice was a smart and extremely focused little girl," said Reynolds about the child who would quickly distinguish herself as among the most gifted students in Putnam County.

"I'd be reading stories like *Goldilocks and the Three Bears,* and the other children's minds would start to stray. Alice would be looking right back at me and scrunching up her little brow like she was trying to make a mental picture of what I was reading. From day one, she could outspell children twice her age. And if she had to recite a nursery rhyme or a verse of poetry, Alice didn't get nervous. She'd get up, recite perfectly and sit back down.

"Lord yes, she had the stuff from the beginning," remembered a beaming Reynolds. "A lot of children passed my way, but Alice Walker was the smartest one I ever had."

Alice's success was all the more striking in a state where legislators, propelled by their trademark concept of "separate but equal," had historically allocated $1.43 for the schooling of a black child, compared to $10.23 for a white one.

3

Roots

FOLKS IN WARDS Chapel were not surprised when they heard, after church services and during neighborly visits, about the extraordinary ability Alice was displaying in school. All the Walker children were known to be bright, and it was common knowledge that their father was one of most intelligent and industrious men in the community.

In fact, East Putnam Consolidated, the school Alice attended, had opened in early January 1948 after being built under the leadership of Willie Lee Walker. Undeterred when the all-white Board of Education refused to provide funding to replace the leaky, dilapidated buildings where black children were being schooled, Mr. Walker rallied area farmers to buy an old barracks from Camp Wheeler, an army base about forty-five miles away. The farmers arranged to haul the barracks to Eatonton and assembled it on a plot of land donated by David Simmons, a Walker relative who had inherited a farm from his mother. Simmons provided enough surrounding space for the children to have a playground in the expansive green fields.

Putting in walls, windows, and floors after they finished their daily chores, the men and women of the community converted the barracks into a clean, cheery schoolhouse. To raise money for materials, Alice later remembered, the workers held dances and "toe-pulling contests," popular parlor games during which women displayed their feet from behind a curtain and the menfolk would choose, by pulling their toes, the ladies they would like to escort for a light-hearted social evening. As with the baby contests, money collected from "toe-pulling" competitions would be used to repair a shed or to help buy groceries for a sharecropping family down on its luck.

Although Alice was young when her first school opened, her memories of the sacrifices poor black farmers made to uplift their children would remain vivid her entire life. "Running in and out of the lantern-lit rooms, what I felt, I think, was simply the warmth and generosity of the grownups as they ate, danced and played after their labor," she later wrote. "There was such security in knowing they were building a place for us."

And folks knew, without question, that Alice's father was instrumental in getting the job done.

BORN IN Eatonton on September 13, 1909, Willie Lee Walker was, at an early age, forced to contend with adult pressures and responsibilities. His parents, Henry Clay Walker and the former Kate Nelson, toiled on a hardscrabble Putnam County farm to raise their five children, of whom Willie Lee was the eldest.

Henry Clay Walker, born July 7, 1888, had grown up in relative prosperity as the son of Albert Walker (Alice's paternal great-grandfather). Married to the former Sallie Montgomery, Albert was a successful cotton farmer who had inherited land from his father, a slaveholder of Scottish descent.

However, Albert lost the farm during Henry's teenage years after a plague of boll weevils destroyed his cotton crop for several years running. Local whites, long envious and resentful of a black man like Albert Walker "rising above his place," had not been sorry to see him fall on hard times. The downturn in his

father's socioeconomic status would have far-reaching consequences for Henry, and decades later for his son Willie Lee,
whose children would also be affected by the pained history of
dispossession in their heritage. Daughter Alice would make especially good use of the Walker family lore she pieced together over
the years. As the youngest child, she was helped mightily in her
efforts by the spellbinding tales of her older siblings, stories Alice
listened to with raptness.

"MY GRANDFATHER Henry, who we called 'Pa-Pa,' was spoiled
because he had grown up like a rich kid, riding around on horses
and wearing fancy clothes," remembered Bill Walker, detailing the
family history before the boll weevils struck. "So when my great-
grandfather Albert lost his land, Pa-Pa couldn't deal with them
having to scuffle and scrape like regular people. He started drinking, gambling and hanging out in jook joints. He got a real bad
reputation."

Where others saw a young man from a once-prosperous black
family going to ruin, Estella Perry saw in her beau, Henry Clay
Walker, a good soul with wounded pride, trying to cope with his
father's ill fortune. Estella was an attractive, high-spirited young
woman who cared about Henry's heart, not his inheritance (gone)
or social standing. Nicknamed "Shug" (short for "sugar"), she
loved to dance and carouse with him in the jook joints, rowdy tav-
erns set deep in the backwoods.

"The Walker family despised Shug Perry because she was considered a loose woman," Bill said. "My great-grandfather Albert
was determined to get Henry out of her clutches and eventually persuaded him to marry another woman, Kate Nelson. Kate was from
a better home and very stable. But Pa-Pa never really wanted her
and kept having affairs."

Born August 31, 1891, Kate Nelson was a quiet, "upright,
Sunday school–teaching" young woman, said Bill about his paternal grandmother. A bright and deeply sensitive boy, Willie Lee could
not help but feel the tension between his mother and his father,

who, having married a woman he did not love, was filled with rage and quick to erupt into drunken tirades.

Willie Lee did his best to shield his younger siblings from the turmoil in the household by helping them with their schoolwork and farm chores. But he could not protect them or himself from the impact of his father's adulterous liaisons, behavior that would lead to a devastating loss when he was eleven years old.

Having suffered years of her husband's widely known philandering and abuse, Kate Nelson Walker found herself vulnerable to the kindness of another man, and the two became lovers for a brief time. "Seeing as she got no love or comfort from Pa-Pa, who really wanted to be with Miss Shug, Kate found it elsewhere," said Ruth, explaining her grandmother's infidelity. "She'd been putting up with Pa-Pa's affairs for all those years, so I guess she looked at the situation and said, 'Well, two can play at this game.'"

But guilt ridden and devoted to her children, Kate soon ended the affair. The man, who had fallen deeply in love with her, wanted the relationship to continue. On July 4, 1921, while walking home from an outing with her son Willie Lee, Kate was accosted by her former lover, who reputedly stepped from behind a bush, pistol in hand. When she rebuffed his pleas to "keep company" again, he poked the gun in her chest and it fired. Kate Nelson Walker died the next day, a month shy of her thirtieth birthday.

"My Daddy sat down on that dusty country road and cradled his bleeding mother," said Ruth, recounting the story as it had been passed down over the years. "She was wearing one of those lace-up corsets and she asked him to unloose it. He had to go all up under her dress to get it untied. Between seeing his mother get gunned down and then having to halfway undress her, my father was thoroughly traumatized."

As a widower with five children, the oldest of whom was eleven-year-old Willie Lee, Henry Walker was eager to find another woman to manage his household (Shug Perry had since moved up North and married). According to Ruth, her grandfather approached a neighbor who had several daughters, hoping that he could hire one of them to cook, clean, and take care of the children. Concerned about the propriety of a young girl keeping house for "a good-look-ing widower who rode a horse," the man suggested that Walker marry the daughter he was willing to lend out, a shy teenager named Rachel who was not much older than Willie Lee.

"Pa-Pa didn't go over there to bargain for a wife, he went to hire a maid or a nanny," Ruth explained. "But Pa-Pa had to marry her to keep it clean, so people wouldn't talk."

After being advised by Rachel's father that she was "smart, a hard worker and so generous that she'd give away everything in the garden and smokehouse," Walker took home his young bride. "It was strictly a marriage of convenience," Ruth continued. "Mama Kate died in July and Pa-Pa married Rachel in August. It didn't have anything to do with love."

For Willie Lee, who was still grieving the violent death of his mother, Rachel's quick arrival only served to deepen his anger and despair. "He eventually learned to love and respect her, but he never called her 'Mama'—she was always 'Miss Rachel' to him," Bill explained.

Psychologically wounded by the tragedy of his childhood, Alice's father coped by working constantly and keeping his deepest emotions to himself. Said Ruth: "You just had to pick up the pieces and carry on."

BY CONTRAST, Minnie Tallulah Grant, born December 2, 1912, gave full expression to her joys and sorrows. "If my Mama felt sad or had her feelings hurt, she'd just break down and cry on you," Ruth remembered. "You didn't have to strain yourself trying to fig-ure out how she was feeling."

In her ability to speak her mind, Minnie Lou (short for Tallulah) had taken after her father, William A. Grant. A Putnam County farmer born on November 2, 1884, Grant was a tall, light-skinned man with a fiery temper who never held back even his most shock-ing thoughts. "He told me that every time one of his children was born, he wanted to take it out to the woodpile and chop its head off," said Ruth, remembering her maternal grandfather. "He claimed he never wanted a single child, but it didn't work out that way because my mother was the fifth of twelve."

For the hardships that came with providing for such a large family, William Grant was quick to blame his soft-spoken wife, the former Nettie Lee. In a scenario that mirrored Henry Clay Walker's forced and ill-fated marriage to Kate Nelson, Ruth said that her grandfather Grant never loved her grandmother Nettie.

"Grandpa Grant really loved another woman," she explained. "But for whatever reasons, he didn't marry her, so he took out all his frustrations on Grandma Nettie. He would beat her for just the least little thing. He was mean as a bruised rattlesnake."

As Minnie Lou got older, she locked horns with her father, never hesitating to confront him whenever he launched into one of his violent rampages. "Mama, being a high-toned Grant, she didn't take nothing," Bill Walker said. "Grandpa Grant would try to defend his manhandling of Grandma Nettie, but Mama wouldn't hear it. She'd get all up in his face and tell him what a lowdown, rotten, no-count husband and father he was."

Opposite in temperament and tone from her mean-spirited father, Willie Lee Walker was precisely the kind of reasoned, hard-working young man Minnie Lou Grant was eager to know. They first met in church, where Willie Lee caught his future wife's eye by directing sly winks at her when there was a lull in the preacher's sermon. He reputedly winked so hard, Minnie Lou later said that she could hear the clicks!

"Mama would be sitting on one side, Daddy would be on the other, and he'd smile and wink at her," Ruth said. "After church they'd chitchat a bit and eventually they started courting."

The young couple quickly fell in love. But their romance sparked only rancor in William Grant, who took a dim view of what he considered to be the "low-life" lineage of Minnie Lou's beau as it was personified by his father, the "jook-jointing, wife-cheating, whiskey-guzzling" Henry Clay Walker.

"Grandpa Grant didn't want his daughter dealing with no part of Willie Lee Walker because he knew the reputation of Pa-Pa," Bill explained. "So when Daddy was dating Mom, she got pregnant.

That guaranteed that her father would put her out. Then she could do what she wanted to do."

What Minnie Lou Grant wanted to do was marry Willie Lee Walker, which she did on June 1, 1930, six months after their first child, Willie Fred, was born. After their marriage, the couple lived, for a short time, with the volatile Henry Clay Walker, who soon learned that his daughter-in-law did not cower before any man. "Mama had to put Pa-Pa in his place a couple of times before he realized he couldn't push her around," said Bill, pridefully. "Because she stood her ground, he came to respect my mother, and after a while, they got along just fine."

Added Alice: "I grew up believing that there was nothing, literally nothing, my mother couldn't do once she set her mind to it. So when the women's movement happened, I was really delighted because I felt they were trying to go where my mother was and where I always assumed I would go."

4

"Shift for Self"

In a photograph taken of Alice's parents in the 1930s, Mr. and Mrs. Walker project an image of unshakable determination and dignity. The darker-skinned Willie Lee, clad in overalls, a gleaming white shirt, and a black fedora positioned nattily on the back of his head, has his right arm extended, protectively, around the shoulder of his wife. Minnie Lou, wearing a stylish outfit and a hat that is also set at a rakish angle, is leaning into her husband's embrace. Depicting maturity, experience, and a sober strength, the portrait leaves viewers with a sense that the couple is prepared to deal with whatever lies ahead.

For black sharecroppers during the Great Depression, daily life, never a "crystal stair" in the words of acclaimed black poet Langston Hughes, became an even greater challenge. The wave of prosperity that had lifted the nation during the Roaring Twenties crested and then crashed in 1929, shortly before the Walkers took their vows. Banks and business empires collapsed into financial ruin, labor violence erupted, and bread lines formed as hunger and homelessness stalked millions of Americans. When President Herbert Hoover, fearing complete social and political collapse, began to create relief programs to stem the economic decline, blacks routinely found themselves discouraged, if not outright excluded, from obtaining support. Guidelines announced by officials in Texas were typical of those that greeted Southern blacks seeking public aid: "Applications are not taken from unemployed Mexican or colored families. They are being asked to shift for themselves."

According to Bill Walker, his parents shifted for themselves the first years of their marriage by sharecropping for the same white family that employed Henry Clay Walker, who had been forced into tenant farming after his father, Albert, lost the land. However, when Minnie Lou and Willie Lee sought payment for their cotton crop at "settling-up" time, they were confronted with a situation that befell many a black sharecropper in Georgia—and one that only intensified during the Depression years. Instead of paying the Walkers, the plantation owner, not too long after Alice's sister Mamie was born in 1932, informed the struggling couple that they owed *him* for the overpriced commissary food and supplies that they'd purchased during the year.

"After working a whole year and with two kids to feed, my parents came home with no money and eighteen dollars in debt," Bill explained. "So after this went down, my father wanted out. He figured he'd better do something else before he ended up killing somebody."

Taking a job previously held by a white man named Ed Little, Willie Lee eventually moved his family to a flimsy, weather-beaten shack on the property of a wealthy matron, May Montgomery. Under the blistering Georgia sun, he began working for her as a dairy man, general laborer, and chauffeur at the salary of six dollars per month, or seventy-two dollars a year. At the time, the average yearly income for white families was about $1,300. Black families earned just under $500 a year, according to U.S. Department of Commerce census data.

A few years later, with conditions worsening for blacks throughout Georgia and Willie Lee fearing for the very survival of his family, he asked Montgomery if she would consider increasing his wages to twelve dollars a month so that his children (there were now six) would not starve. Her reply: "I was only paying Ed Little ten dollars and I would never pay a nigger more than I would pay a white man. Before I'd pay a nigger twelve dollars a month, I'd milk the cows myself."

MONTGOMERY'S CRUEL and unconscionable attitude was not uncommon in a state that consisted, in the mid-1930s, of more than forty percent blacks; they were nearly ninety percent of its tenant farmers. The degradation blacks endured took many forms, ranging from the kind exemplified by Montgomery's humiliating retort to ghoulish public lynchings. Lynch law owes its name to Charles Lynch, a Virginia farmer who reputedly exacted rough justice during the Revolutionary War. Between 1890 and 1940, Georgia frequently led the nation in the number of lynchings, often carried out in a cheering, carnival-like atmosphere.

Georgia's lynch mobs found wide acceptance for their lawlessness—thanks, in part, to elected officials who did not hesitate to announce from the statehouse floor their support of the barbaric practice. "If it requires lynching to protect women's dearest possession from raving, drunken human beasts, I say lynch a thousand Negroes a week," declared a celebrated legislator, echoing the views of many.

And thus were allegations of rape and the chivalric duty to defend "white women's virtue" used by Southern whites to justify their brutal assaults against the black community. In truth, the vast majority of Georgia's lynch victims were innocent and impoverished tenant farmers who challenged, by word or deed, the prevailing white supremacist customs of the day. The evidence of this was manifest throughout the South, as William Faulkner aptly noted in his 1942 novel *Go Down, Moses:* "How to God can a black man ask a white man to please not lay down with his black wife? And even if he could ask it, how to God can the white man promise he won't?"

Having confronted white oppression, as had Willie Lee Walker when he dared to ask Montgomery for a raise, so-called uppity niggers found themselves ready targets for the Ku Klux Klan, a group that used extreme violence to terrorize blacks who refused to accept the subhuman status to which they had been relegated for generations.

Taking its name from *kiklo,* the Greek word for "circle," the Ku Klux Klan was first organized in 1866 by a group of ex-Confederates who opposed the political rights granted to blacks following the Civil War. The group was soon disbanded under pressure from more "liberal-minded" members who disagreed with the Klan's public whipping and hanging of blacks. The Klan re-emerged in 1915, now targeting Catholics and Jews, as well as blacks, after a group of white supremacists climbed atop Georgia's Stone Mountain and breathed new life into the hooded, hate-spewing sect. At the time, the Klan was riding high from the notoriety of D. W. Griffith's *The Birth of a Nation.* Reputedly beloved by President Woodrow Wilson (who selected the movie as the first to be screened in the White House), the unabashedly racist film glorified the Klan's violence and depicted freed male slaves (played by white actors in blackface) as "rapacious savages" lusting after white women.

It was against the backdrop of the Ku Klux Klan and the perhaps less brutal, but similarly debilitating, dominance of "decent" white folks that Willie Lee Walker risked—at a minimum—his livelihood by asking Montgomery to increase his wages. An aging divorcee who could not possibly have managed her farm alone, Montgomery eventually relented and begrudgingly paid him the twelve dollars he requested. As the years progressed, the Walkers, as a point of pride and dignity, demanded better pay from all the whites who employed them. Even so, by the time Alice was born in 1944, the Walkers, with eight children, were earning only two to three hundred dollars per year.

Willie Lee and Minnie Lou Walker weathered the Depression by fighting for their family. The determination they displayed in the photograph was not a theatrical pose, but rather a true portrait of the grit and courage they had to bring forth to battle harsh oppression.

Even with the New Deal programs introduced by President Franklin Roosevelt, the Walkers and other black sharecroppers like them often found public aid withheld from their families. Decades later, Alice would detail one such experience in her story "The Revenge of Hannah Kemhuff." The story, about the tactics a poor black Southern woman utilizes to redress a wrong, is based on an incident that Minnie Lou Walker recounted to her youngest child. Mrs. Walker told Alice that during the Depression, when food was scarce, she was once issued a government voucher to obtain flour from a relief agency in Eatonton. On the day she was readying herself to go into town to use the voucher, she received a box of secondhand clothing from a sister who lived in the North. As was customary during the era, blacks who had fled the rural South for a better life routinely sent clothes and money back to their kinfolk, who were still battling Jim Crow laws.

Grateful for the care package, Minnie Lou Walker selected one of the "new" dresses she had just received to wear on her errands. When she arrived at the relief agency, in her words, "looking nice off of what somebody else threw away," she was confronted by an irate white woman who, angered by Mrs. Walker's tidiness and the fine quality of her dress, refused to give her the flour. "Anybody dressed up as good as you don't need to come here *begging* for food," the woman said resentfully to Alice's mother. Mrs. Walker countered that she was not begging, but rather taking her rightful share of goods offered by the government to needy families (who paid taxes) such as her own. Further enraged by Mrs. Walker's assertive and self-respecting reply, the woman turned away from her and bellowed to a coworker, "The *gall* of niggers coming in here dressed better than me!" And then huffed, according to daughter Ruth, "There are more lies told here than anyplace in Eatonton."

Dispatched home humiliated and without the flour, Mrs. Walker later told Alice that the family made ends meet by trading their surplus cornmeal with friends and relatives who had an abundance of flour. The family also was able to keep hunger at bay owing to the bounty of fruits and vegetables Mrs. Walker cultivated in her spectacular garden. "My mother canned everything," Ruth would later recall. "Peaches, blackberries, okra, green beans, even fried chicken. If it grew, she could put it in a jar."

Despite the discrimination they faced during the Depression, Willie Lee and Minnie Lou Walker persevered, leaving their youngest daughter with an enduring message about justice that would eventually shape and inform all of her writing. Whenever her mother told the story about the flour, Alice would later write, "She automatically raised her head higher than ever—it was always high—and there was a look of righteousness, a kind of holy *heat* coming from her eyes. She said she had lived to see this same white woman grow old and senile and so badly crippled she had to get about on *two* sticks."

"The Revenge of Hannah Kemhuff," the story Alice crafted from her mother's saga, appears in her short story collection *In Love & Trouble*. It was later selected by the Houghton Mifflin Company for publication in its annual literature anthology as one of the best short stories of 1974. Moreover, the research on voodoo that Alice conducted for the piece would lead to the resurrection of Zora Neale Hurston, one of the most distinguished literary figures of the twentieth century. But first, there were Ferris wheels.

5

Booker T.

MISS REYNOLDS said she could see it in her sparkling brown eyes. Sister Ruth felt the charm whenever baby Alice smiled. But Bill Walker knew that his sister was a special child imbued with an uncommon magic the day he looked up and saw her legs dangling from the seat of a Ferris wheel.

Every summer, a traveling fair with amusement rides and carnival attractions came to Eatonton. The Walker children saved their hard-earned pennies in anticipation of screaming on the rides and stuffing their bellies with the roasted peanuts and pink cotton candy the vendors hawked on the midway. On this particular evening in the late 1940s, Bill said that he and several of his siblings were making their way through the crowded fair back to Wards Chapel when they discovered that Alice, who was about five years old, had managed to slip away. Fully aware of the demons that might be awaiting a lone black girl as the bright carnival lights faded and night fell in the backwoods of Georgia, Bill said his whole body tightened and his heart began to pound.

"I searched all over the fairgrounds and couldn't find her anywhere," he remembered. "I was really starting to panic when I happened to look up, and there, at the top of the Ferris wheel, sat this little black figure all by herself.

"To this day, I don't know how Alice, who didn't have any money or tickets, convinced the white man who was operating that Ferris wheel to let her on. But there she was, just sitting up there swinging her little legs back and forth like she didn't have a care in the world. From that moment on, I knew Alice would accomplish great things. There was just no stopping her."

Reveling in his carnival memories, Bill launched into another story that revealed the spunk of his baby sister. He said that about the same time Alice was charming her way onto Ferris wheels, she earned pocket change by gathering eggs from the Walkers' chickens and selling them to Leo Hurt, owner of Eatonton's funeral home for blacks.

"Mama told her that she could collect a dozen eggs each week and the money she earned, fifty cents or so, would be her own," he explained.

"To get to Leo's, Alice had to walk through the roughest part of town, with all the jook joints and honky-tonks. People would be drinking, gambling, and carrying on at all times of the day and night.

"Even though she was just an itty-bitty little girl, Alice would take her basket, sashay on to Leo's and sell her eggs. Now any other kid would have been scared to death of that part of town, not to mention ending up at the undertaker's at the end of the journey. But Alice was never afraid. She was always independent."

Alice's confidence and natural ease in the world also made an impression on Doris Reid, today a slender, hazel-eyed Atlanta homemaker. She said that during her youth, the Reid and Walker families, each with eight children, were so close they considered themselves kin. "My parents had five girls and three boys, the Walkers had five boys and three girls, so we used to joke that we could all just break off in pairs and marry each other," she recalled, with a sly grin.

Reid, whose family lived closer to town, said she used to beg her parents to let her visit Alice during the weekends in Wards Chapel. "We must have been about six years old and Alice would spread a blanket out in a big field for us to lay on," Reid remembered. "I'd be worried about snakes and spiders, but Alice never seemed to be afraid of the outdoors. She'd cross her arms under the back of her head, stare up into the sky, and start talking about the clouds and the trees. Her deep fascination with nature made her stand out from the rest of us children.

"And she was always reading something. I can recall I would say, 'Why on earth do you read all the time?' And she would look back at me real serious-like and respond, 'The more you read, the more you know.'"

A few years later, Alice would demonstrate the depth of her knowledge in an exchange that would captivate Reid's memory for half a century. She said that once when Alice came to her house to play, the two girls visited Reid's paternal grandmother, Ma Jessie, who lived nearby. Hanging in the foyer of Ma Jessie's house—as it had been, Reid avowed, for her entire existence—was a huge, beautifully framed photograph of a distinguished-looking black man. Reid had always assumed the man, elegantly poised and wearing a fine suit, was a distant relative.

He was, in fact, a pioneering educator who Alice, barely eight years old, recognized as soon as she walked in the door. "Ma Jessie! Where'd you get that picture of Booker T. Washington?" Reid remembered Alice exclaiming with awe. "He started a school in Alabama. He knew the president." Stunned by Alice's familiarity with the politically influential founder of Tuskegee Institute, Reid's grandmother, a bit flustered, told Alice she had purchased the portrait in Macon, to which the young girl forthrightly replied, "Why don't you give it to me, please?"

"Within that same hour Alice had not only given a full report on a man I'd been looking at all my life, but had flat-out asked to take Booker T. Washington home with her," Reid recalled with a hearty laugh. "So my grandmother said to Alice, 'No, child, I'm not going to give that picture away because it means a lot to me. But seeing as you're the only person who ever asked me about it, I'm going to give it to you when I die.'"

"I will never forget what happened next if I live a hundred

years," Reid continued. "Alice's face lit up, she turned to my grand-mother and said, 'Oooh . . . You tell everybody that, Ma Jessie. Tell everybody I get that picture when you die.' "

A wonder to herself, Alice later said she wasn't sure "how all this early education happened." "I think it was those long evenings before bed, playing before the fireplace, and the wonderful way people used to talk to each other over meals and just sitting around the yard," she ventured.

She continued, "I remember winning a countywide contest when I was also really little. The principal of the high school offered to give a dollar bill to whoever knew all its symbols—the pyramid, the eye. I suspect my father, a Mason, thirty-third degree, taught me."

6

"I Been Cryin' . . ."

NOT TOO long after Ma Jessie's promise, Doris Reid witnessed another pivotal moment for Alice. She remembered that it was a warm summer evening when she and her parents visited the Walkers at the farm they were sharecropping near Milledgeville, in Baldwin County. Bounding up the porch steps, Reid paid her respects to "Cousin Willie Lee and Minnie Lou" and quickly dashed back to Alice's room. Peeping around the door, she was greeted by a frightening image that, decades later, still made her voice quiver.

"There was Alice, sitting in bed, with this white cloth wrapped around her face that covered most everything except for one eye," remembered Reid, her lush Georgia drawl quieting to a whisper. "You know how kids are, I just blurted out, 'What's wrong with you?' and she told me she'd been hit with a BB gun. Then I asked, 'Does your head hurt? How does it feel? Did you throw up? Is your eye bleeding?' It just hurt me so bad to see her all bandaged up like that.

"Finally, I asked her if she could cry out of the eye that was covered. And she said, 'I been cryin,' as these little tears began to roll down her cheeks."

· · ·

INJURED IN 1952, Alice would not offer a full account of the incident that cost her the vision in her right eye until the 1983 release of her essay, "Beauty: When the Other Dancer Is the Self." First published in *Ms.* magazine, the piece would later be included in her debut nonfiction collection, *In Search of Our Mothers' Gardens*. In the essay, which is presented in a series of flashbacks, Alice writes that she was injured while playing "Cowboys and Indians" with two of her brothers. The boys, ages ten and twelve, had BB guns that had been purchased for them by their parents. Because she was a girl, Alice, age eight, did not get a gun and was "instantly relegated to the position of Indian" with only a bow and arrow. She notes that on the day of the injury, she was on top of the family's tin-roofed carport, holding her bow and arrow, when she felt a piercing blow that blinded her right eye.

"Both brothers rush to my side. My eye stings, and I cover it with my hand," she writes. " 'If you tell,' they say, 'we will get a whipping. You don't want that to happen, do you?' I do not."

The incident, as chronicled in the essay, would have a far-reaching impact on Alice's self-esteem and, ultimately, on her development as a writer. It would also lead to a painful breach fueled by the complexity of family dynamics and the vagaries of memory.

IT IS a sunny, fall afternoon forty-three years after Alice's injury. Curtis Walker, a copper-colored man in his midfifties wearing a red running suit and white mesh loafers, sits on a chair in a disheveled convenience store in Atlanta that is both his place of business and his makeshift home. Patrons going in and out of The Lookout Chicken Fish Steak Sub Restaurant, next door, pop in and utter a low-toned "how ya' doin' " to Curtis, who has had a string of run-ins with the law and is afforded a certain sympathetic sorrow in the gritty neighborhood. But today, "Curt" is not interested in talking about his troubles with eviction notices or slick gambling buddies. Training his eyes on a can of motor oil that sits on a distant shelf, he leans forward and slowly begins another story.

"This is how it went down," said Curtis. "Mama and Daddy had got us BB guns. There was a car shelter in the yard and Alice climbed on top of it. She had Bobby's gun. I had mine. I shot my gun and the BB rose high in the air and hit her right smack in the eye. It was a terrible accident, no doubt about it. And as far as the outcome, it doesn't make a bit of difference, but Alice had a BB gun, too. It was just one of those things that can go wrong when kids are playing."

As for Bobby, he lets loose with a torrent of words when, in a telephone conversation, he recalls that day in the yard. "I can see it as plain as if it were today," he said, his voice direct and methodic. "We were living in a house way back off the road, without hardly any neighbors, and me, Alice, and Curtis had to make up games to entertain ourselves.

"We would play with knives—throwing them and trying to get them to stick in stuff, like a sheet of writing paper. On the day Alice got shot, we were playing 'Cowboys and Indians.' I let Alice use my BB gun because Curtis was selfish. I was up on the carport with her, helping her cock the gun, and Curtis was on the ground below. Curtis pointed his gun up at us, fired, and the BB struck Alice's eye. I knew we were gonna get killed, so I told Alice to tell Mama she stepped on a wire. It was very unfortunate what happened and we all felt bad about it. It was a real sad day."

The perilous mix of firearms and children in Southern culture is made plain in the reflections of an unnamed writer in Alabama: "I was given a BB gun as a Christmas gift when my family thought I was old enough, as were my cousins. As we were all running out the door to try them out that morning my Aunt Flossie Mae called to us, 'Be Careful! You could put an eye out with those!'

"We immediately thought, 'Wow! What a Great Idea!' So, we got in a circle and tried to blind each other. Good thing our aim was bad . . ."

THERE IS no disputing the anguish that settled over the Walker household in the aftermath of the incident that left an unsightly scar and permanently damaged the vision of the sassy, outgoing child who had once happily proclaimed herself to be "the prettiest" in the family. However, contrary to their fears, neither Curtis nor Bobby ever received much punishment for their behavior. Their first line of defense was to persuade their baby sister—as pressure from the shot began to build up blinding pain inside her right eye—to tell her mother that she'd stepped on a wire that snapped back in her face. When they later confessed that Curtis had shot Alice, he and Bobby "got a mild reprimand and that was the end of the BB guns." After a while, "everything went back to normal," Curtis recalled.

But not for Alice. For her, "normal" had meant running, full-out, through the fields with her vision unhampered. It had meant smiling back at a delighted sea of black faces when, in patent leather shoes and frilly dresses, she rose before the church each spring and recited her Easter speech. "Normal" had meant being adored because she was "the icing on the cake and the ice cream, too" as her brother Bill had once lovingly described Alice.

Far from what Curtis believed, and as the entire Walker family would later come to know, for Alice the injury had devastating consequences. "It was great fun being cute," she would write in "Beauty . . ." "But then one day, it ended." Alice had voiced similar sentiments in her 1973 short story, "The Flowers." The story centers on Myop, a black girl whose innocence is shattered after a discovery she makes while picking flowers in the woods surrounding her home.

It seemed to Myop as she skipped lightly from hen house to pigpen to smokehouse that the days had never been as beautiful as these. . . . She was ten, and nothing existed for her but her song.

Her arms laden . . . Myop began to circle back to the house, back to the peacefulness of the morning. It was then that she stepped smack into his eyes. Her heel became lodged in the broken ridge between brow and nose. . . . When she pushed back the . . . debris Myop saw that . . . all his clothes had rot-

ted away except some threads of blue denim from his overalls.
. . . Very near where she'd stepped into his head was a wild
pink rose. As she picked it to add to her bundle she noticed . . .
the rotted remains of a noose. . . .

Myop laid down her flowers. And the summer was over.

UNABLE TO hitch another ride after the white man they flagged
down on the highway refused to help, Mr. Walker and Jimmy
returned home to find Alice on the front porch laid prostrate by the
sharp pains in her head and with scar tissue forming like spilled
milk over her right pupil. The sturdy trunk and sprawling limbs of
a tree growing in the yard would be the last image the eye would
ever discern.

For about a week, the Walkers treated Alice with cool com-
presses, soothing salves, and lily leaves, a home remedy used to
break fevers. "I remember my father, with his sweet band of leaves,
which he placed tenderly around my head," Alice would later recall.
"And I remember my mother frying me my own chicken, a small
bantam that she had raised." But despite their care, Alice's eye
remained cloudy and her body listless. Ruth, who was about thirteen at the time, remembers the agony of watching her baby sister
suffer.

"It was just the most terrible thing you can imagine. Alice was
in so much pain and nothing we did seemed to make her feel better.
Putting washcloths to her eye, making ice packs for the swelling,
massaging her forehead, none of it made a bit of difference. I
remember after I'd change her bandage and rub a bit of ointment
around her eye, I'd hold her for a while and she'd doze off to sleep.
We'd be so grateful for her to get a little rest. Then she'd wake up
drenched in sweat and start crying because her head hurt so bad. It
was heartbreaking because Alice was so young, fragile, and small.
And she'd been such a happy child."

Worried by Alice's lack of response to their treatments and
fearful that a dangerous infection might set in, Mr. and Mrs.

Walker consulted with relatives who chided them for using "folk medicine" and suggested they take their daughter to a *real* doctor, Bill remembered.

"These were some people on my mother's side who lived in Macon and always treated us like country bumpkins," he said. "Because they lived in the city and didn't have to deal with out-houses and slopping hogs, they thought they were better than us. Anyway, they'd apparently found this white doctor who told them he'd charge $250 to operate on Alice's eye.

"I got the money for my parents and they took her to Macon. At that point, we didn't know that she'd been blinded and we were hoping that maybe after the doctor cleaned up the eye, she'd be able to see out of it again. But he hardly examined her at all. In his eyes, Alice was just another poor, ignorant, black sharecropper's daughter. She came home in the same condition as when she left. The only thing different was that the doctor had $250 more to put in his pocket."

Not only did the physician fail to treat Alice (she would later remember being given a bottle of eyedrops), but a gruff pronouncement he made during the office visit would torment her for decades to come: "Eyes are sympathetic," the doctor cavalierly proclaimed. "If one is blind, the other will likely become blind, too."

As much as the doctor's prognosis filled her with a frightful dread, Alice was even more distressed by the "hideous cataract" that had changed her appearance. "Now when I stare at people—a favorite pastime, up to now—they will stare back," she wrote in the essay. "Not at the 'cute' little girl, but at her scar. For six years I do not stare at anyone, because I do not raise my head."

Uprooted by her family's move from the familiar surroundings of Wards Chapel to Milledgeville, Alice also suffered the insecurity of being a newcomer at the school there, a former penitentiary with its execution chamber barely disguised. The "creepy" school deepened Alice's sense of vulnerability. And she missed the soothing purrs of her gray-and-white cat, Phoebe, astray when the Walkers left Putnam County and never found.

Alice later lamented, "All new children and teachers and that awful school with the imprint of the electric chair. I was not known. My disfigured eye was all the new children saw."

Doris Reid remembers the dramatic shift in Alice's personality after the injury, which she says neither her parents nor the Walkers ever mentioned. "Nobody said a word about it," she maintains.

The shroud of silence was no doubt connected to the profound sense of guilt and regret Alice's parents must have felt about buying their sons BB guns and the pain (mental and physical) Alice suffered afterward. For about a month after the incident, with Alice taunted by schoolmates and her grades faltering for the first time ever, the Walkers, thinking it was best for their child, sent her back to Wards Chapel. There, she lived with her paternal grandparents and re-enrolled in East Putnam Consolidated, where she'd been the star pupil in Miss Reynolds's class. After closing shop on Fridays at Stribling's garage, Bill would routinely return Alice to Milledgeville for weekends with the family, Ruth said.

"Up until the eye incident, Alice had been a straight A student, then she started bringing home Bs and Cs," Ruth explained. "The kids in Milledgeville were mean and hurtful, so Mama and Daddy wanted to protect her. With Alice back at the old school, they knew she'd be loved by Miss Reynolds, by our grandparents, and everybody else in the community. Our whole family returned to Wards Chapel that next year. So, looking at the big picture, Mama and Daddy thought they were doing more good for Alice than harm."

It *was* a relief for Alice to be spared the cruel "one-eye" invectives of her Milledgeville classmates. Still, Alice said she felt both abandoned and punished by her parents' decision to send her away from home. Why was it, she wondered, that *she* had to leave the family instead of Curtis or Bobby? To her wounded, eight-year-old spirit, the decision felt like rejection. And if not rejection, it certainly felt unfair. "My parents didn't explain why, what, when, or anything," Alice remembered. "It was decided and off I went."

Ashamed of her appearance and unable to understand why she was "exiled," her brothers left to run free, Alice became increasingly despondent and withdrawn. She took refuge in the books she received from friends and relatives at Christmas and for birthdays—

Gulliver's Travels, Robinson Crusoe, and collections of fairy tales. She also began to write sad poems.

"Before, Alice was inquisitive and extremely outgoing," Reid remembered. "She was the type of child that could charm a rock. After the accident, she wanted to be more alone. She tended to be more to herself. We still had fun, but she wasn't as talkative as before and she spent a lot more time with her books. I could see those changes and because I loved Alice, they just hurt my little heart.

"I looked beyond the eye, whereas I don't think Alice did. I remember telling her, as we got older, 'Oh Alice, you look so pretty. You're just glowing,' and all this and that. And she'd say, 'Oh stop. I'm ugly. Everybody knows I'm not pretty anymore.' "

OVER THE years, Alice's sadness and lack of self-worth would be compounded by the sense of betrayal she felt. The way she saw it, she'd been wronged. By her brothers. By her parents. And perhaps, worst of all, by the lie her brothers had bullied her into telling to save their own hides. About their allegation that she, too, had been a "gun-wielding cowboy," half a century later, Alice would defend herself as she had not been able to do as an eight-year-old girl with a wounded eye: "My instinct is that my brothers have concocted another face-saving story. Again, it is their word against mine. If I had a gun too, the battle would seem fair. Even if I didn't know how to shoot it. At the time of the injury everyone referred to it not only as 'an accident,' but as '*my* accident'—thereby absolving my brothers of any blame.

"The unhappy truth is that I was left feeling a great deal of pain and loss and forced to think I had somehow brought it on myself. It was very like a rape. It was the first time I abandoned myself, by lying, and is at the root of my fear of abandonment. It is also the root of my need to tell the truth, always, because I experienced, very early, the pain of telling a lie."

7

Knights in Shining Armor

ALICE MAINTAINED a public silence about her eye injury because she did not want to be pitied. Not by friends, lovers, future employers—and especially not by literary critics, who, as her career progressed, would be called on to assess her talents as a writer. For Alice, the injury and the circumstances surrounding it were a private matter. Besides, in the years immediately following the incident, she was less concerned about her compromised vision than she was about the "glob" of scar tissue that covered her right eye, making her feel flawed and ashamed.

Writing in "Beauty," she describes her response at age twelve when a visiting cousin, having taken an inadvertent glance at one of Alice's school pictures, innocently inquired, "You still can't see out of that eye?"

No, I say and flop back on the bed over my book.
That night, as I do almost every night, I abuse my eye. I rant and rave at it, in front of the mirror. I plead with it to clear up before morning. I tell it I hate and despise it. I do not pray for sight. I pray for beauty.

Alice would reprise the theme in the opening stanza of her poem "Remember?"

>*Remember me?*
>*I am the girl*
>*with the dark skin*
>*whose shoes are thin*
>*I am the girl*
>*with rotted teeth*
>*I am the dark*
>*rotten-toothed girl*
>*with the wounded eye*
>*and the melted ear . . .*

From all accounts, whatever feelings the Walker family might have had about the despair that had descended on Alice remained largely unexpressed. Not unlike her father in the aftermath of the death of his mother, she was left to contend with the trauma of the injury, primarily, by herself. It was out of her isolation and feelings of being an outcast that, Alice later said, she began to hone her powers of observation. She developed an empathy and sense of kinship with other people she perceived to be "afflicted," including ailing and feeble whites who, before her injury, she had not been inclined to consider charitably. Echoing the sentiments of poet Theodore Roethke, who wrote that "In a dark time, the eye begins to see," Alice, from what she later characterized as her "solitary, lonely position," began to "really see people and things, really to notice relationships and to learn to be patient enough to care about how they turned out."

But the compassion that surfaced in Alice for others she found difficult to afford herself. When she would rise in the morning and discover that her eye had not "cleared up" while she was sleeping, suicide would often present itself as the best answer to her unanswered prayers for "beauty." "I daydreamed—not of fairytales—but of falling on swords, of putting guns to my heart or head, and of slashing my wrists with a razor," Alice told John O'Brien in

Interviews with Black Writers (an excerpt appears in *In Search of Our Mothers' Gardens*).

"For a long time I thought I was very ugly and disfigured. This made me shy and timid, and I often reacted to insults and slights that were not intended. I discovered the cruelty (legendary) of children, and of relatives, and could not recognize it as the curiosity it was. I no longer felt like the little girl I was. I felt old, and because I felt I was unpleasant to look at, filled with shame."

HER CAREER as a beautician (and later, nursing home administrator) curtailed by debilitating back injuries, Ruth started tending children in her Atlanta home. Surrounded by juice-filled baby bottles, rattles, and packages of gleaming white diapers, she settled into a plush reclining chair one afternoon and discussed her family's apparent obliviousness to Alice's emotional pain.

"You see, Alice was such a special, sweet, and delightful little girl that the accident really didn't matter that much to us," Ruth explained. "I mean, it mattered that she couldn't see out of her eye anymore, but it didn't matter that it looked bad in terms of cosmetics. As far as we were concerned, she hadn't changed because Alice was just Alice. She was still that same precious little girl that everybody loved so much.

"I know that Alice has felt, in retrospect, that we didn't take what had happened seriously enough. Speaking only for me, it was years before I realized how betrayed she felt and how much the injury had affected her self-esteem."

Given her family's poverty and lack of access to medical care, Alice had no recourse but to press on as best she could with what she believed to be a blight on her appearance and the doctor's doomsday prediction hanging over her head. Her spirits were lifted somewhat by the support and affection of her seventh-grade teacher at Eatonton's Butler-Baker High School, a woman who, as a child, had also been blinded in her right eye.

"While we never talked directly about the subject, Alice and I had a special understanding that I believe was a comfort to her when she was in my class," said Trellie Jeffers, today chair of the English Department at Talladega College in Alabama.

"I'd lost an eye and it was common knowledge in Eatonton that I wore a prosthesis. By junior high, the children had stopped teasing Alice the way they'd done in grade school, but you could sense that she was still very concerned about her appearance. She could see, I think, that when I stood up in front of the class that I looked fine and that the injury hadn't stopped me from going on with my life.

"Alice wrote a poem to me on a piece of pink stationery and I still remember the first line. She wrote: 'You are my knight in shining armor.'"

A DOLLAR this week. Two the next. Maybe only fifty cents when he wanted to surprise his mother with a fancy hairpin or some new flower pots. Handing over as much as he could spare from his weekly twenty-six-dollar paycheck, Bill Walker, by 1955, had repaid every penny of the $250 he'd borrowed from Dickie Stribling. And at age twenty-one and fed up with "the ways of white folks" in Georgia, Bill quit his job at Dickie's and moved to Boston, where relatives had relocated a few years before. Within days of his arrival Bill was hired at a tire shop. His salary, astronomical for a black man in Georgia, was fifty-five dollars a week. Every time Bill got paid, a crisp twenty, folded inside a letter with a few lines of greetings, made its way back to Wards Chapel.

Bill learned, from letters he received from Alice, that her grades had improved, but that she still felt dejected and excluded by classmates because of her eye injury. Remembering her childhood sass and sparkle, Bill's heart ached as he now thought of his baby sister, dispirited and forlorn.

"It hurt me that Alice didn't have a lot of friends," Bill said. "The older children had left home. Bobby and Curtis were standoffish because they felt guilty. It just seemed to me that Alice was more alone than she'd ever been."

Hoping to cheer her, Bill and his wife, the former Gaynell (Gaye) Joyner, decided to bring Alice up North to visit them during the summer of 1958. At the time, the couple lived in Roxbury, a vibrant blue-collar area of Boston that attracted many Southern blacks seeking better schools and jobs. They extended their invitation to Alice by way of asking her if she would help care for their newborn son, Billy. But the offer was actually a carefully calculated ploy. The quiet dinners and leisurely strolls Bill and Gaye hoped to enjoy while Alice took care of the baby would, of course, provide welcome relief for the hard-working couple. But their true goal was to rectify, as best they could, the "medical treatment" Alice had received in Macon when she was eight.

"We thought the doctors in Boston might be able to help her," Bill later explained. "But we didn't want to tell her the plan right off, because we knew she'd get all excited. She'd been through so much already with the doctors in Georgia that we didn't want her to be disappointed if things didn't work out. So we came up with the baby-sitting idea as a pretense for getting her to Boston, knowing that she'd naturally say 'yes.' Then we could sneak her to the hospital without getting her hopes up high."

Not too long after Alice arrived, laden with books teachers had loaned her (by Hawthorne, Poe, and others) and the blue composition books she filled with stories and poems, Bill went into action. Unfamiliar with the medical facilities in Boston, Bill asked a relative to recommend a hospital where Alice might be treated and was directed to the Eye and Ear Infirmary at Massachusetts General Hospital. An affiliate of the Harvard University Medical School, the Infirmary, founded in 1824, is an international leader in research and patient care for disorders of the eye. Working behind the scene, Gaye took care of the logistics.

On a hot, humid morning, Bill, wearing a dress shirt and pants instead of the navy blue work clothes he usually wore to the tire shop, approached his baby sister shortly after breakfast. "I made a point of starting the conversation real casual," he recalled. "I said, 'I want you to go with me down to the hospital.' She said, 'What for?' I said, 'They're just gonna look at your eye and see if they can do anything about that white spot.' And she said, 'OK.' "

Medical records from Massachusetts General confirm that Alice

Walker, "a 14-year-old girl shot in [the] right eye with a BB gun," was first examined at the facility on July 22, 1958. Thumbing through the documents nearly forty years later while sitting at his dining room table savoring big handfuls of cashews, Bill recalled the experience.

"So me and Alice arrive at the hospital. We get in the wrong line. We go stand in another line and it's the wrong one too. We finally get it straightened out, get the ID card, and go wait in this big room.

"I'll never forget being in that room because there were black people, white people, all kinds of people sitting in that room. Compared to Georgia, it was like being on another planet. After a while, this white receptionist comes out and tells us the doctor is ready to see us. It's a white doctor. He asks us to have a seat and tell him what happened.

"We explain. Then he examines Alice's eye real good and announces right there on the spot that they can treat her, but she has to be admitted because she'll need to stay in the hospital overnight. I was shocked. After all the foot-dragging we'd been through before, I couldn't believe that the doctor had made a decision that quick.

"Alice was standing right next to me, not saying a word. So I put my arm around her and asked, 'Is that OK with you?' In this real quiet voice she said, 'Yeah.' So I signed a whole bunch of consent forms and the doctor gave me some for my parents. When those forms came back from Georgia, I took her to the hospital again and she had the operation."

At 9:20 A.M. on August 6, 1958, Dr. Morriss M. Henry, an unassuming, Arkansas-reared ophthalmologist, performed an extracapsular cataract extraction on Alice's right eye. Describing the procedure in the postoperative report that he dictated the next day, Dr. Henry noted that "the eye was opened with the Von Graefe knife. . . . The remnants of the cortex from the lens were removed by pressure on the cornea and gently milking the material out. . . . The wound was closed by pulling the sutures tight and the conjunctival flap down. . . . The patient tolerated the procedure well and was sent to the floor in good condition."

These days, Morriss Henry can be found in his sunny, plant-filled office in Fayetteville, Arkansas. A courtly, soft-spoken man in his early seventies, Dr. Henry (also a lawyer who has served in the Arkansas State Senate) is lauded throughout the region for his first-rate surgical skills. He has also been celebrated for shunning the limelight his many accomplishments have garnered him. Framed and hung in his examining room is a clipping from a local magazine that attests to Dr. Henry's special status among his peers. It reads, "Morriss M. Henry—Doctor, lawyer, legislator—And boring at all of them."

Sitting in his office in a gleaming white lab coat, Dr. Henry gracefully holds a plastic model of the human eye in the palm of his hands. In plain, everyday language, he shares his memories of the young patient he treated in 1958.

"What I remember most is that she was very mature and we established a really good rapport from the start," Dr. Henry said. "With her being from Georgia and me from Arkansas, we had similar accents. We laughed and joked about how we understood each other. When I asked about her studies, she told me she was interested in a writing career and I thought that was impressive.

"Because general anesthesia was still risky back in those days, I used a local on her eye and asked her to be really still because if she coughed or moved, I'd be in big trouble. The operation took 30 to 45 minutes and she never flinched. Thinking about it today, I'm amazed that a child could stay still for that long.

"The BB pellet had damaged her iris and blood had leaked to the back of the eye, creating pressure that caused great pain. Given the nature of the injury, I knew that the eye had been permanently blinded. So the point of the procedure was to extract the scar tissue, which was pretty unsightly. I would have definitely wanted it removed myself."

After a routine (for the era), five-day period of recovery, Alice was discharged from the hospital on August 11, 1958. In his report, written on the last day he examined her, Dr. Henry noted, "Eye looks good. She wants to go back home as soon as possible."

In "Beauty" Alice writes that the doctor who performed the surgery was named O. Henry. Forty years later, Morriss Henry offered his explanation for having his name confused with that of the famed author, best known for his mastery of the surprise ending.

"On the day of the surgery, after I'd finished my charts, I went to check on Alice. She was understandably tired and maybe a little disoriented. She said she couldn't remember my name. And I said, 'Mo Henry, that's what they call me around here.' She said, 'O. Henry? I can remember that.' "

"And I bet you at the time that clicked with her because she wanted to be a writer. So she called me Dr. O. Henry until the day she left the hospital. And that was just fine by me."

8

A Long Walk

THE SCAR tissue in her eye removed, Alice returned to Bill and
Gaye's house transformed. She was not necessarily a "new" Alice,
but rather a revitalized version of the adorable girl who had
charmed Ferris wheel operators and grandmothers like Ma Jessie.
However, Alice's protective older brother found her behavior immediately after the surgery a bit unsettling, if not downright foolhardy.
Age twenty-four at the time, Bill said he thought Alice should rest
and allow Dr. Henry's handiwork to heal up real strong. But his
fourteen-year-old sister had other ideas. The young girl who'd once
sauntered blithely past rough-and-tumble jook joints was back in
stride. Her injury had left emotional wounds that she'd work to
unravel for years to come. But her outlook colored by the flowers
that blossomed every spring in Wards Chapel, Alice's natural optimism had not been destroyed.

"On the same night she came home from the hospital, Alice
took off and went to a Johnny Mathis concert," Bill recalled, a bit
of bemused irritation still in his voice. "I can laugh about it now,
but at the time, it kind of pissed me off.

"Some relatives who had tickets invited her and she was out the door. Me, I'm thinking she's had an operation, she needs to take it easy. She's not thinking about nothing except Johnny Mathis. After her eye was fixed, Alice's spirits went back up and she didn't want to miss a thing."

Doris Reid, who had exchanged letters with Alice while she was in Boston, remembers the relief she felt when they reunited at summer's end. Mr. Walker had told her parents about Alice's operation. Haunted by memories of the day she had seen her friend with bandages covering her face, Reid, her imagination gone wild, said she feared Alice would return to Eatonton "with big scars or half her head shaved."

"Not that Alice didn't look good before, but when she came home, she was *hot stuff*," remembered Reid, with a saucy laugh. "Her hair was done up all cute and she had these real pretty dresses she'd gotten up there in Boston. Nobody in Eatonton could hold a candle to her."

Alice later said she had no memories of the surgery or of her recovery after the procedure. And as for Johnny Mathis, nearly fifty years later, the mere mention of his name brought a devilish twinkle to her eyes: "I don't remember going to the concert, but I'm not surprised I was there. I loved Johnny Mathis. Talk about a powerful cure! How could I not have felt better after looking at that man?"

Better indeed. In the final pages of "Beauty" Alice would describe the feelings of confidence and self-worth she regained after the scar tissue was removed. "Now that I've raised my head I win the boyfriend of my dreams. Now that I've raised my head I have plenty of friends. Now that I've raised my head classwork comes from my lips as faultlessly as Easter speeches did, and I leave high school as valedictorian, most popular student, and *queen,* hardly believing my luck."

Alice's renewed sense of pride and purpose would also be reflected in her depiction of a black girl who appears in the story "Fame." Published in her collection *You Can't Keep a Good Woman Down,* the protagonist of the story is Andrea Clement White, a celebrated black woman writer and honored guest at a luncheon ("rocklike hen, red ring of spicy, soggy apple") in the

South. "'In *spite* of you I'm sitting here,'" Alice writes, revealing the author's internal monologue as she is feted by a cadre of conformist blacks and "slow, aged . . . Wasps." In the closing paragraphs of the story, Alice introduces the girl who, with a slight bow, offers "a slave song, authorless," in tribute to White. It is only then that the author feels validated.

Alice writes, "It was this child's confident memory, *that* old anonymous song that gave Andrea Clement White the energy to stand up and endure."

Just as the girl in "Fame" knew there was redemptive power in the slave song, Alice would come to honor her eye injury as an "initiation" that helped her to mature and prepare for challenges ahead. The separation from her parents, even temporarily, had been agony. But over time, Alice said she realized that her family, strapped by limited resources, had done the best that they could. "Now I understand the sadness of everyone about what happened," she said. "My parents poor, often sick, and by the time of my birth, really tired, were looking for ways to help me survive.

"But they underestimated my love for them. I could never be happy away from my mother. I loved her so much my heart sometimes felt like it couldn't hold all that love. I didn't care how poor we were."

Alice would evoke the *gift* of her childhood pain in such works as "How Poems Are Made: A Discredited View."

Letting go
In order to hold on
I gradually understand
How poems are made . . .

They are the tears
that season the smile
The stiff-neck laughter
that crowds the throat
The leftover love.
I know how poems are made.

There is a place the loss must go.
There is a place the gain must go.
The leftover love.

Alice was anchored, during her adolescent years, by the love and affection of Porter Sanford III, a smart, handsome young man who also attended Butler-Baker in segregated Eatonton, the only high school open to blacks. The son of a cotton mill laborer and a mother who worked as a cook at Butler-Baker, Sanford said that Alice won his heart when she was in the fifth grade, he in the seventh. Today a prosperous Atlanta realtor and aspiring politician, Sanford recalled, "Our parents would work all week and then on Saturday go into town to shop and socialize. We kids would buy our ice cream or candy and hang out with our friends. I'd see Alice, who I thought was really pretty, and we'd talk a bit. She didn't say much, but Alice had this very compelling aura about her even at that age. I was interested in dating her from the start, but thought she was too young."

Their casual weekend chats over licorice whips and chocolate bars eventually became a bit more charged. The teens started a full-fledged romance after Alice returned from Boston. From then on, Porter and Alice would have a standing date on Saturday nights. "Twisting again" to Chubby Checker records, cheering at sporting events, taking in movies at the Pex Theater—Alice and Porter were always together and easily the most popular couple at school.

About the despair Alice had suffered before her eye operation, Sanford, like Reid, said the injury was barely noticed by her friends. "Alice had so many attractive qualities that most people didn't even pay any attention to her eye either before or after she had the operation," he recalled. "She could outdo everybody in everything. And Alice had a tremendous amount of rebellion in her personality that made her a real force in our community."

At a time when he and the other students at Butler-Baker were reluctant to confront the bigotry blacks endured in the Jim Crow South, Sanford said that Alice did not hesitate to express her anger about injustice. He recounted the day he drove himself, Alice, and their classmate Bobby "Tug" Baines to their jobs at Rock Eagle, a majestic 4-H center on the outskirts of town. The center takes its name from an ancient Indian effigy mound found on the site. Each summer, white youths from all over the country gathered at Rock Eagle to hike, swim, and camp. Blacks were permitted on the property only as janitors, groundskeepers, or kitchen staff. Alice worked in the cafeteria as a "salad girl," washing lettuce and slicing tomatoes for hours on end.

She'd capture the atmosphere in her poem "Eagle Rock." A stanza reads:

> The eagle endures
> The Cherokees are gone . . .
> As paleface warriors . . .
> So cleanly scrubbed
> Of blood:
> They come before the rock.
> Jolly conquerors.

Sanford remembered, "We were in my parents' car and Alice started talking about how unfair it was that we had to walk to school while the white kids had a bus; about how white people got paid more for doing the same work that we did; about how they constantly had their foot on our necks. I said we just had to accept it and there was no use in complaining.

"Alice got so mad at me that she demanded to be let out of the car. She dragged Tug out with her, telling him he should be ashamed to ride with me and they walked the rest of the way to work."

Baines, who later traveled the world as an administrator for the Red Cross, spoke in somber tones when he reminisced about his unplanned trek to Rock Eagle. "Alice never accepted the lowly station of blacks in the South. She was conscious of the injustices long before the rest of us recognized them and started to fight.

"That was a long walk she invited me on that day," he continued, with an easy laugh. "Alice was always real serious about her issues."

. . .

THE SOUTH, in the mid to late 1950s, was undergoing a cataclysmic upheaval on the issue of civil rights. The landmark school desegregation case *Brown v. Board of Education* had been successfully argued before the Supreme Court in 1954. Buoyed by the victory, black political, religious, and civic organizations began a full-scale campaign to dismantle Jim Crow.

For many, the most galvanizing event of the era was the 1955 bus boycott staged in Montgomery, Alabama. The protest was sparked by the defiance of then-forty-two-year-old Rosa Parks, a seamstress who earned about seventy-five cents an hour altering clothes at a local department store.

An active member of the Montgomery chapter of the National Association for the Advancement of Colored People (NAACP), Parks had long complained about the indignities blacks suffered under segregation. She especially deplored the custom on public transit systems, common throughout the South, that required blacks to enter the front of a bus to pay the fare and then reboard through the back door. For "sport," sometimes drivers, after a black passenger had paid, would speed off, leaving the hapless and humiliated rider standing on the street in a stream of exhaust fumes. And when the front section of bus seats (reserved for whites) was filled, black passengers were automatically expected to relinquish their seats in the rear to whites of any age or station.

Exhausted after a long day's work and fed up with the injustice of the system, Parks, on Thursday, December 1, 1955, refused to give up her seat to a white rider, as three other black passengers on the bus had already done. "I'm tired of being treated like a second-class citizen," Parks told driver James F. Blake when he demanded that she, too, abandon her seat. To his warning that he would have her arrested, she calmly replied, "You can do that."

Blake parked the bus and called the police, who immediately arrested Parks and fined her fourteen dollars for "disorderly conduct." Under the direction of Dr. Martin Luther King Jr., a Georgia-born minister who was then pastoring Montgomery's Dexter Avenue Church, the black community rallied around Parks and, inspired by her quiet courage, refused to ride the city's buses for 381 days. Instead, people walked to work, organized carpools, and rode bicycles, thereby ruining the economic machinery of Montgomery and bringing international attention to the degradation of blacks in the South. The protest continued until December 21, 1956, when the U.S. Supreme Court, under pressure to end the crisis, finally struck down Alabama's bus segregation laws. A resounding triumph, the Montgomery boycott ushered in a massive civil rights movement that would rage through the nation in the 1960s.

ALICE'S FEELINGS about the fomenting racial upheaval would infuse the title poem in her debut collection *Once* (1968). Written in fifteen parts, the closing stanza called to mind the 1964 Norman Rockwell painting, "The Problem We All Live With," depicting a black girl in starched white dress and flanked by federal marshals, as she arrives for classes at a previously all-white school.

> *then there was*
> *the*
> *picture of*
> *the*
> *bleak-eyed*
> *little black*
> *girl*
> *waving the*
> *american*
> *flag*
> *holding it*
> *gingerly*
> *with*
> *the very*
> tips
> *of her*
> *fingers.*

9

Order My Steps

ALICE'S FIRST image of Martin Luther King Jr. was beamed back to her from a television screen one day in her mother's living room. She recalls that she was about sixteen. No longer able to continue in the cotton fields, Mrs. Walker, now in her late forties, had started working as a maid and saved up part of her earnings to purchase a small black-and-white set. When she returned to Wards Chapel after cooking, scrubbing, ironing, and dusting for white families, Mrs. Walker would sometimes unwind a bit by watching TV before she started the next round of chores in her own home. And after that work was completed, she turned, with near-religious zeal, to the daily tending of her magnificent garden.

Resplendent with petunias, zinnias, dahlias, rhododendrons, towering sunflowers, deep red pansies, and hollyhocks, Mrs. Walker's garden was legendary throughout Putnam County. A gifted and generous gardener who, in the words of her daughter Ruth, "gave away enough flowers to be the official florist of Georgia," Mrs. Walker had a ready reply for the many admirers of her artistry: "A house without flowers is like a face without a smile."

The influence of Mrs. Walker's gardening and reverence for

flowers is found throughout Alice's work. The image of a wild pink rose nestled against the frayed rope of a noose, lent an ethereal tone to the story about Myop. In "Petunias," which appears in *You Can't Keep a Good Woman Down,* Alice writes of an unnamed civil rights worker in Mississippi whose son returns from Vietnam and shows her how to make bombs. Enraged by the woman's activism, segregationists desecrate the grave of her great-grandmother, who had been enslaved. "One morning I found her dust dumped over my verbena bed," the protagonist announces, unshaken. "And a splintery leg bone had fell among my petunias." The message of the succinct and sardonic tale? Although they might be rendered "fertilizer," the oppressed can continue to bloom.

Alice's writing would likewise be infused with her mother's quilt-making skills. Offering reflections in *A Communion of the Spirits: African American Quilters, Preservers, and Their Stories* (1996), she observed:

> Well, my mother was a quilter, and I remember many, many afternoons of my mother and the neighborhood women sitting on the porch around the quilting frame, quilting and talking, you know; getting up to stir something on the stove and coming back and sitting down. My mother also had a frame inside the house. . . . I feel just really good and protected and blessed . . . when I am under quilts made by my mother. . . . It's the same tradition as sand painting or carving . . . The power is partly about grounding yourself in something that is humble . . . something that you can actually see take form through your own effort.

It was Mrs. Walker's loving smile and the coziness she could always bring to even the most derelict sharecropper's cabin that comforted Alice when she came home from directing dramatic skits or presiding over student council meetings at Butler-Baker.

By the late 1950s, Alice had watched as, one by one, her older siblings fled the "back of the bus" treatment that still prevailed in Georgia despite Supreme Court rulings outlawing segregation. Like countless other Southern blacks, her brothers and sisters had left their birthplace for Boston, Newark, Cleveland, and Detroit— places where they could find decent jobs, drink from any water fountain, and eat a leisurely meal at whatever restaurant they chose to patronize.

As she charted her career in college administration, Alice's eldest sister Mamie traveled extensively. An alumna of Morris Brown College in Atlanta, Mamie noted that her subsequent research on "the impact of colonialism in diverse cultures," took her, in the early 1960s, to such countries as Ireland, Peru, Vietnam, Nigeria, and Lesotho. "My mind did not permit me to remain in Georgia and be mistreated," Mamie declared in a clipped, British-style accent. "Real intelligence will take you to the moon."

Although her days were filled with extracurricular activities and the warmth of her romance with Porter, Alice suffered a certain melancholy each time one of her siblings left Eatonton. Her loneliness was assuaged by the close bond she shared with her mother, who understood Alice's somber moods and the solace she found in books. By her teens, Alice had read most of Shakespeare, her father having rescued the collected works ("everything but *Othello*," she later noted) from a trash heap at the white school in Eatonton. "I learned most of *Hamlet, Romeo and Juliet,* and *Macbeth* by heart." Alice was also fond of Georgia-born writer Frank Yerby, whose story "Health Card" had won a 1944 O. Henry Prize and who was "rumored to be a Negro." And then there was *Oedipus Rex,* the labyrinthine Sophocles tragedy in which the King of Thebes blinds himself upon learning that he has, unwittingly, murdered his father and bedded his mother. Alice said that Bobby Baines introduced her to the drama during a break from his studies at Atlanta's Morehouse College. "Whenever Bobby came home, we'd get together and discuss some of the books he'd read," Alice explained. "He told me about *Oedipus Rex,* which I read and was blown away. I thought it was profound, to-the-bone, literature."

Detailing her mother's affirmation of her passion for books, Alice would later write, "I could go into my room and shut the door and lie on the bed and read, knowing I would never be interrupted.

No matter what was needed, there was no word about making me leave a book.

"I suppose because I was the last child there was a special rapport between us and I was permitted a lot more freedom. Once when I was eight or nine she was about to whip my brothers and me for something, and when she finished whipping the others and got to me, she turned around and dropped the switch and said, 'You know, Alice, I don't have to whip you; I can talk to you.' "

It was against the backdrop of such companionship that Alice and Mrs. Walker settled in front of the television one afternoon in October 1960. Intelligent, probing, and fully aware of the obstacles blacks faced in the South, Alice had been wondering if she, like her siblings, would be forced to leave Georgia to fulfill her ambitions as a writer. For the more she came to understand how Southern racism had limited her opportunities to pursue other vocations, the stronger her commitment to writing grew.

As a young child, Alice's interest in both painting and the piano had been stifled because her parents, on their paltry sharecroppers' income, could afford neither art supplies nor music lessons. In truth, as Alice would later reveal with great sadness, she had studied piano for a few months. She then chose to stop, knowing the fifty cents per lesson was too much for her parents to spare.

Of the mind that science was a worthy endeavor (especially after her eye surgery), Alice had also considered a career as a research scientist. But there were no microscopes, chemistry sets, or other tools of the trade available to black students in Georgia. While she had an innate ability with words and enjoyed the worlds she discovered in books, Alice's predilection for writing was also a matter of practicality; paper and pencil were cheap and plentiful in her circumscribed landscape. Even then, a writing tablet was never purchased without a thought to its cost.

As she sat with her mother, the answer to some of Alice's worries about segregation and its impact on the trajectory of her life appeared on the TV screen. It came in the form of a cool and collected Dr. Martin Luther King Jr. as he was being handcuffed and shoved into the backseat of a police car. His offense? Leading, in the aftermath of the Montgomery boycott, yet another protest against Jim Crow. This time the target was an Atlanta department store whose white owners were all too happy to take the money of blacks wanting to buy new stoves or refrigerators, but who banned them from enjoying so much as a tuna fish sandwich or a cup of tea at the lunch counter. Those who demanded equality were gruffly greeted with, "No Colored Allowed," or worse.

Writing in "Choice: A Tribute to Martin Luther King, Jr.," Alice later described her response to the newscast she watched with her mother: "He [King] had dared to claim his rights as a native son . . . . His whole body, like his conscience, was at peace. At the moment I saw his resistance I knew I would never be able to live in this country without resisting everything that sought to disinherit me, and I would never be forced away from the land of my birth without a fight."

Having been transformed by her very first glimpse of Dr. King, Alice decided, that instant, to remain in Georgia and join the Black Freedom Movement that blossomed after the events in Montgomery. Only eleven when Rosa Parks had refused to relinquish her seat, Alice knew little, if anything, about the victory in Alabama. "Seeing the footage of Dr. King getting arrested was definitely a turning point," she later explained. "He showed me that black people were no longer going to be passive and just accept the inhumanity of segregation. He gave me hope."

Ready to join the front lines of the civil rights struggle, Alice finished her final year of high school in a blaze of glory. One of the highlights of the year, as Doris Reid recalled, was the first-prize trophy Alice brought back to Butler-Baker from a statewide dramatics contest. The award was presented for her direction of excerpts from *Imitation of Life,* the 1933 Fanny Hurst novel about the pained relationship between a black domestic and her light-skinned daughter. Ashamed of her mother because she cooks and cleans for a successful white woman, the daughter rejects black culture and attempts to pass for white. First adapted for film in 1934 and again in 1959, *Imitation of Life,* as interpreted by Alice for the competition, left the audience stunned.

"Alice's staging and the passages she chose for us to read were very powerful," remembered Reid, who was cast as the daughter. "She made you really feel the whole racial dynamic in the South. When she had me say, as the daughter, that I wanted to be white, it was to show how black people, as a consequence of constantly being degraded, had learned to hate themselves. I think the audience was shocked. Alice forced you to look at the ugly stuff, the stuff nobody wanted to face."

ALICE'S SENSITIVITY to Jim Crow's withering impact on the self-esteem of blacks was heightened by her observation of the changes that overtook Mamie after she left Eatonton. By her own admission, Mamie had been "horribly scarred and damaged" by the racial humiliations she suffered as a child. In an interview, she was quick to vent her anger.

"I spit on Eatonton with its big, ugly, red-faced white people," said Mamie, in her early seventies, as she sat in her Atlanta home surrounded by artifacts collected during her travels. "I knew from birth that I was as good as anybody and better than most, black or white. No one in my family really knows me or all the hurts I've been through. As far as my heart and emotions, they didn't seem to care. So I rose above it."

As much as they would have relished ridding the South of segregation, the Walkers had raised their children with all the love and encouragement they could muster. Mamie's rebukes, often leveled against her parents in what they perceived to be accusatory and judgmental tones, left them feeling at best guilty; at worst, inferior, ineffectual, and unrefined, Alice said. Given the criticism Mr. and Mrs. Walker had already endured, Alice was not surprised, as she readied herself for college, to find them a bit wary of higher education and the effect it might have on their youngest child. Besides, one didn't need a Ph.D. to see that not a single black person in Eatonton kept food on the table by being a writer.

"I think my parents had been badly burned by their experience with my sister Mamie," Alice later said. "They'd made a lot of sacrifices for her to get an education. Then when she came home, she criticized the way they lived, the way they talked, what they didn't know. It seemed like she looked down on them.

"If they had any expectation for me, it was perhaps that I would be a schoolteacher. Mostly, they just wanted me to have a good, reliable job. But their main concern was that I not go off somewhere and come back thinking I was 'better' than them. They had already been through that."

With haunting poignancy, Alice later explored, in the poem "For My Sister Molly Who in the Fifties," the issues of self-love and identity with which Mamie struggled. The piece is written from the perspective of a young child in awe of an older sister who:

> *Once made a fairy rooster from*
> *Mashed potatoes . . .*
> *Green onions were his tail*
> *And his two legs were carrot sticks*
> *A tomato slice his crown . . .*
>
> *Knew Hamlet well and read into the night*
> *And coached me in my songs of Africa*
> *A continent I never knew*
> *But learned to love . . .*
>
> *Who read from* Prose and Poetry
> *And loved to read "Sam McGee from Tennessee"*
> *On nights the fire was burning low . . .*
>
> *Who walked among the flowers*
> *And brought them inside the house*
> *Who smelled as good as they*
> *And looked as bright*

Alice writes that the sister, home during college breaks, eventually begins to chide her poor, black family for their "sloppishness." No longer comfortable in her own skin, the sister:

Found much
Unbearable
Who walked were few had
Understood   And sensed our
Groping after light
And saw some extinguished
And no doubt mourned.

The last line reads: "FOR MY SISTER MOLLY WHO IN THE FIFTIES / Left us."

"When I saw the first version of the poem, I thought it was lovely," Mamie later said. "It was so to the point. Alice had captured exactly the way it was.

"But when it was published, the last lines had been added," she continued. "I felt as if Alice had given me praise with one hand and taken it back with the other. One was left with the impression that I had deserted my family or died. On the contrary, everything I learned, I tried to pour into Alice's head. She could absorb my college-level teachings like a sponge when she was a child. I loved her (and do love her) so much. We are both Aquarius, very daring people. But the poem was hurtful."

In the O'Brien interview, Alice explained that the first draft of the poem was for Mamie alone, "and the way I wish her to relate to the poem." She added that she crafted, over a period of five years, nearly fifty versions of "For My Sister Molly" before its 1973 publication in *Revolutionary Petunias & Other Poems*. "As I wrote it, the lines and words went, on the paper, to a place comparable to where they lived in my head."

"My sister was a pioneer," Alice added, decades later, after a public reading of the poem in New York. "She was one of those people who build a bridge to the other side. Many of them find it difficult to return home."

But at age seventeen, Alice, the valedictorian of her fifty-three-member class, still had years to go before rising to the celebrity that would usher her writing to audiences around the globe. For now, she knew that her future would turn on her continued pursuit of education. One need only look at the menial jobs—maid, cook, chauffeur, field hand, factory worker—available to blacks in Wards Chapel to understand it was imperative for Alice to obtain a college degree.

While she would later remember "looking into" Savannah State University, Alice ultimately chose to attend Spelman College in Atlanta. The all-female, historically black institution was highly regarded. Moreover, because of her impaired vision, the school granted Alice a "rehabilitation" scholarship, made available to students with disabilities. Under the headline, "Au Revoir Class of 1961," an announcement about Alice's decision was printed on the front page of the May 23, 1961, issue of the *Butler-Baker News*. "Alice is a recipient of a paid scholarship award at Spelman," the notice read. "After completing her studies there she is planning to strive for excellence in the arts."

Alice stood firm and cast her lot in the red clay of Georgia with people who were now rallying, like Dr. King, to battle the injustices blacks had endured for generations. For her, the motto of the Butler-Baker class of 1961 was more than apt: "With the ropes of the past, we will ring the bells of the future."

Driven to the depot by her father, Alice left Eatonton for Spelman on a Greyhound bus in late August 1961. The elders in the community had shown their support for her achievements by collecting seventy-five dollars, which they gave to Alice to defray college expenses. Mrs. Walker, on her maid's earnings of less than twenty dollars a week, had given Alice "three things she never owned herself," a typewriter, a sewing machine, and a suitcase, "as nice a one as anyone in Eatonton had ever had," Alice would later write. "That suitcase gave me permission to travel and part of the joy in going very far from home was the message in that suitcase."

Emboldened with the spirit of Rosa Parks, Alice deliberately sat in the empty front section of the bus "reserved" for white passengers. Writing years later, she described the experience: "A white woman (may her fingernails now be dust!) complained to the driver, and he ordered me to move. But even as I moved, in confusion and tears, I knew he had not seen the last of me. In those seconds of moving, everything changed. I was eager to bring an end to the South that permitted my humiliation."

As the bus pulled away, Alice, now sitting in the back, turned and looked through the window. She saw her father standing on the side of the road, his hat in his hands. Seeing his sad eyes, she brushed back her tears.

10

Nobody in Atlanta

SHE DIDN'T know it when she arrived on the Spelman campus, but for the second time in her life, Alice Walker was going to be educated in a former army barracks.

Founded in 1881 by Sophia B. Packard and Harriet E. Giles, white missionaries from New England, Spelman was started as a school for black females just out of slavery. Packard and Giles had visited the South the previous year and been appalled by the conditions that blacks—illiterate, landless, and impoverished—faced as they struggled to build independent lives after slavery's end. Concerned also about the plight of newly freed slaves, Rev. Frank Quarles, the influential black pastor of Atlanta's Friendship Baptist Church, arranged for the school, with an inaugural class of eleven girls, to open in his church basement on April 11, 1881. It was christened the Atlanta Baptist Female Seminary. One of the school's early benefactors was Standard Oil Company magnate John D. Rockefeller, who, after hearing about the institution in 1882, pledged the then-princely sum of $250 to the school's building fund. In 1884, thanks to donations from Georgia's black community and continued support from Rockefeller, the school moved to the site of a barracks that had been occupied by Union soldiers during the Civil War. The barracks was renamed in honor of Mr. and Mrs. Harvey Buel Spelman, the parents of Mr. Rockefeller's wife, Laura Celestia Spelman.

With its focus on "industrial education," the early curriculum at Spelman offered courses in printing, sewing, cooking, laundering, and housekeeping, in addition to basic courses in reading and the Bible. The founders placed a high priority on imparting to the young black women in their charge, practical skills that would help them become good homemakers with strong religious convictions that reflected the school's motto, "Our Whole School for Christ." The curriculum eventually expanded to include standard liberal arts classes in literature, geography, mathematics, and English. When Alice arrived in 1961, eighty years after its founding, Spelman's emphasis on gentility and "moral education" was still in full force on the red-bricked, magnolia tree–lined campus.

At the time, annual tuition at Spelman was about $1,200. The fee was less than the $2,500 charged by Wellesley and other elite women's colleges in the North. Still, the tuition was beyond the means of most sharecropper families, and over the years, Spelman had attracted most of its students from the black middle class—the daughters of ministers, teachers, funeral directors, insurance agents, social workers, and librarians. While Alice was not the only scholarship student at Spelman, as the daughter of a tenant farmer she was definitely in the minority. But she did not allow herself to feel inferior. By the same token, she did not expect or curry any special favors because of her eye injury. Alice's objectives at Spelman were to read more books, improve her writing, and get in the thick of the civil rights protests that were erupting on the streets of Atlanta, seemingly everyday.

A staunch supporter of the movement was a tall, lanky, and energetic professor named Howard Zinn. The son of Jewish immigrants, Zinn had earned a doctorate in history from Columbia University, with the tuition paid by the GI bill. Upon graduation, in 1956, he had been hired by Spelman president Albert Manley to chair the school's history and social science departments. Manley, the former dean of the College of Arts and Sciences at North Carolina College, had ended more than fifty years of New England leadership at Spelman when, in 1953, he became the school's first black and first male president.

In his 1994 memoir, *You Can't Be Neutral on a Moving Train,* Zinn records the atmosphere on the campus, which, when he joined the faculty, was surrounded by a twelve-foot-high stone wall. "[Students] were expected to dress a certain way, walk a certain way, pour tea a certain way. There was compulsory chapel six times a week. Students had to sign in and out of their dormitories, and be in by 10:00 P.M. Their contacts with men were carefully monitored; the college authorities were determined to counter stories of the sexually free black woman and worse, the pregnant, unmarried black girl. . . .

"It was as if there was an unwritten, unspoken agreement between the white power structure of Atlanta and the administrations of the black colleges: We white folk will let you colored folk have your nice little college. . . . And in return, you will not interfere with our way of life."

In the early 1960s, the "way of life" for whites in Atlanta was not much different from that depicted by the city's "favorite daughter," Margaret Mitchell, in her 1937 Pulitzer Prize–winning novel *Gone with the Wind.* Unlike the shotgun-totin', moonshine-drinkin' "crackers" who lived in the piney woods of Georgia, white Atlantans, like Mitchell's heroine Scarlett O'Hara, were inclined to express their prejudices against blacks with an aristocratic veneer. Detailing the reaction of local officials when a group of black students challenged the city's color barrier by sitting in the "white" section of the Atlanta Municipal Auditorium, Zinn, who accompanied the students, shows the innovative spin that was put on Jim Crow. "The manager, in consternation, phoned the mayor, who advised him dryly, to dim the lights. Afterward, queried by the press, the manager announced that he had designated those front row orchestra seats 'a Negro section.'"

Both on the Spelman campus and in the often surreal, segregated world of Atlanta, Professor Zinn, attentive and always bearing a warm and welcoming smile, stood in unshakable solidarity with black people. Reared with many hardships in a working-class neighborhood in Brooklyn, Zinn was especially sensitive to the students at Spelman who, like Alice, grew up in poverty. About their first meeting, in 1961, at an honors dinner for incoming freshmen, he would later recall, "I remember my first impression of her: small, slender but strong-looking, smooth brown skin, one eye silent, the other doubly inquiring with a hint of laughter. Her manner was polite, but not in the directed way of a 'Spelman girl,' rather almost ironically polite—not disrespectful, simply confident. We talked, and liked one another almost immediately."

Alice would later remark that Howard Zinn was the first white man with whom she'd ever had a real conversation. "He was funny, friendly, and genuinely cared about the students. Up until that time in my life, whenever white people came around, everybody turned to ice; that was the effect they had on black people. They made it clear that we didn't have anything they considered worthy or valuable, even though they could not eat without our labor. It was obvious that Professor Zinn respected my intelligence."

In keeping with her expressed desire to "excel in the arts," Alice took a broad range of classes her first year at Spelman. They included ballet, elementary French, English composition, fundamentals of speech, general biology, and history of Western civilization. Her transcript reveals that she earned an A in most of her courses, with the exception of physical education and freshman math, in which she received grades C and D, respectively.

Calisthenics and parallelograms may not have been her strong suits, but it was not long before everyone at Spelman became aware of Alice's writing ability, according to Sadie Allen, dean of students at the time. "Around campus, she was gaining a reputation for being very talented and creative," noted Allen, who had graduated from the college in 1941. "There was what the young people today would call 'a buzz' building around Alice. She'd already arrived as a highly recommended student and from what we'd hear in the administration, she was making quite a name for herself in English class." Among the authors Alice studied were Thomas Hardy ("his country world reminded me of my own") and Stendhal ("his ecclesiastical and military one did not").

Decades later, Alice recalled the comments from English professor Esta Seaton on her analysis of the Robert Browning poem "The Bishop Orders His Tomb at Saint Praxed's Church." "She said that all of my papers, including this one, seemed more like stories than papers. . . . She'd read my papers in class and listening to them, always with embarrassment, I wanted to make them better. . . . So I always wrote them over at least once."

HER FRESHMAN year at Spelman completed, Alice, eighteen, took her first trip abroad. With her expenses underwritten by a group of prominent women from Atlanta's black churches (among them Coretta Scott King), Alice was selected as a delegate to the World Festival of Youth and Students, held July 28 to August 6, 1962, in Helsinki, Finland. Before her departure, she would have a brief meeting with King ("bright-eyed, slim and . . . bubbly") who was herself en route to a peace conference in Geneva.

Alice later recounted her first impressions of Finland: "The country seemed incredibly clean and everything smelled of dill. They cook with it a lot I think; and all the potato dishes had an unusual flavor. I was much pursued by Finnish boys; who caught me, a couple of them, and took me dancing. They could dance! And I remember thinking: 'How is it possible that they dance so well and love it so and are having such a good time swinging me about and these are very white people? The blondest of the blond.'"

Organized in the aftermath of Fidel Castro's 1959 revolution in Cuba, the youth festival brought together delegates from all over the world to exchange ideas about peace and freedom through political rallies, cultural seminars, song, dance, and theater performances. Although she has no memory of meeting them there, two women who would later become close to Alice also attended the gathering: a brilliant Brandeis University student named Angela Y. Davis and Gloria Steinem, then a twenty-eight-year-old press officer who was beginning to make her mark in the male-dominated world of journalism.

In her 1974 autobiography, Davis writes that the presentation by the Cuban delegation was the most impressive event at the festival. After a spirited theater piece in which the group satirized the U.S. government's failed 1961 attempt to overthrow the Castro regime at the Bay of Pigs, the Cubans formed a huge conga line and, with drums pounding, danced off the stage and then out of the auditorium. Alice and Angela were among the jubilant masses who joined the group as it snaked triumphantly through the streets of Helsinki.

Also in Helsinki was Julius Coles, an older Morehouse College student Alice had met at a mixer in the beginning of her freshman year. "Compared to some of the other young ladies at Spelman, she was not exactly a beauty queen," Coles would later say about Alice. "But in terms of scholarship, which mattered most to me, she emerged early as a major brain."

Located within the same Atlanta University center complex (a consortium of several colleges that share facilities), Morehouse, the nation's only private, historically black, all-male college, is considered Spelman's "brother" school, with cross-enrollment in classes permitted between the institutions. In fact, Coles had thought of his relationship with Alice as being primarily a "brother/sister," intellectually driven camaraderie until by chance they both ended up at the youth festival.

"I'd been warned against going to Helsinki because 'there'd be all kinds of communists' there," Coles remembered, "but I wanted to attend because I was interested in international affairs.

"So I arrive, and lo and behold, there was Alice," he continued. "We went to some events together and the feelings of attraction between us started getting really strong."

Coles said he remembered the two of them attending a reading by the acclaimed Soviet poet Yevgeny Yevtushenko: "He was a really powerful writer. Alice, who had gotten into Russian literature, was just in heaven."

Yevtushenko was a self-confident and unflinchingly forthright poet, who, in writing about the rewards of political struggle, had crafted the lines "Finished with lies and crooked ways, one day posterity will burn with shame remembering these peculiar times when honesty was labeled courage." As such, Yevtushenko would have been for Alice, soon to be launched into the heat of civil rights battles, a true soul mate and literary comrade-in-arms.

After the festival, Alice and Julius traveled together to the Soviet Union by train. As the old Russian locomotive chugged its way through the countryside, they drank a bottle of Negrita Rum they'd bought in Helsinki and belted out rousing choruses of songs about "the revolution." Their light, carefree, and, in Coles's memory, "sexually charged" moments were interspersed with serious discussions about world affairs. Having been charmed and inspired by the Cubans she'd met in Finland, Alice read, while on the train, Castro's defense of the revolution, *History Will Absolve Me*. The book helped to frame her understanding of the political roots of the uprising in Cuba and provided an overview of Marxist ideology that made her even more conscious of how little she knew about the Soviet Union. "I was so ignorant of history and politics that when I went to Moscow and was taken on a stroll across Red Square, I could not fathom for the longest time *who* the Russians were queuing up to view in Lenin's tomb," she later wrote.

Determined to learn more about the country, Alice enrolled in Professor Zinn's Russian history course "Revolution and Response" when she began her sophomore year in the fall of 1962. The class would prove to be a watershed for the pensive and yearning young woman from Eatonton as the "buzz" about Alice's intellectual powers increased. Decades later, sitting in a café in Berkeley, California, Zinn explained, "I thought I'd liven the history up a bit by having the students also learn about Russian art and literature. Alice didn't say much in class and then her first papers started to come in and she'd written this essay on Tolstoy and Dostoyevsky. It was sensational. It was written with so much grace, style, and critical intelligence that I wanted to share it with my colleagues in the academic world."

"I showed it to a certain professor. Not believing that a black student from rural Georgia could have written such an impressive paper, he said, with a really condescending attitude, that she must have plagiarized it. And I said to him, 'Who could she have copied it from? Nobody I know could have written this. I don't think there's anybody in the city of Atlanta who could have written a paper this eloquent.' "

For Zinn's class, Alice also read Turgenev, Gorky, and Gogol. Curious about Russian women writers, she immersed herself in the works of poet Anna Akhmatova (1888–1966). Born Anna Gorenko, the author, as a teen, had adopted the Akhmatova surname of a maternal ancestor after her father told her he did not want his name linked with poetry. Her work banned as "counterrevolutionary" under Stalin, Akhmatova exhibited her defiance in such poems as "Parting."

> *Not weeks, not months—years*
> *We spent parting. And now finally*
> *The chill of real freedom*
> *And the gray garland above the temples.*
>
> *No more treasons, no more betrayals,*
> *And you won't be listening till dawn,*
> *As the stream of evidence*
> *Of my perfect innocence flows on.*

"I read all the Russian writers I could find . . . as if they were a delicious cake," Alice later noted. "[They] made me think that Russia must have something in the air that writers breathe from the time they are born."

That Alice could craft a commanding essay on Russia's literary giants did not surprise her roommate, Constance Nabwire. Born in Uganda and educated at one of her country's most prestigious boarding schools, Nabwire was among a group of talented African students who, in the early 1960s, had been offered scholarships to colleges in America by the United Negro College Fund. Nabwire said that, unlike most of the students at Spelman who appeared to have few interests "beyond their Friday night dates," Alice made special efforts to befriend African students and was well versed in foreign affairs.

"Alice was informed, political, and had an international perspective that was rare at Spelman," remembered Nabwire, today a social worker in Minnesota. "By chance we were thrown together and it made all the difference for me to room with someone who was intellectually stimulating and engaged with the world."

The exact whereabouts of the Tolstoy/Dostoyevsky paper that bedazzled Zinn remains unknown. Queried about it, Alice deadpanned, "I've heard so much about it, I wish I could read it myself." However, Zinn did save a paper his star pupil wrote on a collection of Russian dissent writings, *The Year of Protest, 1956*. Neatly typed on onionskin paper, a portion of the essay reads, "Zdanov's 'A Trip Home' has a universal ring. It seems that all over the world people can rise from the suffering mass at the bottom to the privileged few at the top and forget that suffering still exists or ever did. Still, in the Soviet Union this brings up the question of 'the new class' which isn't supposed to exist. What is it like? Apparently comfortable at the top and glad to be there. What do the 'new classers' think of the sacrificing workers whose labor keeps the wheels of the country turning? Apparently, if they can manage it, nothing. Perhaps Socrates was right after all. Maybe man would be better off without a body because then he would not be able to sell his soul for physical comforts."

Writing in red ink, Zinn noted that the paper was "perceptive and well-written" and marked it with an A, which was the grade Alice received for the class. With the exception of a B in Bowling and a C in modern dance, Alice earned an A in the majority of the courses that she took her second year at Spelman (among them national government, American history, introduction to philosophy, and literature of the Western world). About her performance in bowling and dance class, Alice later wrote, "Fred Astaire I'm not. I'm a fair bowler but the math involved in scoring fouled me up pretty badly."

Her friendship with Julius Coles "promising, but cooled," she met during her sophomore year two other people who would one day play important roles in her life. One was Robert Allen, another Morehouse student (and son of Spelman dean Sadie Allen). Also a Georgia native, Allen, a senior at the time, first met Alice in Professor Zinn's Russian history class.

"I'd done a year abroad in Germany and later visited the Soviet Union, so I was very interested in socialism, communism, Marxism, and all that," Allen recalled. "This was during a time when a lot of people believed the civil rights movement was part of a communist plot to take over America and that King was under their control. The only place where any of these issues were discussed with any intelligence was in Howard Zinn's class.

"Howard asked students to prepare reports that we'd present to the rest of the class. Alice gave hers one day and I remember sitting in the back of the class and thinking, 'God, she's really cute! She's got really nice legs, too.' I'm ashamed to say that I don't remember a word of her presentation because I was so fixated on how cute she was. Eventually, we got to talking, but nothing major happened right then."

Alice also developed a friendship with David DeMoss, a white exchange student from Bowdoin College in Brunswick, Maine, an all-male institution at the time. DeMoss had grown up near Boston in a working-class family. Interested in learning, firsthand, about the civil rights movement, he was among a group of ten students from Bowdoin who attended classes at Morehouse for about a week during the spring of 1963. Heralding the arrival of "Visitors from the North," a front page article about the exchange in the March 28, 1963, issue of the *Atlanta World* (a local black-owned newspaper) noted that the program aimed to promote interracial understanding by giving whites "some insight into the life of Negro students in the South today."

Thirty-three years later, DeMoss, a trim lawyer and lifelong sailing enthusiast, reminisced about meeting Alice at a "social" during his week at Morehouse. "The feeling I got was that one of her friends had dragged her to this event," said DeMoss, as he sat in the parlor of his comfortable home on the North Shore of Boston. "It wasn't my impression that she did that kind of socializing on a regular basis.

"But we danced a bit and I definitely thought she was attractive. She told me she had a brother in Boston whom she planned to visit during the summer and that struck a chord. I may have written her once or twice after I returned to Bowdoin. But when she came up to her brother's place, I asked her out and we started dating. We were together all the time. I guess you could call it a torrid summer romance."

Alice remembers little about her first encounter with DeMoss other than that she was a wearing a pink faille dress purchased by Nabwire that they both shared and looked, in her own words, "divine" in. That she'd won the heart of a white student from the North hardly raised eyebrows, according to Howard Zinn. "As the only white students around were exchange students, there wasn't much opportunity for interracial dating," he explained. "I don't think anyone at Spelman made a fuss over those few situations."

However, the fiery passion that quickly ignited between Alice and David did have a political component, she later said: "White people from the North would come down all the time, look at our situation and leave. They'd be just passing through. But I could tell that David really cared about the struggle. He'd grown up poor, so he understood how the system kept people down. Still, he was so hopeful and full of optimism.

"David was also very connected to his emotions and knew how to show his affection. He was a wonderful lover. He took me to visit his family and we spent almost the entire time in the guest room they had prepared for me. I had a red corduroy bathrobe then and I used to try to hide him in it. Finally, his mother said, 'If you're going to be in Alice's room, you need to leave the door open.' She'd figured out we were not in there reading *War and Peace*."

BY THE end of her sophomore year at Spelman, Alice was making strides, both in the classroom and in her social life. As for her romance with Porter? They had already parted amicably, before

Alice left Eatonton, with a clear understanding of the goals they each wanted to accomplish in life. "I don't think either of us ever contemplated marriage," Sanford would later explain, matter-of-factly. "As young black kids from the deep South, it was going to be real tough to make it without a college education and we didn't know what lay ahead. We never got very serious because we both had dreams we wanted to fulfill."

"We separated not because we'd stopped loving each other, but because life took us to different places," Alice agreed.

With the encouragement of Esta Seaton, Howard Zinn, and friends like Julius Coles and Constance Nabwire, Alice had made, in two years, steady progress toward her goal of becoming a writer. But the demure, "lady-like" demeanor Dr. Manley and other Spelman administrators expected from students was beginning to wear on her spirits. She found herself stifled in the rarified Spelman environment as other black students throughout the South marched on picket lines and sat boldly at segregated lunch counters. In the words of a popular protest song, Alice, too, woke up each morning with her mind "stayed on freedom." But on a campus where mastering the "social graces" was considered more important than social reform, Alice felt increasingly angry and alienated. It was just a matter of time before the stone wall that surrounded Spelman, and that served as both a literal and a figurative barrier to the outside world, would become as oppressive to her as the whites who were turning fire hoses on black children and screaming, "Go back to Africa."

11

Forbidden Things

ON JUNE 11, 1963, in a fourteen-and-a-half-minute, nationally televised speech, President John F. Kennedy publicly acknowledged the
racial strife in the South by denouncing segregation. Calling the
practice morally wrong, the president said, "We preach freedom
around the world, and we mean it. And we cherish our freedom
here at home." Kennedy continued:

> But are we to say to the world—and much more importantly
> to each other—that this is the land of the free, except for the
> Negroes; that we have no second-class citizens, except for
> Negroes. . . . We face therefore a moral crisis as a country and
> as a people. It cannot be met by repressive police action. It can-
> not be quieted by token moves or talk. It is time to act in
> Congress . . . and above all, in all of our daily lives. . . . Those
> who do nothing are inviting shame as well as violence. Those
> who act boldly are recognizing right as well as reality.

"Acting boldly," at about the same time President Kennedy was
urging the nation to confront its racial crisis, Spelman president

Albert Manley fired Howard Zinn. Manley offered no specific reason for the dismissal (effective June 30, 1963) in the terse termina-
tion letter he mailed to the tenured professor, and in fact, none was
needed. It was common knowledge on the campus that Manley considered Zinn, advisor to the school's Social Science Club, the prime
"instigator" of the growing discontent Spelman women were voicing about the administration's paternalism, conservatism, and
ongoing efforts to restrict their involvement in civil rights protests.

Writing later in his journal about being forced out of his job,
Zinn noted that Manley had always felt threatened by his advocacy
on behalf of students. Moreover, revealing his true sentiments about
the young black women in his charge, Manley had made it clear
that Zinn's support of Spelman students was woefully misplaced.
"Why aren't you interested in other things, students cheating on
exams, students stealing in dormitories, things missing all the
time?" Zinn writes that Manley had once queried him during a tension-filled meeting between the two. "Aren't you interested in these
things?"

By the time Zinn received Manley's letter, Alice had already left
the campus for Boston, where she would live for the summer with
her brother Bill and his family while working as a salesclerk in the
city's Jordan Marsh department store. She heard about the dismissal of her favorite professor from a classmate who phoned her
from Georgia. It was news that left Alice stunned. Even President
Kennedy, with his political future tied to powerful white Southern
Democrats, had stepped forward, realizing that segregation was a
scourge on the nation that could no longer be ignored. How could
it be that Zinn, a tenured professor, had been fired for encouraging
students to put democracy to the test? Was that not his duty as an
educator in a country that purported to "cherish freedom"?

In a letter dated June 20, 1963, Alice, age nineteen, wrote to
Zinn expressing her shock and outrage:

> To be perfectly honest I don't know what to say to you. When
> I left Spelman a little while ago [for summer break] I believed,
> happily, that I would have the next two years . . . to think of

something. Some thing, that is, fine enough to give you at least
a vague idea of what a great and wonderful person you are. . . .
I've tried to imagine Spelman without you—and I can't at all.

There is a break in the text of the letter, and then it begins again,
dated June 21:

Last night . . . I was far too upset to finish my letter. Today I
received a letter from Mrs. Seaton. . . . She let me know that
much of the community as well as the college is also torn up
about this thing. She also said you plan to fight the action. . . .
I'm glad! I shall write again when I have 'gotten myself
together' (smile—chin up, chest out!) You know how much
you mean to us. Whatever I can do to help please *please* let me
know.

On July 8, 1963, Alice again wrote to Zinn (who ultimately took a
job at Boston University), giving him Bill's phone number should he
want to call. Her sadness about the unexpected turn of events was
evident in the forlorn tone with which she ended the letter: "Well, I
must leave for work—I'm a salesgirl at Jordan's downtown. I sell
moth ball crystals and stuff. Give the family my love . . ."

Zinn recalled that Alice later sent a poem, "Contemplation." A
fragment read:

> *Through the lonely streets*
> *Filled with chattering echoes*
> *Rattle the empty souls . . .*

David DeMoss, who worked as a soda jerk in a Boston-area ice
cream parlor during the summer of 1963, remembered that Alice
was "clearly disappointed that the administration at Spelman didn't
appreciate Zinn's abilities as a teacher, but moreover, what he represented as a human being."

"Here was this white man who refused to accept the status
quo," DeMoss explained. "He fought back because he understood

that when black people were degraded, society as a whole was diminished. He was perceived at Spelman to be a troublemaker and he was. But what upset Alice was that they couldn't see that he was the right kind of troublemaker."

DeMoss said that despite Alice's despair over Zinn's plight, the two of them still managed to have a "sweet summer filled with many passionate days and nights," adding that they were vigilant about contraceptives. They went to the theater, to museums, and cheered for the hometown Red Sox at Fenway Park. Sharing his love for the sea with Alice, he took her sailing and on more sedate, but nonetheless romantic, rides on the swan boats in Boston Common. As an interracial couple strolling hand in hand who thought nothing of stealing a kiss on a public street, DeMoss said that he and Alice were subject to many a disapproving glare. "People stared at us and so forth," he remembered, "but to tell you the truth, I didn't give a damn.

"I adored Alice. And I had grown up in a family where it was just ground into us kids that everybody was equal. To be prejudiced against anybody was absolutely not allowed. Call me naïve, but I figured Alice and I would just walk into the sunset and live happily ever after. I couldn't imagine any problem that our love couldn't overcome."

For Alice's siblings (especially her brothers) who had grown up under the threat of the Ku Klux Klan and with strict taboos about "race-mixing," Alice's romance with David DeMoss forced them to see that the free-spirited independence their baby sister had always exhibited knew no bounds. By their standards, Alice, in her unrestrained love relationship with a white man, was exercising freedoms that, given the volatile history of race relations, they felt warranted more discretion. Had the Walker brothers been inclined to court white girls during their adolescent years in Wards Chapel, they knew there would have been hell to pay. And it was hard not to conjure images of the red-necked, straw-chewing, tobacco-spitting landlords of their youth when they thought about Alice and her new beau.

"It seemed to me that with all the dirt white men had done,

Alice could have found a black boyfriend in Atlanta," insisted Bobby Walker. "Morehouse was busting at the seams with black men."

More open-minded, brother Bill still had concerns. "I didn't have any problems with David because he was a very nice guy, well-mannered, polite and all that," Bill later explained. "But it kind of threw me for a loop when Alice took him to Georgia and I got word about how people responded to them down there. To Alice, David was just another guy, but for people in Eatonton, well, the whole town was blown away. You don't just go to a small Southern town with a white man and walk the streets with him and go into shops and restaurants and act like he's as black as you are. Eatonton was not ready to give blacks the kind of freedom and acceptance Alice was demanding. So, I guess she rubbed it in their face. There are people in that town today who are still talking about Alice coming home and walking down the street holding hands with a white boy."

Sister Mamie put it this way: "Alice never asked for permission. She just did." And well she did, in "Forbidden Things," a poem destined for *Revolutionary Petunias:*

> *They say you are not for me,*
> *and I try, in my resolved but*
> *barely turning brain,*
> *to know "they" do not matter*
> *these relics of past disasters*
> *in march against the rebellion*
> *of our time.*
>
> *They will fail;*
> *as all the others have:*
> *for our fate will not be this:*
> *to smile and salute the pain,*
> *to limp behind their steel boot*
> *of happiness,*
> *grieving for forbidden things.*

During that summer of 1963, before Alice and David had strolled bodaciously through the dusty streets of rural Georgia, they had participated in the largest demonstration for racial unity in the history of the nation—the March on Washington for Jobs and Freedom. On Wednesday, August 28, 1963, the young couple was among 250,000 people (an estimated 60,000 of them white) who had gathered in front of the Lincoln Memorial to show their support for the goals of the march, foremost among them the passage of an impending Civil Rights Act. The bill would outlaw segregation in public accommodations, thereby granting blacks "the opportunity to stop at a hotel, or eat at a lunch counter . . . on the same terms as any other American," as President Kennedy had put it earlier in the year. The highlight of the day would be Martin Luther King's impassioned delivery of his now legendary "I Have a Dream" speech.

DeMoss still has the original ticket for the bus he and Alice rode from Boston to join the march. He holds the ticket, crafted out of a strip of pink construction paper and stamped "Bus 3, any seat," as he happily remembers the day: "I don't think we'd planned to go. It was a spontaneous thing that sort of happened at the last minute. The bus left way before dawn, and we stopped for breakfast, I believe, at a Baptist church in the black community of Baltimore. As we made the final few miles into Washington and approached the Lincoln Memorial, there was an electric wave of excitement in the air. Alice and I got swallowed up in a massive throng of people, but we were there. It was a wonderful trip."

Indeed, perched high above the crowd on the limb of a tree far away from Lincoln's statue, Alice heard the day's proceedings as clear as a bell, thanks to the booming loudspeakers. Describing the impact of King's speech in shaping her understanding of the *magnificence* of her black Southern heritage, she would later write: "Martin King was a man who truly had his tongue wrapped around the roots of Southern black religious consciousness, and when his resounding voice swelled and broke over the heads of the thousands of people assembled at the Lincoln Memorial I felt what a Southern person brought up in the church *always* feels when those cadences—not the words themselves, necessarily, but the rhythmic spirals of passionate emotion, followed by even more passionate pauses—rolls off the tongue of a really first-rate preacher. I felt my soul rising from the sheer force of Martin King's eloquent goodness . . .

"And when he spoke of 'letting freedom ring' across 'the green hills of Alabama and the red hills of Georgia' I saw again what he was always uniquely able to make me see: that I, in fact, had claim to the land of my birth. Those red hills of Georgia were mine, and nobody was going to force me away from them until I myself was good and ready to go."

In addition to civil rights leaders such as Dr. King, A. Philip Randolph, Bayard Rustin, and Student Nonviolent Coordinating Committee (SNCC) chairman John Lewis, scores of famous athletes and entertainers also participated in the march. Among them were Lena Horne, Jackie Robinson, Paul Newman, Mahalia Jackson, Harry Belafonte, Marlon Brando, and Charlton Heston. Of all the celebrities who addressed the crowd, it was perhaps Parisian dance hall queen Josephine Baker who best spoke, without flourishes or high platitudes, to the significance of the love Alice and David shared.

A St. Louis native who had immigrated to Paris in 1925, Baker had become one of the biggest stars in France. Her appearance at the march was viewed by many as evidence of the success attainable by blacks who escaped the debilitating crush of racism in America. Visibly moved by the sight of thousands of people, black and white, "united in a common dream," Baker, in a burst of emotion, shouted out to the crowd, "You are on the eve of a complete victory. You can't go wrong. The world is behind you. Salt and pepper. Just what it should be."

12

Fit for Myself to Know

ALICE RETURNED to Spelman in the fall of 1963 dispirited, but determined to complete the education she knew she needed to contribute to the empowerment of blacks in the South. Likewise committed to the ideals Martin Luther King Jr. had spoken about in Washington, David DeMoss, who had graduated from Bowdoin in June, took a teaching job at a predominantly black high school in Prince Edward County, Virginia. He and Alice maintained their relationship through letters, phone calls, and passionate weekend visits. As DeMoss recalled their trysts, poignant memories emerged.

"When I flew back to Virginia from Atlanta, after I first saw Alice that fall, I was very much in love," DeMoss said. "There were a bunch of white sorority-type girls on the flight who'd seen me say good-bye to Alice at the airport. On the plane, they stared at me and kind of turned up their noses. I was so distraught about leaving Alice, I just broke down and cried."

In a letter Alice wrote to Zinn dated September 20, 1963, she told her former professor about the new love in her life: "I'm pinned! . . . The 'fellow' involved is <u>wonderful!</u> . . . He wants so much to meet you . . . because he knows how close I feel to you."

On campus, Alice continued her studies and, as president of the school's Social Science Club ("I feel sort of lost without you around as advisor," she wrote to Zinn), tried to inspire her classmates to battle the complacency that Manley and other administrators seemed to believe would fare them best in the world. Not about to be silent about Zinn's dismissal, Alice, within days of returning to Spelman, fired off a letter to the student newspaper, *The Spotlight*. Remembered years later by many of her classmates as the most "confrontative" action ever taken by a student in the school's history, the letter read:

Dear Editor:

I was very distressed to find upon my return to the campus this fall that Dr. Howard Zinn, to whom Spelman College owes so much of its present more modern and progressive character, had been dismissed quite abruptly and completely without warning. . . . In plainer terms Dr. Zinn was fired and received notice of this fact on the very same morning that he and his family were to leave the campus presumably for summer vacation.

As one who has watched with keen interest the developments of the movement for civil rights on this campus I cannot but wonder if this action on the part of the college against Dr. Zinn does not testify to what was said in many a stormy session last spring on "liberty at Spelman" that freedom of expression and to dissent does not, indeed, exist at Spelman. . . .

[Dr. Zinn's] competency as a teacher is not to be questioned; his character speaks for itself. . . . It is the writing of Dr. Zinn on the Negro movement in general and the Negro student movement in the South in particular that is about the best in the country; being both intelligent and objective. It was to Dr. Zinn's classes that all really serious and inquiring students aspired to attend. Finally, but not really, it was to Dr. Zinn that each person on this campus was truly an individual and infinitely more important than a new building or a smooth green lawn.

I am not sorry for Dr. Zinn in the usual sense of the word, the world takes care of its own and history favors great men—the more injustices overcome and profited from, the greater the personality. I am sorry though for us, as a group of presumably mature and civilized individuals, if we can settle down to "business as usual" with only a second thought to what we have lost and to what we have become. . . . How many of us I wonder are still familiar with the poem which begins—"I have to live with myself, and so, I want to be fit for myself to know . . . "

Let us not desert the battle because a leader has moved to another part of the field. It was for us, the student body, Spelman College itself, that Dr. Zinn fought. We have accepted a debt which is fast becoming overdue. . . .

This letter is not meant as an accusation, though it will likely be taken as such: it is written not in anger, but from regret. It is my intention to rumple the complacency of my Spelman sisters so that if they do not share my regret they can at least properly appreciate our loss.

Sincerely,

Alice Walker

In her correspondence to Zinn on September 20, Alice enclosed a copy of the letter. About her effort, she wrote, "In some ways it is not what I'd like to express at all—What I'd really like to do is show such anger and wrath that Sisters Chapel would dissolve into a shuddering heap of rusty old bricks and pious old ladies! However, whatever I am saying I mean it and am glad that I do."

"It was heartening to have Alice come to my defense that way," Zinn later said. "There was, in fact, an outpouring of support for me among the students, but no one expressed that more eloquently than Alice."

So impressed was Zinn by Alice's literary talents during his sojourn at Spelman, that he'd once attempted to "keep up" by crafting a poem for her birthday. *Fortunately* (emphasis is his), he said he only remembered the first stanza:

> *Alice, Alice, in the palace*
> *of your mind*
> *odd thoughts do dwell . . .*

Beverly Guy-Sheftall, a Memphis native who was a year behind Alice at Spelman, remembers the shock waves Alice's letter sent through the campus (blacks comprised seventy-five percent of Spelman faculty and staff). "Folks were truly upset with Alice because while what she said was true, they couldn't stand her criticism of the college."

"All of her views were consistent with my assessment of the school," continued Guy-Sheftall, who is today director of the Women's Research and Resource Center at Spelman. "But I was too young, obedient, and conformist to say it. I always admired Alice for speaking out because the environment was clearly stifling. Her Zinn letter was very powerful in that it laid out all the problems at Spelman in a way that couldn't be denied."

Enraged that Manley had fired "the most distinguished member of his family," Staughton Lynd, a Harvard- and Columbia-trained historian whom Zinn had brought to Spelman, also rose to his defense. Like Zinn, Professor Lynd had also been wowed by the papers Alice had written in his American history class ("There was something about the way she put her sentences together that knocked me out") and applauded her willingness to confront Manley.

"There was a really strange scene going on down there," Lynd said, recalling his years at Spelman. "The students would go downtown and picket segregation and then come back to this walled-off campus with nitpicky, antiquated rules put in by a generation of black administrators who were basically helping to keep Jim Crow alive. As I recall, Alice was disciplined for having her light on one night 'after hours,' while she was reading French poetry. That was emblematic of the dozens of inane, repressive restrictions the students endured."

In a note to Zinn on September 29, 1963, Lynd, fed up with Spelman, asked his former department chair for a letter of recommendation, saying he had decided to resign and seek another job. "My one concern is to help Alice Walker transfer as her letter in *The Spotlight* will be the end . . . ," he added, before signing off.

Buoyed by the natural beauty of the campus, despite its administration's strictures, Alice, rooming in the French House with Constance Nabwire, persevered as best she could for the rest of the year. In a letter datelined "Autumn," she wrote to Zinn, "The crooked dogwood in front of the infirmary is a flaming torch—and the sun is as warm as in June. Connie and I have somehow managed to dig out our old gay spirits to match the cheerful rustling of the bright leaves and we often look searchingly across the campus half-expecting to see the man in the olive green suit—our favorite Prof. and friend. . . . Just to liven up the French House some, Connie and I have distributed a beauteous supply of Renoir nudes—they're all over the place and tomorrow Mrs. Manley [the president's wife] is coming to check the general tastefulness of the house. . . . I shall always feel that I reached Spelman many years; five, to be exact, too late. But then—better to have come and known than not to have known at all—n'est-ce pas?"

Alice was intrigued by the French language, the culture, and, especially, the role of France in African politics. Still, disaffected by the problems at Spelman, she refused a school fellowship that would have enabled her to study in Paris. The $2,000 award was underwritten by the brokerage firm Merrill Lynch. The Merrill family, like the Rockefellers, had long been generous financial supporters of historically black colleges. As chairman of the board of trustees of Morehouse College, Charles Merrill (a family heir) had heard about Alice, who, he said, was uniformly described to him as "brilliant." Nominated by Spelman faculty to receive the Merrill fellowship, Alice declined the honor. "I could see that Spelman was part of the colonizing machinery," she later explained. "They offered no support whatsoever for the black students who were putting their lives on the line trying to bring down Jim Crow. Yet, there was money to send us off to Europe, which, being white, the administration perceived as the 'cradle of civilization.' I was really suffering behind this, so I turned the fellowship down."

Proclaiming, "Here's one we tried to help, but she refused it," President Manley, Merrill later said, informed him that Alice had rejected the award bearing his family's illustrious name. Apprised that she was the daughter of struggling tenant farmers, Merrill found himself bemused by Alice's decision, which was unprecedented in the history of Spelman. "I guess she figured she'd just end up walking along the Seine having one more imaginary argument with Dr. Manley, whom she despised as a timid, paternalistic conformist," Merrill later recalled. Still, it seemed to him a bit rash that a "needy" student such as Alice would turn down the cash.

As much as Merrill (brother of the celebrated poet James Merrill) fashioned himself a liberal, socially responsible philanthropist, committed to using his vast fortune to uplift the dispossessed, he had failed to understand how his upper-class breeding colored his perceptions of Alice. Until, that is, she wrote a blistering poem, inspired by a real-life exchange in which she took him to task for his cavalier dismissal of her writing aspirations. This he had done, with what Alice perceived as a condescending air, one day when he was on the Spelman campus and they happened to cross paths. Still perplexed by her refusal of the award, Merrill had asked Alice, whom he'd come to know through his frequent visits to Morehouse, precisely what she intended to do with her life.

First mentioned by Merrill, the poem, now lost, describes a white man (Merrill) who encounters a poor black student (Alice) during a heavy rainstorm. The man is wearing expensive shoes crafted of fine leather. The student, in summer shoes with slats, feels water soaking her feet as she stands in torrential rain defending her desire to become a poet despite the man's intimations that people of her "station" would be ill equipped for such a lofty career.

"I mailed the poem to Charles Merrill," Alice would later remember, "and to his credit, I think he learned from it. We've kept in touch over the years."

About what he now refers to as Alice's "memorialization of my arrogance," Merrill said, "She is honest. 'If I had carried a gun, I would have shot him,' is one of the lines I remember from her poem. Alice felt patronized and she let me know about it in no uncertain terms. She never compromises to be politic or nice."

Although she felt there was much she could contribute to the college ("unwanted though [it] may be"), Alice, by the end of 1963, had come to realize that her evolution as a writer, thinker, and activist would forever be thwarted at Spelman. This was due in no small part to the guidelines she'd been given, the previous year, for a term paper in one of her classes. Dispatched by a speech and drama professor to attend a lecture by Dr. King (then pastor of Atlanta's Ebenezer Baptist Church), Alice was admonished to assess only the form of his presentation, "not King's politics."

About the folly of the assignment, she later remarked, "And so I had written a paper that contained these lines: 'Martin Luther King, Jr. is a surprisingly effective orator, although *terribly* under the influence of the Baptist Church so that his utterances sound overdramatic and too weighty to be taken seriously.' I also commented on his lack of humor, his expressionless 'oriental' eyes, and the fascinating fact that his gray sharkskin suit was completely without wrinkles—causing me to wonder how he had gotten into it."

After attending the march on Washington, she'd been outraged by her understanding of the insult the professor had leveled against both her intelligence and the importance of the civil rights movement: "Here's a man who was changing the face of the nation. And all they cared about at Spelman was if he had 'organized his thoughts' properly."

Reflective of Alice's growing psychic disengagement from the school, her coursework began to suffer. She received a C in introduction to African civilization, a class in which, given her passions, she should have thrived. The writers on her Spelman syllabus—Catullus, Ovid, Austen, the Bronte sisters, Hemingway—had their merits. But as Alice later noted in her essay, "Saving the Life That Is Your Own: The Importance of Models in the Artist's Life," she now hungered for literature woven from "the historical and psychological threads" of her forebears.

"The absence of models, in literature, as in life . . . is an occupational hazard for the artist," Alice asserted in the piece, which opens *In Search of Our Mothers' Gardens* (1983). "Simply because models, in art, in behavior, in growth of spirit and intellect—even if rejected—enrich and enlarge one's view of existence.

"What is always needed . . . is the larger perspective," she continued. "Black writers seem always involved in a moral and/or physical struggle, the result of which is expected to be some kind of larger freedom. . . . And yet, in our particular society, it is the narrowed and narrowing view of life that often wins."

Alice shared her unhappiness about the narrowness of her college life in another letter to Zinn that fall: "There is nothing really here for me—it is almost like being buried alive. It seems almost a matter of getting away or losing myself—**my self**—in this strange, unreal place."

In yet another, she told Zinn that she'd been reading Emerson and had found much to ponder in the writer-philosopher's essay "Self-Reliance." She ended that letter with a quotation from Emerson's journal (April 12, 1834) that underscored her frustrations with the white-gloved artifice of Spelman: "All the mistakes I make arise from forsaking my own station and trying to see the object from another person's point of view."

LIKE ALICE, Alabama native Marilyn Pryce (now Hoytt) was a politically active Spelman student who had also been valedictorian of her high school class. Arrested for joining civil rights protests, Pryce said that it was only a liberating year abroad in Paris that enabled her to survive the oppressive atmosphere at the school.

Pryce had returned to France after graduating from Spelman in the spring of 1963 and was not surprised to learn, while there, of the despair that had descended on the friend with whom she'd marched in demonstrations and bemoaned compulsory chapel.

A drama major at the college, Pryce also noted that she'd cast Alice in an excerpt from Eugene Ionesco's *The Bald Soprano,* which she'd directed her senior year. ("She was a little bit shy, but she did a beautiful job"). And it was to Pryce that Alice would later dedicate "Chic Freedom's Reflection," a poem in which she extolled her classmate's ability to freshen her makeup in the shine of a sheriff's badge before being hauled off to jail:

> *One day*
> *Marilyn marched*
> *beside me (demon-*
> *stration)*
> *and we ended up*
> *at a county farm*
> *no phone*
> *no bail . . .*
> *which irrelevance*
> *Marilyn dismissed*
> *with a shrug*
>
>   *She*
> *had just got*
>   *back*
> *from*
>   *Paris . . .*
>   *she*
>   *smelled . . .*
>   *like spring*
> *& love*
>   *&*
> *freedom . . .*

"We were both rebellious, but Alice also had a certain vulnerability that left her unprotected at Spelman," said Pryce. "With the civil rights movement in full swing, it truly hurt her that people with real integrity and substance were not valued at the school. Some of us could grit our teeth and find a way to make the best of it, but not Alice. From the beginning her standards were very high and Spelman did not deliver."

Alice felt alienated by the naïveté and passiveness of the middle-class milieu at Spelman. Her family's grinding poverty and the permanent damage to her right eye were daily reminders of her need to keep fighting. She'd never known any of the comforts that could give rise to complacency.

Having been witness to her struggles at Spelman, David DeMoss offered full support when his lover began to speak openly about leaving. "She needed to be in a bigger world, around people who were alive and more willing to take chances," he said. "Alice brought a great deal of passion to everything she did. With all its fuddy-duddy rules and regulations, the college was suffocating her."

All her life Alice had watched white landowners, with their "Come here boy" and "Where you going gal?," infantilize blacks and beat them down. She did not now intend to be treated like an unruly child by Albert E. Manley and the other bourgeois blacks at Spelman who had blithely accepted his dismissal of Howard Zinn. In the poem "Compulsory Chapel," Alice distilled her dismay.

A quiet afternoon
the speaker
dull
the New Testament
washed out
Through the window
a lonely
  blue-jay
makes noisy song.

The speaker crashes
on . . .
Over his left
ear
the thick hair
is beginning
to slip

Upon her graduation from Spelman in 1929, a student named Alma Ferguson Crockett had declared, "I owe the world a woman, I shall earnestly strive to pay my debt." Taking her words seriously, Alice, no longer able to tolerate Spelman's emphasis on "ladies," withdrew from the college in December 1963 after completing the first semester of her junior year. More than twenty years would pass before she'd again set foot on the campus and be cheered by the blossoming dogwood trees.

PART TWO

To Have
and
to Hold

13

Make Yourself Useful

IN HER 1945 book *Field Work in College Education*, social philosopher Helen Merrell Lynd had written about the need to "break down the duality between life and letters." She noted that students who were encouraged to engage in the world outside of college walls were most apt to realize their full potential and that "individuals who have gone as far as possible in realizing their potentialities are the stuff of a democratic society."

So it was that Staughton Lynd, having vowed to assist Alice before he left Spelman, wrote to his mother in hope of securing a place for his former student at Sarah Lawrence College. Helen Lynd (coauthor with her husband Robert of the classic sociological study *Middletown*) had been a member of the Sarah Lawrence faculty for nearly forty years. Impressed by Alice's academic record and political activism, and confident that she'd flourish at an institution that linked education to "the experiences, interests and capacities of the individual student," Helen Lynd helped to arrange Alice's transfer (on full scholarship) to the elite, then all-women's college, in early 1964.

Ruth recalled, "Nobody in the family was shocked or upset when

Alice told us she'd withdrawn from Spelman. My parents were very supportive of her. They figured she knew what was best."

Located in Bronxville, New York, an affluent village about twenty-five miles north of New York City, Sarah Lawrence College was founded in 1926 by William Van Duzer Lawrence, a wealthy land developer. The college, named in honor of his wife, Sarah Bates Lawrence, had carved out a rarified niche for itself in higher education by abolishing letter grades, formal lectures, and required courses. Instead, each student at Sarah Lawrence (which counts broadcaster Barbara Walters and performance artists Meredith Monk and Yoko Ono among its alumnae) was paired with a faculty member who guided her through a personalized course of instruction for which she received an evaluation detailing her progress as an "educated human with an obligation to the larger community." The annual tuition when Alice arrived at the campus was a hefty $3,000 (today, the cost is about $40,000), making Sarah Lawrence then, as it is now, one of the most expensive colleges in the United States.

As Alice's primary contact at the college, Helen Lynd became her "don," or faculty advisor, helping her to get settled on campus and to select classes. About Lynd, who died in 1982, Alice would later write, "She was the first person I met who made philosophy understandable, and the study of it natural. It was she who led me through the works of Camus, and showed me for the first time, how life and suffering are always teachers, or, as with Camus, life and suffering, and *joy*. . . . Since studying with her, all of life, the sadness as well as the joy, has its magnificence, its meaning and its *use*."

In keeping with Sarah Lawrence's founding principles, students took only three courses each year, exploring each intensively in small seminars and private conferences with their professors. In addition to several courses in writing, Alice, guided by Lynd, would turn her attention to studies in theory building, Western Europe in the twentieth century, comedy, and a rigorous examination of Cicero and Petrarch.

Unlike the stodgy, regimented approach to learning Alice had endured in most of her classes at Spelman, she was encouraged to write as she pleased and to develop her own voice at Sarah

Lawrence. Even the design of the campus—dormitories, classrooms, and administrative offices all interspersed in the same ivy-covered Tudor buildings—promoted a sense of unity and reflected the school's philosophy that life and art were fundamentally intertwined. For Alice, who lived her first year at the college in Room 27 of MacCracken Hall, the building that also housed the library, the contrast with Spelman could not have been more stark, as she would later note: "I had written at Spelman, but very few people seemed to care. For the most part, writing was considered decorative. At Sarah Lawrence everybody understood that writing was about your heart and your soul and you did it because you had to. Students of dance, danced. Musicians made music. Writers wrote and painters painted. I hardly looked in a mirror the entire time I was there because unlike at Spelman, nobody cared about what you wore or if your hair was done the right way. I was consumed by my work. It was wonderful."

Although Alice felt affirmed as a creative writer at Sarah Lawrence, as a self-described "daughter of the rural peasantry" she was initially taken aback by the tremendous wealth of her new classmates. At Spelman, "wealthy" students hailed, for the most part, from the ranks of the black middle class. At Sarah Lawrence, the majority of Alice's classmates were "of the manor born." Their family names graced banks, prestigious museums, and international corporations. Still, as young white women for whom privilege came as a birthright, they found license, in the 1960s, to rebel against their ruling class status by playing out the "rags-to-riches" role—in reverse. For Alice, who'd been raised in paper-thin shacks without electricity or indoor plumbing, the apparent enchantment of her classmates with "deprivation" was a constant source of bewilderment.

"I arrived in the winter when it was very cold and I didn't even have a coat," Alice said. "I was given a stipend, so I eventually got one. In the process of getting adequate clothes, books, and all the other things I didn't have, coming from Georgia, it was really strange for me to see so many women from wealthy families, yet they all dressed in rags. It took me a while to understand this aesthetic of the rags and 'dressing down' because my struggle had been not to wear rags. And because my mother and Ruth created dresses and outfits for me that were often masterpieces, I never did."

Samuel B. Seigle, a classics professor who joined the Sarah Lawrence faculty in 1964, confirmed Alice's impressions of her classmates and their attempts to distance themselves from their lineage by way of "fashion statements."

"There was a dress code for going into the actual town of Bronxville, but otherwise students ran from door to door in their nightgowns. For at least four years, these young women from the highest echelons of power were allowed to be part of the counterculture. They could go to class barefooted, wearing tattered clothes or barely anything at all. And most of them did."

Alice's encounters with the wealthy students at Sarah Lawrence called to mind her contretemps with Charles Merrill. Just as she'd been unbowed before one of the nation's financial titans, she also enlightened her well-heeled classmates at Sarah Lawrence, showing them, by word and deed, her allegiance to people who measured their worth in the currency of dignity and self-respect.

One such student was Helen Berggruen, the daughter of a wealthy art dealer who counted Pablo Picasso among his cronies. Spurred by her friendship with Alice, Berggruen would spend a summer in Alabama working with rural blacks, five or six generations of whom could have been educated with the money her family spent on lithographs.

"If I hadn't met Alice, I probably never would have had my eyes opened to the *real* America," said Berggruen, today a California-based painter whose work is exhibited in international galleries. "I was rich, white, northern, naïve, and sheltered. I'd never had to confront the issues that were part and parcel of her daily life.

"But Alice didn't make me feel guilty. She talked to me one-on-one with a calmness and clarity that helped me understand how I could get involved in the movement. And when I got to Alabama, I truly felt welcomed. Nobody cared about my background. Their attitude was, 'Hey, little sister, glad you came. Now make yourself useful.' "

Useful. Alice's dedication to both politics and her development as a writer would cause her to cut a wide swath on a campus where most students, cushioned by their wealth, struggled to find purpose and meaning in life. If Spelman had been like a prison, Sarah Lawrence was an open laboratory where Alice was given free rein to experiment and explore the social responsibilities of an artist.

With her creative aspirations supported as they'd never been before, Alice began to think more seriously about her future as a writer. Did she have talent? And if so, could her writing really help people—people like the sharecroppers in Wards Chapel and the "toe-pulling" contest women who had offered up their feet to build a school?

As she pondered such questions among the moneyed set at Sarah Lawrence, Alice discovered a different void. It was clear that she'd needed to leave the South. Still, she longed for the earthy vibrancy of her roots. Just as her mother had turned to gardening, cooking, and the crafting of exquisite quilts to feed the impoverishment of her soul under segregation, Alice now turned to art for affirmation on a campus where black faces were rare. With earnings from baby-sitting and clerical jobs, Alice bought three inexpensive prints: *Alice* by Modigliani; *Three Tahitian Women* by Gauguin; and *Four Studies of the Head of a Negro* by the Flemish master, Rubens.

"After I hung the prints in my room, I felt less lonely," Alice revealed, three decades later, to a reunion gathering of Sarah Lawrence alumni. "They became my friends."

AT AGE seventy-five, Jane Cooper, a delicate woman with gray hair styled in a girlish pageboy, sits in her sun-drenched apartment in New York City. The rooms are painted in muted shades of white and pale green, and everywhere the eye rests, there are books. Adrienne Rich here. Lucille Clifton there. The works of Audre Lorde and Grace Paley on a gleaming coffee table. And on a distant bookshelf near a window, seemingly placed so as not to draw any attention to themselves, are two books of her own, *Scaffolding* (1993) and *Green Notebook, Winter Road* (1994).

On the faculty of Sarah Lawrence from 1950 to 1987, Cooper calculates that she taught dozens of talented writing students. But mention Alice Walker and Cooper—now debilitated by a lifelong autoimmune disease—squares her shoulders and her luminous gray eyes blaze from behind oversize glasses. "What's different about Alice is that she had the most incisive way of telling the truth," said Cooper, who worked primarily in conference with Alice on fiction. "When you're teaching eighteen- to twenty-two-year-olds, there is a lot of confusion. But by that point, Alice had already been involved in the civil rights movement and she was very clear about where she stood. She had so much integrity and strength of character that I used to think that when I went to heaven, it wouldn't be St. Peter at the pearly gates, it would be Alice."

Cooper noted that unlike most beginning writers, Alice, from the outset, was able to transmit her confidence and clarity to the printed page. Her voice was fresh and precise, so precise that readers unfamiliar with her creative landscape could sometimes be taken by surprise. "She'd written a story in which she described the land as being red, so when she came to conference, I told her she had the color of the earth wrong," Cooper remembered. "Alice looked me dead in the eye and said, 'No, you've got it wrong. The land is red where I come from. And that's the way it's going to be in this story. Period.' "

"It was astounding how as a student, Alice could make you question yourself and fine-tune your thinking. She had a wild intelligence that she refused to hold back."

As a white woman who had grown up in an affluent family in the Jim Crow South, Cooper also noted that she was especially sensitive to the racial themes Alice addressed in her writing. Indeed, speaking with a faint lilt of her native Florida, Cooper credited Alice with helping her to better understand the special role a family member had played in shaping the nation's views about blacks. Asked to explain, she paused and then slowly recited a comment once made about her by another writer—a remark she used as an epigraph to a poem in *Green Notebook, Winter Road*: "The most amazing thing I know about Jane Cooper is that she's the niece of King Kong."

"You see, my uncle Merian Cooper wrote and produced the movie *King Kong*," said Cooper, about the 1933 film that critic Pauline Kael later denounced as a "phallic joke carried to the level of myth."

"It is filled with all kinds of racist symbolism about blackness and the 'savagery' of Africa," Cooper continued. "With Alice in my class, writing so provocatively about racial oppression, I could see exactly how *King Kong* reinforced and contributed to the cruelty I saw perpetuated against black people every day when I was a child. Because a member of my family had put out this terrible cinematic vision, I felt I had an even greater responsibility to help fight for the dignity of black people."

As if she had been preordained to counter, in one fell swoop, the simplistic and demeaning imagery of *King Kong,* Alice wrote, while working with Cooper, a haunting story about an encounter between an African man and an African American woman who cross paths in England. Thirty-five years later, Cooper speaks in deeply respect-ful tones as she describes the impact "The Suicide of an American Girl" had on the literary community at Sarah Lawrence.

"Whenever a student wrote something truly exceptional, the work would be mimeographed and the entire writing faculty and a group of senior students would get together and discuss the piece," Cooper said. "Well, everybody was completely bowled over by Alice's story. It was a complex, extremely prescient piece that explored the tensions between Africans and blacks in the U.S. Alice still had many of the formalities of fiction that she needed to learn, but what she was doing as a student was remarkable. She wrote with a daring and force that separated her from the rest."

Never published, "The Suicide of an American Girl" deals with a chance meeting between Ana Harriman, a twenty-six-year-old American black woman, and Djin Jdin, a Ghanaian who has left his village to live in London. Ana, a native of Georgia who finds her-self unable to pledge allegiance to the American flag because she "cannot speak and spit at the same time" has spent ten years teaching in Africa, searching for a sense of belonging and acceptance that she cannot find in America.

Much to Ana's dismay, she discovers that the Africans she had hoped would welcome her as a devoted "returning daughter" instead treat her with indifference. "And even this was not complete," Alice writes, "for, since it was obvious that Ana was not a white American and therefore not aligned with power, she did not deserve the same respect, but something less, something not love, nor even friendliness, but a familiar disrespect based on an awareness of her servitude."

A few days before she is to leave London and return to America, Ana spends an evening chatting with Djin in a residence hall where they are both staying. Rife with the pain of displacement on both sides, their conversation moves into a sexually charged debate about racial loyalty and the meaning of home. In twenty-eight pages, Alice explores, in unflinching detail, the deep yearning among black Americans and their African counterparts for a relationship that can transcend an explosive mix of passion, longing, suspicion, envy, and mistrust that exists between them; a relationship that has always, at its core, the horrific history of the slave trade. Alice later noted that the piece was influenced by the writing of Doris Lessing, reared in Zimbabwe and author of such widely hailed works as *African Stories* (1962) and *The Golden Notebook* (1965), a novel about a woman writer's struggle to discover the meaning of "self."

Alice also named Kate Chopin, the Brontës, and Simone de Beauvoir as writers who likewise helped to shape her craft at the time: "[They] are well aware of their own oppression and search incessantly for a kind of salvation. Their characters can always envision a solution, an evolution to higher consciousness on the part of society, even when society itself cannot. Even when society is in the process of killing them for their vision."

Written in the mid-1960s, "The Suicide of an American Girl" was prophetic in that the gender conflicts and issues of racial allegiance Alice considers in the story would fall at the center of the

Black Arts Movement about to emerge among writers like Nikki Giovanni, Sonia Sanchez, Ed Bullins, and LeRoi Jones (later Amiri Baraka). Interestingly, a one-act play, "The Suicide," was among the works published in *Black Fire* (1968), a pioneering release from the Black Arts era. The drama (written by Carol Freeman) opens with the suspicious death of a black man alleged to have jumped off a bridge. The none-too-subtle theme of the piece is white oppression of black people.

As many would soon come to know, Alice's literary reach would extend far beyond the flashpoint political issues of the day. Having moved on from Spelman, Alice now dedicated herself, as she had written about Ana, to the achievement of "technical perfection in her art as well as consistency in her character." In that effort she would continue to have a staunch ally in Jane Cooper, who in her 1974 essay, "Nothing Has Been Used in the Manufacture of This Poetry That Could Have Been Used in the Manufacture of Bread," would detail the many barriers faced by women writers.

Over the next two years, Alice would also be greatly influenced by another member of the Sarah Lawrence faculty, a large-boned woman with a lion-like mane of dark hair. Angered by the accolades heaped on Sylvia Plath only after the poet had committed suicide at age thirty, this professor had pushed what many considered the boundaries of decorum by writing a poem that in its entirety read:

> *I'd rather be Muriel*
> *Than be dead and be Ariel.*

14

Reclaimed

THE DAUGHTER of a successful businessman whose company had supplied the concrete for many of Manhattan's skyscrapers, Muriel Rukeyser had been groomed, as she later noted, to become a suburban matron who married a doctor and played golf.

Instead, after leaving Vassar College (sans husband or degree), the radical poet had gone to Alabama, where she was arrested while reporting on the 1931 "Scottsboro Boys" trial of nine black youths falsely convicted of rapes against two white women. In subsequent years, Rukeyser's passionate melding of politics and poetry would propel her to travel the world in fierce pursuit of "an education with no edges."

She went to Barcelona to cover the Spanish Civil War; to West Virginia in support of exploited miners; to North Vietnam as a witness for peace; and to Ireland, where she indulged in a festival of sex and drinking, later chronicled in her book, *The Orgy* (1967).

Hailed as one of her generation's most undoctrinaire literary minds, Rukeyser, a member of the Sarah Lawrence faculty from 1956 to 1967, recognized in Alice a gifted writer who, like herself, steadfastly refused to conform to societal norms. In Rukeyser, Alice found a teacher who revered poetry as "usable truth" and who pledged allegiance only to her own beliefs.

"What I learned from Muriel is that poetry, done well, is always about the truth; that it is subversive; that you can't shut it up and that it stays," said Alice about Rukeyser, with whom she also studied contemporary writers and the South. "Muriel had a very large imagination that wandered over vast terrain. More than any specifics about structure or technique, she taught me that it was possible to be passionate about writing and to live in the world on my own terms."

Years later, Alice would recall Rukeyser's ecstasy when she read aloud the Gerard Manley Hopkins poem "Pied Beauty":

> *Glory be to God for dappled things—*
> *For skies of couple-colour as a brinded cow;*
> *For rose-moles all in stipple upon trout that swim;*
> *Fresh-firecoal chestnut-falls; finches' wings;*
> *Landscape plotted and pieced—fold, fallow, and plough . . .*

"She made us feel the poem as an intense song of praise to nature," noted Alice for whom the verse held great meaning. "She showed me that for real people, poetry is as necessary as bread."

By turn, Alice demonstrated a dedication to the art and craft of writing that Rukeyser recognized as extraordinary. In her first evaluation of Alice's work, Rukeyser offered unstinting praise for the contemplative young woman who had arrived on the campus, midstream, from Georgia: "Many times this semester, this student was valuable to the entire class—through clear description, penetrating analysis, candor, and grace . . . and she has not hesitated to make the personal application of her findings. . . . There is a beginning in another kind of work . . . the painful and fertile bringing together and holding of many elements. A student of remarkable capacities."

Writer Grace Paley was also on the faculty at Sarah Lawrence during the 1960s. A devoted friend of Rukeyser, she observed that the poet was prone to awkward speech patterns that were often difficult to untangle. "Muriel, whom I loved very much, had a way of talking that was so dense hardly anybody could understand her sometimes," Paley remembered. "Alice had graduated by the time I got to the college. But Muriel sang her praises all the time. There was no question but that Alice Walker was her prized student. And I used to wonder what this black kid from the South, plainspoken, direct, what she made of it, you know, Muriel's obfuscation?

"In any one sentence she'd have a couple of extra clauses, contradictions, strange syntax. Muriel was a brilliant poet. A genius, really. But on personal matters, and it was understood that her relationship with Alice was very personal—she could be vague to the point of unintelligible."

ALICE'S DETERMINATION to achieve (and perhaps exceed) her promise was immediately imperiled in the fall of 1965, when she arrived at Sarah Lawrence, in her own words, "healthy, brown, loaded down with sculptures and orange fabric—and pregnant."

During the summer, Alice had returned to the South, where she joined a group of civil rights workers registering voters in rural Liberty County, Georgia. There, they'd been attacked by a swarm of angry whites, while local police, refusing to protect "nigger-loving, outside agitators," leaned against their patrol cars and blithely watched the melee.

"As those rocks and bottles whizzed past my head, I realized I could easily lose the sight in my other eye," remembered Alice, who promptly relinquished her post. "There was no support for us in the community and I wasn't ready to be a martyr just then. I had a fallback position, so I quit."

Alice's "second choice" for the summer was to visit Africa. Traveling with The Experiment in International Living, a Vermont-based foreign study group, Alice fled the hate-spewing mobs in Liberty County and flew to Kenya, where, working in the middle of a pineapple plantation, she helped to build a school out of sisal stalks. Like many black Americans who first visited Africa in the 1960s, she had been inspired by the independence movement that had swept across the continent beginning in the late 1950s. Still, as with segregation in the American South, Africa's long history of colonization made bittersweet and achingly fragile the "freedom" that emerged in countries like Zaire, Nigeria, and, most notably, Ghana under the famed black African statesman Kwame Nkrumah. As much as she was elated to visit the homeland of her African forebears, Alice was sickened by the wrenching poverty and rampant exploitation of the people, as manifest in the rotting teeth, rheumy eyes, and infected earlobes of the men, women, and children who toiled daily next to her in the pineapple fields.

This was not the "motherland" of pyramid-laden splendor, proud warriors, and majestic queens that, by the mid-1960s, was being vaunted by black radicals wearing dashikis and pounding conga drums on American street corners. This was human misery and despair of the highest order inflicted on people *on their own land*. The polluted waters, hunger of the elders, tear-stained cheeks, and shuffling gaits of little girls as they emerged from their ritual "bath" would forever tarnish the glory of Mt. Kenya and stain Alice's memories of her first pilgrimage to Africa.

"The colonizers had pillaged the land and poisoned the culture," Alice later said. "Of course, I was happy to be in Africa, to connect with my roots and to see the people still fighting for survival. But it was very hard."

Continuing her journey, taxing though it was, Alice also visited Uganda, the native home of her Spelman roommate Constance Nabwire. It was there, in a small village outside of Kampala, that she conceived. The father of the child? David DeMoss, then a Peace Corps worker in Tanzania who had visited her unexpectedly.

Though the couple had officially ended their romance, they were still friends, reflecting the bond Alice would attempt to maintain with all of her lovers. Thousands of miles away from home and drained physically and emotionally from her journey, she was thrilled to see David, one of her most ardent and attentive beaus. There was just one problem. Having not intended to be intimate with anyone during her summer travels, Alice had left her birth control pills in New York.

"The pill had just become available and there were still lots of questions about side effects, so I figured why take it, unless I really needed it," Alice later explained. "I didn't know David was coming to Uganda. It was a total surprise. So, caught up in the joy of the moment, we had sex. I knew immediately that I was pregnant."

The news of DeMoss's impending fatherhood was delivered to him in a manner that, decades later, still brought a pained grimace to his face. Back in Tanzania, one day a bag of mail was tossed from a truck, landing with a thud on the road near his village. In the bag was a neatly written letter from Alice, "informing me that she was pregnant and I was the culprit," DeMoss said somberly, his cheeks flushing scarlet.

"The letter was very matter-of-fact," he continued, "just like Alice. She wanted to get an abortion. I was against it. But of course, it was her choice."

Not exactly. For with abortion illegal in 1965, the "choices" available to Alice, as a poor, black, unmarried student, were next to nil and downhill, with a vengeance, from there. She didn't have any money. She didn't know any doctors. Since arriving at Sarah Lawrence, she had hardly stepped foot in New York City, except to research its architecture for one of her classes.

Calm and composed though Alice may have seemed to David in her letter, she was facing a major crisis. And she knew it, deep in her bones. Describing the dilemma her unplanned pregnancy presented as she began her final year of college, Alice would later put it this way: "It was me or it. One or the other of us was not going to survive."

AMONG THE group of women Alice had befriended at Sarah Lawrence was Diana Young, a blue-eyed, sandy-haired native of Texas. Beginning at age ten, Young had worked as a janitor, cleaning toilets and mopping floors in her father's prosperous heating and ventilating equipment business. Although a daughter of privilege, Young had never been pampered. And early on, she'd transgressed the color line in her community by joining forces with the black troops at Girl Scout camp.

On a campus filled, in her view, "with lots of pretentiousness and avant-garde intellectual hype," Young was drawn to Alice's authenticity, straightforwardness, and depth. "I loved to visit and sit and soak up all of Alice's intense and amazing stories," Young recalled. "We'd talk about segregation, growing up in the South, not the arty obsessions that consumed so many of the women at Sarah Lawrence. And I was still a virgin, so hearing about Alice's love life was just fascinating to me. Alice had deep passions and a lot of experience in the world. She was real."

As the weeks passed, the stark reality of Alice's unplanned pregnancy began to set in. Young was among the few Alice had apprised of her condition. She said it was "torture" to watch Alice, her abdomen rapidly expanding, as she struggled to resolve the crisis. Some days, Young ruefully remembered, she'd find Alice sitting on the floor of the library, hunched over stacks of medical books, determinedly reading page after page. Other days, Alice would be holed up in her room, ravaged by morning sickness and so weighted down by depression she could barely speak.

Young recalled, "Abortion was a 'crime,' and Alice didn't know who to trust or where to turn for help—none of her friends did. She kept getting bigger and bigger and we could see that she was running out of time. It was terrifying. For Alice's sake, we tried to hide it, but all of her friends were in an absolute panic. Her future was at stake—and everyone knew that Alice had a wonderful future."

THE OUTLOOK for an American woman wishing to choose when she was ready to bear a child would improve dramatically with the 1973 *Roe v. Wade* Supreme Court decision legalizing abortion. Until then, women wanting to terminate an unplanned pregnancy were forced, at best, to travel abroad for the procedure. At worst, they endured clandestine and costly abortions performed in the United States by doctors, many of them unsympathetic, who exploited the women's fears and vulnerabilities. And untold scores of women suffered, at the hands of so-called back-alley butchers, massive bleeding, ruptured organs, and deadly infections. Thus did pro-choice advocates cheer *Roe v. Wade* as a decision that "stopped the killing overnight."

THE PANIC that gripped Alice's friends was warranted, without a doubt. For at age twenty-one and with her education not yet completed, Alice had decided that having a child was unequivocally not an option. Unlike countless other women of the era who spared their children the shameful brand of "illegitimacy" by marrying the men who had impregnated them, Alice had no interest in "holy matrimony" with David DeMoss. And she had ruled out adoption.

Feeling she had no other recourse, Alice had resolved to commit suicide if she could not obtain an abortion. She'd placed a razor blade under her pillow, which she used to "mime" the slashing of her wrists so she'd be swift and proficient when the fateful moment arrived.

"I felt there was no way out," Alice would later write about the tension-filled days in the fall of 1965. "And so, when all my efforts at finding an abortionist failed, I planned to kill myself, or—as I thought of it then—to 'give myself a little rest.' I stopped going down the hill to meals because I vomited incessantly, even when nothing came up but yellow, bitter bile. I lay on my bed in a cold sweat, my head spinning."

In the absence of choice and with "unwed motherhood" carrying a crushing stigma, Alice's life was held in a precarious balance. As she passed the tenth week of her pregnancy, the razor stood ready to end all the pain. Alice's turmoil would later be reflected in her poem "Suicide":

> *First, suicide notes should be*
> *(not long) but written*
> *second,*
> *all suicide notes*
> *should be signed*
> *in blood*
> *by hand*
> *and to the point—*

that point being, perhaps
that there is none.
Thirdly, if it is the thought
of rest that
fascinates
laziness should be admitted
in the clearest terms.
Then, all things done
ask those outraged
consider their happiest
summer
& tell if the days it
adds up to
is one.

Informed of Alice's pregnancy and her intention to abort or commit suicide, Ruth said she tried to dissuade her sister from taking such drastic steps. If Alice was in trouble, Ruth was there for the rescue. She'd keep the baby. No judgments made. No questions asked.

"I pleaded with Alice to go ahead and have the baby," said Ruth. "I told her that I would raise it, keep it until she finished college, until she got married, however she wanted to handle it, she had my full support.

"But Alice wouldn't hear it. Her choices were abortion or suicide. There was no middle ground. I couldn't storm the gates and force her to give birth."

"What I remember is silence," Alice countered. She said that Ruth, unable to conceive children, was incapable of understanding her plight. "She wanted me to have the baby—for her," Alice noted.

Among other family members, only Mamie (never married and unforthcoming about intimacies) knew that Alice was pregnant, according to Ruth. Mamie responded to the news with a tongue-lashing, telling her baby sister, "in forty-five minutes of long-distance, carefully enunciated language—that I was a slut," Alice later recalled.

"Be that as it may. I was not having a baby. Not under any circumstances. I could barely manage my own life."

While Alice brushed off Mamie's harsh criticisms, she *was* pained by the hurt and embarrassment she felt her pregnancy would bring to family and friends in Georgia. These were good, solid Christian people who had sent her off to Spelman with the highest hopes, not to mention seventy-five hard-to-come-by dollars they had earned with the sweat of their brow. Now she had gone off to New York, dispensed with her home training, and gotten knocked up—and by a white man, no less. Talk about scandalizing the name of the Lord!

Chronicling the crisis in the O'Brien interview, Alice noted, with a restraint that surely belied her despair: "I realized [my family] would be shocked and hurt to learn of my death, but I felt they would not care deeply at all, when they discovered I was pregnant. Essentially, they would believe I was evil. They would be ashamed of me."

But she was spared. Just as Alice had made peace with her decision, another classmate, Brooke Newman, found a doctor on the Upper East Side of Manhattan who performed abortions. His fee? An otherworldly $2,000 cash, the equivalent of about $12,000 today.

"It was more money than I had actually ever held in my hands," Alice later said, with a weary sigh. "And scraping it together as quickly as I had to was not easy. Society accused us of being sinful, shameful, and criminal for wanting to have abortions. The way I see it, the 'crime' was that doctors could get away with profiting off of our desperate need."

The funds for the abortion were hurriedly collected from worried classmates like Diana Young who either loaned or donated outright to Alice what they could spare. Emptying his paltry Peace Corps bank account, David DeMoss eventually sent about two hundred dollars from Tanzania. But the lion's share of the money came from Carole Darden, who, along with Alice, was one of the few black women attending Sarah Lawrence at the time. A slender woman with piercing brown eyes, Darden had grown up in New

Jersey and frequently invited Alice, a cherished friend, to spend weekends with her family. Removed from the college grind, Carole and Alice would play gospel music, recite poetry, and enjoy scrumptious home-cooked meals—savory stews, candied yams, macaroni and cheese, collard greens, smothered chicken—dishes that "make you wish you were a plate," as the saying goes. The rich bounty transported Alice back to childhood days when her mother, dipping from a large blue bowl, made a feast of the lima beans, potatoes, rice, peas, and corn she'd cultivated in her garden. "And in the light and warmth that was *Her*, we dined," noted Alice, who would later treasure the chipped blue earthenware bowl as a monument to her mother's love. Confident that her culinary skills could whet the appetites of the masses, Darden and her sister Norma Jean would go on to coauthor *Spoonbread and Strawberry Wine* (1978), the bestselling recipe book and compendium of black dining traditions.

Sitting in her elegant Manhattan apartment with a dazzling view of the Hudson River, Darden discussed her crucial role in keeping Alice alive: "We were just a small group of students, all barely in our twenties, but we were hell-bent on seeing Alice through. My father was in real estate and had given me what seemed like a fortune back then, five crisp $100 dollar bills when I left for Sarah Lawrence. He wanted me to have some cash on hand in case of an emergency, so I stashed this $500 in a little souvenir lighthouse from Atlantic City that had once been filled with saltwater taffy and hid it in the back of my closet. Finally, at the eleventh hour, when it all came together, I gave Alice the money. All of her friends were so relieved that things turned out well."

Darden continued her reflections, her words now tumbling out as if she'd been waiting to share them for a long time: "There were only a few black women at Sarah Lawrence and we all gravitated toward Alice, because she was stunning. Most of us were just so used to being demeaned or beaten down by racism that we'd accepted it on some level. But that was not Alice's posture.

"We were in Muriel Rukeyser's class together and I'll always remember Alice, speaking in a soft and quiet voice, just laying out white people for all the evil they'd done. Her tone wasn't hostile, but it was direct. She had an edge. Compared to the rest of the black women on campus, Alice was extremely sophisticated with her language and in her thinking. We admired her for that, a great deal."

EUPHORIC NOW that she'd been unburdened of an unwanted pregnancy, Alice stayed up all night writing streams of poems that, as sunrise broke, she stuffed under the door of Rukeyser's classroom— an old gardener's cottage in the middle of the campus. The poems, mostly about Africa, suicide, and the South, were written with bold and succinct strokes, as if Alice, in the aftermath of the abortion, had pared life to its most pure and vital essence. For example, among the poems waiting for Rukeyser each morning was one with a stanza that read:

> *One day in*
> *Georgia*
> *Working around*
> *the Negro section*
> *My friend got a*
> *letter*
> *in*
> *the mail*
> *—the letter*
> *said*
> *   "I hope you're*
> *having a good*
> *time*
> *fucking all*
> *   the niggers."*
> *"Sweet." I winced.*
> * "Who*
> *wrote it?"*
> *"mother."*
> * she*
> * said.*

"I didn't care what Muriel did with the poems," Alice later remembered. "I only knew I wanted someone to read them as if they were new leaves sprouting from an old tree. The same energy that impelled me to write them carried them to her door."

Having forsaken the razor blade, Alice also wrote a short story that affirmed her newfound joy in living. "To Hell with Dying" centers on Mr. Sweet, an elderly, guitar-playing black man, "constantly on the verge of being blind drunk," who is "saved" by the loving affection of children each time his health falters—the result of too many heartaches and shattered dreams. With its poignancy and wry humor, "To Hell with Dying" stands as a marked contrast to "The Suicide of an American Girl." It would become Alice's first published work of fiction, included in the 1967 collection, *The Best Short Stories by Negro Writers*, edited by Langston Hughes. In 1988, the story was published as a children's book with shimmering illustrations by California artist Catherine Deeter.

"Mr. Sweet was a fixture, a rare and honored presence in our family and we were taught to respect him," Alice later explained in "The Old Artist: Notes on Mr. Sweet," an essay about the origins of the story. "No matter that he drank, loved to gamble and shoot off his gun, and went 'crazy' several times a year. He was an artist. . . . I wrote the story with tears pouring down my cheeks. . . . I was fighting for my own life. I was twenty-one."

HER COURSEWORK completed, Alice received her bachelor of arts degree from Sarah Lawrence on a cold, snowy day in January 1966. The ceremony, attended by a handful of other winter-term graduates, was held in the home of college president Paul L. Ward, who, with a champagne toast, offered standard, "light up the world, blaze new trails, no obstacle too great" commentary. Little did he know.

Removed from the rhythms of Sarah Lawrence by poverty, history, culture, and distance, none of Alice's family members traveled to Bronxville to celebrate the event. But she was not alone. Julius Coles, her Morehouse friend and Helsinki traveling partner, accompanied her to the ceremony, beaming with pride as she accepted her diploma.

Then a graduate student in international affairs at Princeton University in New Jersey, Coles had dated Alice during her stay in Bronxville and fallen deeply in love. So bedazzled had he become by the young woman with whom he chugged rum and bellowed revolutionary chants in Russia that he hoped she'd become "Mrs. Coles." He'd already practiced his marriage proposal. But to his great shock and dismay, Alice declined.

"After the ceremony, I drove Alice to Boston," remembered Coles, today an administrator at Morehouse. "On the way up I asked her to marry me and she said 'No.' I was devastated.

"Years later she told me about the abortion and how she needed to reclaim her life and concentrate on her writing, but at the time, I was crushed. Pretty soon, I proposed to another woman and we got married. I loved her, but to be truthful, I was also trying to heal my wounds after being rejected by Alice Walker. I thought I could make her happy. But she needed to move on."

15

New York

HAVING REJECTED Julius Coles, and as she later said, been "thrust into the world with no idea of how to proceed as a writer," Alice moved to Manhattan's Lower East Side. The low-rent neighborhood had long been a sanctuary for immigrants, artists, and rebels of all stripes. Writing about the community in the 1880s, one resident had proudly proclaimed it "the borderland where black and white races meet in common debauch."

To be sure, people were drawn there in the 1960s by its brash, "anything goes" ambience. But as a major crossroads for the counterculture, the community was also a vibrant center of progressive art and politics. A decade earlier, a fiery young black playwright named Lorraine Hansberry had settled in the neighborhood after leaving the University of Wisconsin, a few credits short of earning her degree. It was there, in a cramped apartment, that she began to make notes for the characters that would later emerge in her historic Broadway drama *A Raisin in the Sun*. Clearly, the wild hippie gatherings and sweet aroma of marijuana that would mark Alice's arrival in the Lower East Side belied the fact that not everyone who lived there had followed Timothy Leary's directive to "tune in, turn on, drop out."

In fact, while she looked forward to focusing on her writing, Alice, hardly one to "drop out" of society, had taken a job as a case worker with the city's welfare department. "It's what most of the writers, dancers, painters, and other artists did back then," she remembered. "We were all radical movement people who wanted to save the world. We believed that working for the welfare department would give us a chance to help people." The position also spared Alice from waitressing stints like the one she'd endured to earn extra money while at Sarah Lawrence. "I got tired of the white people grinning up at me and saying, 'You look just like Leslie Uggams,'" Alice sighed, referring to the then-popular black entertainer. "I didn't last long."

Before starting the welfare job, Alice used part of the seventy dollars Muriel Rukeyser had given her as a graduation present to rent a well-worn, two-bedroom apartment on East 12th Street between Avenue A and Avenue B. In addition to its commanding view of a nearby Con Edison utilities plant, the apartment building offered tenants another special feature: it did not have a front door. Instead, one entered the building through an open, unsecured archway that permitted not only residents, but also local winos and other assorted vagrants to roam the building's poorly lit hallways day or night.

For Alice, who cherished the privacy and order that had been in short supply in a family of eight children, the apartment had obvious drawbacks. Still, it was inexpensive and she was happy to share it with Diana Young, now a film librarian, who had also moved to Manhattan after graduating from Sarah Lawrence. Among their close neighbors were poet Allen Ginsberg and his lover Peter Orlovsky. "Peter wore a ponytail!" Alice remembered. "It was so refreshing."

Gazing at a photograph of the litter-strewn sidewalk in front of the apartment building taken the day she moved in with Alice, Young recalled, "There were always bums that Alice and I had to step over, passed out on the front stoop. It was a pretty shabby place." For Alice, the neighborhood rekindled memories of her family's fight for dignity in tawdry sharecroppers shacks. "Living in those conditions showed me exactly what people on welfare needed to prevent them from hitting bottom," she later observed. "That is, the ones who weren't already picking themselves up off the floor."

As a case worker, Alice was charged with, among other duties, assisting welfare recipients being treated in New York City hospitals. She later recalled the special anguish she felt working with patients at Bellevue, the city's infamous psychiatric facility. "It was heartbreaking because no one was doing anything to address the problems that were pushing these people over the brink," she explained. "Most of the patients were poor, barely educated. They didn't have decent jobs. They lived in squalor. Why wouldn't they be insane?

"But instead of dealing with that, the hospital staff would throw Valium or some other sedative at the patients. The system was not radical enough."

It was her belief in the need for radical reform—not only of New York's welfare department, but also of most of the country's domestic and foreign policies—that led Alice to join the swell of protestors who were taking to the streets in opposition to the war in Vietnam—a "campaign against communist aggression" in which the United States had been involved since the 1950s. And if the government-sanctioned killing in Southeast Asia was going unchecked, the situation was no better in Mississippi or Alabama, where state-supported violence continued to be unleashed on blacks. By the mid-1960s, deadly racial clashes were erupting in the North too, as blacks, fed up with years of prejudice and police repression, rioted in Detroit, Newark, and Chicago. Fueled by the government's role in Vietnam and deteriorating race relations at home, the civil unrest Alice had first experienced in the South was spreading like wildfire.

Reflective of the upheaval in the nation's body politic, fervent chants of "Burn, baby, burn" and "Make love, not war" were joining "We Shall Overcome" as the signature anthems of the day.

. . .

IN A reversal of their roles at Sarah Lawrence, Alice lent Diana money and moral support when, soon after their move to New York, she chose to end a pregnancy. "My spirits were low and, because Alice had already had an abortion, she took me under her wing," Young said. "She was going on a long walk one day with one of her friends. I was in my room feeling depressed and she invited me along knowing that being outside, strolling in the park, would make me feel better."

Reproductive choice would be at the thorny center of Alice's story, "The Abortion," which appears in *You Can't Keep a Good Woman Down*. The narrator is Imani, a young black woman who, like Alice, ends an unplanned pregnancy while in college. Imani recalls being liberated by her decision, "bearing as it had all the marks of a supreme coming of age and seizing of direction in her own life." Now married and the mother of a toddler, Imani becomes pregnant again. Torn, she decides not to bear another child. "Take care of yourself," her work-obsessed husband Clarence whispers, with a quick peck on the cheek, as she leaves their small Southern town for an abortion in New York. Upset by his nonchalance, Imani lays down the law, upon her return: "Have a vasectomy or stay in the guest room. Nothing is going to touch me anymore that isn't harmless."

Completing the circle of Alice's postoperative chat with Dr. Morriss Henry, "The Abortion" would garner a 1981 O. Henry Prize. "I was pleased," Alice later said. "Synchronicity is such a sign of life."

THE FRIEND who cavorted in the park with Diana and Alice was Garland Jeffreys, a self-described "bohemian artist" with whom Alice had a brief romance shortly after moving to the Lower East Side. Jeffreys had just returned from Italy, where he'd studied Renaissance art, and lived a few blocks away from Alice and Diana. A black man with sandy-colored hair, Jeffreys remembered asking Alice for a date after noticing her on the street and being attracted to her calm and quiet demeanor. "She was jamming on the physical side, too," he added with a rakish grin.

"This was during the time when there was a lot of shouting and screaming from the black militants to get back to our African roots," said Jeffreys, today a musician, as he sat in his Manhattan apartment surrounded by stacks of compact disks. "What I liked about Alice was that she wasn't all caught up in the political fray.

"Don't get me wrong," he continued. "Alice was definitely committed to black liberation. But she had already been to Africa and didn't fall for that 'Black Queen' rap or any of the other jargon that the black revolutionaries were preaching. We connected on a spiritual and artistic level. I was studying yoga. She was into her writing. We were both really focused on our art."

Jeffreys was quick to note that his sexual relationship with Alice was "nothing heavy," saying they both dated other people while they were involved. Still, he was visibly moved as he revisited their love affair. Rising from the sofa, he began to pace back and forth, seemingly overcome by emotion. Finally, he stopped in the center of his living room, looked straight ahead and quietly said, "I have a birth defect. It's not that noticeable, but my right eye is funny. And I'm nearly blind on that side. The doctors think my mother probably went through some kind of trauma when she was pregnant with me. Alice and I never talked about it. I think the topic might have been too sensitive for both of us at the time. But neither Alice nor I had eyes like regular people. We were both unusual in that way."

UNUSUAL ALSO at the time for an unpublished black writer was that the poems Alice had delivered to Rukeyser were being reviewed by Monica McCall, a respected literary agent whose client list included journalist Pete Hamill and acclaimed novelist Graham Greene. Remembered by veteran New York book editor Joyce Engleson as an "extremely handsome woman with an elegant accent," McCall, a native of England, also represented Rukeyser.

And although Alice would remain unaware of their relationship for decades to come, McCall and Rukeyser were lovers, according to Jan Heller Levi, author of a forthcoming biography of the poet. The irony of it was that at the time of Rukeyser's death in 1980, the line "What would happen if one woman told the truth about her life? / The world would split open," from her poem "Kathe Kollwitz," would be trumpeted by lesbians worldwide and used as a rallying cry to fight gender oppression. But in 1966, Rukeyser's sense of radical politics stopped short of discussing her love for women—except in extremely veiled language. Alice later said that it would have "helped me enormously and cleared up a lot of confusion" had she known that Rukeyser and McCall had an intimate relationship. But she hadn't a clue. "This is the sorrow of not telling the whole truth about who you are," she mused.

Mincing no words, Levi, who also worked as a personal assistant to Rukeyser, offered an intriguing analysis: "I wouldn't be surprised if Muriel was sexually attracted to Alice. As much as she nurtured Alice as a student, and could recognize, immediately, what she would become as a writer, my sense is that Muriel needed to keep a certain distance because her feelings were so intense. She had an extremely charged and powerful connection with Alice. The mentoring relationship between them had to be fraught with land mines."

Decades later, Alice expressed astonishment at Levi's hypothesis: "Wow," she marveled. "Who knew? I was so young and naïve."

WHATEVER THE underlying currents might have been, Rukeyser was certain that McCall could usher into the literary mainstream the student she had lauded, in her final faculty evaluation, as "one of the best with whom I have ever worked." McCall had recently placed a novel that had been received with glowing reviews and was confident, because of the book's critical success, that she could find a publisher for Alice's collection of thirty poems, titled *Once* and dedicated to Howard Zinn. And aside from Rukeyser's appraisal, McCall was impressed with the manuscript on its own merits. She thought it was masterful, the themes provocative, the words splendidly crafted. But at a time when only a handful of black writers,

most notably James Baldwin, were being published by major commercial houses, few in the industry shared McCall's enthusiasm for
Alice's manuscript with its poems about Kikuyu villages, martyred
civil rights workers, suicide notes, and the "medicine" that could be
found in a black grandmother's long unbraided hair.

The great flowering of black literary talent that had emerged in
the 1920s and come to be known as the Harlem Renaissance had
waned. Although writers such as John O. Killens (*Youngblood*,
1954), Paule Marshall (*Brown Girl, Brownstones*, 1959), Ann
Petry (*The Street*, 1946), and Dorothy West (*The Living Is Easy*,
1948) had garnered critical praise in the 1940s and 1950s, few publishers paid much attention to the black artistry that began to blossom, again, during the 1960s.

Such works as Truman Capote's *In Cold Blood* (1966) and
Jacqueline Susann's *Valley of the Dolls* (1966) were the publishing
sensations of the day. Editors were wild to sign up the next book
that would fly off the shelves. A poetry collection? By an unknown
black woman writer? Not a chance.

"The conventional wisdom was that there was just no market
for books about the black or African experience," remembered
Mitch Douglas, a former assistant to McCall. "Monica told me that
she'd send Alice's manuscript out and editors would return it the
next day. She'd get on the phone and try to impress upon them the
big mistake they were making; that some day they'd kick themselves
for having missed the chance to publish Alice Walker. But nobody
cared."

Had they inquired, the powers-that-be in the publishing world
would have discovered that Alice was not exactly losing any sleep
over their lack of interest in *Once*. The poems had come in a torrent of relief after her abortion and helped her heal from a traumatic experience. Getting them published had never been her goal.
Moreover, she was unaware that Rukeyser was circulating her
work. "Muriel gave the poems to Monica; I didn't have anything to
do with it," Alice later said. "I had needed to write them, but I
didn't care if they ever got published. That was irrelevant to me."

With the poems being sent out from McCall's office to meet their fate, Alice concentrated on other writing projects when she returned home from her "tedious and totally draining job." Her affair with Jack Heyman, a muscular, curly-haired colleague at the welfare department, took a bit of the boredom out of the "hard forty."

Remembering their brief liaison, Heyman, today a labor organizer in Oakland, California, said that he and Alice were "kindred spirits in complete rebellion against the status quo."

"Society was changing, but there were still lots of taboos about blacks and whites going out together," explained Heyman, who, like Alice, had been born in Georgia. "Alice and I were united in our desire to fight the system. We had a strong sexual attraction to each other. And as political radicals, we just naturally resisted anybody telling us what we could or could not do."

The West End Bar near Columbia University on Broadway at 116th Street was one of the unofficial headquarters for political activists living in New York at the time. Zipping uptown from the Lower East Side on his motorcycle, Jack and Alice would regularly meet friends at the bar. Over beers and with strains of Otis Redding and Janis Joplin blaring in the background, the young rebels would debate the ongoing squirmishes in Hanoi and Birmingham.

Determined also, in Heyman's words, to "trespass in enemy territory," he and Alice also rendezvoused in places where their presence, as an interracial couple, was likely to turn heads. He especially remembers a dinner they shared at The Pen and Pencil, an elegant Upper East Side bistro "that had a nice ring to it, seeing as Alice was a writer." "We walked into the restaurant and it was like a bomb had been set off or that we'd dropped in from an alien planet," Heyman recalled. "People were staring so hard, we thought their eyes were going to pop out of their heads into their dinner plates. So me and Alice order a big filet mignon, a bottle of nice wine, the works. And we sit and gaze dreamily at each other through the entire meal. Our attitude was, 'Screw you. We're lovers and we're not going to hide in the shadows.'"

Said Alice: "I loved the motorcycle! And Jack was cute. He reminded me of Marlon Brando in *One-Eyed Jacks*."

Her love life was thriving. In addition to her relationships with

Jeffreys and Heyman, Alice was also enjoying, as she would later slyly note, "an attachment" with Robert Allen, the friend from Morehouse, now a graduate student in sociology at the New School for Social Research in New York. A tall, soft-spoken man, Allen had spent childhood summers visiting kinfolk in Buckhead and Sparta, rural communities within twenty miles of Wards Chapel. Familiar with the red clay, country churches, and lovingly tended cemeteries in which poor blacks took such pride, Allen said he felt a "rooted kindredness" with Alice that deepened as he learned more of her writing aspirations and determined commitment to "the folk."

"I had a sense of Alice's struggles coming out of Spelman and Sarah Lawrence," Allen explained. "Given the circumstances, I was really in awe of her focus and the fact that she was basically finding her own way. There was also the physical, sexual attraction kind of thing and that led to a summer fling, I guess you'd call it. We had really strong feelings for each other. But I was already engaged to someone else."

And so it was in the open, free-spirited days of 1960s. As the Beatles crooned, "All you need is love."

ALICE WAS engaged and energized by the vibrant art scene and political fervor pulsating in various enclaves all over New York. Draping the walls in colorful African fabrics, and filling the rooms with flowers and lush plants, she and Diana had transformed their drab apartment into a warm and welcoming home. The problem was that Alice was never in it. And when she was, the soul-murdering strain of her job at the welfare department undermined her creative muse. Unwilling to sacrifice her writing for the sake of a paycheck, Alice, after about six months of "trying to personally save the walking wounded," called it quits.

In a letter dated June 4, 1966, she shared the news with Muriel Rukeyser, who also lived in Manhattan. "I have been thinking about you often this past week and wanting to call and yet not wanting really to talk—if you can imagine the feeling—but wanting you to know that all is well with me," she wrote to her former teacher. "I quit my job a week ago and have been pleased to find that all my ideas were not squeezed out by the routine of 9–5."

In what would be a consistent pattern in her life, Alice was soon rewarded for "stepping out on faith." Bemused by, but respectful of Alice's decision to forgo the fellowship endowed by his family (to say nothing of the poem), Charles Merrill had kept in touch with Alice after she left Spelman. One day, not too long after she'd resigned from the welfare department, he came to visit her from Boston, where he had founded the Commonwealth School, an innovative urban academy. A patron of the arts, Merrill also painted.

"He saw this ramshackle place where I was living, in a building without a front door, and basically offered me the same grant I had turned down when I was a student," said Alice, who would later own one of Merrill's paintings. "I accepted it because Charles Merrill had since proven to me that he appreciated my work and supported what I was trying to accomplish. Because the award was no longer tied to me being a student at Spelman, I didn't feel that I was compromising my morals or integrity."

Relieved of her job and now with two thousand dollars, Alice began making plans to return to Africa. She decided on Senegal, where she could "learn French from black people and immerse myself in the culture." But a magazine story changed everything.

Just as Alice was preparing to leave New York, she read yet another article on the latest civil rights standoff in the South. Looking at the photos of dull-eyed, ragged black children sitting on the steps of dilapidated shacks (just like the ones she'd been raised in), she felt compelled to "wade in the water," again. What was the point of studying French in Senegal, she asked herself, when black parents in Biloxi and Tuskegee couldn't vote, when their children were given secondhand books (if any) from white schools inscribed with "Nigger" and "Long Live the Klan"? None that she could tell.

So, instead of Dakar, Alice booked a flight to Mississippi, where she'd work with the NAACP Legal Defense and Educational Fund, Inc. (LDF). As she packed her books, clothes, African sculptures and prints, she could not help but think about all the times her parents had been forced to search for new housing when white landowners no longer needed them to chop cotton or milk cows. Remembering their panicked desperation, she arranged, after clearing the plan with Diana, for a needy family she'd worked with at the welfare office to take over her apartment before she said farewell to the Lower East Side.

16

Live or Die

THEY CALLED it "Mississippi," meaning "great river." For the Choctaw, Chickasaw, and Natchez Indians who first inhabited the region, the landscape was considered sacred because of its spectacular beauty and the mighty river that traversed the terrain and sustained an abundance of wildlife. But by the time civil rights struggles erupted in the South in the late 1950s, the word *Mississippi* had taken on a new meaning. For blacks fighting for equality, it had become synonymous with the most brutal racial violence the nation had witnessed since slavery.

The Magnolia State had earned its ignoble reputation as "the bottom line for white supremacy" shortly after Reconstruction. With the highest percentage of blacks of any state (most of them destitute sharecroppers), Mississippi lawmakers sought to crush the nascent power of the black citizenry by taking away its vote. To that end, the lawmakers enacted a variety of voting restrictions, ranging from absurdly difficult literacy tests to exorbitant poll taxes that guaranteed, *ipso facto*, that blacks would remain disenfranchised. Denied decent jobs, schooling, health care, and basic human rights far beyond the scale blacks in other parts of the South suffered, the average black person in Mississippi had a better chance of dying before age thirty than finishing third grade.

Over the years, the few blacks who dared to challenge Mississippi's political system were apt to find, at best, their crops ablaze or their livestock mysteriously poisoned. At worst, blacks bold enough to demand their constitutional rights could expect to be savagely beaten or lynched. The vicious assaults were usually orchestrated by members of "White Citizens' Councils," influential civic leaders (otherwise known as the "white-collar" Klan) who had organized throughout the state to intimidate blacks and keep them "in their place."

Because Mississippi functioned, prior to the 1960s, primarily as a closed society under ironclad white rule, few people outside of the South knew of the terror blacks there endured. But by the time Alice left New York to join the freedom fighters gathering in Greenwood and Jackson, the Magnolia State had been revealed as the roiling cauldron of racial hatred generations of blacks had known it to be.

Unveiled, Mississippi emerged as the place where Emmett Till, a mere boy of fourteen, had been murdered for reputedly "making overtures" to a white woman. It was the place where NAACP field director Medgar Evers had been gunned down on his doorstep. It was where the dedicated civil rights workers James Earl Chaney, Andrew Goodman, and Michael Schwerner (the latter two viewed as "white traitors" from the North) had been killed, at the outset of Freedom Summer 1964, by a gang of "Good Old Boys" that included the county sheriff.

So deeply entrenched was bigotry in Mississippi that Governor Paul Johnson, making stump speeches in the mid-1960s, could count on grandstand cheers from white supporters when he unabashedly proclaimed that the NAACP stood for "Niggers, Alligators, Apes, Coons, and Possums."

The state's contemptuous and consistently cold-blooded stance on race relations had thus made Mississippi ground zero for civil rights struggles. A protest song recorded by Nina Simone in 1964 reflected the sentiments most blacks held about the Magnolia State: "Alabama got me so upset, / Tennessee make me lose my rest, / but everybody knows about Mississippi, God-dam!!!!!!!!!!"

Anyone examining the life of Alice Walker in the summer of 1966 could not help but wonder why she was carting herself off to Mississippi ("What has four 'eyes' and can't see?" went the riddle chanted by black children) just as she had received a fellowship that would have enabled her to write full-time in the nation's premier publishing center or to travel to Senegal. She had survived Jim Crow Georgia, a traumatic childhood injury, political strife at Spelman, a transfer to Sarah Lawrence, suicidal depression, and an illegal abortion that might well have ended her days. Driven nearly insane (and permanently scarred, in the minds of many) by the racial violence he had endured in Mississippi, native son Richard Wright had been forced to leave the state to forge a writing career. Now comes Alice, by her own volition, into the belly of the beast? Her family was horrified.

"Mississippi was such an awful place that I didn't want Alice to even fly over the state," her sister Ruth later said, without a trace of humor. "I was scared to death for her to go down there where everybody knew white folks would just as soon kill you as say 'Good morning.' "

For Alice, it was precisely because blacks lived under such brutal conditions in Mississippi that she felt it was a "life-or-death" matter to go there and confront the repression head on. "All my life Mississippi had been the epitome of evil for black people. I knew that if I was to be able to live at all in America, I needed to be able to live unafraid, anywhere. I had to face up to the system that had almost done me in and so many of my people. Mississippi was the test."

EN ROUTE also to Mississippi that summer was another resident of Lower Manhattan who, like Alice, was determined to make America fulfill its promise of "liberty and justice for all." But unlike Alice, twenty-three-year-old New York University Law School student Mel (short for Melvyn) Leventhal had been to the Magnolia State before. Offered an internship with the Boston-based Law Student's Civil Rights Research Council, Leventhal had been assigned to Jackson (the state capital) the previous summer to help draft the many lawsuits that were being filed against Mississippi in response to its flagrant disregard of federal desegregation decrees. Undeterred by the bricks, rocks, bottles, and random gunshot blasts that routinely greeted civil rights workers in the state, Leventhal had returned to Jackson the summer of 1966 as an intern with the NAACP LDF. The director of the office was future children's advocate Marian Wright (later Edelman). A Spelman graduate, Edelman went on to Yale Law School and in 1965 became the first black woman admitted to the Mississippi bar.

"I couldn't just be an observer and follow what was happening in the South in the newspapers," Leventhal later said. "I felt compelled to do something concrete to help the people. All my life, I had been an empathetic person who could not stand to see anybody mistreated. And what was happening to blacks in Mississippi was as wrong as wrong could be."

The depth of the bigotry in Mississippi may have been new to Leventhal, but he had experienced hurt and humiliation firsthand. A native of Brooklyn born on March 18, 1943, and the grandson of Jewish immigrants, Leventhal's parents divorced when he was about nine years old. When his father remarried, he took his eldest son with him, leaving Mel and a younger brother to be raised by their mother (who never remarried) on a paltry bookkeeper's salary. "I don't think I saw my father more than two or three times, after my parents divorced," said Leventhal, recalling his youth. "One day when I was about twelve, I took my baby brother over to my dad's house, just so he could get a better idea of what his father looked like. The man slammed the door in our face."

Educated in local public schools and yeshiva (Jewish day school), Leventhal said his status as an "outsider," rejected by his own father, made him naturally sympathetic with blacks when civil rights battles began in the early 1950s. He marked the abuse suffered by Jackie Robinson when he joined the Brooklyn Dodgers, becoming the first black man to play major league baseball, as a transforming event in his life. "I was outraged and disgusted by the way white people treated Jackie Robinson," Leventhal said, adding that he had numerous black childhood friends. "I felt his hurt deep in my heart and vowed right then to do everything I could to end that kind of discrimination and hate."

A decade later, Leventhal found himself in Mississippi, where his allegiance to blacks invariably brought him the invectives "nigger lover," "communist," and "homosexual"—the slurs commonly used against liberal whites—and made him a prime target for the state's signature brand of brutality. "If I had ever studied up on exactly how dangerous it was to try to end segregation in Mississippi, I might not have had the courage to go," he later noted with a wry laugh. "I could not have imagined the level of racism down there. My ignorance is what saved me."

If ignorance "saved" Leventhal from fully grasping what he was up against as a white man working for racial justice in Mississippi, the relationship he would begin the summer of 1966 with a young black writer from Georgia would soon make the situation perfectly clear.

ALICE ARRIVED at the Jackson airport at about noon on a hot and humid day in late June. She was met, as she recalled, by a worker from Edelman's office. "Marian had been a beloved student activist at Spelman, but as she'd graduated before I arrived, I had never met her," Alice later said. "I admired her commitment and was really happy to get involved with the projects being organized out of her office."

She hastened to add, "The 'Inc. Fund,' as we called it, was much more radical and progressive than what people think of as the NAACP. It was a completely separate organization."

Hungry and a bit nervous about what her Mississippi summer would bring, Alice was relieved when her companion suggested they have lunch before she got settled. Tossing her luggage in the backseat of the car, they took off for Steven's Kitchen, a black-owned, soul food restaurant in downtown Jackson where civil rights workers routinely gathered to fill their stomachs and replenish their spirits after battling Jim Crow. Sitting at a table that day, savoring a rib-sticking lunch of smothered chicken, greens, and cornbread, was Mel Leventhal.

"I was introduced to Mel when I arrived at the restaurant and I remember thinking he was cute," Alice later said. "But at the time, I was very mistrusting of white people in the Movement. I believed what SNCC had been saying about how whites needed to be in their own communities doing civil rights work. I agreed that they were often a detriment in the struggle because of the way blacks in the South had been conditioned to automatically defer to whites."

The Student Nonviolent Coordinating Committee, SNCC, pronounced "snick," was an activist group founded primarily by black college students who had been staging peaceful sit-ins at segregated lunch counters since the early 1960s. Over the years, as the SNCC demonstrations gained increasing media attention, more whites joined the protests and were welcomed into the group's leadership. But by the mid-1960s, the black students who were the driving force in the organization had grown weary of having milk thrown in their faces and catsup poured down their backs in response to their simple request for a cup of coffee.

Angered by the inability of the older black establishment to dismantle Jim Crow with "the weapon of love," SNCC had taken a more radical turn. And in SNCC's growing militancy, the role of whites, no matter how sincere or dedicated, had become a major flashpoint. Moving closer toward the Black Power stance that had been taken by Muslim leader Malcolm X, many SNCC members now felt that blacks should separate from whites and take control of their own destiny. In his memoir *Walking with the Wind* (1998), former SNCC chairman John Lewis describes the conflict that raged through the group: "The subject we kept coming back to again and again was the relevancy and even the possibility of an interracial democracy. . . . [Some SNCC members] published a position paper that expressed their views that black people needed all black organizations to establish their own identities and develop their own direction. This idea caught fire with many SNCC members. . . . A motion was passed to keep whites in SNCC but to have them work only in white communities. Everyone could see it would be only a matter of time before they were ousted completely."

But white people had not been "thrown out" of the movement just yet. When Alice returned South, Mel Leventhal and the other white civil rights workers like him were still ensconced in the struggle in the Magnolia State.

ALICE HAD expected that she would be put to work in Jackson registering voters as she had done the previous summer in Georgia. But because of her writing skills, she was assigned to nearby Greenwood to take depositions from poor blacks who had been evicted—thereby losing their "homes"—for attempting to register to vote. On August 6, 1965, President Lyndon Johnson had signed the Voting Rights Act, rendering illegal the literacy tests and poll taxes that had prevented blacks from using the ballot.

Discrimination in public accommodations had been banned the previous year with the passage of the Civil Rights Act. If Mississippi whites continued to ignore the law of the land, they were going to pay for their defiance with a never-ending series of lawsuits. The evidence Alice gathered would be used in such cases, and she fully intended to help the sharecroppers describe, in the most unvarnished terms, every indignity they had endured.

As she set off for Greenwood in a battered "movement car" (replete with bullet holes in the chassis), Alice knew she was using her education, as she had hoped, in the service of her people. She could not help but feel that powerful spiritual forces were also at play. For by chance, the cute law student had been assigned to work with her, giving Alice the opportunity to discover exactly what Mel Leventhal was all about.

17

In a Biblical Way

ALICE AND Mel arrived in Greenwood (about ninety miles northwest of Jackson) the night before they were to take depositions from the town's beleaguered sharecroppers. Once there, they checked into a local motel. Glaring with open disgust at the black woman and white man standing before him, the motel clerk who registered Mel and Alice did little to hide his feelings about their patronage. Mississippi whites did not even feign to comply with civil rights legislation, and the state's schools, libraries, hotels, hospitals, and restaurants were as segregated as they had been at the end of Reconstruction.

In *We Are Not Afraid*, a 1988 book about freedom struggles in the South, authors Seth Cagin and Philip Dray described Greenwood as a city with a special antipathy toward improved race relations. "A defiant crowd of Greenwood blacks marched to city hall. Hundreds of white bystanders lined the curb cursing and urging the cops to unleash the dogs. 'Turn 'em loose. Sic 'em! Sic 'em! We killed two-month old Indian babies to take this country. And now they want us to give it away to the niggers,' they said."

Having been raised under Jim Crow, Alice knew how deeply whites resented integration and the "outside agitators" they believed were destroying their time-honored "way of life." She was not at all surprised by the hostile treatment she and Mel had received at the front desk, and later found herself irritated by Mel's response.

"Mel was shaking his head in disbelief and saying, 'I can't believe they don't want to let you stay here,' and other remarks that reflected the naïveté that so many Northerners displayed when they came to the South. Did he think that just because some laws had been changed, white people were automatically going to start treating blacks like human beings? That kind of attitude infuriated me."

After obtaining their keys from the clerk, Alice and Mel went to their respective quarters. But as darkness fell, they grew fearful that Greenwood's "good old boys," apprised of their presence by the motel staff, might come pay them a visit. Rattled, but refusing to abandon their mission, they decided to spend the night in the same room. They figured that if push came to shove, they would have a better chance of defending themselves together than apart.

"It was understood that the local Klan was informed whenever civil rights workers came into a town in Mississippi," Alice explained. "That kind of threat and intimidation was standard procedure. They tried to terrorize both you and the black people in the community you were trying to organize."

Too nervous to sleep, Alice and Mel, in separate beds, decided to read aloud the only book in their room—the Bible. As they took turns reciting passages from the Song of Solomon, Alice began to see her coworker in a different light.

With its vivid and joyful verses extolling sexual desire ("your breasts are the clusters of dates and I will climb up into the palm to grasp its fronds"), the Song of Solomon is a paean to sensuality. Whatever its interpretation among biblical scholars, the everyday eroticism of the scripture about two lovers burnishes on the page.

"I could tell by the way Mel read those passages that he was a deeply committed, passionate man," Alice said. "Nothing romantic happened that evening, but our souls had touched. We really bonded over the Song of Solomon."

The late-night visit Alice and Mel had feared did not come to pass. Instead, they received their "welcome" the next day after they had taken depositions from several tenant farmers and then stopped for lunch. "Alice and I were sitting in the restaurant when an old white man comes up to us and says, 'Don't let the sun set on you in Greenwood,' " Mel said, recalling the incident. "He was such a caricature of a racist 'cracker' that we couldn't help but laugh.

"As we still had a number of sharecroppers to interview, Alice and I finished lunch and then went back to work out in the countryside. But as night fell, I noticed a pickup truck following our car. There were two white men in it, and they looked pretty ominous."

With his eyes trained on the rearview mirror, Mel began to drive cautiously through the dark and desolate backroads of Greenwood. Everytime he sped up, "the truck would go faster and be right on my tail," he remembered. "So finally, I turn to Alice and tell her, 'We've got a problem. We better get out of here.' "

Through the hazy beam of his headlights, Mel could see the highway up ahead that led out of town. But there were several intersections marked with stop signs to navigate before they'd be on the open road. Not wanting to draw the attention of any "officers of the law," who were known to lurk in the backwoods waiting to arrest civil rights workers on trumped-up charges (or do something worse), Mel restrained himself from pressing the gas pedal to the floor.

Although he tried to remain calm, his fear was rising. Glancing at Alice, Mel thought about all the movement people who had been struck down in Mississippi and wondered if he and Alice were about to join their ranks. He had just made it through one intersection, with what he was now certain were Klansmen dead on their heels, when the pickup truck was hit broadside by another car.

"I heard this big crashing sound, and I shot out like a light," Mel remembered. "When I looked through the rearview mirror, I saw this elderly black man getting out of a station wagon. I could tell from the bend of his body and the bow of his head that he was apologizing to the white men in the truck, who were, of course, hoppin' mad."

Safely on the highway, Alice and Mel drove back to Jackson without further incident. The next day they learned that the "accident" had been staged by the local NAACP as a diversion to help them get out of town. "Word had gotten back to the black leadership that we'd been threatened, so they came up with a fake crash to cut off the men they knew would be trailing us at the end of the day," Mel explained. "A lot of folks have this image of blacks in Mississippi at that time being subservient, always with their hats off kowtowing to white people. But they did what they could to fight for their own freedom. If it hadn't been for that 'wreck,' Alice and I just might have been strung up in Greenwood."

DESPITE THEIR close call, Mel and Alice continued the dangerous task of interviewing sharecroppers. Touched by his gentleness, integrity, and willingness to risk his life for poor black people, Alice's attraction to Mel grew. Still, she could not help but wondering, as she later remarked, "if the man was brave or someone who was just really stupid."

She got her answer one evening when she, Mel, and another movement friend ventured to the Ross Barnett Reservoir in Jackson. Desperate for relief from Mississippi's brain-broiling heat, they had decided to take a cooling dip. A black woman, a white man, and a white woman, frolicking together, at night—in Mississippi? Well, there could only be one explanation for that. Rightly deducing that the three were civil rights workers, state troopers drove up and began harassing them.

Quick to distance herself from Alice, the white woman, now clinging to Mel, tried to appease the officers. But Mel, incensed by their hateful jeers, "stuck with me," Alice recalled. "Most white people in a situation like that would have automatically abandoned the black person," she said. "Mel passed a major test that night because when he stood up to those state troopers and aligned himself with me, he showed a lot of courage. We started sleeping together shortly afterward because he'd proven to me who he truly was."

Similarly, Alice said that as she and Mel became lovers, she found herself drawn to voices that, in their *authenticity*, inspired hopefulness, no matter the odds. "At about this time, I was reading

James Baldwin and listening to B.B. King, who has done as much to instill optimism in my soul and work as any book. I was also learning from the work of Malcolm X that the truth . . . simply because it *is* the truth always has an element of delight. . . . Truth is the orgasm of what is right."

NOW CONFIDENT that she could trust him with her deepest vulnerabilities and emotions, Alice began sharing her writing with Mel. She let him read short stories she had completed at Sarah Lawrence and others she had strained to polish late at night in her Lower East Side apartment, after exhausting days at the welfare office. Removing the neatly typed pages from a manuscript box one morning over breakfast at Steven's Kitchen, she watched quietly as Mel mused over the poems for which Monica McCall hoped to find a New York publisher. He was charmed from the start. "Poverty was not a calamity for me," Alice had written, quoting Albert Camus on the opening page of *Once*. "It was always balanced by the richness of light . . . circumstances helped me. To correct a natural indifference I was placed halfway between misery and the sun. Misery kept me from believing that all was well under the sun, and the sun taught me that history wasn't everything."

Leafing through the pages, he went on to such pieces as Alice's poem "South: The Name of Home":

> *all that night*
> *I prayed for eyes to see again*
> *whose last sight*
> *had been*
> *a broken bottle*
> *held negligently*
> *in a racist*
> *fist*
> *God give us trees to plant*
> *and hands and eyes*
> *to love them . . .*

And in the section "African Images, Glimpses from a Tiger's Back" he read:

> *A small boat*
> *A placid lake*
> *Suddenly at one's hand*
> *Two ears—*
> *Hippopotamus.*

Before choosing law, Mel had given serious thought to a career as a playwright. That Alice—intelligent, attractive, and committed—was also a writer made him desire her all the more. "I was smitten by Alice the first day I saw her, but I fell in love with her when I read *Once*," Mel later said. "There was so much passion and sensitivity in her work. The images in her poems stayed with you for a very long time. They were real."

Alice would later note that some of the poems in the collection were influenced by Zen epigrams and the artistry of haiku poets such as Basho and Shiki. "I was delighted to learn that in three or four lines a poet can express mystery, evoke beauty and pleasure, paint a picture," she said.

Alice and Mel's romance quickly grew serious. Theirs was no light-hearted fling stirred up in the heat of battle that would fizzle when the couple left Jackson, each going their separate ways. As the summer progressed, falling into each other's arms at night, both knew that they had found their soul mate.

While interracial relationships had blossomed among civil rights workers from the outset of the movement, such liaisons were not without their complications. At the very core of the Jim Crow system, and central to its continued existence, was the vicious stereotype of the sexually charged, violent black man obsessed with ravishing white women. As for black women, lurid myths about their licentiousness and "loose" morals had made them prey to sexual exploitation by white men since slavery. For civil rights activists, this painful history colored every interracial pairing. Having sat at lunch counters together, been spat on together, and jailed together, mixed-race couples might well find their love a target of derision from their peers.

"We were a group of young men and women with natural attractions to one another, regardless of race . . . which did not make everyone overjoyed," explained former SNCC chairman John Lewis in his memoir. "It was that issue of segregation versus integration, an issue that would always be a wedge for us. There were men and women in our organization who considered it a betrayal to our race, a denial of our identity, to become romantically involved with a white person. . . . And like so many of our problems at that time [this sentiment] would grow rapidly."

In Mississippi, the bias against interracial unions was codified, with the overkill characteristic of segregationists, in the state constitution, which decreed, "The marriage of a white person with a Negro or mulatto, or person who shall have one-eighth or more of Negro blood, shall be unlawful or void. . . . The purpose of forbidding marriage between white persons and Negroes or mulattos is to prevent such persons from living together in the relationship of husband and wife."

But if anybody working with Mel and Alice in Jackson in 1966 had trouble with their relationship, they kept it to themselves. Besides, such disapproval wouldn't have mattered to the young lovers; having survived a summer in Mississippi, they were now ready to take on the world. Those inclined to look on interracial romance as "transgressive" would find Alice's response in her poem "While Love Is Unfashionable," which she dedicated to Mel.

> *While love is unfashionable*
> *let us live*
> *unfashionably . . .*
> *love our blackest garment.*
> *Let us be poor*
> *in all but truth, and courage*
> *handed down*
> *by the old*
> *spirits . . .*

While love is dangerous
let us walk bareheaded
beside the Great River.
Let us gather blossoms
under fire.

If there was to be walking "under fire," Alice felt that Georgia was a good place to take the next step. Proud of the role she had played in helping poor black sharecroppers fight Jim Crow, Alice decided to visit her parents in Eatonton after she finished her job with the NAACP. She invited Mel, who would be returning to New York to finish law school, to join her for a few days. The couple had begun their Mississippi sojourn reading the Song of Solomon in a modest motel room. A passage from the same text seemed to speak to their future as Alice departed with Mel for her hometown: "I found him whom my soul loveth: I held him, and would not let him go, until I had brought him into my mother's house, and into the chamber of her that conceived me."

18

Tulips

THE FOUR-HUNDRED-MILE drive from Jackson to Eatonton passed through many a violent segregationist stronghold. While the June 1964 murders of Chaney, Goodman, and Schwerner had drawn major media attention, the gruesome stories of many other civil rights workers and random victims of racist vigilantes who had perished in Southern hamlets in the decade since Rosa Parks had dared to remain in her bus seat were rarely reported in the *New York Times* or the *Atlanta Journal-Constitution*. Who knew, for example, of Johnnie Mae Chappell? A devoted mother of ten, Chappell was slain by whites in March 1964 as she walked to a neighborhood store in Florida to buy ice cream for her children. Most often, a stony silence was the only response to the deaths of such unknown martyrs who'd been felled in the midst of trees, rivers, and sprawling fields of cotton, where hatred had triumphed over humanity.

Knowing the danger of her journey with Mel, Alice, before leaving Jackson, called Ruth and put her on emergency alert, providing names of movement friends to contact if she and Mel did not arrive in Eatonton as planned. For Ruth, who had never wanted her baby sister to set foot in Mississippi, the thought of Alice being harmed *on the way home* was almost too much to bear. But not wanting to alarm the rest of the family, Ruth kept to herself the details of her conversation with Alice.

"I was a nervous wreck that whole day, waiting for them," Ruth recalled. "Finally, at about three o'clock in the morning, I heard these footsteps coming up the front porch and I peeped out the window. It was Alice and Mel. I was just so thankful they were both alive."

With their children supplementing their thirty-dollar monthly rent, the Walkers had since moved to a nice house in town, painted white with green shutters. There were pecan trees in the yard, a hedge for privacy, and a porch swing. The family had prepared a bed for Mel in the living room. Alice bunked with Ruth. Out of respect for her parents, she would never have slept with any lover, let alone a white man, under their roof. Bone weary from the strain of the drive, both Alice and Mel went to bed within minutes of their arrival. Formal introductions could wait until daylight.

In fact, it wasn't as if Mel came to the Walker household a complete stranger. Mrs. Walker knew from Alice's letters that Mel was a white law student committed to the black freedom struggle. She was also aware that he was Jewish, a faith about which she had little knowledge. And what she did know had been colored by the teachings delivered from the pulpit of Wards Chapel AME (African Methodist Episcopal), where, because of her generosity and devotion, she was the esteemed "mother of the church." This Christian bias was in full evidence when Mrs. Walker, later in the day, officially met Mel.

"Alice introduced me to her mother and the first words out of her mouth were, 'You're one of those who killed Christ,' " he remembered. "So I replied, 'Well, Mrs. Walker, I don't think I was there at the time,' and we both kind of chuckled. I didn't find the remark particularly offensive. It was said more out of a lack of understanding than any kind of hatred or disrespect."

Remembering the exchange, Alice said she had felt "completely mortified." "I was very concerned about Mel's feelings and not wanting him to be hurt. I knew that my mother's heart was entirely open to him. But she had never met a Jew before. And when it dawned on her where she had heard about Jewish people, she just blurted out what the preachers said in church."

Mel would later remember Mr. Walker as an "intense, extremely intelligent man" who, despite his reserve, "talked up a blue streak" on the topic of politics. Having risked life and limb to become, in the 1940s, one of the first black men to vote in Putnam County, Mr. Walker had a lot of wisdom to impart to the aspiring civil rights attorney. "Working in Mississippi, I'd come to know what kind of courage it took for a black man to defy Jim Crow and register to vote," Mel said. "That Mr. Walker had voted at a time when so many other black people had been afraid to challenge the system made him very unusual. As far as I was concerned, that made him as much of a freedom fighter as anybody else. Though he did talk to the point where it gave me a headache."

After sitting a spell with her parents, Alice and Mel visited the cemetery across from Wards Chapel AME. There, as Alice later noted, she "introduced him to that amazing collection of Walkers" buried in the expansive family plot. They also took quiet walks through the nearby fields and meadows where she had found so much comfort during her youth. On seeing, through Alice's eyes, the resplendent sweep of a willow or the shimmering yellow of a wildflower, Mel immediately understood why *Once* was filled with poems regaling her "passionate courtship with trees" and overarching reverence for nature. Poems that had enthralled him in Steven's Kitchen, such as "South: The Name of Home," captivated him anew:

> *The earth is red*
> *here—*
> *the trees bent, weeping*
> *what secrets will not*
> *the ravished land*
> *reveal*
> *of its abuse?*

Mel still had sharecroppers to canvas in Mississippi before he would return to New York, so he only stayed in Eatonton a few days. For Ruth, the memory of his departure was even more dramatic than had been his early-morning arrival with Alice.

"I was standing right out on the porch the evening that Mel left," Ruth said. "Alice walked him to the car and they kissed. Now, I knew that Mel and Alice were good friends, but it hadn't occurred to me that they were an item. After Mel drove off, Alice came back into the house and she had tears in her eyes. She told me, 'I'm going to marry him.' That just about shocked me to death because *Mississippi* and *interracial relationship*—well, those were dangerous words that just didn't mix. I didn't understand how she could even think about falling in love with all the stress and strain she and Mel had gone through in Mississippi."

Allowing that she'd been accepting of Alice's romance with David DeMoss, Ruth said her astonishment had less to do with Mel's color than the fact that "Alice was so independent, I didn't see her marrying anybody—black, white, purple, or blue. It was *that* combined with the word *Mississippi* that took me by surprise."

For Alice, the explanation was simple: "I loved Mel because he was passionate about justice and he was genuinely passionate about me. He was soulful, expressive, and didn't hold back any of his feelings. It was so obvious he enjoyed every moment we were together." And together they intended to be.

AN AVID swimmer, Mel had taken a job as a lifeguard at a New York University pool to support himself during his last year of law school. As part of his compensation, the university had also given him a rent-free room overlooking Washington Square Park. It was there that Alice joined him when she returned to New York from Georgia. The first order of business was to create a space where Alice could write in the cozy but cramped quarters. To that end, Mel borrowed a metal folding table from his mother, which they draped with a madras bedspread and *voilà*—a desk for Alice. Having been raised by a mother who designed everything from her garden to her canning jars to the clothes she crafted out of flour sacks, Alice was ever attentive to beauty. On her desk was a lovely sculpted earthenware vase that she and Mel kept filled with pink peonies or white daisies.

Sitting at the sturdy Smith-Corona typewriter her mother had given her when she left for Spelman, Alice began to write a novel about an impoverished sharecropping family. Sometimes the rural characters would fall silent, refusing to compete with the blaring car horns and screeching sirens of the city. On those days, Mel, welcoming a break from studying torts and contracts, would close his law books. They'd head to the university pool in the basement of the building. There, with his muscular body gliding through the water, Mel taught Alice how to swim. Patient as she mastered the eccentricities of clutches and stick shifts, he also taught her to drive his bright red Volkswagen Beetle.

Diana Young had met Mel shortly after he and Alice started living together and she was surprised by the seriousness of their relationship. She was especially concerned that the couple planned, as Alice confided, to return to Mississippi after Mel graduated from law school, in less than a year.

"It was clear that Alice and Mel weren't just doing the casual 'free love' thing everybody was doing in the 1960s. They were really committed," Young explained. "I admired their courage, especially as an interracial couple. But I was also concerned that perhaps Alice was going to put her writing on the back burner. I was afraid of Mel's career taking precedence over hers. Not that Mel was overbearing, I was just worried that, like a lot of women, Alice might lose herself."

But far from losing herself, Alice, encouraged by Mel's love and unflagging support, began to write with an even stronger focus and intensity. That winter, with her Southern characters uninspired by the snow that blanketed New York City, Alice put aside her novel and began an essay on the civil rights movement that she would later submit to a national magazine contest.

Remembering how Alice crafted the piece, Mel said, "She was at her desk, and I was over in a corner reading the newspaper. The typewriter was clicking furiously. After a while, she hands me ten or fifteen pages. I remember thinking, 'Well, this is just the first draft.' I was wrong. The essay had come to her in full form, and it was magnificent. She may have tinkered with it a little, but what you see on the printed page is pretty much what she handed to me straight out of the typewriter. For me to write an essay that polished would have taken at least six months. And she wrote the whole thing in one sitting while I was fiddling with the newspaper."

"The Civil Rights Movement: What Good Was It?" won first prize and would appear in the Autumn 1967 issue of *American Scholar* as Alice's first major published work of nonfiction. In the essay (reprinted in *In Search of Our Mothers' Gardens*), Alice argued that regardless of the outcome, the movement had sparked a sense of pride in blacks that would live forever. In poignant passages she compared her life, shaped in the fervor of freedom struggles, to that of her mother, who, demeaned by Jim Crow most of her years, would sometimes lose sight of her self-worth. Alice noted that her mother was especially prone to such lapses after watching soap operas ("tales of hypocrisy and infidelity"), a habit she had developed while working as a domestic for whites.

"My mother, a truly great woman who raised eight children of her own and half a dozen of the neighbors' without a single complaint, was convinced that she did not exist compared to 'them,' " Alice wrote, describing Mrs. Walker's response to the television images she absorbed. "She subordinated her soul to theirs and became a faithful and timid supporter of the 'Beautiful White People.' Once she asked me, in a moment of vicarious pride and despair, if I didn't think that 'they' were 'jest naturally smarter, prettier, better.' My mother asked this: a woman who never got rid of any of her children, never cheated on my father, was never a hypocrite if she could help it. . . . She could not bring herself to blame 'them' for making her believe what they wanted her to believe: that if she did not look like them, think like them, be sophisticated and corrupt-for-comfort's-sake like them, she was a nobody."

Offering a stark contrast, Alice wrote that it was after seeing Dr. King on television that she was inspired to join the civil rights movement, a decision that ensured "the influence my mother's soap operas might have had on me became impossible."

"Because of the beatings, the arrests, the hell of battle during the past years, I have fought harder for my life and for a chance to be myself, to be something more than a shadow or a number, than I had ever done before in my life," Alice continued. "Before, there had seemed to be no real reason for struggling beyond the effort for daily bread. Now there was a chance at that other that Jesus meant when He said we could not live by bread alone."

In its intimate and impassioned analysis of the impact of racism on the black psyche, Alice's essay echoed sentiments that had been expressed by James Baldwin in his masterwork, "The Fire Next Time." Like Baldwin, who, despairing at the plight of his childhood friends, had wondered, *What will happen to all that beauty?*, Alice too exhorted blacks to "walk without shame" and honor their heritage. And like Dr. King in *Letter from Birmingham City Jail*, Alice spoke directly to those who criticized civil rights efforts but saw no evil in the injustices that compelled blacks to "agitate." Read together, the three essays offer insights into the 1960s freedom struggle that are perhaps unparalleled in their candor, vision, and eloquence.

But even before the essay hit the newsstands, Alice had been accepted to a writing residency at the MacDowell Colony in Peterborough, New Hampshire. There, in a cozy cabin with a wood fire to warm her and the soaring gospel music of Mahalia Jackson and Clara Ward playing in the background, Alice continued to work on her novel. At home in the rural landscape, her characters Margaret, Mem, Brownfield, and Grange emerged with a compelling vividness and force, affirming Alice's instinct that their pained and complex story was better suited to telling in the rolling hills of New Hampshire than on the gritty asphalt of New York.

Missing Alice, Mel too escaped to the countryside. Every weekend, after loading his Volkswagen with flowers, oranges, and grapefruit, he made the five-hour drive to MacDowell, where he and Alice snuggled next to the crackling fire.

Secure in their love and with Mel only a few months from graduation, Alice, fulfilling her pledge to Ruth, decided to marry the man she'd first eyed with skepticism in Steven's Kitchen. Just as she'd weighed the impact of whites in the movement when she began her romance with Mel, politics also influenced her decision to join him in matrimony.

"If we were going back to Mississippi, then we'd be going as husband and wife," Alice explained. "There was a long tradition of white men having black mistresses in the South. That was not going to be my path. So I proposed to Mel, and he happily obliged. Apart from our love, it was important politically for us to be legally married." Although concerned about what the future held for Alice and Mel, the Walker family generally accepted the news. "We understood Alice had a mind of her own," said Ruth.

Joined by just a few friends (among them Carole Darden), Melvyn Rosenman Leventhal and Alice Malsenior Walker were married, without fanfare, in a brief civil ceremony conducted on March 17, 1967, in the chambers of New York City Family Court judge Justine Wise Polier. Having eschewed wedding gifts, Alice and Mel presented Judge Polier with a stunning bouquet of pink tulips. The flowers, they later explained, were offered in celebration of the sanctioning of a union that tore at the very fiber of white supremacy. For in 1967, as Mel and Alice prepared to return to Mississippi, intermarriage remained an outlawed offense in the South, odious in the extreme to the proud sons of Dixie with their stranglehold on freedom.

19

Beyond Daily Bread

THEY DID not express their disdain with violence, murderous threats, or hateful curses about "mongrelization"—the stock in trade of arch segregationists in the South. But the truth could not be denied. Many blacks *were* opposed to the interracial relationships that had flourished in the heat of civil rights battles and that had led to a rise in marriages between blacks and whites from about fifty thousand interracially married couples in 1960 to sixty-five thousand a decade later—a thirty percent increase.

A greater willingness in the nation to address, if not accept, the long-standing racial taboo was signaled, cinematically, by the 1967 premiere of *Guess Who's Coming to Dinner?* Released the same year Alice and Mel wed, the landmark film told the story of a black doctor (portrayed by Sidney Poitier) struggling, with his white fiancée, to break the news of their engagement to her parents. After much liberal angst, the young woman's parents (played by Katharine Hepburn and Spencer Tracy) eventually give their blessing to the pair. However, Poitier's parents, especially Roy Glenn Sr. in his role as an old-line "race man," are considerably less thrilled about their son crossing the color line.

Unlike the rest of Alice's family, Bobby Walker had similar misgivings. "I didn't have anything against Mel, personally," Bobby remembered. "But straight up, I told Alice that if I could find a black woman to marry, I didn't know why she couldn't find a black man."

And as much as Carole Darden cherished her friendship with Alice and respected Mel Leventhal for being "one of the sweetest and bravest people on earth," she did not, even as she stood by their side in Judge Polier's chambers, smile on the couple's union. Then involved with SNCC, which by the late 1960s had purged most whites from its ranks, Darden said she was saddened by Alice's decision to marry a white man. To her mind, whites had brutalized blacks for generations. How could any of them, even a white man as righteous as Mel, now be trusted "to love and protect" a black woman's heart?

"As good as Mel was, I was not into seeing 'love for love's sake,'" Darden later said, "it was just a jarring juxtaposition. Neither Alice nor I wanted to get into anything that would hurt the other, so for a while, we kept some distance."

For Mel's mother, "distance" offered scant consolation. Leaving no question as to how she felt about her son's marriage to a *schvartse* (the pejorative Yiddish term for a black person), Miriam Leventhal sat shiva, mourning him for dead.

Unbowed by the disappointment of some friends and family members, the Leventhals set out to craft a loving and politically meaningful married life for themselves. As was customary during the era, Alice had taken Mel's surname in marriage. She would maintain her birth name, always, professionally.

Upon their arrival in Jackson in the summer of 1967, the couple bought, for $13,000, a three-bedroom bungalow at 1443 Rockdale Drive. The home, in a well-tended enclave of professional-class blacks, had previously been owned by Marian Wright Edelman, who, impressed with Mel's past work in her office, had hired him as a staff attorney at an annual salary of about $5,000.

"What distinguished Mel was his huge level of energy and absolute insistence that Mississippi be a just place," said Edelman, president of the Children's Defense Fund. "He was one's ideal civil rights lawyer. I thought the world of him."

About Alice, whom she'd also come to know the previous summer, Edelman added, "Her gifts and talents as a writer were an inspiration to me."

In a few months, the newlyweds had established a home, community ties, and a measure of economic security, thereby defying the forces that deemed the mere presence of the Leventhals "a crime against the state." "We intended to stand our ground," Alice said, emphatically, more than thirty years later. "We came to Mississippi to kill the fear it engendered as a place where black life was terrifyingly hard, pitifully cheap."

THAT MEL and Alice's arrival in Jackson had not brought blazing crosses on their front lawn or firebombs hurled through their window did not mean, however, that there was not danger lurking ahead. After all, this was the town where editors at the local *Clarion-Ledger* had alerted readers, the next day, to the historic 1963 March on Washington with a banner headline that read, "Washington Is Clean Again with Negro Trash Removed." As a tenacious NAACP lawyer fighting school segregation, Mel was, in the words of a neighbor, "steady on the television," making him a ready target for the Klan. Indeed, in a newsreel typical of dozens from the era, Mel assails Mississippi politicians for their bull-headed stance against integration. These were people, who, when faced with federal desegregation decrees, responded by removing air conditioners, cafeteria trays, bleacher seats, and athletic equipment from public schools mandated to admit blacks. They'd be damned if "apes and coons" gained access to what they clearly believed to be the cornerstones of a Mississippi education. "It's an absolute disgrace," said Mel, in the news clip, reviling the actions of his adversaries. "But it is time for reconciliation with the present and the future. We *will* have quality education for every child."

With his increasing notoriety as "Mr. Civil Rights" in Mississippi, Mel found it prudent to keep a loaded weapon, both at home and in his huge Oldsmobile Toronado, a car that did little to lower his visibility. For added protection, he and Alice also kept dogs. The first, a mixed breed, Alice christened Myshkin, in honor of a character in Dostoyevsky's novel *The Idiot* who finds himself entangled in a cruel and corrupt world. After Myshkin was stolen ("leaving us to search and weep"), the couple adopted Andrew, a handsome German shepherd.

While Mel traveled filing lawsuits, Alice labored on her poems and stories and returned to the novel she had put aside the previous winter in New York. In keeping with Virginia Woolf's directive that a woman have "a room of her own," the couple had hired a carpenter to convert one of their bedrooms into a writing studio for Alice. There, sitting at her custom-made desk and surrounded by her beautifully crafted bookcases, Alice worked devotedly on her writing, stopping only to tend the garden she had begun to cultivate in their small backyard.

As if to affirm her efforts, soon came the official announcement from *American Scholar* about her winning essay. In truth, Alice had received advance notice of her award from the magazine's editor, Hiram Haydn. By chance, Haydn was also the editor at Harcourt Brace & World (later Jovanovich) whom Monica McCall, after countless rejections from others, had finally persuaded to publish Alice's collection of poems. In a typewritten letter to Muriel Rukeyser dated August 8, 1967, Alice, in a rush of excitement, shares news of her success with her former teacher: "Don't breathe a word of this to anyone . . . but, there was an essay contest in the *American Scholar* and I won it and now I will be in that rather crusty magazine—isn't that nice! Hiram called me all the way from Washington to tell me—and they will pay me three hundred great big dollars! But I promised him I'd tell no one. You must remember that I did not."

Before the publication of her piece (which had bested several hundred entries), Alice was asked to submit biographical data that might also be printed in the magazine. She began the sketch with an overview of her childhood (there was no mention of her eye injury) and then proceeded to discuss her education at Spelman ("the college butted into my life") and later at Sarah Lawrence ("a magnificent job of not bothering me").

In closing passages about her life with Mel in Mississippi, she revealed, "At present, when I am not paralyzed by the rioting and the war in Vietnam or the generally sorry and chaotic condition of the country, I am writing my first novel, still untitled. . . . I am not interested in writing 'The Great American Novel,' but would be proud to write some great human novels, a la Victor Hugo."

In her aspiration to emulate the French master famed for *Les Misérables* and *The Hunchback of Notre Dame*, Alice was making clear her intention, as a writer, to examine the suffering of humanity. Her years in Mississippi would put such suffering in bold relief and help her gain perspective on her youth in Georgia.

"The stories were knee-deep," Alice would later say about her sojourn in Mississippi. "The first two years passed in a fever to get everything down—in poems, stories, the novel I was writing, essays. . . . It was a period of constant revelation, when mysteries not understood during my Southern childhood came naked to me to be embraced."

20

That Alice?

THE HYPOCRISY of religion as practiced by racist whites in the South was among the "mysteries" Alice examined in her writing after she and Mel settled in Jackson. The theme is at the center of her story "The Welcome Table," in which an elderly black woman is forcibly removed from a church.

"It was the ladies who finally did what to them had to be done," Alice writes in the story, which appears in *In Love & Trouble.* "Daring their burly, indecisive husbands to throw the old colored woman out they made their point. God, mother, country, earth, church. It involved all that, and well they knew it. Leather bagged and shoed, with good calfskin gloves . . . they looked with contempt at the bloodless gray arthritic hands of the old woman, clenched loosely, restlessly in her lap. Could their husbands expect them to sit up in church with *that?*"

Apoplectic in their indignation, the whites fail to see that the humble black woman they now reject as a "desecration" is the same one who nursed their children and prepared their meals. As crafted by Alice, she stands as symbol for the unheralded generations of black women who kept the white Southern cosmos from collapse.

Dragged, *literally*, from her pew and hurled out of the stained-glass sanctuary, the woman finds herself "back under the cold blue sky." Bewildered, she gazes into the distance and behold!—a Jesus figure appears. The man ("long brown hair, parted on the right side") mirrors a picture the woman had once "taken out of a white lady's Bible" while toiling as a maid. Whether real or imagined, this "Jesus" comforts her. But as the story ends, a subtly drawn question is left for readers to contemplate: Can faith placed outside of oneself ever lead to redemption?

The story is grounded in Alice's childhood observations of the "faithful" whites in Eatonton who, fresh in their finery, dutifully kept each (segregated) Sabbath with the Lord. It was further shaped by an incident during the Spelman years when Alice (wearing the vaunted pink faille dress) ventured with Constance Nabwire to services at a church in Atlanta. "The white American missionaries had come to Uganda and taught us that it was important to worship God, to read the Bible and to pray," Nabwire said. "When Alice and I tried to enter the church, the door was slammed in our faces. I didn't understand. For several months, I did nothing but cry."

In the O'Brien interview, Alice impassively remembered white men "in blue suits and bow-ties materializing on the steps above with axe-handles in their hands. We turned and left. It was a sunny day."

Alice unraveled and refined such memories through her work with the older black women she came to know as a consultant in black history for Friends of the Children of Mississippi (FCM). FCM was a component of the federal Head Start program, founded in 1965 with a mandate of providing free meals, health care, and preschool education to underprivileged children *of all races*, ages one to six.

As a consultant, Alice was charged with developing a black history curriculum for Head Start teachers, many of whom, because of Jim Crow, had not been educated beyond fifth grade. Undermining the mission were the Mississippi politicians who condemned Head Start as a "communist plot" and who blocked funding for the children's applesauce, milk, crayons, and coloring books whenever they could. Despite such opposition, Alice, like her husband, persevered.

"These were women I identified with, women who'd do anything for the good of black children," Alice later wrote. "I felt, on my first day before my class, as if the room were full of my mothers. Of course, teaching them black history in two weeks of lecturing, films, pictures was something else again. . . .

"Try to tell a sixty-year-old delta woman that black men invented anything, black women wrote sonnets . . . that kinky hair is delightful. . . . It was hard."

Faced with such obstacles, Alice determined that the best way to help her "earnest but educationally crippled" students gain a sense of self-worth that they could, in turn, impart to the Head Start children was to ask the women to write their autobiographies.

From their stories, in which many of the women revealed both a reluctance to call themselves "black" and an unshakable pride in the black race, Alice hoped they would come to see their contradictions, as well as "the faith and grace of a people under continuous pressure." For her part, Alice found that the women's moving accounts of their suffering and occasional triumphs brought more depth and nuance to her own writing. For example, offering a student's response—"Around 1942?"—to her question, "When was the period of slavery?," Alice would later note, "How could I underestimate the value of that answer."

However, finding little merit in the black history booklets Alice created with her students, state officials soon withdrew funding for her position (effectively firing her). But her brief stint with the Head Start teachers would prove invaluable to Alice as she sat in her study crafting stories that probed the complex emotional landscape of black women—women like Mrs. G. S., who, in her autobiography for Alice's class, had written, "My mother raised her family to work for what they wanted, and to be honest, proud of your color. . . . She taught us a white person wasn't no better than a black person, a man was just a man, no matter what color he is. My mother said the reason we are black is this: a curse from God."

∙ ∙ ∙

IN HIS memoir *Words & Faces*, Hiram Haydn would explain how Alice Walker, age twenty-three, came to join a publishing house with a list that included Virginia Woolf, E. M. Forster, Italo Calvino, T. S. Eliot, and Günter Grass, to name a few of the authors whose books carried the Harcourt Brace Jovanovich insignia. Respectfully remembered by his peers for giving new writers a chance, Haydn would also, in the late 1960s, persuade Harcourt to acquire a bold first novel about the intersecting lives of a gay, white male professor and a young black man: *A Glance Away* (1967) by a then-unknown author named John Edgar Wideman.

> In 1967, Monica McCall . . . sent me a script of poems by a young black woman. Monica urged me to do the daring thing, accept a first book of poems and publish it *first*. Alice Walker, she said, wanted to write a novel, and if we published the poems, we would certainly have the novel, too.
>
> The poems were strong, some of them with a primitive vitality, others delicately evocative. . . . Both Bill Jovanovich and I were impressed by them, but their quality did not insure the writer's ability as a *novelist*. . . . We finally, with real regret, decided against acceptance.
>
> Some months later I was surprised to receive the script back, with a note from Monica saying that she had tried other publishers and all had balked. . . . She was still convinced that we were the people to do it, and hoped we'd reconsider our decision. . . . We decided to go ahead.
>
> *Once* has sold more than three thousand copies, a figure unusual for any book of poems. . . . Its tiny, fiery author will go on and on, Alice Walker will, and I look forward with joy to every moment of her fulfillment.

With a simple blue cover, its title in white "boxcar" letters displayed diagonally across the front of the book, the hardcover first edition of *Once* sold for $4.50. Alice, who in the early fall of 1968 received copies in Jackson, remembered being pleased by her achievement, "but not elated or anything."

"The book came in the mail and it was really amazing to hold it in my hand," she later said. "But it was also strange because so much time had passed since I'd written the poems, none of which I had intended to publish. It was the *writing* of the poems that had been meaningful, because they emerged after my abortion and clarified how very much I loved being alive."

About the evocative title of the collection, Alice explained, "It is meant to reflect the ancient story-telling tradition of *Once upon a time.* . . . The 1960s in America was such a mythical time. Centuries of history were being played out in people's lives every day. If we could have just stayed with it, I truly believe we could have saved the world."

To be sure, any joy Alice might have felt about the publication of her first book had been severely diminished by cataclysmic events earlier in the year. By early 1968, Alice and Mel were expecting a baby. Initially concerned about the impact a child might have on her writing, both Alice and Mel soon came to revel in the prospect of parenthood—an added benefit of which was that, as a "family man," Mel might be exempt from active duty in Vietnam (the war was now in full force). But only a few days in April had passed before Alice suffered a miscarriage. It was her anguished response, she believed, to the April 4 assassination of Martin Luther King Jr. as he stood, laughing, on the balcony of the Lorraine Motel in Memphis, Tennessee.

Feeling compelled to join the masses arriving in Atlanta to pay their final respects to the fallen civil rights leader, Mel and Alice left Jackson to attend King's funeral, held April 9, 1968. As they walked behind the mule-drawn wagon bearing the coffin of the thirty-nine-year-old man who had implored his future eulogists not to mention his Nobel Peace Prize, but instead to honor him in death as "a drum major for justice," Alice was overwhelmed with sorrow.

Remembering the event decades later, Alice said her heartache was compounded by the "surreal" street scenes she witnessed as she marched, dazed, in King's funeral cortege: "It was as if the last light in my world had gone out."

"People were extremely solemn because we were all thinking about the horror of what had happened and what King's loss meant for the future of the movement," she explained. "Then suddenly, these vendors with little carts appeared and people started leaving the procession to buy Coca-Cola and hot dogs.

"Now, it had been a really difficult day and I know that people have to eat and drink, but the whole atmosphere immediately changed to something grotesque. There you were, almost dead from shock and grief, walking next to somebody champing on a hot dog. What had started out in stateliness and dignity degenerated into this ugly scene."

Devastated emotionally, Alice also had a profound physical response to King's death: "The week after that long, four-mile walk across Atlanta, and after the tears and anger and the feeling of turning gradually to stone, I lost the child I had been carrying. I did not even care. It seemed to me, at the time, that if 'he' (it was weeks before my tongue could form his name) must die no one deserved to live, not even my own child."

As for Mel, more than three decades later, he could barely speak about the events of April 1968. "It was tough," he responded stoically, and then fell silent.

UNAWARE OF the pained history of *Once*, Alice and Mel's new friends in Jackson greeted the book's release with admiration and awe. Carolyn Parker, a black activist who was also married to a white civil rights lawyer, remembered being "floored" when she discovered that Alice was the author of a poetry collection her husband, Frank, had brought home from the office one day. Although the Parkers and the Leventhals socialized at backyard barbecues and card parties (Mel being a whiz at both poker and bid whist), Carolyn said she had no idea that Alice was a writer.

"Alice was a quiet person who didn't talk that much," Parker recalled. "So when my husband showed me the book, I didn't connect the name on the cover with the same shy, reserved person I knew. It just didn't compute. Finally, I said to Frank, 'You mean to tell me *that Alice*, the one married to Mel, is the person who wrote this book?' And he said it was.

"Growing up in Mississippi I had never laid eyes on a black writer. And come to find out that Alice, a woman I actually knew, had written a book. Talk about being impressed!"

Harcourt demonstrated its appreciation of *Once* (which had immediately gone into a second printing) by including the book in a large newspaper advertisement trumpeting the company's new poetry releases. Printed in the October 20, 1968, issue of the *New York Times Book Review*, the ad itself had an intriguing history.

The original manuscript for *Once* had included a poem titled "The New York Times, For Some Reason." The poem had been inspired, Alice later explained, by a *New York Times* article describing a trip Massachusetts Senator Edward Kennedy had made to war-ravaged Vietnam. According to the October 26, 1965, story filed by *Times* reporter Neil Sheehan, Kennedy attempted to play soccer with local children, who, after a few half-hearted kicks, outright refused to play. Perplexed by the children's behavior, Kennedy then handed the ball to a little girl, who, as the *Times* put it, "for some reason," immediately burst into tears. Alice's poem suggests that the newspaper story made light of the distress of Vietnamese children, who, in her view, had every reason to fear "a big, white American man" wielding an object they might have construed as a bomb.

Worried that a poem critical of the influential *New York Times* might prove to be an impediment to the career of a fledgling writer, Haydn had removed it from the manuscript. As the poem had already been published (in the March 1966 issue of *The Activist*), Alice found herself bemused by Haydn's actions. She was not, nor would she ever be, the least concerned about "offending" the *Times*.

"I didn't understand it then, but Hiram was trying to protect me," Alice later said. "He knew all about the politics, the backroom dealing and gamesmanship that goes on in publishing. I didn't care."

As for Alice's debut effort as a writer, *Once* was never reviewed in the *Times* but would garner glowing reviews in numerous other publications. Writing in *Poetry* magazine, Lisel Mueller praised the collection, noting, "I am again shocked into recognition of how the history of this country has, for the Negro, created a reality in which color, rather than any individual consideration, has become the touchstone of identity. [Walker] is a sensitive, spirited and intelligent poet. Feeling is channeled into a style that is direct and sharp, honest speech pared down to essentials." Mueller offers readers a few lines from Alice's poem "Karamojans":

> *The Noble Savage*
> *Erect*
> *No shoes on his*
> *Feet*
> *His pierced ears*
> *Infected*

And then adds, "One would like to keep quoting such small beauties."

Chicago Daily News critic DeWitt Beall exclaimed, "At last there is a poet I find really exciting. Her name is Alice Walker . . . and not hung up on anybody's course in Modern Poetry or anybody's dogma about the Black Revolution. She just calls 'em the way she sees 'em and that, in this dogmatic age, is refreshing."

Lauding Alice's ability to "evoke a living image," the influential book trade *Publishers Weekly* declared, "Her poetry is pure, candid, earthy . . . sophisticated, sometimes . . . cryptic . . . but warmed by her redeeming grace—an ability to feel love for one person in one place, one time."

In truth, the talent that was now beginning to enthrall the literary establishment had already been affirmed and acknowledged by the "Shakespeare of Harlem," namely, Langston Hughes, the leading black poet of the day. An acquaintance of Muriel Rukeyser through leftist politics, Hughes had been delighted with "To Hell with Dying," which she had sent him in 1965, during Alice's last year of college. He published it two years later in *The Best Short Stories by Negro Writers* (1967). Heralding Alice's story in a collection that showcased work by distinguished writers such as Jean Toomer and Gwendolyn Brooks, Hughes, in his introduction, bemoaned the lack of funding for black writers and singled out Alice as especially deserving of support: "As a first choice for a subsidy, then why not the astounding Miss Alice Walker? Neither you nor I have ever read a story like 'To Hell with Dying' before."

That "Langston had nabbed Alice first" was what rankled John Henrik Clarke, himself an esteemed black writer and historian. Editor of the 1966 collection *American Negro Short Stories*, Clarke had hoped to include Alice's work in his book, "but couldn't get to her in time."

"Oh yes, I had desperately wanted 'To Hell with Dying,' but Alice was in motion and I could never seem to catch up with her," Clarke mused, shortly before his death in 1998. "So, Langston liked to rib me about it, you know, in a light-hearted joking manner. He was very proud to have published Alice's story before anyone else. He knew she was going far."

To Alice's amazement, not only did Hughes heap praise on her writing, but he extended himself to her as a devoted mentor and friend. Unconcerned when she, educated at both Spelman and Sarah Lawrence, shamefacedly confessed that she had not read "one line of his work," he happily gave her an armful of his books. Hughes always answered her letters (in "optimistic green ink") and had taken special pains to send Alice a big, frilly card wishing her joy in her marriage to Mel ("a major act of grace at the time"). Likening Alice to "a young Ruby Dee," the elegant black actress who rose to fame for her role in *A Raisin in the Sun*, Hughes delighted in Alice's passion for art and commitment to social justice. Decades later, Alice marveled at the warmth and generosity Hughes bestowed on her at such a formative time in her life. "We fell in love with each other on first sight," she said, still visibly moved. "He became a good part of my sun."

·   ·   ·

A PROFOUND grief swept through the black literary arts community when Langston Hughes died unexpectedly at age sixty-five, on May 22, 1967. A few days earlier, Alice had found it curious that Hughes, always prompt in his correspondence, had not answered one of her recent letters. The explanation for his uncharacteristic silence would come by way of a telegram inviting Alice and Mel to a private memorial service for Hughes to be held at the Benta Funeral Chapel in Harlem. Among the mourners was Muriel Rukeyser, continually looking over the head of her former student "for someone more important to talk to," Alice would later note.

Transforming her sorrow, Alice would go on to honor the memory of the man she'd come to regard as her "literary father" in her first book for children: *Langston Hughes, American Poet* (1974). In a brief afterword, she expressed her gratitude for his open heart and unwavering faith in her future as a writer.

"After my first meeting with Langston Hughes, I vowed I would write a book about him for children someday. Why? Because I, at twenty-two, knew next to nothing of his work, and he didn't scold me; he just gave me a stack of his books. . . . I will always be grateful that in his absolute compassion and generosity he fulfilled my deepest dream (and need) of what a poet should be."

And just as Hughes had hoped that Alice's talents would be affirmed financially, she responded to the practical needs of a writer who, despite his celebrity, never made much money at his craft. It was not lost on her that Hughes had titled his last book (published posthumously) *Black Misery* (1969). Nor that lacking health insurance, he probably could not have paid for his last hospital stay, had he survived.

"About two weeks before he died, I took a sack full of oranges to Langston Hughes," Alice would later recall. "The joy I felt in giving that simple gift is undiminished by time."

21

Nude

ALTHOUGH RUKEYSER'S behavior at Hughes's memorial service had been hurtful, Alice maintained contact with her former teacher after she and Mel moved to Jackson. In a letter dated November 10, 1967, Alice complimented Rukeyser on the title of her forthcoming book *The Speed of Darkness* ("all your titles have themselves and an echo") and asked her to convey best wishes to Monica McCall, who was in London at the time. Before closing, Alice gave Rukeyser an update on the progress of her novel: "I think it will be good—but it is very different from anything I've ever done before. . . . The agonizing thing is to not flinch from the honesty of discarding subtle cliches. One wants to talk the old language in a very new way."

As for her part, Rukeyser continued to publicly applaud Alice's achievements. Jerry W. Ward Jr., then a doctoral student in English, remembered meeting Rukeyser in 1968 at an antiwar rally in Albany, New York. Upon learning that Ward's adoptive home was Mississippi, she urged him to meet the extraordinary writer now living in his state.

"Muriel Rukeyser told me all about Alice and how she and her

husband were going to be involved in the movement in Jackson,"
recalled Ward, who later joined the faculty at Tougaloo College on
the outskirts of the city. "She wanted me to get to know this woman
whom she said would 'soon be making waves.' "

And when *Once* was released, Rukeyser provided a ringing
endorsement of the collection that had first been crafted in her classroom. "Brief slashing poems—young, and in the sun," she
declared—words that would later appear on paperback editions of
the book.

Despite the accolades, Alice, always a careful observer of
human nature, felt a growing strain in her relationship with the
woman whom poet Anne Sexton, alluding to Rukeyser's forceful-
ness, had proclaimed "the mother of everyone." Removed from the
tumult of her years at Sarah Lawrence and the dynamics of their
student-teacher bond, Alice came to realize that she didn't really
know Muriel Rukeyser. And much to her surprise, the person now
beginning to emerge exhibited some disturbing character traits.

"Muriel wanted to be thanked, constantly, for helping me to get
published," Alice later remarked. "No amount of flowers and letters of gratitude ever seemed to be enough."

In "A Student's Memoir of Muriel Rukeyser," poet Sharon
Olds recalled incidents that bring texture to Alice's reflections.
The essay chronicles a poetry workshop Olds took with Rukeyser
in the mid-1970s. "She talked about the importance of beginning
the poem, how it must suck in, call, seduce the reader from the
first so the reader cannot turn aside," Olds wrote in the piece,
which appears in *By Herself: Women Reclaim Poetry* (2000). In
other passages, Olds offered a glimpse of Rukeyser's bitterness at
her plight in the publishing world. Although respected for her
dedication to poetry as a form of social activism, Rukeyser never
achieved wide public acclaim. "She mentioned how powerful
anthologists are—how they can keep a poet's work away from
readers for twenty years, a whole generation of readers. This had
happened to her, she said, and there was a full body of loss in her
plain statement about it."

Olds later described Rukeyser as forlorn and withdrawn after a public reading her workshop class attended. "We lined up with the others in the reception room to thank her, but felt her loneliness, a kind of hollowness in the air around her, our inability as star-struck students to give her much back."

The angst is clear in Rukeyser's poem "From a Play: Publisher's Song":

> *I lie in the bath and I contemplate the toilet-paper*
> *Scottissue, 1000 sheets*
> > *What a lot of pissin and shittin*
> > *What a lot of pissin and shittin*
> *Enough for the poems of Shelley and Keats—*
> *All the poems of Shelley and Keats.*

DETERMINED, AS she had vowed after her eye injury, to "tell the truth, always," Alice was grateful for having the full sweep of the day to devote to her writing. The novel she had been working on for two years was a harrowing tale, inspired in part by the 1950s murder of an Eatonton woman, the mother of one of Alice's classmates. Her husband had shot her. Her battered corpse was later prepared for burial at the funeral home where Alice delivered eggs and Ruth worked part-time as a cosmetician.

Outraged by the viciousness of the assault, Ruth had urged her then-thirteen-year-old sister to visit the mortuary and "bear witness" to the injuries that had been inflicted on the woman. Alice would later remember gazing quietly at the cadaver, her eyes taking in the gaping gunshot wound in the woman's head and then traveling the length of her body until her eyes rested, finally, on the woman's callused foot, clad in "a run-over shoe with a ragged hole, covered with newspaper, in its bottom." For Alice, the woeful image would come to represent the vulnerability of black women, an image she now labored, in her novel, to bring to life.

"I had to look at, and name, and speak up about violence among black people in the black community," Alice would later write about the evolution of her first novel, which she had titled, in draft form, *What Can the Righteous Do?* "How can a family, a community, a race, a nation, a world, be healthy and strong if one half dominates the other half through threats, intimidation and actual acts of violence? Could I make the reader realize this fact?"

The novel would also be shaped by Alice's observations of abuse in her own family. Although Henry Clay Walker and William A. Grant both mellowed in their elder years, Alice was well aware of her grandfathers' mistreatment of women. "As young men, middle-aged men, they were brutal," she'd remember. "One grandfather knocked my grandmother out of a window. He beat one of his children so severely that the child had epilepsy. Just a horrible, horrible man."

As much as he abhorred racial injustice, Willie Lee Walker, too, would give sway to sexist attitudes and behavior. The angle of his vision skewed by childhood trauma, a tyrannical father, and the humiliations black men suffered under Jim Crow, Alice's father adhered to the dictate that women should "love, honor and obey." It was a stance that prompted many spirited confrontations with a wife and youngest daughter who were not inclined to submit.

"The way Daddy saw it, cooking and cleaning was women's work," Ruth remembered. "So, my brothers really didn't have to lift a finger around the house. Alice sure enough told Daddy that she thought it was unfair."

Added Alice: "My father picked up a lot of negative stuff from the slave-owning culture that his grandparents grew up under. When [he] looked back at men and white men were the only ones that were 'men' for many years, he saw men who had a bullwhip. He was influenced by the dominant culture."

Alice's poem "The Democratic Order: Such Things in Twenty Years I Understood" would evoke the turmoil of a man burdened by private wounds and societal constraints. That she understood the roots of her father's behavior did not make it any easier to bear.

My father
(back blistered)
beat me
because I
could not
stop crying.

He'd had
Enough 'fuss'
He said
For one damn
Voting day.

ALICE CHERISHED the solitude that enabled her to grapple, creatively, with the difficult themes in her novel. At the same time, she was eager to engage with other artists. To that end, she was pleased to make the acquaintance of the esteemed writer and scholar Margaret Walker (no relation). Walker was on the faculty at Jackson State University, which, like Tougaloo, was another of the historically black colleges in the area.

Two years before Alice was born, Walker had won the 1942 Yale Series of Younger Poets award (the first black person so honored) for her soaring volume *For My People*. She would be hailed again in 1966 for *Jubilee*, an epic novel about slavery rendered in the voice of the enslaved. As with Alice, Langston Hughes had encouraged Margaret Walker in her writing. Indeed, it was he who had suggested that the two women meet.

"I arrived in Jackson and discovered Margaret Walker," Alice would later remember. "[She was] a natural force, creating work under unimaginable pressures and by doing so keeping alive, in the thousands of students who studied under her, not only a sense of art but also the necessity of claiming one's birthright at the very source."

Equally impressed with Alice, Dr. Walker had organized a book party to celebrate the release of *Once*. And later, when the professor took a sabbatical, she recommended that Alice be brought in to teach her black literature class. "I met with the president of the college and told him to hire Alice," Dr. Walker recalled. "She'd already been published and her credentials were superb. I couldn't think of a better candidate for the job."

Although their face-to-face meetings were infrequent, Walker noted that she was taken by Alice's independence and clarity of purpose. She said that unlike other black writers she'd met, Alice was not "searching for the limelight."

"In looking homeward to blacks in the South, Alice stood out from most of the young writers coming up at that time," Walker said. "Her mission was not of the moment. Which is why she is still here."

Alice prepared for the class with the same rigor and dedication she had brought to her work with the Head Start teachers. She wanted the students to treasure, as she did, their magnificent black literary heritage. But much to her dismay, their spirits were not uplifted after reading Langston Hughes regaling Susana Jones in her red dress—"*come with a blast of trumpets, Jesus!*"—nor when they entered the world of Louisiana writer Ernest Gaines, whose short stories (especially "The Sky Is Gray") Alice greatly admired. But she could have never imagined that the students would dismiss, as "old-timey," the work of the professor in whose class they were officially enrolled, her immediate position notwithstanding. Talk about the weary blues (as Langston had put it)—the students were bored by "For My People"!

How could Margaret Walker's praise song to blacks—"praying their prayers nightly to an unknown god, bending their knees humbly to an unseen power"—leave them unmoved? "For My People" was already one of the most exalted poems in the black literary canon. Yet, the students found it "square."

" 'Oh these older poets! They never tell us to fight!' " Alice would later write, repeating a young woman's lackluster response to the poem. "I realized that she had read the poem, even read it passionately, and had not understood a word of what it was about."

The students' disaffection with their course work was emblematic of a rift over art and politics that was, by the late 1960s, becoming more pronounced in the black community. Just as a younger generation of civil rights activists had grown impatient with the nonviolent strategies of Martin Luther King Jr., there was now a young group of black artists decrying racism in more militant tones. After all, the young folk argued, Dr. King had preached peace and what had it gotten him? A bullet in the head. Emboldened by the radical stance of the Black Power movement and, for many, transformative trips to a newly decolonized Africa, these younger writers scoffed at what they viewed as the "pleading" posture of their literary forebears. They found just cause to agree with the harsh assessment of Richard Wright, who had dismissed the relevance of much early black writing, saying that such work "entered the court of American public opinion dressed in the knee pants of servility, curtsying to show that the Negro was not inferior."

This group of writers now capturing the attention (and adulation) of black youth nationwide was fed up with lawsuits and prayer meetings. They aimed to vanquish racism by "fighting fire with fire," in their art and in the streets. Framed philosophically as the "new black aesthetic," the literary outpourings of these emerging writers would come to be known as the Black Arts movement, with "death to whitey" one of the signature themes of their poems, stories, and plays.

Her artistic voice was not as brash as that of Amiri Baraka, Nikki Giovanni, or the other young writers whose incendiary work (i.e., "nigger can you kill") had brought instant fame in Black Arts circles, but Alice was angry about the suffering of black people too. She knew that the outcome of her BB gun injury might have been radically different had the white man driving on the Milledgeville highway not refused her father a ride. She'd watched as her parents and each of her siblings struggled to withstand the punishing blows of racism and knew full well the price they had paid to hold fast to their dignity. As difficult as it was, some days, to reject the "eye for an eye" thinking that was now gaining ground among blacks, Alice did not believe that black liberation would rise up from hatred. That blacks should demand their rights was understood. However, the greater challenge, she felt, as a writer and a human being, was for blacks to resist emulating the behavior of bigots. They had to find the courage to claim their own souls. In addition to Dr. King, she took as her model freedom fighters like Fannie Lou Hamer, who, when criticized by segregationists for "seeking equality" with whites, had replied, "I don't want to go down that low. I want the true democracy that'll raise me and the white man up."

With regard to the white man with whom she now shared her life, Alice later said that she refused to allow the Swahili-obsessed "revolutionaries" living in Newark and Chicago to denigrate a marriage forged in the menacing face of the Klan. Spurred by their commitment to freedom, she and Mel had purposefully moved to Mississippi and felt no need to justify their love to anyone. Truth be told, more than a few of the righteous black militants now screaming "all power to the people" with clenched fists thrust in the air had, themselves, tasted of the "forbidden fruit." There was even a name for it: talking black and sleeping white.

Idolized as one of the most radical voices of the Black Arts movement, Amiri Baraka had himself once been married to a white woman. With their thunderous paeans to "Nubian queens," none had dared to confront Eldridge Cleaver when he revealed, in *Soul on Ice* (1968), that he had "practiced" rape on black women before assaulting his more desired white prey. Instead, his best-selling book had been lauded as a major contribution to the "black aesthetic" and brought Cleaver rock star–caliber fame.

But black women who refused to limit their love interest to black men could expect fierce retribution. In her poem "The Girl Who Died #2," Alice would pay tribute to a student at Sarah Lawrence who'd committed suicide after being scorned, by blacks, for one such "offense." The student ("a little brownskinned girl from Texas, away from home for the first time") had enrolled at the college after Alice graduated.

No doubt she was a singer
of naughty verse
and hated judgments
(black and otherwise) . . .

Behold the brothers!

They strut behind
the casket . . .
Thinking whom
to blame
for making this girl
die . . .

This girl who would not lie;
and was not born
to be "correct."

As the 1960s came to a close, Alice was sick to death of hypocrisy and violence. In her life and in her art, she was driven even more to offer a racially embattled America a vision of the ennobling power of love (arduous though it was to achieve). It was a vision she'd voiced in the middle section of her poem "Once":

It is true—
I've always loved
the daring
  ones
Like the black young
man
Who tried
to crash
All barriers
at once,
  wanted to

swim
At a white
beach (in Alabama)
Nude.

For Alice and Mel, the affirmation of their daring would reveal its human face when, at 7:06 P.M. on November 17, 1969, their daughter, Rebecca Grant Leventhal, was born.

22

Watered with Blood

THROUGHOUT THE South, white men had fathered children with black women, forcibly, for generations. Before the civil rights era, interracial relationships that might have been forged in a mutuality of love and respect had, by the necessity of Jim Crow, been kept in the shadows. White Georgia writer Lillian Smith would spark a national uproar over her unsparing treatment of the miscegenation taboo in *Strange Fruit*, her 1944 novel about the secret love between Tracy Deen, son of a Southern white doctor, and Nonnie Anderson, a college-educated black woman employed as a maid.

In 2003, Essie Mae Washington-Williams, a seventy-eight-year-old retired schoolteacher, would claim her heritage as the daughter of a black woman and U.S. Senator Strom Thurmond, who had once run for the presidency on a segregationist platform. Her mother, Carrie Butler, had worked as a maid in the home of Thurmond's parents.

The powder keg that was miscegenation colored the perspective of the medical staff that greeted Mel when he arrived at Jackson's University Hospital to comfort his laboring wife and then, many hours later, to bask in the joy of Rebecca's birth. They named her, Mel later said, in loving memory of his maternal grandmother.

After being assured that his wife and daughter (who had weighed in at nearly ten pounds) were resting peacefully, Mel left the hospital. When he next returned, his arms were laden with an eye-popping bouquet of red roses that he presented, with great flair, to Alice in her room. At the time, it was such a rarity for a white man in the South to claim, let alone rejoice in, the birth of a child he had fathered with a black woman that the white hospital workers were left dumbfounded. Their shock was registered on the margins of Rebecca's birth certificate where, next to the designation for the race of her parents (Mel "White"/ Alice "Negro"), a clerk had penciled in "correct" so as not to have the entry deemed a mistake. A photocopy of the document clearly reveals the notation.

"They put that little note on the side so no one would think it was a typographical error—that Rebecca's father was white, and her mother black," said Mel who, upon receiving word that Alice was soon to deliver, had rushed home from New Orleans, where he was arguing a school desegregation case. "In 1969, there were not many interracial couples like us in Mississippi—openly married, starting a family, refusing to bow down to the repression in the state. I had actually expected a lot more flack."

As the person whose body had been poked and prodded in the pain-racked hours before Rebecca's birth, Alice had a less forgiving view of how she and Mel had been received in the maternity ward. Ever mindful that the white male medical establishment in Jackson was not likely to welcome the black wife of the Jewish NAACP lawyer "forcing" the city's schools to integrate, Alice had been treated, throughout her pregnancy, by the only female gynecologist on the hospital's staff. The woman (white) was rumored to be a lesbian supportive of civil rights efforts. But as Alice struggled to bring Rebecca into the world, she found the physician's bedside manner "chilly and abrupt." Preoccupied though she may have been, Alice had enough of her wits about her to discern that the woman was clearly rankled by their union.

"No one could believe we were together, married, to have our neither black nor white child," Alice would later write, describing the response she and Mel elicited. "We were a major offense. And yet [what] I have consciously remembered is the look in [Rebecca's] eyes when she emerged. . . . It felt so much like an old acquaintance re-entering a room we happened to be in."

AFTER A few days at the hospital, Alice returned home. By a stroke of fortune, she had completed her novel (now officially titled *The Third Life of Grange Copeland*) three days before Rebecca was born. By the time she had penned the final sentence of *The Third Life* there was not a single line in the entire 247-page novel that had been in the first draft. And Alice knew there were more novels, poems, and stories she wanted to write. As a young mother married to a man in the crosshairs of a political system that would have just as soon seen them all dead, she had no illusions about the difficulties in sustaining the serenity and solitude she needed for her work. "I often felt overwhelmed," she would later say about the first years after Rebecca's birth. "I was afraid I could not be a successful writer and a mother at the same time. I was torn between my desire to do justice to my art and the demands of my marriage in a place where the tree of freedom was constantly being watered with blood."

Reflective of her own concerns, Alice would later be drawn to *Second-Class Citizen* (1974), a novel by Nigerian writer Buchi Emecheta. The protagonist of the largely autobiographical work is Adah, an aspiring author who successfully integrates her career with motherhood. Unaided by a husband who is both a failure at his civil servant job and misogynistic (he destroys her first novel), Adah pursues her art nonetheless. Over time she comes to think of her three children not as "impediments," but rather as cherished future readers for whom she is inspired to perfect her craft. "And it is here that Adah makes the decision that seems to me impressive and important for all artists with children," Alice would note in "A Writer Because of, Not in Spite of, Her Children," a review of the Emecheta work that appears in *In Search of our Mothers' Gardens*.

"Since [Adah's] novel is written to the adults her children will become, it is okay with her if the distractions and joys they represent in her life, as children, become part of it. I agree that it is healthier, in any case, to write for the adults one's children will become than for the children one's 'mature' critics often are."

The conflicts over family and career that weighed on Alice's psyche might have felt less burdensome had she been able, immediately after Rebecca's birth, to discuss her feelings with other women in the creative arts. But she was yet unacquainted with such peers. Oddly enough, the rising black poet Audre Lorde, also interracially married and with children, had recently come and gone as a writer-in-residence at Tougaloo, without she or Alice ever crossing paths. In New York, June Jordan, several years divorced from her white husband, was beginning to pursue her writing career while raising a young son. Maya Angelou's *I Know Why the Caged Bird Sings* (1970) was soon to be published, as was *The Bluest Eye* (1970), a novel by an Ohio native born Chloe Wofford, later to be known as Toni Morrison. Both women had children. As did poets Sonia Sanchez, Nikki Giovanni, and Gwendolyn Brooks, who, in 1950, had become the first black person to win a Pulitzer Prize, for her collection of poems, *Annie Allen* (1949).

But Alice, at age twenty-five, had yet to meet these black women, all of whom had embarked on the path she now tread. And in Jackson, beyond Margaret Walker (thirty years her senior), there was not another black woman bodacious enough to call herself a professional writer.

That is not to say that Alice lacked caring friends or supportive neighbors during her sojourn on Rockdale Drive. Mildred and Willie Belt, a kindly older couple, both of them teachers, lived next door and were always willing to lend a helping hand. And on the other side was James Graves, the quick-witted owner of a janitorial service, and his warmhearted wife, Clotie, a nurse.

And there were other families in the community with whom Alice and Mel periodically socialized, including the Parkers. But as sweet and generous as these friends were, they didn't necessarily marvel, as Alice did, at the work of Anna Akhmatova or "A Black

Man Talks of Reaping," a poem by Arna Bontemps that had "tingled the bottom of my toes," she later exclaimed. And why, these neighbors wondered, if James Baldwin wanted people to buy tickets to *Blues for Mister Charlie*, had he promised to leave audiences "waiting for nurses to carry them out," his avowed intention for his blistering drama about race and retribution in the South? Alice understood. Mel did too.

But with Mel constantly on the road and keeping late hours at the NAACP office, the couple didn't spend much time together anymore. And more often than not, it was Alice who was left to contend with the threatening phone call or hate-filled letter ("the 'eyes' of the Klan are upon you") that always seemed to arrive just as she was polishing a paragraph or trying to nurse a hungry and agitated Rebecca. Alice later noted that she was awestruck and humbled by her newfound understanding of the significance of bearing a child.

"It finally dawned on me what an incredible thing women do in peopling the world," she said. "Everyone you see has come out through a woman and usually a woman who has endured enormous pain. This is what has been hidden; the heroic nature of giving birth and its sublime hopefulness."

To be sure, Alice had a room of her own. But unlike Virginia Woolf, Alice wrote with the threat of a firebomb being tossed into her home at any minute, and there was not a Bloomsbury Group with whom she could calmly sip afternoon tea and discuss her fears. Unburdening herself in the flurry of press interviews that would come with the release of her novel, Alice would soon tell reporters, "It's very intimidating in Jackson. Living in a hostile community can dry up your creativity. . . . People either turn away from us or ignore us or say things like . . . well, I went to a restaurant with Mel and . . . a white man turned around and said, 'They're letting niggers into everything now.' That sort of thing."

23

"Conformity is not Community"

UNFLINCHING IN its depictions of the dehumanization of a share-cropping family in Georgia, Alice's first novel, *The Third Life of Grange Copeland*, was released in the summer of 1970. The protagonist is Grange, who, bullied and belittled by a white landowner named Shipley, lashes out in frustration at his wife, Margaret, and son Brownfield.

"You'd think he'd be satisfied, me feeding him and her fucking him!" Margaret laments when Grange, in drunken torment about his plight, takes up with a prostitute whom he openly parades. Offering as legacy a stony-faced silence, murderous threats, and a fatal shrug about his inability to support his family, Grange succumbs to the plantation owner's "shiftless and irresponsible" stereotype of black men and flees to the North. First mistreated and then abandoned, Margaret takes refuge in suicide by poisoning herself. "To most of the people at the funeral, Shipley's presence was a status symbol and an insult," Alice writes. "Though they were not used to thinking in those terms."

Continuing the cycle of misplaced violence, Brownfield terrorizes his wife, Mem, a cheery schoolteacher with whom he'd had hopeful dreams before he, too, became defeated by the degradation of tenant farming. The name Mem was inspired by the French *la meme* ("the same"), Alice later explained, and symbolized the oppression of women worldwide. Describing the blind rage that consumes Brownfield, as it did his father, Alice writes:

> His crushed pride, his battered ego, made him drag Mem away from school-teaching. Her knowledge reflected badly on a husband who could scarcely read and write. It was his great ignorance that sent her into white homes as a domestic, his need to bring her down to his level! It was his rage at himself, and his life and his world that made him beat her . . . His rage could and did blame everything, *everything* on her.

Emotionally stronger than Margaret, Mem fights back. One day, after suffering yet another of Brownfield's vicious beatings, she grabs a shotgun and trains it at his testicles. "You going to take the blame for every wrong you do and stop blaming it on me . . . and everybody else for fifty miles around. . . . You going to respect my house . . . and you ain't never going to call me ugly or black or nigger or bitch again, 'cause you done seen just what this black ugly nigger bitch can do when she gits mad!"

But Brownfield, having mastered the "sins" of his father, eventually breaks Mem's spirit. Burdened by unwanted pregnancies, her health falters. She loses her passion for books (which Brownfield uses for "kindling") and stops tending the flower garden in which, like Minnie Lou Walker, she had once taken such pride. Convinced (wrongly) that Mem is having an affair with the kindly white man for whom she now toils as a maid, Brownfield lies in wait as his wife, laden with holiday groceries and gifts, returns from work one Christmas Eve. Despising her for "flaunting" his impotence as a provider, Brownfield fires a shotgun blast that rips off his wife's face. And thus did Alice create a history for the brutalized corpse Ruth had beckoned her to witness when she was age thirteen.

Meanwhile, Grange Copeland is awakened to his complicity in the corruption of his soul. This Alice puts forth with dramatic effect when Grange, now in New York, encounters a pregnant white woman in Central Park who, abandoned, is suffering her own private despair. Both fearful of his presence (read: rapist) and outraged by Grange's empathy ("there she sat . . . her big belly her own tomb"), the woman, attempting to flee, falls into an icy pond. Grange lets her drown after she rebuffs his assistance and calls him "nigger" with her last breath. The incident sets him off on a violent spree during which Grange assaults Italians, Poles, Jews, anybody who "acts whites."

At first Grange justifies his behavior as "payback" for the cruelties he'd endured in the South. "He had killed a thousand, ten thousand, a whole country of them in his mind," Alice writes. But his blood thirst is soon vanquished by a nagging conscience and craving for love and self-respect. "Each man would have to free himself. . . . Make a life that need not acknowledge them. . . . At least love was something that left a man proud that he *had* loved. Hate left a man shamed, as he was now."

In this, his transformative "third life" of spiritual reflection, Grange returns to Georgia, where he confronts Brownfield (still blaming "whitey" for all his problems) and becomes a wise and loving companion to his granddaughter, Ruth. Here Grange admonishes his son:

I *know* the danger of putting all the blame on somebody else for the mess you make out of your life. I fell into the trap myself! And I'm bound to believe that that's the way the white folks can corrupt you even when you done held up before. 'Cause when they got you to thinking that they're to blame for *every*thing they have you thinking they's some kind of gods! You can't do nothing wrong without them being behind it. You gits just as weak as water, no feeling of doing *nothing* yourself. Then you begins to think up evil and begins to destroy everybody around you, and you blames it on the crackers. *Shit*! Nobody's as powerful as we make them out to be. We got our own *souls*, don't we?

Writing in an afterword to a paperback edition of the novel, Alice elaborated on its prevailing theme: "An inevitable daughter of the people who raised and guided me, in whom I perceive the best as well as the worst, I believe wholeheartedly in the necessity of keeping inviolate the one interior space that is given to all. . . . The white man's oppression of me will never excuse my oppression of you, whether you are man, woman, child, animal or tree. Because the self I prize refuses to be owned by him. Or by anyone."

Among the first reviews was a short piece in the *Library Journal* written by Victor A. Kramer, an English professor at Georgia State University in Atlanta. "The novel, compacting the Copeland family life through three decades from 1920 presents hatred . . . within a plot that seems near fantasy," Kramer declared. "Walker's characters are not pretty ones. Yet this is the point: dignity can be maintained amidst intense degradation."

On August 13, 1970, Kay Bourne offered her views in the Boston-area *Bay State Banner*: "Most poignant is the relating of the lives of black women, who were ready and strong and trusted, only to so often be abused by the conditions of their oppressed lives and the misdirected anger of their men. *The Third Life of Grange Copeland* is more personal than the historical novel form. Alice Walker wants to talk to the living about the living and she has succeeded."

More reviews would follow, in publications such as the *Chicago Sun-Times* ("Black, but no polemics") and the *Washington Post* ("occasionally ponderous"). However, it was a critique of *The Third Life* that appeared in the August 22, 1970, *Saturday Review* that prompted Alice, as had been her lifelong habit, to respond immediately to what she perceived to be an injustice. Three other novels by black authors were also discussed in the piece written by Josephine Hendin, a white woman who had published a study of Georgia author Flannery O'Connor.

"Can one still shed tears for blacks of the lower middle class?" queried Hendin in the opening sentence of her review. "Is their mis-

Alice's maternal (Grant, seated foreground) and paternal (Walker, standing second row, far left and right) forebears with their children, 1937.

Mary Poole. Alice's great-great-great-great-grandmother. As a slave, Poole walked from Virginia to Georgia with a baby on each hip. Alice notes, "It is in memory of this walk that I embrace my 'maiden' name, Walker."

Alice's brother, Curtis Walker, at the Georgia gravesite of their great-grandmother, Sallie Montgomery Walker, who was born a slave.

A 1930s-era portrait of Alice's parents, Minnie Lou and Willie Lee Walker. Mr. Walker courted his future bride during church services, winking so hard "you could hear the clicks."

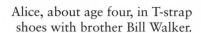

Alice, about age four, in T-strap shoes with brother Bill Walker.

Alice, about age six.

Ophthalmologist Morriss Henry. Dr. Henry removed the scar tissue that had formed over Alice's right eye in the aftermath of a blinding childhood injury.

Alice's first-grade teacher,
Birda Reynolds.

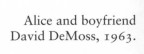

Alice's high school
memory book, 1961.

Alice and boyfriend
David DeMoss, 1963.

Alice (far right) with Spelman College class-mates, early 1960s.

Alice and historian Howard Zinn. About her former Spelman College professor, Alice says, "It meant a lot to have an example of someone who stood by what he believed."

Alice and Sarah Lawrence College professor Muriel Rukeyser. The poet supported Alice's development as a writer.

Sarah Lawrence College professor Jane Cooper. She recalled, "Alice had a wild intelligence that you couldn't hold back."

Carole Darden. A Sarah Lawrence College classmate who cleaned out her coffers to help Alice in a dire moment of need.

A late 1960s photo of Alice and Mel Leventhal in their Jackson, Mississippi, backyard with pet dog Andrew.

Alice, Mel, and their daughter Rebecca celebrating the 1970 publication of Alice's first novel, *The Third Life of Grange Copeland.*

Alice, Mel, and Rebecca, 1970.

"The Problem We All Live With." A 1964 painting by Norman Rockwell captured the school desegregation conflicts that arose during the civil rights era. Shortly after graduation from Sarah Lawrence, Alice returned to her native South to join the struggle.

Mississippi police responding to a group of freedom fighters. Alice and Mel lived in the state during the height of the civil rights movement.

The Sisterhood. A group of black women writers in New York who met informally during the 1970s. Back row, left to right: Verta Mae Grosvenor, Alice Walker, Lori Sharpe, Bessie Smith [in photo], Toni Morrison, June Jordan. Seated, left to right: Nana Maynard, Ntozake Shange, Audrey Edwards.

The inscription Langston Hughes wrote to Alice in commemoration of the publication of her first story, "To Hell with Dying."

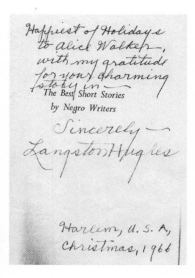

Happiest of Holidays to Alice Walker, with my gratitude for your charming story in
The Best Short Stories
by Negro Writers
*Sincerely —
Langston Hughes*

*Harlem, U. S. A,
Christmas, 1966*

"The Shakespeare of Harlem" as rendered in the 2002 reissue of Alice's first children's book, *Langston Hughes, American Poet.*

The June 1982 cover of *Ms.* magazine. The issue included a profile of Alice that was the first to herald her as "a major American writer."

Gloria Steinem (left) and Alice at a benefit for the San Francisco Women's Building.

Estella Perry (circa 1930s). Although Alice never met Perry, she'd provide inspiration for Shug Avery in *The Color Purple.*

Robert Allen, Alice, and Rebecca Walker, early 1990s.

Alice and Robert during the construction of Walker's forty-acre Northern California retreat, Temple Jook House, circa 1990. Inspired by the artistry of Shinto temples and Japanese farmhouses, Alice would design parts of the home herself.

Oprah Winfrey, Rebecca Walker, Alice, and Quincy Jones during the 1985 filming of *The Color Purple*.

Alice and Rebecca, early 1990s.

Alice with her mother, Minnie Lou Walker, 1979. "She showed me the bounty of the earth," says Alice of the woman she honors as the most influential in her success.

The headstone Alice placed on the unmarked grave of Zora Neale Hurston. The Fort Pierce, Florida, cemetery is now visited by scores of Hurston admirers who adorn her plot with photos, talismans, and charms.

Alice with author Ding Ling (front, center) during a 1983 trip to China. Standing behind Alice is writer Paule Marshall. Tillie Olsen is seated (front, right).

Alice, in a room of her own, with a portrait of Virginia Woolf.

Alice with Cuban president Fidel Castro during a 1995 visit to Havana. "I figure that Fidel's imperfections are about as big as he is. But still he is formidable. If only he could dance!" she says.

Alice's sisters, Ruth Walker Hood (left) and Mamie Walker.

Alice, brother Bill, and sister-in-law Gaye Walker.

Brothers Curtis (to the left of Alice), Jimmy (on the right), and Fred (seated), and sister Ruth, late 1990s.

Family friend visiting Alice's brother, Bobby Walker, in Eatonton, Georgia, 1998.

Completed Temple Jook House with Luna Mahala goddess sculpture by David Walker (no relation) in foreground.

Admirers of Alice Walker under Eatonton, Georgia, street sign erected during the late 1980s, in her honor.

Alice with great nephews, niece, sister Ruth, and Jean Weisinger (far right).

Alice and William Poy Lee at the centennial celebration of Langston Hughes's birth, 2002.

Tracy Chapman (left) and Alice picnicking in Northern California, mid-1990s.

Alice's fiftieth birthday celebration. Back row, left to right: Tracy Chapman, Clarissa Pinkola Estes, Ruth Walker Hood, Gloria Steinem, Jean Shinoda Bolen, Angela Davis, Carole Darden, Joan Miura. Front row: Wilma Mankiller (seated on railing), Belvie Rooks, Alice, Aneta Chapman, June Jordan.

Although Alice never met writer James Baldwin, she loved and admired him as a "spiritual brother." "He rather adored her," recalled a friend, speaking of Baldwin's affection for Alice. "He understood they were cut from the same cloth."

Alice in velvet dress, early 1990s. Her mantra: "It's all about love."

ery too ordinary, their suffering too quiet to arouse the compassion of an age addicted to extremes of violence?"

Turning her attention specifically to *The Third Life*, Hendin went on to criticize its author, writing that Alice, as a Southern black woman, "hated the self-hatred" of her characters so much that she could not objectively dissect their plight. Put off, as a reviewer, by her perception that Grange assuaged his despair by randomly assaulting whites, Hendin effectively dismissed the novel: "Miss Walker disappoints by [using] political cliches. . . . Has any man's soul ever been healed by politics? [Her] solution ignores the depth and force of the loveless agony she describes."

By no means did Alice ignore the review. Firing off a letter to *Saturday Review* book editor Rochelle Girson, she responded to her critic in the same questioning style:

Can Josephine Hendin really express such mid-Reconstruction condescension and be taken seriously . . . ? And if she can be, then all those tears allegedly shed for us "quietly suffering blacks" have been misdirected. We ain't needed 'em half as much as y'all.

As a black writer, I say yes to the universe. And not quietly, either . . . [Hendin] has read into *The Third Life of Grange Copeland* perhaps all that she is capable of comprehending, which is not much, and rather tiresome, anyhow. A case in point is her declaration that my main character cures himself of self-hatred "presumably" by beating up as many white people as he can. This insults my imagination, and is ridiculous besides. Not that I think beating up one's oppressors isn't a great idea. Nothing else seems to have worked. However, it simply happens that in this novel what motivates the old man to change is love of self (not love or hatred of white folks—because to him as to me, white folks are mainly irrelevant unless they are standing directly in one's sunlight; which, of course, they too often are). . . .

The reason I bother to write this letter at all is because it occurs to me that *Saturday Review* could do a teeny bit better. Why try to discuss, intelligently, four full length novels on one page, for example? . . . It is ironic that Miss Hendin presumed to write a book about *The World of Flannery O'Connor*, for I cannot imagine her coming to grips with her subject. Miss O'Connor herself recognized that "no matter how favorable all the critics in New York City may be, they are an unreliable lot, as incapable as on the day they were born of interpreting Southern literature to the world." And [she] meant that they couldn't even interpret <u>white</u> Southern literature. . . . She was right, of course.

But I am a black Southern writer and that, I know, presents its own problems for a reviewer like Miss Hendin. Which is why I blame *Saturday Review* for allowing her to display her rather hackneyed ignorance of black life and black art in such an irresponsible and influential way.

"For Justice only" was the salutation Alice wrote before signing her name.

Alice made several copies of the letter, which she dispatched to a wide range of friends and colleagues including John Henrik Clarke, Charles Merrill, Muriel Rukeyser, Jane Cooper, Margaret Walker, Hiram Haydn, civil rights activist Jesse Jackson, and writer Studs Terkel—the latter two she had recently met in Chicago while on a publicity tour for the book. In a cover letter, Alice explained why she had felt it necessary to respond to Hendin's review:

It is imperative that black artists protest racist interpretations of their work, cavalier and insensitive handling of it, and white people's unfailing ability to be dishonest, when it comes to evaluating the work of black artists. . . . I refuse to accept other people's warped vision of what I am or what my experiences have been, but will challenge them wherever they are found, not only in relation to my own work but also in relation to that of other black writers and poets. . . . Let me put it this way: all my heroes died during the last ten years, and they did not die for me or my people to continue to be insulted by people who apparently spent the decade reading Updike.

This letter she closed with the salutation "On all fronts, Alice Walker."

That Alice had challenged both Hendin's assessment of *The Third Life* and her purported expertise on Flannery O'Connor (1925–1964) was reflective of Alice's allegiance to her Southern heritage, despite its obvious inequities. As it happened, O'Connor, the only child of wealthy white landowners, had been raised in Milledgeville, the town where Alice's parents had once struggled as tenant farmers and where Alice had been blinded in her right eye. Decades later, her brother Jimmy would remember having delivered milk to "Miss O'Connor" at Andalusia, the sprawling country manor to which the author had returned to write (and raise peacocks) after being stricken with lupus while living in the North.

O'Connor was a clear beneficiary of the riches that had come to Southern whites at the expense of exploited black families like the Walkers, but Alice recognized truth and honesty in her work, which she had first read at Sarah Lawrence. About the author of sardonic and racially charged stories such as "Revelation" and "Everything That Rises Must Converge," Alice would later write:

It was for her description of Southern white women that I appreciated [O'Connor's] work . . . because when she set her pen to them not a whiff of magnolia hovered in the air . . . and yes, I could say, yes, these white folks without the magnolia . . . and these black folks without melons and superior racial patience, these are like the Southerners that I know. . . .

[O'Connor] destroyed the last vestiges of sentimentality in white Southern writing . . . and she approached her black characters—as a mature artist—with unusual humility and

restraint. . . . The magic, the wit and the mystery of Flannery
O'Connor I know I will always love, I also know the meaning
of the expression "Take what you can use and let the rest rot."

As with Hendin's review, an article about *The Third Life* that
appeared in *Jet* magazine was another that Alice felt compelled to
publicly refute. The unbylined piece (published September 3, 1970)
was a severely edited version of an earlier United Press International
story in which Alice had expressed her despair with the "inhumanity" of most whites. Featured with the *Jet* piece was a photo of
Alice, Mel, and infant Rebecca that had been taken in Central Park
during Alice's publicity tour in New York.

Under the headline, "Teacher Writes Book, Assails Whites," the
expurgated *Jet* article read, "Alice Walker is Black and her book, a
first novel, is no pacifier. . . . [It] tells how white oppression leads to
despair. . . . Yes, Alice Walker said, it was her opinion that Blacks
must not look to whites for anything. Blacks must treasure their
families, treasure other Blacks. . . . '[White people] don't inspire me
in any way,' Walker continued. 'I could stand to go years and years
without seeing one.'

"What about her white husband, Mel? He is one person, an
individual, Alice Walker explained."

In a letter to the editor of *Jet*, Alice immediately responded:

My primary objection to your article (as opposed to the UPI
article which was your source), is that a few of your readers
have been led astray by it. I have received indignant letters
from women who are enraged by what they consider my
"hypocrisy." What they mean is that from the way *Jet* con-
densed, mutilated and otherwise presented my point of view, I
appear to be apologizing for, or attempting to "justify" my
marriage to a white man. . . . Perhaps my choice of words was
poor, but the complete article shows my basic feeling that
<u>generally</u> whites do not exhibit much character, humanity or
love, but that I, personally, have a husband and white friends
who do . . .

I am aware that some of your readers have trouble with this explanation. One lady wrote me that she feels that "if she could love one white person, she could love them all." And such uncomplicated thinking is apparently what you encourage in your readers. It is a pity that this should be so. . . .

Whether you agree with my point of view or not . . . you owe it to your readers and to me and to yourself to present it fully, rather than seeking to chisel my words to neatly fit a category you have invented.

Alice signed off with "Conformity is not Community," before mailing her letter to the black-owned novelty magazine.

AS DISTRESSING as the *Jet* article was for Alice, its publication enabled childhood friends like Doris Reid to fully understand the contours of her life. Reid said she first learned of Alice's marriage to Mel when, shortly after the event, she overheard a conversation between her father and Mr. Walker. At the time, Reid was back in Eatonton after having lived overseas many years with her husband, a career military officer.

"My Daddy and Cousin Willie Lee were sitting out on the front porch, which I just happened to be sweeping," Reid said, recounting the scene.

"So my Daddy asks, 'How are the children?'"

"Mr. Willie Lee says, 'Alice done got married.'"

"Daddy says, 'Yeah? Who she marry?'"

" 'White man.'"

" 'White man?' my Daddy says, shocked."

" 'Yeah,' cousin Willie Lee answered. 'White man from up North.' "

"Back then, you didn't question your parents, even if you were grown," Reid continued, adding that she noted resignation, not disapproval, in Mr. Walker's voice. "So, as much as I was dying to hear more about Alice, I knew better than to open my mouth. But in my mind, I was thinking to myself, as I just kept a-sweeping: 'Alice married a white guy? Then she must have loved him. She must have loved him. That's all.' "

Reid said her feelings were confirmed when she was reading a copy of *Jet* several years later and chanced upon the photo of Alice, Rebecca, and Mel. "Looking at that photo, it really hit me, you know, the magnitude of what Alice had done," Reid explained. "Because hey, marrying a white man was something that black women in the South didn't even consider. For Alice to have gone down that road, I knew she must have loved Mel with all her heart."

But where Reid saw love, others saw a "race traitor" and began to speak harshly of Alice and her aspirations after the *Jet* article appeared. They accused her of "putting down the black man," of thinking that she was "better than everybody else," Reid remembered. "These were mostly old high school friends who somehow took Alice's marriage as a personal slap in the face. It was completely juvenile," she added.

And as for Alice's strides as an author, Reid said the article gave her all the more reason to stand up for her friend. Unlike the day she overheard the exchange between her father and Mr. Walker, Reid refused to stay silent when Alice's critics began to carp. "I knew Alice was always writing, but it wasn't until I read *Jet* that I realized she had gone as far as publishing a book," Reid said, with a joyful laugh. "So, when folks would start bad-mouthing her, I'd defend Alice to the death. I'd say, 'Excuse me, I don't recall seeing anything you've written lately.' "

IT WOULD not appear until a year after the novel's release, but of all the reviews of *The Third Life of Grange Copeland*, it was one published in *Freedomways* and written by Mississippi native Loyle Hairston that Alice felt best realized what she had been trying to achieve.

A quarterly journal founded in 1961, *Freedomways* had taken a lead role in publishing the emerging voices of the civil rights movement. "The Diary of an African Nun," Alice's story about a novitiate's "marriage to Christ," had appeared within its pages in

1968. "Must I still ask myself whether it was my husband, who came down bodiless from the sky . . . and claimed the innocence of my body?" muses the spiritually conflicted Ugandan woman. "Or was it the drumbeats, messengers of the sacred dance of life and deathlessness on earth?"

Writing in the No. 2, 1971, issue of the publication, Hairston likened *The Third Life of Grange Copeland* to the literature of authors such as Chekhov, Dostoyevsky, and Pushkin, adding that the novel (which Alice had dedicated to her mother and to Mel) was most reminiscent of Maxim Gorky's searing portraits of "common people under the yoke of oppression."

"With the skill of the Russian masters," Hairston observed, "Miss Walker has peopled her novel with characters whose passion for life seethes with a fury that borders on the demonic in its frustration. . . . And yet there are passages . . . that make the reader weep, so effectively does the author evoke pathos through her prose, so profoundly does she probe the depths of tormented men's souls. . . . To be sure, there are flaws in the novel but the author's craftsmanship minimizes their effect on the overall impact of the work."

Hairston's review was significant, Alice later explained, because where others had charged her with creating "stereotypically brutal" black male characters, Hairston was among the few critics who emphasized the transformation Grange Copeland underwent in the course of the narrative. She added that Hairston, well versed in Russian literature ("where you get 'meanies' and 'goodies' "), understood the harsh realism of her novel, that the brutality she depicted was not "unnecessary" or "extreme," but rather a truthful rendering of the conditions Alice wanted readers to address. In short, there was meaning in the misery that raged through her novel.

"*The Third Life* is very realistic. . . . I didn't want there to be any evasion on the part of the reader," Alice continued. "I wanted them to know that people like Grange and Brownfield exist and that you are going to have to deal with them. I wish people would do that rather than tell me that this is not the right image."

Before the publication of *Once*, Alice had made clear her intention to pursue her artistic vision regardless of the dictates of the literary establishment, be it black or white. Queried about "responsibility" in a January 1968 *Negro Digest* article headlined "Black Writers' Views on Literary Lions and Values," Alice had forthrightly replied, "Black writers should direct their work towards an audience, some imaginary ideal audience that will appreciate what they have to say, and profit from it. To write solely for a black audience is limiting and presumes too much; that they will appreciate your efforts; that they will try to understand you; that they will care enough about your work to buy your books; and that white people could never get anything (be made better; one might say) from what one writes. . . . I think it is only important that we write from within ourselves and that we direct our efforts outward. Period."

In her allegiance to an independent voice, Alice was taking a stance far different from the proponents of the Black Arts movement, who insisted, at least rhetorically, that black artists cultivate a collective black consciousness that spoke exclusively to the sociopolitical concerns of a black community under siege by "whitey." "The Black Arts Movement is radically opposed to any concept of the artist that alienates him [*sic*] from his community," wrote Larry Neal in the influential 1968 manifesto "The Black Arts Movement." "Black Art is the aesthetic and spiritual sister of the Black Power concept. As such, it envisions an art that speaks directly to the needs and aspirations of Black America . . . the Afro-American's desire for self-determination and nationhood."

Having written a novel in which the theme of black accountability superceded the racism of whites—one in which the needs of Mem and Margaret were equal to those of Brownfield and Grange—Alice was clearly not in step with Black Arts ideology as it had been defined by movement forces like Neal and Amiri Baraka (an approach Alice would later characterize as "two-thirds 'hate whitey's guts' and one-third 'I am black, beautiful, strong, and almost always right' ").

Indeed, writing in "Black Art," a poem that would be widely emulated during the era, Baraka had called for "Dagger poems in the slimy bellies of the owner-jews / Black poems to smear on girdle-mamma mulatto bitches / . . . poems . . . setting fire and death to whities ass / . . . Another bad poem cracking steel knuckles in a jew-lady's mouth."

Given that criteria, Alice, the wife of a Jew and mother of a biracial daughter, was considered sorely deficient. Her "failings" were publicized with a special disdain by *Negro Digest* editor Hoyt Fuller, who, admitting he had never read her novel, nonetheless trashed *The Third Life* on the basis that a white reviewer had found it meritorious, Alice later recalled. And suspicions about her racial allegiance would crescendo when, in May 1971, the novel was excerpted in *Redbook* magazine, an issue that trumpeted a profile of Hollywood handsome Robert Redford on the cover with the words: *Husband, Father, Sex Symbol.*

Thirty years later, poet Sonia Sanchez described the ideological conflicts that erupted, constantly, during the Black Arts years: "It was the early 1970s when black writers were first starting to get reputations and certain 'perpetrators' put people in different political camps. A lot of these brothers wanted to cop big book contracts and they viewed Alice as competition and as a sell-out because she'd married a white man. I was in the nationalist group and not necessarily appreciative of Alice's interracial marriage, so I found myself in the midst of this madness, but I always admired her work. My goal, as a writer, was to lift up Africans and bring us back onto the human stage. Alice and I may have chosen different roads, but our destination was the same."

Like Sanchez, Nikki Giovanni remembered the political pressure to choose which writers embodied *real* black feeling, black judgment, black thought. As to her first encounter with Alice Walker, Giovanni said that she was so enthralled by *The Third Life* that she phoned Alice and boldly asked if she (and her young son Thomas) might stop in Mississippi to meet her on their way home from a vacation. Alice graciously agreed.

"I'd read the novel while in Barbados and was just knocked out by its brilliance," Giovanni recalled. "I knew Alice was married to Leventhal and living in Jackson. So I called the international operator, got her number, and asked if we could visit before returning to New York. Seeing as Thomas and Rebecca were about the same age, I figured they could play together."

"It was my first trip to Mississippi," Giovanni continued. "Alice took us around. I saw Medgar Evers's house. I met Margaret Walker. We were there three or four days and it was really fun to stay in Alice's home and just hang out."

As it happens, Alice's memories of the impromptu visit are far less winsome than those of her former guest: "Right off, Nikki asked me why I had married a white man and told me she didn't want to hear anything about 'love.' She asked me how I could lay down every night with somebody I wanted to kill.

"I told her there were a lot of white people who upset me, but Mel wasn't one of them, and I certainly didn't want to kill him. At the time, our lives were so stressful that her comments hurt a lot."

24

The Children Grow in Love

HARLEM-BORN POET and essayist June Jordan was another writer who journeyed South to visit Alice while she was living in Jackson. On the faculty of Sarah Lawrence in the early 1970s, Jordan said she had never heard of Alice Walker until one day when the college buzzed with talk about a "famous" black alum. The woman, a beloved student of Jane Cooper and Muriel Rukeyser, had accepted a lecture invitation. Rumor had it that she would be returning to the campus with her white husband, a decidedly uncool move in the minds of a small but vocal group of militant black students then enrolled at the school, which had gone coed in 1968.

"There was a huge uproar about this event," Jordan recalled. "At the time, I didn't know a thing about Alice and couldn't have cared less about the color of her husband. I was torn about attending the lecture because it was at night, which meant I'd have to arrange for a baby-sitter. But folks were in such a 'nationalist' frame of mind and getting so bent out of shape about this woman, I figured I'd show up to make sure she wasn't attacked."

According to Mel, such scenarios were not uncommon. "Alice and I almost always got 'bad vibes' when I joined her at readings or talks," he remembered. "But I loved being there and never stopped going. We just took it in stride."

With Mel proudly seated in the audience, Alice, revisiting her childhood, delivered an eloquent address titled "The Black Writer and the Southern Experience." "The richness of the black writer's experience in the South can be remarkable, though some people might not like to think so," Alice observed in remarks later published in *In Search of Our Mothers' Gardens*.

A shack with only a dozen or so books is an unlikely place to discover Keats. But it is narrow thinking indeed to believe that Keats is the only kind of poet one would want to grow up to be. One wants to write poetry that is understood by one's people, not by the Queen of England. Of course, should she be able to profit by it too, so much the better, but since that is not likely, catering to her tastes would be a waste of time.

Alice continued:

In large measure, black Southern writers owe their clarity of vision to parents who refused to diminish themselves as human beings by succumbing to racism. Our parents seemed to know that an extreme negative emotion held against other human beings for reasons they do not control can be blinding. Blindness about other human beings, especially for a writer, is equivalent to death.

Although the atmosphere in the room was tense during Alice's presentation, no one was rude to her or disrespectful, Jordan recalled. Decades later, she said what she most remembered about the lecture was the soothing timbre of Alice's voice and the simplicity of her attire.

"Back then, like a lot of black writers, I had a huge Afro and wore a trench coat, boots, and dark sunglasses, day or night," Jordan said, letting loose with a peal of laughter. "Alice showed up in this nice, plain, ordinary dress. Her outfit was not political at all."

Alice's message about the creative gifts black writers could find in their communities also touched Jordan, herself a fiercely political author who'd already published a poetry collection (*Who Look at Me*, 1968) and a novel (*His Own Where*, 1972). She would continue, over the next thirty years, to write nearly as many books, including her final work, *Some of Us Did Not Die*, a collection of essays published posthumously in 2002.

Making her way to the podium at the end of the lecture, Jordan realized she had found in the soft-spoken, simply dressed Alice a powerful artistic ally. A few months later, when she traveled to Mississippi to write about the civil rights movement for the *New York Times Magazine*, Jordan visited Alice and Mel and featured them prominently in her article.

"Mel is the chief engineer of legal moves beyond mere mirage-desegregation," Jordan noted in "Mississippi 'Black Home,' A Sweet and Bitter Bluesong." "His wife is the distinguished black poet and novelist Alice Walker, a gentle, elegant person who is the daughter of sharecroppers. . . . Alice says she 'always wanted to get back to the people . . . Country people. Very remarkable people, who make you realize maybe for the first time what it means to be brave.' "

Jordan continued, "Prospects of violence shadow the mobility of Mel and Alice. They do not go to the movies on a Saturday night, when the theater is likely to be crowded with white teenagers, and they try to shop in the larger supermarkets."

Then she again quoted Alice, who, resolute, had declared, "Southerners will never make me feel afraid. . . . They won't make me feel ashamed. . . . I'm a Southerner. This is my home."

Inspired though she was by the commitment of her new friends, Jordan said that the ominous sense of danger surrounding the couple remained with her for years. "When I got to Jackson, I could see firsthand how vulnerable Alice and Mel were," Jordan remembered. "The white folks were trigger happy. It was like being clinically insane to live under that kind of intimidation."

.   .   .

THE REPRESSION came in myriad forms. For instance, Alice, seeking a break from her writing, one day decided to go bowling with her neighbor Clotie Graves. Alice had taken classes in bowling (a sport with origins in ancient Egypt) while at Spelman to fulfill a physical education requirement. Although she had never quite mastered the scoring of "spares" and "strikes," she enjoyed the game.

As was typical of public accommodations in Mississippi, the Jackson bowling alley Clotie and Alice selected had been closed to blacks until the passage of the Civil Rights Act of 1964. Years later, the owners were none too happy about being "forced" to open to blacks not only their bowling lanes, but the facility's on-site child care center as well. Aware of the service, Alice and Clotie planned to leave their toddlers, Rebecca and James Jr., at the center while they bowled.

But when the women entered the nursery with their children, they were met by white workers who, red faced and blustering, summarily announced that "no black kids" were allowed. Outraged, Alice stood her ground as she calmly informed the workers that she'd sue the bowling alley "down to its last pin," if the children were not admitted. In short order, James and Rebecca were inside.

For Clotie, a lifelong resident of the Magnolia State, Alice's response was a revelation. "It was the first time I'd ever seen a black person stand up to whites," she remembered. "Because even after the laws changed, there was still segregation and most blacks just accepted it and stayed in their place. But not Alice. After that incident, I started speaking up too, because she'd inspired me."

Before long, fearful that the child care staff might retaliate, Alice and Clotie decided to forgo their outing. "Knowing they were angry at us, it was hard to concentrate because we were worried the white folks might hurt our kids," Clotie explained. "I don't think we bowled more than a couple of balls before we decided to just leave and go home."

To be sure, white resistance to black demands for equality remained doggedly entrenched. No sooner had Alice faced down the bowling alley operators than she was compelled to call the city's bus drivers to account. In a letter (circa 1970) to the manager of the public transit system, she leveled her complaint:

> Dear Mr. Gibson,
> On yesterday, March 12, at around two o'clock in the after-noon, on bus #2406, one of your drivers referred to me as "girl." I assure you I am grown-up, married, and I teach. I often take this bus . . . and I would not like this to happen again. I recommend that you instruct your drivers that it is customary for bus drivers to refer to their passengers (the female ones) as "Miss," "Madam," or "Lady."

In a terse postscript after signing the letter, Alice made it clear to Mr. Gibson that she expected to see swift and dramatic improvements among his staff. "If courtesy titles are not used, with all passengers," Alice warned, "I think I can promise you that you will be sued."

And then, there was the library. Not anticipating any difficulty obtaining a library card issued in her own name, as opposed to one that identified her as "Mrs. Melvyn Leventhal," Alice applied for a new card. Of the mind, apparently, that since she just *had* to marry a white man, she should be satisfied to carry his (Jewish) name, the library refused to issue a card to "Alice Walker." To obtain one, she had to present evidence of a legal name change from "Leventhal" to "Walker," which she did.

The mental anguish suffered by civil rights workers was well understood by Josephine Diaz Martin, a white psychiatrist who would come to treat many of them as patients. A New Yorker who arrived in Mississippi in the mid-1960s to work with impoverished children, Dr. Martin soon found her office filled with freedom fighters, both black and white, desperate for relief from the psychological torment of their experiences with Jim Crow. At times, the activists were so severely traumatized that they required hospitalization. Fearful of what might befall civil rights workers seeking psychiatric treatment in the South, Dr. Martin frequently sent her patients, secretly, to facilities in the North.

That Alice could craft poems and stories in the midst of such racial strife (white police would gun down two black students at Jackson State in 1970) was an amazement to Jordan. She also noted that Alice, refusing to succumb to the political "ugliness" all around, had transformed her writing studio itself into a "work of art," replete with fresh flowers, gorgeous ceramics, and hand-woven tapestries.

"When I first arrived at their house, Alice took me to this stunningly beautiful room and told me that she didn't do anything in it except write," Jordan remembered. "I said, 'Get outta here.' Maybe white people had that kind of set-up, but no other black writer I knew had that kind of space.

"Mel's support was vital," she continued. "But more importantly, Alice was determined to become a writer. After seeing that room, it was obvious, even in the hell that was Mississippi, that Alice had arranged her life in such a way that she could pursue serious art. I knew right then that she was going to become a big-time writer and I told her precisely that."

As for Alice's feelings about her future, Jordan remembered her being less certain of triumph. "In that really quiet voice of hers, she said. 'Do you really think I'll succeed?' " Jordan's reply? "Absolutely. You can bank on it." Jordan added that Alice's work was distinguished by an emphasis on mystery and transcendence at a time when the country was enmeshed in seemingly intractable battles about race. By way of example, she cited "Medicine," a poem in *Once*:

> *Grandma sleeps with*
> *my sick*
> * grand-*
> *pa so she*
> *can get him*
> *during the night*
> *medicine*
> *to stop*
> * The pain*

In
the morning
clumsily
I
wake
them

Her eyes
look at me
from under-
  neath
his withered
arm

The
medicine
Is all
In
her long
un-
braided
hair.

It was just such transcendent love that kept Mel and Alice in Jackson, battling on in the hope that their efforts would help to defeat bigotry and create a more just world for their child. Offering her final impressions of Mississippi, Jordan had written, in her article, "The dead are remembered. The children grow in love."

She then put flesh to her words by describing an infant she'd seen nestled against her father's chest. The father was Mel Leventhal, asking aloud as he kissed the crown of his daughter's head, "Who would hurt you, Rebecca? Who would hurt you?"

25

A Kindred Lover of Beauty

As MUCH as Clotie Graves admired Alice's courage and looked to her as a role model in the fight for justice, she was increasingly pained by the psychological toll Mississippi seemed to be exacting on her friend. Never prone to idle chatter, Alice became even quieter and often appeared to be depressed. Knowing her fondness for nature and hoping an outdoor adventure might boost her spirits, Clotie and James one day invited Alice to go fishing with them when Mel was out of town. While her neighbors hauled in nets full of catfish and snapper, Alice sat under a tree and read.

Upon her arrival in Jackson, Alice had immersed herself in "a college of books." The spurt of concentrated reading had been prompted by her realization that her studies at Spelman *and* Sarah Lawrence had left, as she later noted, "crucial areas empty." "My lessons had, in fact, contributed to a blind spot in my education that needed desperately to be cleared if I expected to be a whole woman, a full human being, a black woman full of self-awareness and pride."

To that end, Alice consumed works by W. E. B. Du Bois (*The Souls of Black Folks*, 1903; *Black Reconstruction*, 1935) and

Gwendolyn Brooks ("If there was ever a *born* poet, I think it is Brooks"). Her reading also included books by Elechi Amadi (*The Concubine*, 1966), Camara Laye (*The Radiance of the King*, 1954), Bessie Head (*Maru*, 1971), and Gabriel García Márquez (*One Hundred Years of Solitude*, 1967).

"These writers do not seem afraid of fantasy, of myth and mystery," Alice explained. "Their work deepens one's comprehension of life by going beyond the bounds of realism. They are like musicians: at one with the cultures and their historical consciousness."

A lifelong lover of music, Alice was inspired by gospel artists such as Clara Ward and Mahalia Jackson. About her passion for a blues legend, she exclaimed, "I love the very *idea* of B.B. King." She was also influenced by Austrian virtuoso Wolfgang Amadeus Mozart, whose melodic symphonies, concertos, and sonatas marked the height of the Classical age. "I can't remember a time since I was introduced to his music at Sarah Lawrence that Mozart didn't transport me into the joy of wholeness," Alice would later note. "I wish I knew more about his mother. Because my sense is that a lot of his music comes from lullabies and folk songs from her side of the family."

Steeped in such expansive literature and music, Alice experienced the repression in Mississippi all the more intensely. Friends like Clotie could sense that she was on the brink of spiritual collapse. "It seemed like Jackson was starting to close in on Alice," she remembered. "She needed to be away from the conservatism, the racial restrictions, and the small-mindedness. Blacks who'd been raised in Mississippi had developed certain survival skills. But it was hard on movement people like Alice and Mel because the white folks were relentless."

IN SEPTEMBER 1970, a dozen years after Dr. "O. Henry" removed the scar tissue from her eye, Alice, eager for a respite from Dixie, submitted an application that would return her to the Boston area as a writing fellow at the Radcliffe Institute in Cambridge. Founded by a Radcliffe president, Mary Ingraham Bunting, and renamed in her honor in 1978, the institute targeted women with family responsibilities who also wished to pursue creative or scholarly projects, "each according to her own design." In addition to office space, institute fellows were granted library privileges at Radcliffe and Harvard and could audit, with faculty permission, classes at either school.

In her application, Alice wrote that she was at work on a novel about a young woman at a "genteel" black college in the South. The woman, on a quest to integrate her African and black American identities, travels to East Africa, where she falls in love and marries. "I want to explore some of the discoveries that might stem from a misplaced nostalgia and romanticism," Alice wrote, detailing the theme of her work-in-progress. "This is not a sociological novel, nor a political one. It is a love story in which the beloved is both a man and a continent."

Continuing, Alice noted that she would also use her fellowship to refine her technical skills: "There is a good bit I'd like to learn about The Novel—especially in regard to the many ways it can be written—because, although I have recently published my first one, I am sometimes not sure I know what a novel is."

And finally, having mentioned the success of her residency at MacDowell, Alice told the selection committee that she longed to return to a vibrant community of writers and scholars: "In this regard, Mississippi has been anything but inspiring," she flatly volunteered.

EVEN AS he traversed the state, working, in his own words, "murderous" hours to bring justice to Mississippi, Mel was mindful of the difficulties Alice faced as a creative artist living in Jackson. It was true, he had abandoned his playwrighting ambitions for court pleadings, but his soul was still stirred by the poetry of Shakespeare, the sharp wit of Oscar Wilde. A firm supporter if not a practitioner of the arts, he shared Alice's frustrations with a community where the gridiron was king and a demolition derby a shoo-in to outdraw the symphony. And on the rare nights when Alice and Mel ventured out to take in a local movie or dance concert, they had to brave whites shouting, "Nigger go home," and other invectives that belied the much-vaunted Southern grace and hospitality. That Alice, after three years, was ready to trade Jackson for the snowy winters in Cambridge did not surprise her husband at all.

"Alice was unhappy in Mississippi and it was not just because of the pressures of being part of an interracial couple," Mel would later observe. "She felt stifled because we were living in a barren, cultureless, unsophisticated part of the country. I don't think she would have felt any different had she been married to a black man."

"It was a love/hate relationship," he continued. "Alice loved the land and natural beauty of the South, but she could not abide the backwoods mentality and the lack of intellectual stimulation."

With regard to his own emotional health, Mel insisted that aside from his grueling workload, he "managed fine" in the Magnolia State. Thirty years later, neighbors would offer a different perspective. "If Mel had sat still and really thought about all the white folks who wanted to kill him, I truly believe he would have cracked up," said James Graves, husband of Clotie. "He'd laugh about the Klan when we were sitting around drinking Tanqueray and playing poker, but with a wife and a child, I know he had to be scared to death. I think he dealt with his fear by throwing himself into his work. The man lived and breathed the NAACP."

In the early 1970s, Henri Norris, a black woman just beginning her law career, arrived in Jackson to assist the NAACP with desegregation cases. Like Graves, she said that Mel was subject to many hostilities. As it happened, Norris was also a graduate of Spelman. Today, a political activist in San Francisco, she recalled, "I was really looking forward to meeting Alice, who was legend at Spelman for all her principled positions. And truth be told, I was very curious to know why this powerful sister had married a white man. When I met Mel, I understood completely. He was so gentle, thoughtful, and helpful. I was really impressed and instantly fell in love with them both."

Norris continued: "One day, Alice was invited to a reception in the home of some middle-class black people. I was invited, too. Mel, typically, was working into the night and arrived late. When he walked in, these colored folks were very chilly. It was obvious to me that Mel wasn't welcomed because he was white. I was highly disturbed by this because I was working to be a civil rights lawyer and wanted people to be treated equal. It was the first time I acknowledged that black racism existed. I remember thinking how brave Alice and Mel had been to come to Mississippi where they were clearly catching hell on both sides."

WHILE SHE awaited word from Radcliffe, Alice continued to write and to teach at Tougaloo College, where she'd been a guest lecturer since 1970. She was heartened to find the academic climate a bit more rigorous than it had been at Jackson State. Indeed, she would later remember a "brilliant" Ralph Ellison holding forth on the Black Arts movement during a visit to the campus. Ellison, author of the celebrated 1952 novel *Invisible Man*, had evoked the ire of the new generation of black writers because of what they viewed as his paternalistic response to their cries for rebellion. Blacks would be better served, Ellison seemed to suggest, if they troubled themselves with addressing the question "What is the value of self-knowledge?" rather than "offing" the white man.

"He was not buying the fashionable black nationalist party line of the day," said Alice, about Ellison's provocative lecture, which she attended with Mel.

The daring of Tougaloo students under Alice's tutelage was evident in *Pound*, a literary journal that she helped them to compile and release. Writing in her preface to the twenty-four-page collection of prose and poetry (two of her poems were also included), Alice praised the student-authors for their candor and honesty. "What is striking is how rooted [the work] is in the world and experiences that produced and shaped it," Alice observed. "Yet it is not exclusive. It is unfailingly evocative of a private world that is, unselfconsciously, open to visitors. . . . This is a major accomplishment in any age. And I applaud it."

Although she didn't single out any of the contributors by name,

Alice was sure to have found special meaning in such works as
"Pregnant?" a poem written before the court decision on *Roe v.
Wade*, by a student identified only as Lynn:

> *Why is it so very
> sinful to be Pregnant?
> Is not this one of the
> least miracles we can
> take part in?*
>
> *Yes, I am pregnant.
> Why? Why am I full
> of love and beauty?
> Well, I just couldn't
> hold it back. I had
> to let it show.*
>
> *Please don't embarrass
> me by asking questions.*
>
> *You want to feel my
> Love bulging out?
> Put your hand gently
> on my stomach.*

In addition to the racial and sexual themes she planned to
explore in her new novel (provisionally titled *Atonement and
Release*), Alice knew, as she drafted early chapters, that she needed
a structure that would challenge her artistically and keep her creatively engaged. *The Third Life* had been chronological in sequence.
Now, ready to expand her reach, Alice set upon writing a nonlinear
narrative that, like a crazy quilt, would "jump back and forth in
time and work on the mind in many different patterns." Quilting
with needle, fabric, and thread was an art form in which black
Southern women had flourished for generations. But could Alice

transfer such artistry to the printed page? For inspiration, she turned to the prose poem acclaimed as the literary masterpiece of the Harlem Renaissance—*Cane*.

"I remember reading *Cane* for the first time with a passionate recognition of a kindred lover of beauty," Alice later said, "and weeping over the poem about there always needing to be, and there always being, someone who becomes the seed that gives us once again the singing, shining tree."

Written by Nathan Eugene (later, Jean) Toomer and published in 1923, *Cane* is a richly textured montage of stories, sketches, and poems evoking black life in the South, with an especially sensitive treatment of black women in Georgia. The opening passage reads:

> *Men had always wanted her, this Karintha, even as a child . . . Old men rode her hobby-horse upon their knees. Young men danced with her at frolics when they should have been dancing with their grown-up girls. . . . This interest of the male, who wishes to ripen a growing thing too soon, could mean no good to her.*

And later in the text, Toomer offers the poem "Song of the Son":

> *O Negro slaves, dark purple ripened plums*
> *Squeezed, and bursting in the pine-wood air*
> *Passing, before they stripped the old tree bare*
> *One plum was saved for me, one seed becomes*
>
> *An everlasting song, a singing tree . . .*

Applauding Toomer's rich overlay of narrative styles, the distinguished literary scholar Darwin T. Turner wrote, "Poems link, separate, echo, and introduce stories with themes of nature's beauty, man's disruption of nature's harmony, work, tributes to Black folksong, love, dreams of escape, false gods and true gods. . . . Imagistic, impressionistic, sometimes surrealistic [*Cane*] is redolent . . . with sensuous appeals to eye and ear."

Although she'd already published, by age twenty-six, a collec-

tion of poetry, a novel, highly praised short stories, and essays, Alice
was driven, with *Cane* as a model, to elevate her skills. Aware that
a novel of such scope would require her full concentration, Alice
decided to send Rebecca, now about eighteen months old, to nursery school three days a week. She was cheered to discover an excellent one, run by a black teacher in her Rockdale Drive home, half a
block away. An ardent crusader for civil rights, Barbara Cornelius
had infused her school's curriculum with the spirit of the freedom
struggle. To be sure, Rebecca would learn her ABCs, and the "ee,
yi, ohs" of "Old MacDonald," as well as the rousing choruses of
the Negro national anthem ("Lift Ev'ry Voice") and protest songs
like "Ain't Gonna Let Nobody Turn Me 'Round."

"She is stout and black-skinned and warm . . . exactly the sort
of person I wanted my daughter's first teacher to be," Alice later
wrote, admiringly, of Mrs. Cornelius. "The nursery school is a
large, spotless room. . . . I gaze at the small chairs and tables almost
with longing."

In her decision to make writing a priority, Alice was forging new
ground. In the South, black women were, by definition, expected to
be paragons of domesticity for their blood kin, as well as for whites.
Although the landscape had improved somewhat, thanks to civil
rights gains, the South remained rife with black women who, barred
from other occupations, spent more time rearing white children
than their own. Such was the price of survival.

Now comes Alice, dispatching her toddler to nursery school
because of the demands of a *novel*? It was an act scarcely conceived,
let alone realized for black women.

"Alice's writing wasn't a hobby," asserted her neighbor Clotie,
"she took it seriously. But back then, that was a strange concept for
people to understand."

"I supported her one hundred percent because I knew it was
hard for Alice to write with a small child in the house; with Mel
always in court, with her mother, who she sorely missed, being in
Georgia. She'd show me the little twenty-five- and thirty-dollar
checks she got when a story or poem got published and I knew that
money didn't come easy. So, James and I were always happy to fill

in if Alice was still writing after Rebecca came home from nursery school or whenever she needed a baby-sitter."

If *Once* was an expression of the joy she felt after surviving an abortion and *The Third Life* her first attempt at an extended work, Alice was determined, with her second novel, to achieve an even greater mastery of her craft. In the absence of identifiable guidelines for black women writers, she'd devise her own; she'd invent her own methodologies. Truth be told, Mrs. Cornelius and her sun-filled nursery school were central to Alice's creative vision.

"By the time Rebecca was born, I had no doubts about being a writer. (Doubts about making a *living* by writing, always)," she would later say. "Write I did, night and day . . . and it was not even a choice, as having a baby was a choice, but a necessity.

"With Mrs. Cornelius, Rebecca was in the best school I expected her to know," Alice continued, "where she could hear the story of Harriet Tubman . . . and see Harriet herself in her teacher's face."

Describing his state of mind as he labored on the manuscript that would become *Cane*, Jean Toomer offered words that now resonated with Alice: "Now I wanted a book published as I wanted nothing else. I wanted it because it would be a substantial testament of my achievement. I felt it would lead me from the cramped conditions . . . I had outgrown, into the world of writers and literature. I saw it as my passport to the world."

26

A Kiss on Both Sides

In her 1963 book, *The Feminine Mystique*, Betty Friedan had bemoaned the plight of middle-class white women purportedly "trapped" in the suburbs with their talents stunted and their potential unrealized. "We can no longer ignore the voice within women that says: 'I want more than my husband and my children and my home,' " Friedan had thundered in the book, setting off a media frenzy. "The longer [an American woman] conforms, the less she feels as if she really exists."

Never having enjoyed a privileged existence from which to "liberate" themselves or otherwise flee, most black women greeted the feminist movement that emerged in the early 1970s with skepticism, if not outright scorn. Given the lowly economic status of their families, black women had, by necessity, labored outside of their homes for generations. Writing in *When and Where I Enter* (1984), black historian Paula Giddings would later explain, "Not only were the problems of the White suburban housewife (who may have had Black domestic help) irrelevant to Black Women, they were also alien to them. Friedan's observation that 'I never knew a woman, when I was growing up, who used her mind, played her own part in the world, and also loved, and had children' seemed to come from another planet."

Although black women were not drawn to the feminism fashioned by affluent white women, they were acutely aware of the constraints on their lives, the Black Power movement notwithstanding. In her refusal to sacrifice her writing to marriage and motherhood, Alice was undeniably more "radical" than many of her contemporaries, but she was not alone. Just as Friedan had probed the disaffection of white women, writer-editor Toni Cade (later Bambara) would, in 1970, publish a collection of prose and poetry that addressed gender issues from a black female stance. At the time of its release, the volume, aptly titled *The Black Woman*, was unprecedented in American letters. But in contrast to the hoopla surrounding Friedan's work, the black feminist discourse on such topics as education, economics, abortion, and child rearing was largely ignored.

Decades later, jacket copy from *The Black Woman* offers ample evidence of the tradition from which Alice's literature would emerge in the 1970s and, by turn, serve to uplift and expand: "Today America is witnessing two great human revolutions. One is that of the burgeoning Black pride militancy. The other is the rising demand by women for liberation from their chattel-like roles in a male dominated society. This volume presents the eloquent writings of those vitally involved in both—Black women, speaking of themselves and for themselves."

With offerings from Audre Lorde, Sherley Anne Williams, and Paule Marshall among others, the collection featured work from black women on the cutting edge of the artistic and political landscape. "The Diary of an African Nun," Alice's story about the oppressive demands of religion, was reprinted in the volume, which also included "Who Will Revere the Black Woman?," in which jazz singer Abbey Lincoln contemplates "black power" as practiced by many of the leading militants of the day:

"When a Negro 'likes white girls,' his woman (the Black Woman) is the first he wants to know about it. White female rejects and social misfits are flagrantly flaunted in our faces as the ultimate in feminine pulchritude . . . Evil? Evil, you say? The Black woman is hurt, confused, frustrated, angry, resentful, frightened and evil! Who in this hell dares suggest that she be otherwise? These attitudes only point up her perception of the situation and her healthy rejection of same."

New York poet hattie gossett kept close ties with Bambara (1939–1995) as both a devoted friend and sister-in-arms. To her mind, *The Black Woman* belies any notion that African American women stood on the sidelines of women's liberation.

"If you really examine that book, you have to wonder why the black nationalists didn't drop an atomic bomb on Toni," gossett later said. "The book blew the debate wide open. It challenged the concept of pussy power that was so rampant among the brothers; the position that they were under so much pressure battling whitey that they could just walk all over black women and we had to accept that 'ten paces behind' bullshit."

DETERMINED TO take a hard look, through her art, at the challenges facing black women, Alice was happy to receive, on March 2, 1971, a letter from Radcliffe granting her a $5,000 writing fellowship for the academic year beginning that fall. Aside from the obvious merits of her application, the selection committee had perhaps also been swayed by a reference letter provided by Jane Cooper: "Alice Walker is one of the strongest, most humane, most interesting young writers I know. . . . Who else writes, from the inside, of the lives of black sharecroppers in the South? . . . I too am applying for a Radcliffe grant, but I'm not just being noble when I say that I'd put her application before my own; it's that important for her."

Alice's former teacher would be awarded a Radcliffe/Bunting Fellowship about twenty years later.

Before she left for Cambridge, Alice journeyed to California (without Rebecca or Mel) to visit Diana Young, who had joined a commune near San Francisco. She also took a stroll down memory lane with Robert Allen, who'd moved to the area from New York in the late 1960s. Author of a riveting eyewitness account of the assassination of Malcolm X, Allen had gone on to become a writer-editor for various activist publications. His work had taken him to Czechoslovakia, Cambodia, and Paris, as well as Hanoi just as American forces were beginning to bomb North Vietnam. Upon his return to the states, Allen, a draft resister, traveled the country ("as far as I could go in a raggedy old Nash Rambler") giving lectures about his experiences abroad. Like Alice, he'd also married interracially, to a white woman who'd been an exchange student at Spelman and active herself in Mississippi freedom struggles. Before leaving New York, the couple had opened (and closed) the Browser Bookshop near City College. "It lost all the money we put into it," Allen said, with a good-natured laugh. "But it was a great fun and we enjoyed it. Alice even came up and did a poetry reading."

About his reunion with Alice in California, Allen recalled, "She fell in love with the Bay Area right away. She liked the hills, the trees, and the ocean. We exchanged a very warm greeting because I think the feeling we had for each other was still there."

Throughout her years in Jackson, Alice had kept in touch with Diana. In advance of her arrival in the summer of 1971, she dispatched to her former roommate a letter in which she shared news of her Radcliffe award and her hopes for the future: "Mel wants to remain in Mississippi and we love each other so it is very hard to decide to stay apart. . . . We are fearful about this experiment but are hopeful it will succeed. I know, however, that if I continue here without doing the things I want to do I'll become a thin-lipped, disgruntled harridan. . . . These are chaotic times for me, but I will try not to come unglued. In the meantime, I send my love to you and a kiss on both sides of your head."

READY TO focus her attention on *Atonement and Release*, Alice was settled, with Rebecca, in a furnished apartment at 50B Linnaean Street in Cambridge by early September 1971. The $240 monthly rent was to be deducted from her $5,000 Radcliffe award. And in a request not commonly made by fellowship applicants,

Alice had appealed, in her proposal, for funds "to provide small payments to the East Africans I will have to interview." That $250 was likewise subtracted from her grant, as was the projected costs of Rebecca's day care for the ten-month stay (nearly $1,500).

In short, after expenses, only about $1,000 of Alice's award would remain to supplement her writing. Of course Mel, who planned to visit whenever there were lulls in his court cases, would add to the coffers as best he could. But Alice was now effectively on her own. She had resigned herself to the fact that there'd be little room in her budget for the movies, museums, concerts, and other cultural attractions that had been lacking in Jackson. Such was the price of her reprieve from Aunt Jemima memorabilia and Mississippi's sports-crazed citizenry.

With money tight, Alice was determined to optimize the educational benefits of her fellowship. Exercising her auditing privileges, she immediately signed up for an English class at Harvard. Apparently unimpressed, Alice could recall neither specific subject matter nor instructor when later queried about the class. "I don't remember a thing about it," she shrugged.

But she was not soon to forget the virulent epidemic of Hong Kong flu that swept through New England shortly after her arrival. Unaccustomed to the harsh winter climate (subzero temperatures, compared to the sixty-five-degree winter average in Mississippi), both Alice and Rebecca fell victim to the virus and contracted lengthy, debilitating colds. After several days with no improvements in Rebecca, Alice braved the weather and took her two-year-old daughter ("burning with fever and whooping cough") to a well-known pediatrician for care. Already taxed by the upheaval in her life, Alice was not cheered in the least by the doctor, a man who was clearly stunned to discover a black mother and child waiting among the Boston bluebloods in his medical suite. "[I] hate it when his white fingers touch her," Alice would later write about the doctor's imperious response to Rebecca. During the 1970s, the Boston area was mired in a ferocious school busing conflict. The widely reported controversy made Alice all the more sensitive to race matters in a city that exalted itself as a "cradle of liberty."

As she struggled to nurse herself and her ailing toddler back to health, Alice's writing plans fell, increasingly, by the wayside. But what she lost in concrete progress on her new novel, Alice gained in a deeper understanding of "Strong Horse Tea," a short story she had written years before Rebecca was born (it would later be published in *In Love & Trouble*). In the story, Rannie Toomer, a rural black mother, is unable to obtain medical treatment for her infant son who is grievously ill. "Why did colored folks always want you to do something for them?" grumbles the white mail carrier who refuses to deliver Rannie's urgent plea for help to the town doctor. Desperate, Rannie resorts to a folk remedy (horse urine), which she collects from a mare during a raging thunderstorm. But before she returns with the "tea" to her shoddy cabin, her baby dies.

"When would this one know . . . that she could only depend on those who come," Alice had written in the story, alluding to Rannie's naïve faith in the "goodwill" of Southern whites. With its focus on the travails of an impoverished black woman fighting for her child, "Strong Horse Tea" evokes "A Worn Path," a 1941 story by famed Mississippi writer Eudora Welty (1909–2001). But unlike Alice's rendering of Rannie Toomer, Welty's portrait of protagonist Phoenix Jackson is marred by caricature. By the time Jackson finishes her December backwoods trek to get medicine for a grandson who's swallowed lye, she's been "spooked," in stereotypical minstrel show fashion, by scarecrows, snakes, buzzards, *black* dogs, and "big dead trees, like *black* men with one arm" (emphasis mine).

In a closing flourish, a white hunter Jackson encounters near the end of her journey "jokingly" points a gun at her, having already chortled, "I know you old colored people! Wouldn't miss going to town to see Santa Claus!" In Welty's hands, what might have been intended as satire instead exudes a discomfiting segregationist air. As it happened, Alice would go on to interview Welty, who, by the 1970s, had long been feted as the literary doyenne of Jackson, Mississippi, where she'd been born to a prominent family with black servants in its employ. First published in the *Harvard Advocate* (Winter 1973), the exchange would be reprinted in *Conversations with Eudora Welty* (1984) edited by Peggy Whitman Prenshaw.

In introductory passages, Alice sets the scene for the interview that she conducted at Welty's stately English Tudor home: "When we face each other, talking at first in starts, I think how odd it is that I feel entirely relaxed, entirely comfortable. . . . For this *is* Mississippi . . . and black, white, old, young . . . all these labels have meaning for a very good reason: they have effectively kept us apart, sometimes brutally. So that, although we live in the same town, we inhabit different worlds. . . . Still, I am undaunted, unafraid of discovering what I can."

Proceeding, Alice queries Welty about her publishing history (then, eleven books), her favorite poets (Yeats, John Donne), and her thoughts on women's liberation ("I haven't any bones to pick"). Understandably curious about Welty's views on race relations, Alice inquires, tactfully, "Did you think there was anything *wrong* with Mississippi in those days, when you were young? Did you see a way in which things might change?"

Welty's reply: "Well, I could tell when things were wrong with *people* . . . that we knew or knew of, they were very real to me. . . . And I think this is the way real sympathy *has* to start. . . . People are first and last individuals, and I don't think of them in the mass when I feel for them most."

An artist in eternal pursuit of enlightenment (preferably gleaned firsthand), Alice later said she was grateful for her chat with the author whose talents were perhaps best summed up by Flannery O'Connor. Offering a dissenting critique of "Where Is the Voice Coming From?," a celebrated Welty story about the assassination of Medgar Evers, O'Connor declared, "The more you think about it, the less satisfactory it gets."

"I liked Eudora's calm, clear, gray-eyed gaze," Alice remembered. "She was very present, very there. Of course I felt again the security all around her, as with Flannery, as with Bill [Faulkner]; in a large, handsome house her father had built and left to her, a society in which she was prized. Still. She had a deformity of the upper back/spine. And this is probably what saved her."

Similarly, Alice said that her encounter with the arrogant pediatrician who'd treated Rebecca had enabled her to *live* Rannie

Toomer's plight as she'd only imagined it when she was crafting "Strong Horse Tea." "Illness has always been of enormous benefit to me," Alice would later write about the insights she gained during the flu-ravaged winter of 1971. "It might even be said that I have learned little from anything that did not in some way make me sick."

NOW AGE twenty-seven, Alice also knew, as she began her residency at Radcliffe, that it was the inspiration, solace, and grit she'd found in the artistry of black women writers that was having the greatest impact on her creative life. Committed to bringing more readers to Phillis Wheatley, Nella Larsen, Francis E. W. Harper, Paule Marshall, and Toni Morrison (to name a few of the black female authors largely ignored by the literary establishment in the early 1970s), Alice designed a course in black women writers and was hired, while living in Cambridge, to teach it at nearby Wellesley College.

Like many colleges in the aftermath of the civil rights struggle, Wellesley was attempting to expand its enrollment beyond the affluent whites who had attended the all-female institution for more than a century. Among the handful of black students enrolled at the college in the early 1970s was Yakini Kemp, an Atlanta native with sights on a medical career. She vividly recalled her participation, during the spring of 1972, in what is now generally believed to be the first black women's literature class taught in the United States.

"As a biology major, I took the class, initially, to get a break from all the science," Kemp said. "We were mostly black women and Alice created a womblike atmosphere, so we felt as if we were in a protected space, which was important at Wellesley. Within the first few meetings, it was clear this was going to be my most important course in college.

"Alice had us read books by all these black women we'd never heard of," she continued. "She unearthed a part of our history that we had been denied."

Included on Alice's syllabus were Jordan's *Who Look at Me* and

The Street by Ann Petry, both first works that had received scant scholarly attention. She also assigned her students *Maud Martha*, the evocative 1953 novel by Gwendolyn Brooks that was rarely (if ever) taught on college campuses. Indeed, one of Alice's colleagues at Wellesley, Patricia Spacks, would publish a 1973 book entitled *The Female Imagination* without as much as a mention of Brooks, who, two decades after *Annie Allen*, remained the only black woman to claim the Pulitzer Prize. That Brooks and other women writers of color had been omitted from Spacks's study (and dozens more) underscored the importance of Alice's dedication to teaching their poems, stories, and novels.

Decades later, the black literary scholar Mary Helen Washington would attribute the reassessment of the eighteenth-century poet Phillis Wheatley (c. 1753–1784) to Alice's early championing of the enslaved writer's work. Writing in her essay, "In Search of Our Mothers' Gardens," Alice argued that Wheatley, the first African American to publish a book, was undeserving of the derision with which her poetry had historically been met, especially among black academics. "We now know that you were not an idiot or a traitor; only a sickly little black girl, snatched from your . . . country and made a slave," Alice declared in defense of a poet whose *Poems on Various Subjects* (1773) had been dismissed as conformist and "fawning" to whites. "It is not so much what you sang, as that you kept alive in so many of our ancestors, *the notion of song.*"

Washington had first met Alice, not long after she moved to Jackson, while conducting doctoral research on black women writers. Today a professor of English at the University of Maryland and the author of such works as *Black-eyed Susan*s (1975), *Midnight Birds* (1980), and *Invented Lives* (1987), she cheered Alice's compassionate embrace of the poet. "Black literature needed Alice's voice on Wheatley," Washington maintained. "Her essay gave us the first intimate picture of the poet and the obstacles she faced. Afterward, everybody cut Phillis some slack."

Wheatley's entry in the respected *Norton Anthology of African American Literature* (1997) would attest to that fact: "Wheatley

first had to write her way *into* American literature before she or any
other black writer could claim a special mission and purpose for an
African American literature. She had no models other than
European American ones for her poetry, and she could not assume
that her white readers would want to know what a slave woman
thought or felt unless she could demonstrate her capacity to express
her ideas and feelings in a manner sanctioned by the dominant culture. . . . No single writer has contributed more to the founding of
African American literature."

Along with the splendor of her reading list, Alice gave students
unconventional homework assignments that forced them to grapple
personally (as had Phillis Wheatley in her *very life*) with racial
oppression. One such exercise was the preparation of a "slave narrative" based on each student's life.

"It was instructive to see what some of the women wrote about
slavery based upon their skin color or family background," Kemp
remembered. "Alice's teaching style was very intimate. She didn't
deal in abstractions or unintelligible theory. She was completely
down to earth."

Transformed forever by the course, the former pre-med student
had changed her career goals by semester's end. "I am an English
professor today because of Alice Walker," said Kemp, now a distinguished faculty member at Florida A&M University. "I wanted to
teach about creative expression just as she'd done. She affirmed the
literature of black women and gave us hope that it was possible to
be an artist."

27

Love the Questions

OFF STRIDE with her writing because of illness and the demands of motherhood, Alice knew, even before she'd begun teaching at Wellesley, that the novel slated to become *Meridian* was more likely to be completed if she could continue her fellowship. It was also clear that Rebecca, having been wracked with ailments throughout the winter, needed to return to a warmer climate. So Alice and Mel agreed that their daughter would spend more time in Jackson, where the family had celebrated the holidays at the end of the year.

Conflicted though she was about the turn of events, Alice was confident that with another year at Radcliffe, she could ready her novel for publication. For despite the turmoil she'd endured since arriving in Cambridge, she'd managed to complete a second volume of poetry (*Revolutionary Petunias & Other Poems*), which had already been accepted for publication by Harcourt.

"During the second year, I would forge ahead with the new novel, which, hopefully, hasn't deserted me altogether," Alice had written to Radcliffe officials in early 1972, requesting an extension of her residency. "I feel really caught . . . and can only advise that perhaps the single most important thing the Institute has given me is a chance to break out of, for a while, a confining social and private atmosphere. . . . A renewed fellowship would give me a much needed sense of freedom and possibility."

In short order, her request was approved: "I know how difficult this year has been for you and how many hard decisions it has involved," read the letter granting Alice a renewed appointment (without stipend) from July 1972 to June 1973. "I hope the affiliation will continue to be useful in carrying out your writing."

As MUCH as he had hoped to spend time with Alice in Cambridge, Mel had been unable to get away from Jackson because of his court cases. For him, Alice's decision to extend her stay at Radcliffe signaled a crossroads in their union. It was obvious that Alice had grown weary of life in the South. He wanted to stay in Mississippi and battle the state's bigotry—lawsuit by arduous lawsuit, if that's what it took to win justice.

"After five years, Alice had reached her limit," Mel said. "She was reminding me that I had told her we were not going to be in Mississippi forever. But I had grown very close to my partners and litigated some very important cases. I had accomplished a great deal. The situation was hard on both of us."

"Hard." Well, the way Alice now saw it, conditions were worse than that and she could only withstand so much. What was she to make, for example, of the audience response to *Georgia, Georgia*, a movie she and Mel had ventured out to see one night? Based on a screenplay by Maya Angelou, the 1972 film tells the story of a black singer (played by Diana Sands) who has an affair with a white photographer in Sweden. For her "treachery" the woman is strangled to death in a macabre scene that, to Alice's horror, brought the largely black audience to its feet in triumph.

"People actually cheered," Alice later remembered, woefully. "Mel was upset too, but it was my image and reflection that was being snuffed out on the screen."

Similar displays of the ongoing Southern antipathy toward interracial couples would be recounted by the esteemed black poet Rita Dove in her book, *The Poet's World*. A writer-in-residence at Tuskegee Institute in the early 1980s, Dove noted that she and her husband, the German writer Fred Viebahn, one day left a supermarket to discover a white man attempting to slash the tires of their car. On another occasion, the couple, driving near Auburn University, passed a fraternity house festooned with a huge Confederate flag. Enraged by their mixed-race union, a swarm of frat boys lunged toward the couple's car screaming "racial epithets that I was too scared to actually understand. . . . It was a relief to return to Arizona."

At an impasse in her marriage, Alice remained in Cambridge while Mel soldiered on in Jackson. As she'd done at other difficult times in her life, Alice turned to art for insight on the uncertainty and confusion that pressed heavily on her psyche. In the poem "Reassurance," which would appear in *Revolutionary Petunias*, she laid open her heart:

> *I must love the questions*
> *themselves*
> *as Rilke said*
> *like locked rooms*
> *full of treasure*
> *to which my blind*
> *and groping key*
> *does not yet fit.*
>
> *and await the answers*
> *as unsealed letters*
> *mailed with dubious intent*
> *and written in a very foreign*
> *tongue.*

> *and in the hourly making*
> *of myself*
> *no thought of Time*
> *to force, to squeeze*
> *the space*
> *I grow into.*

THE SHIFTS that were taking place in Alice's private life in the early 1970s were being mirrored in her professional ties. While her relationship with Monica McCall had been fruitful, there had never been a warm rapport between Alice and her literary agent. The mismatch was primarily a matter of temperament. McCall, perhaps because of her British roots, communicated with a marked formality and reserve. Not a person who could ever be described as "chatty," Alice, as a Southern black woman, had nonetheless been raised with more effusive traditions. After all, she hailed from a culture where "gimme some sugar" (a kiss) and "hug my neck" were standard greetings.

In search of a more compatible fit, Alice, after the release of *The Third Life*, ended her affiliation with McCall and signed on with the literary agent Wendy Weil. A Wellesley graduate who was on the ascent in the publishing world, Weil had been recommended to Alice, at about the same time, by writers June Jordan and Julius Lester. "I knew Wendy was looking for fiction writers," Jordan recalled.

Then a New York radio show host and author of the notorious black nationalist tract, *Look Out, Whitey!, Black Power's Gon' Get Your Mama* (1968), Lester had interviewed Alice during her book tour for *The Third Life* and they'd later begun corresponding. "I was drawn to Alice because her work was rooted in the South," recalled Lester, who'd later pen new interpretations of the *Uncle Remus* stories. "It engaged me emotionally. And I liked her, personally, because she was down-to-earth and had no pretenses. . . . It was simple intuition that prompted me to recommend Wendy to Alice."

Alice said that, as with many black militants of the era, Lester's incendiary public persona belied a more complex reality. That his book damned whites ("a cracker is a cracker is a cracker," read a typical passage) did not preclude his genuine friendship with a black woman married to "the enemy." "Julius was finding his direction," Alice remembered. "He was into white women, *always*. So I don't think my marriage to Mel was at all a stretch for him. Or think about Leroi Jones [Baraka]. All the while he was railing he had that white wife, Hettie Jones, who finally wrote us all about it." The book, *How I Became Hettie Jones*, was released in 1990.

Alice said her decision to change literary agents was purely a business transaction. The shift was made without any malice or lack of gratitude for the pivotal role McCall had played at the beginning of her career. "Monica sold everything I wrote and sent her that was worth selling," Alice would later say about McCall. "But I couldn't communicate with her well. It was always so stressful for me whenever we talked."

But what Alice considered a clean and necessary break would be perceived by Muriel Rukeyser as an act of betrayal. Mel, Muriel, Mississippi, Cambridge. Love and trouble summed up the scenario quite well.

ONE OF the early transactions Wendy Weil negotiated on Alice's behalf was the placement of her short story "Roselily" in the August 1972 issue of *Ms.* magazine. Initially launched in 1971 as a one-time insert in *New York* magazine, *Ms.* took its name from the sixteenth-century appellation for "mistress." The term was commonly found in secretarial handbooks of the 1950s as suggested usage when it was not known if a woman was married or single. With its groundbreaking articles on topics such as abortion, sexual harassment, and workplace discrimination, *Ms.* would go on to become the leading feminist periodical in the nation. Still in circulation thirty years later, the magazine survived all its critics. Chief among them was then–ABC Evening News anchor Harry Reasoner, who, in on-air comments about the debut of *Ms.*, had jeered: "I'll give it six months before they run out of things to say."

A cofounder of *Ms.* who would achieve international fame for her activism, Gloria Steinem was Alice's immediate ally. However, it was a less publicly celebrated *Ms.* staffer who'd been involved in civil rights struggles while attending college in Jackson who first brought Alice's writing to the attention of the magazine.

"I'd read Alice when I was in Mississippi, so when her story arrived, I was thrilled," remembered Joanne Edgar, a founding editor at *Ms.* who works today as a communications specialist in New York. "We published early Margaret Atwood, early Mary Gordon, early Ursula Le Guin and many other wonderful writers. But Alice's work stood out because it was beautifully written and angry at the same time. There was an edge to her writing that was often missing in other authors."

"Roselily," for which *Ms.* paid Alice about four hundred dollars, is the story of a beleaguered single black mother hoping to escape the hardships of her life in Panther Burn, Mississippi, by marrying a Black Muslim from Chicago. As the couple stand before the preacher on their wedding day, the words of the traditional marriage ceremony ("Dearly beloved, we are gathered here . . .") are interwoven with Roselily's thoughts about the price she is about to pay for financial security and social acceptance ("She thinks of ropes, chains, handcuffs, his religion").

Her sense of unease rising, Roselily begins to think of her mother and other dead relatives for whom she still grieves ("She thinks of cemeteries and the long sleep of grandparents mingling in the dirt. She believes that she believes in ghosts. In the soil giving back what it takes"). But despite her reservations, Roselily remains outwardly silent and resigns herself to whatever unfolds. ("She wants to live for once. But doesn't know quite what that means. Wonders if she has ever done it").

Underscoring the volume's focus on the black woman's quest for wholeness, "Roselily" would open Alice's debut short-story collection, *In Love & Trouble*. Like *Revolutionary Petunias*, the book showcasing thirteen black women Alice characterized as "mad, raging, loving, resentful, hateful, strong, ugly, weak, pitiful and magnificent" had been completed while she was at Radcliffe. Both would be published in 1973.

Bringing in advances of $750 and $1,500, respectively, *Revolutionary Petunias* and *In Love & Trouble* also garnered Alice a rush of accolades and awards. Writing in the *Christian Science Monitor*, June Goodwin noted the universality of the short-story collection Alice introduced to readers with excerpts from two works that echoed her concerns. Taken from *The Concubine* by Elechi Amadi, the first recounted the anguish of an African girl whose parents promised her in marriage when she was eight days old. In a nod to Alice's future focus on female genital mutilation, the excerpt read, in part, "Ahurole had unconsciously been looking for a chance to cry. For the past year or so her frequent unprovoked sobbing had disturbed her mother. When asked why she cried, she either sobbed the more or tried to quarrel with everybody else."

Next came a passage from *Letters to a Young Poet* (1934) by Rainer Maria Rilke.

People have (with the help of conventions) oriented all their solutions toward the easy and toward the easiest side of the easy; but it is clear that we must hold on to what is difficult; everything in Nature grows and defends itself in its own way and is characteristically and spontaneously itself, seeks at all costs to be so and against all opposition.

Goodwin also hailed the specificity of character, setting, description, and dialogue in such stories as "The Welcome Table," in which Alice offered a vivid portrait of the black woman rejected by white "Christians": "She was angular and lean as the color of poor gray Georgia earth, beaten by king cotton and the extreme weather. . . . On her face centuries were folded into the circles around one eye, while around the other, etched and mapped as if for print, ages more threatened to live again."

"Somewhere in growing up, [Walker] learned to watch people,

to put in words what must have been their wordless hopes and ago-
nies," Goodwin exclaimed.

As she had in "Roselily," Alice examined the divided loyalties of
black women in "Really, *Doesn't* Crime Pay?" The protagonist is
Myrna, an aspiring writer whose husband Ruel ("I think of the song
'Rule Britannia' ") scorns her artistry: "No wife of mine is going to
embarrass me with a lot of foolish, vulgar stuff," he sneers. In an
innovative storytelling device (by 1973 standards), Alice unveils the
saga through Myrna's journal entries. For a white literary establishment distanced, historically, from the voices of black women,
Alice's narrative choices broke new ground in form and content.
Readers learn that Myrna, in her isolation, welcomes the friendship
of Mordecai Rich, himself a writer who engages her in provocative
conversation about culture and art.

Uplifted by Mordecai's admiration of her writing ("You could
be another Simone de Beauvoir!") and the dazzle he brings to her
otherwise dreary existence, Myrna goes to bed with him. "How
else could I repay him?," she confides to her journal. Mordecai
answers by stealing one of her prized story ideas and publishing it
as his own.

Betrayed, Myrna suffers a mental collapse and abandons her
dreams of writing. Instead, scribbling in her journal, she details her
shopping extravaganzas and obsessive indulgences in fragrant
lotions and perfume. "I wait, beautiful and perfect in every limb,
cooking supper as if my life depended on it." Eager to start a family, Ruel is thrilled to now have a wife who'll concern herself only
with his needs and "the pitter-patter of sweet little feet." Docile and
obliging, Myrna offers no resistance when, nightly, he climbs on her
"with his slobber and his hope."

Read as parable, "Really, *Doesn't* Crime Pay?" is reminiscent of
"Good Country People," the Flannery O'Connor story about a
scheming Bible salesman who steals the artificial leg of an educated
white woman disenchanted with farm life. But where O'Connor
leaves her protagonist in a hay loft, pleading, "Give me my leg!," as
the ruthless salesman tosses it into his valise, Alice crafts a different
outcome for Myrna, who, writing in a final journal entry, reveals a

master plan: "I intend to do nothing but say yes until [Ruel] is completely exhausted. . . . When he is quite, quite tired of me I will tell him how long I've relied on the security of the Pill. When I am quite, quite tired of the sweet, sweet smell of my body and the softness of these Helena Rubenstein hands I will leave him and this house. Leave them forever without once looking back."

The perfectly pitched saga of a poor country woman who comes to see her reflection in the magnificence of her homemade quilts, "Everyday Use" would be celebrated as one of Alice's most anthologized stories. Infused with the childhood memories that Alice said gave rise to her poem "For My Sister Molly," the story turns on the tensions between Mrs. Johnson and her daughter Dee, who, disdainful of her roots, has rejected her "slave name" for the fashionably Afrocentric, Wangero Leewanika Kemanjo.

Accompanied by her Muslim boyfriend (given to serpentine "soul" hand shake and incessant "Asalamalakim"), Dee one day visits her mother and younger sister Maggie in the rustic cabin where, to Dee's abiding disgust, they still "choose to live." Dee abhors as "backward" the lifestyle Mrs. Johnson and Maggie (badly scarred in a fire) cherish for its naturalness and simplicity. Alice writes:

> I will wait for her [Dee] in the yard that Maggie and I made so clean and wavy. . . . A yard like this is more comfortable than most people know. It is not just a yard. It is like an extended living room. When the hard clay is swept clean as a floor . . . anyone can come and sit and look up into the elm tree and wait for the breezes that never come inside the house.

Still, Mrs. Johnson finds herself shaken ("I never had an education") by Dee's stinging rebukes. Evocative of Minnie Lou Walker's soap opera–inspired musings, Mrs. Johnson dreams of an appearance on a television show (i.e., the 1950s-era *Queen for a Day*), during which she is honored for her sacrifices and transformed into the sophisticated woman "my daughter would want me to be." In this vision, Dee showers affection on her mother and pins on her dress a large orchid, even though, Mrs. Johnson confesses, "she has told me . . . orchids are tacky flowers."

It is only after Dee—her condescension trumped by covetousness—stakes claim to two handmade quilts her mother has promised to Maggie ("chin on chest, eyes on ground") that Mrs. Johnson fully embraces the artfulness of her life. For it is Maggie, ashamed of her burn scars but attuned to *inner* beauty, who helps her mother recognize the precious history of the Lone Star and Walk Around the Mountain heirloom quilts. Then in a powerfully poignant plot twist, Maggie quietly announces that she need not *own* the quilts ("[Dee] can have them, Mama") to treasure their value. And thus does she free her mother from a hurtful and disempowering bond with Dee, who, ever disparaging of her family's "uncouth" behavior, had bemoaned the quilts being put to "everyday use." Here, Alice describes Mrs. Johnson's response to her youngest daughter's magnanimity:

> She stood there with her scarred hands hidden in the folds of her skirt. . . . This was Maggie's portion. This was the way she knew God to work. . . . When I looked at her like that something hit me in the top of my head and ran down to the soles of my feet. . . . I snatched the quilts out of Miss Wangero's hands and dumped them into Maggie's lap. . . . After we watched the car dust settle I asked Maggie to bring me a dip of snuff. And then the two of us sat there just enjoying.

In her widely read essay, "The Contrary Women of Alice Walker," the black literary scholar Barbara Christian noted that *In Love & Trouble* signaled a dramatic shift in black writing. For even in their "defeat," Christian argued, such characters as Myrna, Maggie, Roselily, and Rannie Toomer, of "Strong Horse Tea," exhibited an independence and ingenuity that countered prevailing black nationalist images of obedient and *unthinking* black women in blind submission to external forces. Whether tricked, trapped, thwarted, confused, exploited, or denigrated, the women held fast to self-ennobling ideals of liberation.

"Focal to Walker's presentation is the point of view of . . . women who must act out their lives in the web of conventions," Christian maintained. "Her women are not presented through a perceptive male narrator, but through the private voices of *their* imaginations or through their dearly paid for words and acts.

"What [Walker] does is interpret contrariness as healthy, as an attempt to be whole rather than a defect of nature or as nonexistent," she continued. "And in exposing the contrariness, in demonstrating its appropriateness, she assesses the false paths of escape from psychic violence—those easy conventions we are wont to see as solutions."

That black women had strong feminist traditions unrecognized in anthems like Helen Reddy's 1972 smash hit "I Am Woman" ("Hear me roar") was at the center of *Revolutionary Petunias* (winner of the Lillian Smith Award from the Southern Regional Council). Alice's stance is clear in the poem "Women," featured in a section of the volume titled "In These Dissenting Times."

> *They were women then*
> *My mama's generation*
> *Husky of voice—Stout of*
> *Step*
> *With fists as well as*
> *Hands*
> *How they battered down*
> *Doors . . .*
> *How they led*
> *Armies*
> *Headragged Generals*
> *Across mined*
> *Fields*
> *Booby-trapped*
> *Ditches*
> *To discover books*
> *Desks*
> *A place for us*

> *How they knew what we*
> Must *know*
> *Without knowing a page*
> *Of it*
> *Themselves.*

In a review of *Revolutionary Petunias* for the *College Language Association Journal*, Tougaloo professor Jerry Ward praised Alice's purposeful engagement with a heritage many black writers of the era had derided as a throwback to a humiliating agrarian past. "What especially recommends this volume . . . is Miss Walker's sensitive and intelligent use of black Southern roots," wrote Ward, who had been apprised of Alice's talents by Muriel Rukeyser. "It is a sure understanding of how to apply ancestral wisdom that informs these precise, lucid and skillfully crafted poems. The promising seeds she planted in *Once* have blossomed into poems of extraordinary grace, wisdom and strength."

Publishers Weekly ventured that Alice had established her place in literature with a collection that included such poems as "Perfection."

> *Having reached perfection*
> *As you have*
> *there no longer exists*
> *the need for love.*
> *Love is ablution*
> *the dirtied is due*
> *the sinner can*
> *use.*

"This is poetry of total purity, lean of line, direct and forceful," the magazine proclaimed.

The *Library Journal* had deemed "uneven" some of the stories in *In Love & Trouble*. Offering tempered praise for *Revolutionary Petunias*, the unapologetically nationalist *Black World* (formerly *Negro Digest*), slammed the second half of the collection as an indictment against black radical activities of the 1960s. For Alice, who'd come to view her work, increasingly, as gifts to ancestral spirits, "professional" assessments—good, bad, or indifferent— were less significant than her *human* development as an artist and activist. "One of the functions of art really is to help you grow, to help you become whole, and to help you become a better person," she'd later muse.

With spiritual growth her driving motivation, Alice was heartened by the response to her new work from such early influences as Jane Cooper. Still struggling to get more of her writing published, Cooper had been stunned, upon receiving an advance copy of *In Love & Trouble*, to find her name among those on the dedication page. In a letter dated October 7, 1973, she shared her response:

> It is a wonderful book. Each work of yours . . . seems to me more moving, as your writing matures, deepens, as the grief opens bottomlessly through the violence and the humor achieves a higher and wilder kind of freedom. . . . All the stories share the desperation for justice that is so blazingly (meaning warmly and powerfully) a part of you. . . . Your gift of the dedication is very great—part of a long generosity of black people toward white that is enough to confound any white person who stops to think about it. . . . Reading your book made me think of [my work] in a different way. What a lot of obstacles I've let anxiety and genteel upbringing put in my way as a writer, when the problems I've had to contend with are just nothing compared to what most people have.

In Love & Trouble would also resonate with another writer. But for this one, well, gentility was not a burden, decorum definitely not a concern. And as for productivity, this author had published more than a dozen novels before writing the diaries (seven volumes) that would bring her international fame—or infamy, in the minds of some. Not long after the release of her collection, Alice received a missive penned in purple ink. It read:

Dear Alice Walker:

This is my only fan letter in years—I love your short stories, was very moved by content and beautiful writing—"In Love and in Trouble" [*sic*]—My editor John Ferrone of Harcourt gave them to me too late to comment on them but if ever you need praise from me write me. I respect admire and love you.

Anais Nin

28

Good Night, Willie Lee

HE HAD stood, with his hat in his hand, and watched as his youngest child left for college on a segregated bus. And thanks to her efforts and that of countless other freedom fighters, Willie Lee Walker had lived to see conditions improve for blacks in the South in ways he could never have imagined. But by 1973, the years of poverty and exploitation had taken a toll on a man whose prospects for wholeness had been shattered the day he saw his mother gunned down on a country road. Suffering the complications of emphysema, diabetes, and pneumonia, Willie Lee Walker died on January 26 of that year. He was sixty-three years old.

"I couldn't understand why my father, who'd struggled twenty years to become a man, another twenty raising a family, and then another twenty being sick, would get a few more years and then just die," remembered Jimmy Walker. "I couldn't fathom the purpose of him suffering through all that he did, seemingly, for nothing. I finally came to realize that God has *His* purpose and those of us left behind must have faith in the greater plan."

The damage he'd suffered was deep, unexamined, and irrevocable, but Mr. Walker had not died without obtaining a sense of resolution, if not total peace about his mother's violent death. According to Ruth, in the early 1940s, some twenty years after the incident, a lawman appeared at the Walker's home in Wards Chapel. She said the officer inquired after Mr. Walker, who was working in the cotton fields.

"I was playing out beside the house where Alice would be born when the sheriff walked up and asked me where Daddy was," remembered Ruth, noting that she was about five at the time. "I was scared to death because I thought Daddy had done something.

"Well, it turned out they'd caught the man who murdered Mama Kate," Ruth continued. "Seeing as Daddy was the only eyewitness, the sheriff took my father to town to identify him. And then they put the man on trial and he went to prison."

Ruth said she couldn't recall the sentence served by the alleged assailant, and no court records can be found. However, she is firm in her memory of a conversation she had with her father, who told her that the men crossed paths, at a neighbor's house, after the man was paroled.

She remembered, "All those years my Daddy had hated this man's guts and there he was as free as a bird. Daddy told me that he wasn't eager to talk. But the man tried to make him understand that he'd loved Mama Kate and it hadn't been in his mind to shoot her, let alone kill her. He told Daddy that he'd regretted, every day of his life, what he'd done. Daddy had always thought he'd want to kill the man if he had a chance. Instead, Daddy said that he looked at the man's hands and they were so lumpy and roiled from arthritis that he felt sorry for him and just walked away."

It would take Alice years to reconcile the death of a man she loved, but battled, primarily because of his unyielding embrace of traditional sex roles. Over time, she would also understand that the Walker children had essentially been raised by two different fathers: Fred, Mamie, Bill, and Jimmy by a man who, while burdened, still had energy and a zest for life that burned bright from his soulful brown eyes. With the arrival of Ruth, Bobby, Curtis, and Alice, any vitality that might have remained in Mr. Walker had been crushed by racism, poor health, and the soul-murdering insult of three hundred dollars for 365 days of back-breaking toil. By contrast, Alice would soon come to pay each year, in taxes, more money than both her parents earned in their entire lives.

"Whenever I talk to the elder set I am astonished at the picture they draw, for the man they describe bears little resemblance to the man I knew," Alice would later write about her father. "The man I knew was almost always sick . . . but with so many children to feed he couldn't afford to lie down. . . . In his whole life my father never had a vacation."

Not surprisingly, Mr. Walker had never "overcome" the trauma of witnessing the murder of his mother, nor his father's rushed and begrudging remarriage to Miss Rachel. Crazed by grief and anger, the adult Willie Lee Walker found a ready target in his daughter Ruth, who spoke with the same inflection as Kate Walker and resembled her physically. When the teenaged Ruth showed an interest in boys, Mr. Walker, transported, mentally, to the bloody aftermath of his mother's romance, beat and locked her in a room. He threatened to disown Ruth if she ever became pregnant. At the same time, Willie Lee Walker encouraged all of his sons to experiment with sex. The more *women*, the better. His credo: "Like bulls, a man *needs* to get a little something on his stick."

Drawn into her father's frequent clashes with Ruth, Alice defended the sister who had smothered her with kisses, sewn her stunning scallop-hemmed dresses, and plaited, to beauty shop perfection, her hair. "I never wanted to be at odds with my father, but I have felt, especially when I was younger, that he gave me no choice," Alice would later note. "Perhaps if I could have relaxed and been content to be his favorite, there would have been a chance for closeness, but because a sister whom I loved was clearly not favorite material, I did not want to be, either."

Remembered Ruth: "Alice always stuck up for me," the painful memories giving rise to an uncharacteristic sadness in her voice. At the same time, Ruth was not unmindful of the complexity of her father's outbursts. "When relatives would come visit us from up North, or even Macon, they'd be bragging about their houses and cars and how much money they had in the bank. My father would say, 'Well, all I have is my children.' And he would say the words with such pride and it made us feel good. Because the relatives would tease my mother about her having married a black dirt farmer who'd never be anything except a sharecropper and a dairy man."

In a *Life* magazine interview, Alice elaborated on her father's dramatic mood swings and the discord his behavior brought to the Walker household: "I couldn't stand it. . . . But what I didn't understand (until years later) is that he didn't know why he was acting this way. That's why I love therapy and counseling and talking and all those things. Because they do help you understand your patterns."

Alice had explored the tensions in a father-daughter relationship in "The Child Who Favored Daughter," which appears in *In Love & Trouble*. The protagonist in the graphic tale is a black man with an obsessive love for his sister, a woman who is destroyed by her love affair with a white man. Unable (in the tradition of Grange and Brownfield Copeland) to direct his ire at its true source, the man develops a seething hatred of all women, including his daughter, whom he discovers has also "given herself to the lord of his own bondage." The father confronts his daughter and demands that she deny the white lover he has learned of by reading her mail. When she refuses, he lashes out in a frenzy of rage and repressed desire that he quells by slicing off her breasts and flinging the flesh "to the yelping dogs."

In *Black Women Writers at Work*, Alice would speak candidly about the story's origins in her liaison with David DeMoss. "I wrote [the story] out of trying to understand how a black father would feel about a daughter who fell in love with a white man. This was very apropos because I had just come out of a [relationship] with a young man who was white, and my father never accepted him. I did not take his nonacceptance lightly. . . . I needed to comprehend what was going on with him and what would go on in any black man of his generation brought up in the South . . . whose child fell in love with . . . 'the enemy.' "

While Mr. Walker never expressed any direct opposition to

Alice's subsequent marriage to Mel, her rebelliousness and refusal to conform to societal expectations for women would always confound him. If he'd read *Once, The Third Life of Grange Copeland*, or "To Hell with Dying," he never offered a word of praise or condemnation to his daughter. "I am positive my father never understood why I wrote," Alice would later recall. "It is frustrating, because I will never know."

Impaired by the circumstances of his life, Willie Lee Walker may not have ever fully *seen* his daughter, but he nonetheless bequeathed gifts to her as valuable as the typewriter, sewing machine, and suitcase Mrs. Walker had given to Alice when she left home for Spelman. In addition to an abiding passion for oysters (Willie Lee Walker, averse to the kitchen, still made a delectable oyster stew), Alice would share her father's love of nature, of naturalness, and of absolute abhorrence of lies, "because the listener might be delighted with the truth."

Indeed, he'd impressed upon her the benefits of truth telling when Alice was about five years old and had accidentally broken a fruit jar. She believed her father knew she was the culprit, but wasn't certain and therefore considered "bluffing her way through" to avoid a probable whipping.

About the incident, she would later write, "I've never forgotten my feeling that he really wanted me to tell the truth. And because he seemed to desire it . . . I confessed. . . . So embraced did I feel by the happy relief I noted on his face and by the fact that he didn't punish me at all, but seemed, instead, pleased with me. I think it was at that moment that I resolved to take my chances with the truth, although as the years rolled on I was to break more serious things in his scheme of things than fruit jars."

Cowed by the threat of *their* punishment, Alice would, however, lose sight of her father's lesson the day she covered for Bobby and Curtis, falsely claiming that her eye had been poked by a wire. It was an abdication of self she would be disinclined to repeat.

At her father's funeral service, Alice stood beside her mother as Mrs. Walker viewed her husband, in an open casket, at eternal repose. "Good night, Willie Lee, I'll see you in the morning," Alice overheard her mother say, "without smiles, without tears, without regrets." "It was then that I knew that the healing of all our wounds is forgiveness," Alice would later write in a title poem that graced a volume, dedicated, in part, to the memory of Willie Lee Walker's shining eyes.

29

We Are a People

IN A brief preface to *Revolutionary Petunias*, Alice noted that the volume was inspired by "those few embattled souls who remain painfully committed to beauty and to love even while facing the firing squad."

The distinctive title of the collection paid tribute to Alice's mother and her practice of brightening whatever inelegant sharecropper's cabin the family found themselves in by planting petunias (in addition to all her other flowers) in the front yard. Mrs. Walker had started the tradition years before Alice was born when one day she and Mr. Walker, traveling by horse and wagon, passed a deserted house where there remained a single lavender petunia poking up from the ground. Charmed by the flower's tenacity and splendor, Mrs. Walker took it home and planted it in a big stump in her yard. Every time the family moved, Mrs. Walker would gather up the petunia cluster, replant it, and watch with pride as it inevitably bloomed in each new setting. When Rebecca was born, more than thirty years after Mrs. Walker had first rescued the petunia, she gave Alice a cutting from the plant, which continued to hold forth in riotous glory.

Comparing the people she honored in her new poetry collection to the petunia, Alice later explained, "It . . . never died. Each winter [the flower] lay dormant and dead-looking, but each spring it came back, livelier than before. In a way, the whole book is a celebration of people who will not cram themselves into any ideological or racial mold. . . . Because of this they are made to suffer. They are told that they do not belong, that they are not wanted, that their art is not needed. . . . Their answer is resistance."

She then offered the poem "Be Nobody's Darling" as an example of the sentiments she wished to convey.

> *Be nobody's darling;*
> *Be an outcast.*
> *Take the contradictions*
> *Of your life*
> *And wrap around*
> *You like a shawl,*
> *To parry stones*
> *To keep you warm.*
>
> *Watch the people succumb*
> *To madness*
> *With ample cheer;*
> *Let them look askance at you*
> *And you askance reply.*
>
> *Be an outcast;*
> *Be pleased to walk alone*
> *(Uncool)*
> *Or line the crowded*
> *River beds*
> *With other impetuous*
> *Fools.*
>
> *Make a merry gathering*
> *On the bank*

Where thousands perished
For brave hurt words
They said.

Be nobody's darling;
Be an outcast.
Qualified to live
Among your dead.

On August 15, 1973, spurred by her love for a "revolutionary petunia" who had died in obscurity, Alice traveled to Florida to place a headstone on the unmarked grave of Zora Neale Hurston. The act would, in effect, symbolize the culmination of her writing residency at Radcliffe, which had ended a month before. "The Revenge of Hannah Kemhuff," the Hurston-inspired tale dealing with voodoo, was among the stories Alice had completed while in Cambridge.

As Alice notes in her essay "Saving the Life That Is Your Own," the story is a reckoning of Mrs. Walker's humiliating Depression-era encounter with the white relief worker who denied her request for food supplies. In Alice's recasting, Mrs. Kemhuff, shamed after a similar incident, seeks solace from Tante Rosie, a rootworker she hires to put a hex on Mrs. Holley, the white woman who has dressed her down.

In the voice of Mrs. Kemhuff, Alice writes, "My spirit never recovered from that insult. . . . I dream and have nightmares still about the little moppet, and always I feel the moment when my spirit was trampled . . . within me while they all stood and laughed and she stood there grinning behind her hands."

Assisted by an apprentice who narrates the story (read: Alice), Tante Rosie concocts a spell for Mrs. Holley that includes a lengthy curse-prayer ("O great One, I have been sorely tried by my enemies . . . I pray that the moon shall not give them peace"). Mrs. Holley learns of the voodoo plot against her, but, ever defiant, brays that she's "not afraid of nigger magic." However, she becomes increasingly unnerved by the very *thought* of Tante

Rosie's powers and then frantic, worrying herself to a sordid and agonizing death.

Alice dedicated "The Revenge of Hannah Kemhuff" to Zora Neale Hurston, having noted, in the text of the story, that the curse-prayer was taken, in total, from *Mules and Men*. "Had [the collection] been lost, my mother's story would have had no historical underpinning, none I could trust, anyway," Alice explained in "Saving the Life That Is Your Own." "I would not have written the story, which I enjoyed as much as I've enjoyed writing anything in my life, had I not known that Zora had already done a thorough job of preparing the ground over which I was then moving."

Alice would later recall that it was Margaret Walker who, in the late 1960s, first made mention to her of Zora Neale Hurston. But more admiring of such writers as Richard Wright, whose graphically rendered *Native Son* (1940) skyrocketed to best-seller charts, Walker presented the pioneering author-anthropologist as "little more than a literary footnote," Alice remembered. It didn't surprise Alice that Walker—of an era when black male authors overshadowed the artistry of black women writers—appeared to hold Wright in more esteem than Hurston. Margaret Walker had also been a close friend of Wright and in 1988 would publish a controversial biography, *Richard Wright: Daemonic Genius*, in which she claimed a pivotal role in the crafting of *Native Son*.

That Margaret Walker had given short shrift to the writer who'd thought self-assuredly of herself as the "cosmic Zora" did not, however, prevent Hurston from making her presence known. She used other tactics to reach Alice. For at about the same time, another of Alice's friends in Jackson, Frankie Walton White, alerted her to Hurston's triumphant 1937 novel, *Their Eyes Were Watching God*. The first black woman lawyer to join the staff of the Mississippi attorney general, White had read the book while a student at Tougaloo. She'd met Alice and Mel through the "movement circuit" shortly after they arrived in town.

"What made me gravitate to Alice was that, like me, she'd been reared on the land and brought that sensitivity to her writing," White remembered. "I'd taught literature before studying law, so

Alice and I were always talking about our favorite books. One day, I was just raving about *Their Eyes* . . . , which Alice said she'd never read."

Not long after White's prompting, Alice discovered that Hurston had been staring her in the face (arms crossed, toes tapping) for several years. As it happened, Langston Hughes had also included the writer's 1933 release, "The Gilded Six-Bits," in *The Best Short Stories by Negro Writers* collection in which "To Hell with Dying" had appeared. Hurston's poignant tale centers on an unexpected breach in the union of Missie May ("If you burn me, you won't git a thing but wife ashes") and her husband Joe ("Ah'd ruther all de other womens in de world to be dead for you to have de toothache"). Hurston's story was right there on page seventy-four of the anthology.

"So, as early as 1967, I'd seen Zora's name," Alice said. "But I didn't even read Zora's story. Or if I did read it, it meant little. It wasn't until Frankie told me about *Their Eyes Were Watching God* and I read it that I fell in love with Hurston."

The woman whose life and literature bedazzled Alice ("there is no book more important to me," she'd later exult about the novel) had been born January 7, 1891, in Alabama and moved with her family to Eatonville, Florida, by age five. Located on the outskirts of Orlando, Eatonville was one of the first incorporated all-black towns in the United States. Hurston, whose father served as a mayor of the industrious village, would later write of the love she found in a community of "five lakes, three croquet courts, three hundred brown skins, three hundred good swimmers, plenty guavas, two schools and no jail house."

She'd elaborate on her childhood in her 1942 autobiography, *Dust Tracks on a Road*:

> We had a five-acre garden . . . so we were never hungry. We had chicken on the table often; home-cured meat, and all the eggs we wanted. . . . There were eight children in the family, and our house was noisy from the time school turned out until bedtime. After supper we gathered in Mama's room, and everybody did

their lessons for the next day. . . . How I hated the multiplica-
tion tables—especially the sevens! . . . Mama contended that
we had plenty of space to play in . . . plenty of us to keep each
other company. . . . She said there was no point for us to live
like no-count Negroes and poor-white trash. . . . Things like
that gave me my first glimmering of the universal female gospel
that all good traits and leanings come from the mother's side.

But Hurston's idyllic youth was shattered following the death of
her mother when the quick-witted and independent girl was about
thirteen. After being passed from one relative to another, she soon
set out on her own, taking menial jobs for survival. Ever mindful of
her mother's directive to "jump at the sun," Hurston was determined to complete her education and eventually earned degrees
from Howard University and Barnard College. While at Barnard,
she studied with the renowned anthropologist Franz Boas, who
affirmed her gifts as a writer and encouraged her interest in African
American folklore.

In 1935, Hurston published *Mules and Men*, the collection of
folktales Alice consulted while writing "The Revenge of Hannah
Kemhuff." "Here was this perfect book!" Alice would later exclaim
about the treasury of tall tales, work songs, fables, and conjure rituals. For example, in the section "Formulae of Hoodoo Doctors,"
Hurston offered a remedy for "Court Scrapes": "Take the names of
the opponent of your client, his witnesses and his lawyer. Take all
their names on one piece of paper. Put it between two whole bricks.
Put the top brick crossways. On the day of the trial set a bucket or
dishpan on top of the bricks with ice in it. That's to freeze them out
so they can't talk." As such, the book's relevance for her story was
not difficult for Alice to discern. Alice was also pleased to note that
both she and Zora had grown up in farm families of eight children
and that their respective hometowns (Eatonton/Eatonville) had
nearly identical names.

Alice's delight with *Mules and Men* was only surpassed by her
adoration of *Their Eyes Were Watching God*. Written in seven
weeks while Hurston was on a research trip in Haiti, the 1937 novel

tells the story of Janie Crawford, a black woman on a personal quest for love and self-knowledge. After failed marriages with men who undermined her desire to blossom like "a pear tree in the spring," Janie finds a soul mate in Tea Cake Woods, who, in asking only that she be herself, fulfills her dreams for an equal and honest relationship.

Throughout the novel, Hurston celebrates the richness of black folk language. In an exchange during which the local menfolk discuss their "God-given right to beat women," Janie immediately counters: "Sometimes God gits familiar wid us womenfolks too and talks His inside business. He told me how surprised . . . y'all is goin' tuh be if you ever find out you don't know half as much 'bout us as you think you do. It's so easy to make yo'self out God Almighty when you ain't got nothin' tuh strain against but women and chickens."

Describing the novel's impact on her, Alice would later write,

> Reading *Their Eyes* for perhaps the eleventh time, I am still amazed . . . that it speaks to me as no novel, past or present, has ever done; and that the language of the characters, that "comical nigger 'dialect' " that has been laughed at, denied, ignored, or 'improved' so that white folks and educated black folks can understand it, is simply beautiful. There is enough self-love in that one book—love of community, culture, traditions—to restore a world. Or create a new one.

Their Eyes was generally well received by white critics, including a reviewer for the *New York Times* who declared it "a well nigh perfect story." But the leading black literary figures of the day were not impressed. Most influential among them was Richard Wright, who, in a review for *New Masses*, assailed the novel for its "minstrel technique," adding, in a damning dismissal, that *Their Eyes* carried "no theme, no message, no thought." Ironically, writing a few years later, Wright would shower a torrent of praise on *The Heart Is a Lonely Hunter*, the 1940 debut novel by Carson McCullers.

"To me the most impressive aspect . . . is the astonishing

humanity that enables a white writer, for the first time in Southern fiction, to handle Negro characters with as much ease and justice as those of her own race," Wright raved in the August 5, 1940, issue of the *New Republic*. According to Margaret Walker, he had expressed similar enthusiasm for the Gertrude Stein work *Three Lives* (1909), hailing her portrait of a title character, Melanctha ("a graceful, pale yellow, intelligent, attractive negress").

Lacking the resources that cushioned writers such as Stein and McCullers (to say nothing of their *whiteness*), Hurston pressed on and in February 1943 became the first black author to appear on the cover of the *Saturday Review*. But giving lie to the myth of "the strong black woman" who can withstand any burden, Hurston was ultimately vanquished by a series of crises. Betrayed by friends and rejected by publishers who scorned her later work, she lost faith. Perhaps most debilitating to her spirit was a false child molestation charge leveled against her by an acquaintance. "I have resolved to die," lamented a crushed Hurston, who was (irrefutably) in Honduras on the date of the alleged incident.

Never able to regain her stride, at the time of her death on January 28, 1960, Hurston's seven books were out of print, her pioneering research on black folklore largely forgotten. With no estate to cover funeral costs, donations had to be solicited to bury the sixty-nine-year-old writer in a segregated cemetery in Fort Pierce, Florida.

IN A short introduction to a 1971 edition of *Dust Tracks on a Road*, Black Arts writer Larry Neal would provide a cursory overview of Hurston's life. A year later, Alice learned of Hurston's fate in "Zora Neale Hurston and the Eatonville Anthropology," an essay by white scholar Robert Hemenway that appeared in *The Harlem Renaissance Remembered*, a 1972 collection edited by Arna Bontemps. "[Hemenway] was the first critic I read who seemed indignant that Zora's life ended in poverty and obscurity," Alice would later write. "It was [his] efforts to define Zora's legacy and his exploration of her life that led me . . . to an overgrown graveyard in an attempt to locate and mark Zora's grave."

Alice's commitment to restoring Hurston to her glory was also fueled by the chilling knowledge that her own life and art could one day just as easily be "consigned to a sneering oblivion." Like Hurston, Alice had detractors who disapproved of her artistic choices and found fault with her refusal to conform (read: marriage to Mel). Despite her published work, Alice was still a young writer, understandably vulnerable to self-doubt. She could not help but wonder what might happen if she, too, embraced Hurston's zeal and lived "more like an uncolonized African than . . . contemporary American blacks."

"After reading the misleading, deliberately belittling, inaccurate, and generally irresponsible attacks on [Hurston's] work and her life by almost everyone, I became for a time paralyzed with confusion and fear," Alice later wrote. "Would I also be attacked if I wrote and spoke my mind? And if I dared open my mouth to speak, must I always be 'correct'? And by whose standard?"

Born of a mother who stood up to white landowners for the sake of her children's education and a father who braved segregationists to vote, Alice would ultimately resolve to face her fears squarely. The standards she would live by would be her own. "I began to fight for Zora and her work; for what I knew was good and must not be lost," Alice later explained.

TODAY, VISITORS to the Garden of the Heavenly Rest will find a well-manicured cemetery in a struggling but earnest black community in Fort Pierce (about seventy miles north of Palm Beach). As one enters the grounds through the arched gates on Seventeenth Street, Hurston's headstone, framed by an arbor of evergreen, commands the landscape. But on the sweltering day when Alice first visited the site, it was choked with waist-high brambles and weeds. Following the crude map she'd been given by the mortuary that oversaw Hurston's funeral arrangements ("there's a circle, she's buried right in the middle of it"), Alice made her way through the tangle of brush. But finding *any* grave in the wild morass masquerading as a cemetery was a challenge, and Hurston's lacked a headstone. Frustrated, Alice finally called out Hurston's name for "divine help." She moved forward and promptly found herself standing in a sunken rectangle "about six feet long and about three or four feet wide." Paying heed to the diagram, but more importantly, to her intuition and respect for ancestral spirits, Alice was confident that she'd found the final resting place of Zora Neale Hurston. She marked the location and, fending off swarms of insects and sandspurs, marched back through the brush to buy a memorial plaque.

Unable to afford the majestic black headstone ("Ebony Mist") that she felt best reflected Hurston's achievements, Alice instead chose a plain gray marker, for which she paid about $250. For the inscription, she selected "A Genius of the South," from the poem "Georgia Dusk" in Jean Toomer's *Cane*. Beneath that, she directed the engraver to carve "Novelist. Folklorist. Anthropologist."—testaments to Hurston's genius in each realm. "It was what I could do, and what I could do was just what was required," Alice later remarked about an effort she considered "neither grand nor historic. . . . The profit was love."

Alice would provide an elaborate account of her pilgrimage in the essay "In Search of Zora Neale Hurston," first published in *Ms.* magazine (and reprinted as "Looking for Zora" in *In Search of Our Mothers' Gardens*). Just as she'd had been inspired by *Mules and Men*, millions of readers would discover Hurston through Alice's reclamation of her life and art.

Superbly crafted, the essay includes fragments of Alice's conversations with black community elders who had known Hurston before her decline. Not wanting to "inspire foot-dragging" in people with information they might have been reluctant to reveal to a stranger, Alice had arrived in Florida armed, as she noted, with a "profoundly *useful*" lie. Alice had reasoned that her "tall tale" was not likely to offend Hurston's daring spirit. To wit, she identified herself, throughout the expedition, as "Zora's niece."

"The lie comes with perfect naturalness to my lips," Alice confesses in the piece. "Besides, as far as I'm concerned, she *is* my aunt—and that of all black people as well."

Thus embraced by the elders, Alice introduces readers to a cast of Hurston's past acquaintances such as Dr. Benton and Mathilda Moseley. At age eighty-two, Alice notes in the essay, Mrs. Moseley is "a neat old lady in a purple dress," zoomin', as Aretha Franklin might have put it, behind the wheel of a vintage black-and-white Buick sedan. "I like her because she stands there *straight* beside her car," Alice writes. "With a hand on her hip and her straw pocketbook on her arm. She wears white T-strap shoes with heels that show off her well-shaped legs."

Mrs. Moseley shares memories of Hungerford, the all-black school that she and Hurston attended. "It *was* only to the eighth grade," she tells Alice, in the essay. "But our teachers were so good that by the time you left you knew college subjects. When I went to [college], the teachers there were just teaching me the same things I had already learned."

Moseley's response gives Alice perspective on the stance Hurston had taken against integration. During civil rights struggles of the 1950s, it was a position for which she'd been vehemently criticized. "I think of the letter [NAACP leader] Roy Wilkins wrote to a black newspaper blasting Zora Neale for her lack of enthusiasm about the integration of schools," Alice notes in the essay. "I wonder if he knew the experience of Eatonville she was coming from. Not many black people in America have come from a self-contained, all-black community where loyalty and unity are taken for granted. A place where black pride is nothing new."

Alice writes that Dr. Benton is "one of those old, good-looking men whom I always have trouble not liking." Like Moseley, he tells her that he knew Hurston well. " 'She was always studying,'" Dr. Benton remembers. " 'Her mind . . . just worked all the time. She was always going somewhere, too. . . . And although Zora wasn't egotistical, what she thought, she thought; and generally what she thought, she said.' "

AND SO it was that in 1977, when Robert Hemenway published the first book-length study of Hurston (*Zora Neale Hurston: A*

Literary Biography), Alice agreed to write a foreword in which she declared:

> Zora was funny, irreverent (she was the first to call the Harlem Renaissance literati the "niggerati"). . . . She loved to give parties. Loved to dance. Would wrap her head in scarves as black women in Africa, Haiti, and everywhere else have done for centuries. . . . Her critics disliked . . . her apparent sensuality: the way she tended to marry or not marry men, but enjoyed them anyway. . . . They hinted slyly that Zora was gay, or at least bisexual—how else could they account for her drive? The accusation becomes humorous—and of course at all times irrelevant—when one considers that what she *did* write [*Their Eyes Were Watching God*] is one of the sexiest, most "healthily" rendered heterosexual love stories in our literature.

Alice continued:

> Zora was before her time, in intellectual circles, in the life style she chose. . . . In my mind, Zora Neale Hurston, Billie Holiday, and Bessie Smith form a sort of unholy trinity. Zora *belongs* in the tradition of black women singers, rather than among "the literati," at least to me. There were the extreme highs and lows of her life, her undaunted pursuit of adventure, passionate emotional and sexual experience, and her love of freedom. . . . She refused to separate herself from "common" people. . . .
>
> *We are a people. A people do not throw their geniuses away.* And if they are thrown away, it is our duty *as artists and as Witnesses for the future* to collect them again for the sake of our children, and, if necessary, bone by bone.

And with that, Alice lifted Hurston, figuratively, from the grave.

RECOUNTING HER support of his efforts, Hemenway later said, "Alice was so encouraging of me as a white man struggling to write about a black woman. I wondered if I had anything to say, and if so, would it be of any value. She assured me that my voice needed to be heard.

"I had all these disparate facts," he continued, "so one day, when I was talking to Alice, she just honed in and asked, 'Well, what kind of flowers did Zora like?' That simple question changed my entire approach to the biography."

In the aftermath of Alice's *Ms.* essay and her Hemenway foreword, scholarship on Hurston (partial to poppies, azaleas, morning glories, and gardenias) continued to flourish. By the 1990s, experts in black culture and art would proclaim Hurston, subject of nearly thirty books, "the most widely taught black woman writer in the canon of American literature." And in keeping with a woman who dedicated herself to "the Negro farthest down," community leaders in Eatonville initiated a "Zora Festival" that each year draws not only the literati, but multitudes of "common folk" who make a pilgrimage to Florida to honor her life.

Assessing Alice's role in Hurston's elevation, Valerie Boyd, author of *Wrapped in Rainbows: The Life of Zora Neale Hurston* (2003), put it this way: "In placing the marker on Zora's unmarked grave, Alice Walker almost single-handedly started the Hurston revival. No one has done more than Alice to resurrect Zora's memory and celebrate her legacy."

Alice later said that in Hurston she saw a reflection of herself— a black woman who reveled in her roots and who refused to bow down to convention. "Zora and I share a culture that we both knew was larger than its grievances. We both thought black people were hilarious and smart. We thought they were good-looking and sexy. Raunchy and raucous. And it was O.K. with us. Why? Because we knew we were just the same."

FAR LESS known than Alice's part in the resurrection of Hurston is her early championing of another writer: Toni Morrison.

In 1972, Alice had included Morrison's then-out-of-print first

novel, *The Bluest Eye*, in the Black Women Writers course she
taught at Wellesley and later at the University of Massachusetts,
Boston. In 1973, Morrison, then an editor at Random House, published *Sula*, a rich and mournful saga that chronicled the complex
friendship between two black women—one a rebel, the other wed
to tradition.

Writing in the *New York Times* on December 30, 1973, Sara
Blackburn offered a mixed review of *Sula* and then, allowing that it
was a "classically unfair carp," went on to criticize the book's
author for "limiting" her gifts to "the black side of provincial
American life."

"If [Morrison] is to maintain the large and serious audience she
deserves, she is going to have to address a riskier contemporary
reality than this beautiful but nevertheless distanced novel,"
Blackburn declared. "And if she does this, it seems to me that she
might easily transcend that . . . classification 'black women writer'
and take her place among the most serious, important and talented
American novelists now working."

Alice was among the many admirers of Morrison's work. She
read her writings closely and had, in an early exchange with Julius
Lester, recommended *The Bluest Eye*. In a letter dated February 19,
1971, Lester shared his response. "The novel of Toni Morrison's
you mentioned, 'The Bluest Eye,' is so beautiful. I reviewed it for
Life magazine, but they decided the book wasn't important enough
to review. Fools! It's an amazing novel."

Equally impressed with *Sula*, Alice was primed when the *Times*
review appeared. She immediately dispatched a letter that was
excerpted in the January 20, 1974, edition of the paper. "I really
liked the novel, so I had to speak up for it," she recalled. A more
substantive rendering of the letter reads:

Dear Sir,
I am amazed (on many levels) by Sara Blackburn's review of . . .
Sula. Is Ms. Morrison to "transcend" herself? And why should
she and for what? The time has gone forever when black people felt limited by themselves. We realize we are, <u>as ourselves,</u>

unlimited, and our experiences valid. It is for the rest of the world to recognize this if they choose. . . .

It is precisely <u>because</u> Ms. Morrison writes so movingly about the inner lives of young black women (and others) in a setting which Ms. Blackburn calls "provincial" . . . that she has such an impact on everyone who reads her. . . . She invariably tells us things we did not know or recognize before. . . . The people of the mainstream just haven't realized it yet. But then, they are often so late.

Alice mailed a copy of the letter to Morrison who, in a January 1974 reply, thanked her for her support.

Dear Alice Walker:
. . . You said precisely the things I felt only you were able to put them with far more coolness and precision than I could ever have imagined. Thank you very much for your kindness but particularly for your intelligence. Yours was really a splen-did letter.

In 1993, Toni Morrison would be awarded the Nobel Prize for Literature.

30

Changes

THE MISSISSIPPI that Alice returned to in 1973 after her writing residency in Cambridge was far different from the one she and Mel had encountered in 1967 when they moved to the South. Antimiscegenation laws had been struck down, public schools had been integrated, and white supremacists, now fearing prosecution, were less prone to rampages of burning crosses, threatening phone calls, and gun shot blasts they had used to intimidate blacks and their supporters in the struggle for equal rights.

Mel's role in the transformation of Mississippi was monumental. Anyone who doubted the impact of the desegregation cases he won needed only to witness the scenario when Alice, having returned to Jackson, one day met her husband for lunch at a local motel.

"We sat relaxing in the restaurant and as we ate watched a young boy of about fifteen swimming in the [motel's] pool," Alice would later write about her lunch date with Mel. "Unlike the whites of the past, the ones in the pool did not get out. And the boy, when he was good and tired, crawled up alongside the pool, turned on his back, drew up his knees—in his tight trunks—and just lay there, oblivious to the white faces staring down at him from the restaurant windows."

"I thought of the time, when I was a child, when black people were not allowed to use the town pool," she continued, "and the town leaders were too evil to permit the principal of my school to build a pool for blacks *on his own property*."

Heartened though she was by the progress that had been made in the South, Alice was ready to move on. She had responded to the call when Dr. King had exhorted freedom fighters to "Go back to Mississippi; go back to Alabama . . . go back to Georgia . . . knowing that somehow this situation can, and will, be changed." Looking back on her work with voter registration, Head Start teachers, the students at Tougaloo and Jackson State, Alice, age thirty, was satisfied she had made a lasting contribution. In keeping with the saying, "blossom where you are planted," Alice had done precisely that. She now needed fresh water, new soil, a different garden.

While the decision was not unexpected, Alice's insistence on leaving the South was unsettling for Mel. He reveled in his work as a civil rights lawyer, executed it superbly, and had imagined staying in Mississippi indefinitely to help make the state completely free (racially) for his daughter. But Mel knew it was futile to ask his wife (who was now seeing a psychiatrist for depression) to remain in a state where white people, as she later observed, "attacked and murdered our children, called us chimpanzees from their judge's benches," in short, conducted themselves like "the Hitlers of our time."

And Mel could hardly disagree with Alice's assessment of the dismal "arts scene" in Jackson. Admiring of Alice's research and writing on Hurston, Mel had taken an early photo of the anthropologist to a stationery shop and had special notecards with Zora's image made for his wife. "What a sweetie!," Alice remembered. Still, in what would be an enduring source of mystery, if not deep disappointment to her, he never read *Their Eyes Were Watching God*. "It was as if [he] drew a line, in this curious territory," she would later write.

That Mel had reasons (never voiced) for his apparent disinterest in the love that blossomed between Janie Crawford and Tea Cake, Alice was willing to accept. As for her continued residence in the South, well, on that matter, she had drawn a line too.

About the ultimatum she presented to him, Mel later said, "One day Alice told me, 'Mel, it's our marriage or Mississippi. You've got to make up your mind.' Since the marriage was more important, we packed up and left."

Their destination? New York City, where Mel could continue his civil rights litigation in a metropolitan office of the NAACP Legal Defense and Educational Fund. Decades later, daughter Rebecca offered reflections on the changes in her family life: "As a child, I didn't really understand that my parents were different colors. All I knew was that they were doing something important and people wanted to be around them all the time. And everybody believed in my existence as a mixed-race baby. Everything was so much fun. But the transition from the integrationist stance to the militant black power consciousness affected my parents. My father worked so hard only to be told that there was no place for whites in the movement. On a theoretical level, he understood it was important for black people to go through their process and have that moment, but emotionally, it was devastating for him. There were demands on my mother to prove her blackness. Instead of getting the support they needed as a couple to negotiate these issues they did what they had to do to survive. I totally understand their decision and respect it. But I could sense that my father was hurting and that my mother was very sad."

Even in her resolve, Alice did not bid her final farewell to Mississippi until she'd apprised her friends and neighbors of the deep love her heart held for them. Paramount among them was Clotie Graves. To the woman who'd tried to lift her spirits when she was low, she gave the sewing machine her mother had bought her when she left Eatonton for college.

"Here it is," Graves proudly proclaimed, nearly thirty years later, as she set the gleaming sewing machine on her kitchen table. "Needless to say, it is one of my prized possessions."

"I hated to see Alice leave," she continued, with tears welling in her eyes. "But I could feel the pressure on the marriage. Alice was cooped in. Jackson was too small and small-minded for what she needed as a writer."

But decades later, such friends as Margaret Walker would remain unswayed by the argument that Alice needed to broaden her horizons. That Mississippi was oppressive and culturally limited, she would not deny. Still, Alice had written several books while living in Jackson. And Mel had brought segregationists to their knees. Suspicious of the swelling tide of feminism in the North, Walker questioned the sudden (to her) departure of two successful, stalwart civil rights servants from her beloved community.

"I was surprised when I heard from Mel that he and Alice were leaving, because they were both doing so well," Margaret Walker remembered. "I know Mississippi was hard for Alice, but it seemed to become intolerable for her after June Jordan came to visit from New York. Now from what I hear, June is bisexual, so maybe that was part of Alice's problem with this part of the country. We see lesbians every day, but we're not accustomed to bisexuals."

As it happened, Alice did not learn, until years later, that Jordan had once been married to a white man, let alone that she'd had female lovers. "She didn't say a word," Alice maintained. "In retrospect, I don't understand it. At that time in my life, I wasn't even aware that [bisexuality] was possible. I think that if June had made mention of either her marriage or loving women, it would have been very helpful. I could have been a lot freer, earlier. That I know."

Alice would later remember her seven years in Mississippi as "a time of intense friendships, passions, and loves among people who came South (or lived there), and who risked everything to change an oppressive, racist system."

"I became an adult there, to have been in the crux was very important," she continued. "Mel and I made a difference. But we paid a price."

The cost would be evident on her face when, in the late 1980s, during a videotaped interview for the Lannan Foundation Literary Series, Alice recounted her exchange with a white man she'd recently met at a book signing in Washington, D.C. She said that the man, a well-connected resident of Mississippi, queried her as to why she consistently declined speaking invitations that he knew had been extended to her by officials at Ole Miss (the University of Mississippi). " 'We really want you,' " Alice recalled the man saying, in a rush of enthusiasm. A generous lecture fee was understood.

The tape rolling, Alice paused and then with tears streaming down her cheeks, continued, "I told him that it was too painful, that it just hurt. I told him that what I remembered from those [Mississippi] years was one white man after the other saying the exact *opposite* and then backing up [their words] with such incredible violence."

Now reaching for a tissue as she wiped her eyes, Alice noted that "perhaps the lesson" could be taken from the man's response to her anguished memories. She said that with his head hung low, the man looked back at her "with real feeling," and replied, "I'm so sorry. I'm so very sorry."

GLORIA STEINEM was among those who eagerly awaited Alice's arrival in New York. Raised in Toledo, Ohio, during the 1950s, Steinem had been determined to achieve the success that had been denied women of her mother's generation. Armed with a degree from Smith College, political insights gained from a sojourn to India, and a fierce activist bent, she descended on New York in 1960 and immediately took the city by storm. Indeed, her cofounding of *Ms.* magazine was the culmination of a series of publishing triumphs that had garnered Steinem admiration and awe as the feminist movement became a major force in the 1970s. It was hard to dismiss the ingenuity (the intelligence was a given) of a woman who had entered the gender debate by taking an undercover assignment as a Playboy bunny. Reprinted in her 1983 book *Outrageous Acts and Everyday Rebellions*, Steinem's riveting expose of the degradation endured by cocktail waitresses in Hugh Hefner's Playboy Clubs ("the men call [black] girls chocolate bunnies") would later prompt the skin pix mogul to order a hit piece on feminism for *Playboy* magazine. "These chicks are our natural enemies," Hefner had raged in a memo. "It is time to do battle with them. . . . What I want is a devastating piece, a really expert, personal demolition job on the subject."

Playboy insiders cannot recall the publication of such a smear in the magazine. On the contrary, a former *Playboy* editor said her pitch to profile Steinem in the magazine's vaunted "*Playboy* Interview" section was readily approved. Steinem rejected the idea. "I pitched [the Steinem interview] to . . . the executive editor when he offered me the job as his associate editor in 1978, as a condition of my accepting the job," recalled Susan Margolis, today a writer in San Francisco. "He gave me the assignment. . . . I pursued Gloria for months and eventually she declined. She felt it would be wrong for her to appear in a magazine which she believed demeaned women. I had argued that it would be a great way to raise the consciousness of the men who read the magazine."

As one of the leading voices at *Ms.*, Steinem wanted a magazine that reflected the passions of a multiplicity of women, both in the United States and abroad. She had first met Alice during a political benefit in Jackson not long after *Ms.* published "Roselily." When she learned that Alice and Mel had decided to leave Mississippi for New York, she immediately offered Alice a job as a contributing editor at the magazine. From her previous stint as a New York welfare worker, Alice knew that a full-time job would leave little time for her writing. And unlike in the 1960s, she now had family responsibilities. Unwilling to sacrifice her art, Alice accepted Steinem's offer on the condition that she would come to the office only two days a week. Moreover, she did not want to attend any meetings. Capping several years of publication in *Ms.*, Alice's name would appear on the masthead beginning in December 1974. Her annual salary was $11,500.

"I first fell in love with Alice on the page," Steinem later said. "I was drawn to her and her work because she seemed to be such a true person, just like a touchstone. I was very happy when she agreed to join the *Ms.* staff. The fact that she didn't want to work full-time and refused to come to meetings was fine."

For Alice, the arrangement was perfect. She and Mel bought a spacious home with stained glass and eight fireplaces at 55 Midwood Street in the historic Lefferts Manor section of Brooklyn, a multiethnic enclave with glorious trees. Granted, "the ruin" needed major renovations, but after Mississippi mere home repair was a welcome challenge. And as she had in Jackson, Alice was able to secure child care for Rebecca right in the neighborhood. Wonderful in every way that Mrs. Cornelius had been, the new baby-sitter was a vibrant woman from the Caribbean who cooked and then taught five-year-old Rebecca how to prepare her favorite food: arroz con pollo (chicken and rice). In a letter dated February 6, 1974, Alice told Jane Cooper of the new developments in her life. "We bought an old house, a brownstone, it was in sad shape. I started working at *Ms.*, going in twice a week, which I'm beginning to feel might have more good points, than bad. . . . But I still don't like editorial meetings."

Alice was appreciative of but not well suited to the free-form communal ambience at *Ms.*, where there were no private offices and children of staffers played merrily in the work area throughout the day. She'd later speak of challenges that were not readily perceived by colleagues at the magazine, who, wowed by her writing and political activism, knew little of the isolated young woman at Sarah Lawrence who'd purchased Gauguin prints of Tahitian women to assuage her loneliness.

"It was hard to be among the first wave of black people to integrate white institutions, even feminist ones, like *Ms.*," Alice explained. "I got the feeling that some of the women thought I was standoffish because I didn't talk much or participate in meetings. I also insisted on a private office. It helped a lot that Gloria understood my needs."

31

How Rare We Were

As ALICE gained increasing recognition for her literary achievements, her stature among some blacks was cast in stark relief. For example, *Essence*, a magazine for black women, had been launched in 1970, a full year before *Ms*. Started by a group of black businessmen, the magazine published a few of Alice's short stories. Still, it was not lost on those who read her works regularly and later watched her ascent at *Ms*. that Alice could have contributed mightily to the evolution of *Essence* had her talents been pursued. Instead, the founders of *Essence* brought in photographer-filmmaker Gordon Parks (soon to direct *Shaft*) as editorial director and all-around marketing guru for the groundbreaking magazine.

"I felt strongly that as one of the most daring black women writers at the time, Alice Walker should have at least been consulted about *Essence*," asserted hattie gossett, who was involved in the planning stages of the magazine. "But whenever I'd mention her name, people would say stupid shit like, 'Well, all she's ever done is write a lot. That doesn't mean she's any good.' "

"The people at *Essence* resented Alice because she wasn't going through the gatekeeping niggerati," gossett continued. "She had ties to Langston Hughes and Sarah Lawrence connections. But what really pissed them off was that she had the nerve to have the white boy. And not just any white boy, but one who was in her corner. So *Ms.* eventually got Alice, and the sisters lost out. Today *Essence* is like a sacred cow and nobody wants to hear this. But I was at those meetings and that's exactly how it went down."

Branded "too militant," gossett was herself fired before the magazine's debut. Among the stories hawked on the cover of the May 1970 premiere issue were "Sensual Black Man, Do You Love Me?" and "Dynamite Afros." The magazine's interest in Afro hairstyles did not, however, extend to publishing pieces by Bessie Head, Buchi Emecheta, or Ama Ata Aidoo, African writers whose work Alice would soon bring to the pages of *Ms.* Aimed more toward amassing advertisers than showcasing talent, *Essence* would trail, rather than help to shape the discourse on black women's writing that emerged in the 1970s.

"The fact that *Essence* didn't appreciate Alice speaks more to where most black women were back then than any problem with Alice," observed Esther Jackson, former publisher of *Freedomways*. "She was ostracized because the sisters were not fully formulated yet. Alice was ten, maybe fifteen years ahead of everybody in her thinking."

And thus it was at Alice's direction that *Ms.* magazine, not *Essence*, secured the rights to excerpt Ntozake Shange's debut novel, *Sassafras, Cypress & Indigo* (1982). Author of the landmark 1976 Broadway play *For Colored Girls Who Have Considered Suicide When the Rainbow is Enuf*, Shange (who struggled with substance abuse after her success) would later thank Alice for remaining a supporter after her star began to fade.

"If you weren't about makeup or shopping, *Essence* just didn't seem to be that interested," Alice later said about her strained relationship with the magazine. "And what might have been worth reading could hardly be found with all the ads for hair straighteners, skin lighteners, and pictures of women looking up at men like basset hounds. Unlike at *Ms.*, I never got the sense that my voice was really valued or understood at *Essence*, even when they published my work. I didn't fit their slick, packaged image." By way of example, Alice noted that editors at *Essence* often recoiled at the earthy language of black Southern characters such as Mrs. Kemhuff, who, in her futile request for flour from the white relief worker, had pleaded, "My children is hungry." "They said my characters sounded country and 'backward,' which is only insulting if you believe the criticism white people have hurled at your blood kin."

In addition to her marriage, it was, in fact, Alice's affiliation with *Ms.* that continued to make her "suspect" as the 1970s progressed. To be sure, there were those (i.e., Carole Darden) who had reconciled themselves to Mel. After all, his commitment to black people could not be denied. But what to make of Alice's relationship with Gloria Steinem? The long-legged, miniskirted white woman who, with her trademark aviator glasses, had become "the face" of feminism and synonymous with *Ms.*? Well, that was a different story.

"I was certainly a fan of her writing, but also a little standoffish because Alice was so firmly connected to *Ms,*" remembered Marcia Ann Gillespie, editor of *Essence* from 1971 to 1980. "Back then, black women were extremely suspicious of women's liberation and the media's elevation of Gloria as the leader of the movement."

And then there was the fallout from blacks who took umbrage at Alice's refusal to respond to a growing sense of "ownership" her literary triumphs evoked in them, Gillespie explained. She recalled the 1973 gathering at Radcliffe where Alice first read "In Search of Our Mothers' Gardens." The essay is an impassioned analysis of the historical barriers to black women's creative expression, a piece in which Alice famously asked,

> What did it mean for a black woman to be an artist in our grandmothers' time? In our great-grandmothers' day? It is a question with an answer cruel enough to stop the blood. Did you have a genius of a great-great-grandmother who died under some ignorant and depraved white overseer's lash? Or was she required to bake biscuits for a lazy backwater tramp, when she cried out in her soul to paint watercolors or sunsets

or the rain falling on the green and peaceful pasturelands? Or was her body broken and forced to bear children (who were more often than not sold away from her)—eight, ten, fifteen, twenty children—when her one joy was the thought of modeling heroic figures of rebellion, in stone or clay?

"By the time Alice finished, you could hear sisters sobbing all over the room," Gillespie remembered. "It was as if she'd brought forth all the ancestors and allowed us to collectively grieve what black women had never been able to achieve.

"When I found out the essay was going to be published in *Ms.*, I was irate," she continued. " 'The white girls don't even get this; they don't deserve it,' is what I recall thinking to myself. I later came to see that 'Our Mothers' Gardens' is really about the human experience and it was wrong of me to think that only black women could relate."

In a twist of fate, the irony of which she realizes, Gillespie would later become an editor of *Ms.* magazine and a close friend of Gloria Steinem. "I needed to get over myself, plain and simple," she said.

It was the pernicious and seemingly endless battles over "claiming rights" that Alice had hoped to conquer when in 1974 *Revolutionary Petunias* was nominated for a National Book Award, one of the publishing industry's highest honors. The other female nominees in the field of eleven were Eleanor Lerman (*Armed Love*, 1973), Audre Lorde (*From A Land Where Other People Live*, 1973), and Adrienne Rich (*Diving into the Wreck*, 1973).

In feminist solidarity, Alice, Lorde, and Rich agreed not to compete with each other, deciding instead to accept the award on behalf of all women, should any of them win. The arrangement, devised in a series of phone calls, did not appeal to Lerman, who, protesting that she did not wish to "mix politics with poetry," declined to participate, as Rich later recalled.

Announced as cowinner, with Allen Ginsberg (*The Fall of America*, 1973), Rich delivered from the podium at Alice Tully Hall in New York's Lincoln Center, the statement on which she, Alice, and Lorde had agreed: "We together accept this award in the name of all the women whose voices have gone and still go unheard in a patriarchal world, and in the name of those who, like us, have been tolerated as token women in this culture. . . . We believe that we can enrich ourselves more in supporting and giving to each other than by competing against each other; and that poetry—if it *is* poetry— exists in a realm beyond ranking and comparison. We symbolically join together . . . in declaring that we will share this prize among us, to be used as best we can for women." And to that end, the women donated the award ($1,000) to the Sisterhood of Black Single Mothers, an advocacy organization in New York.

Thirty years later, Alice offered reflections on the event: "We knew, Audre and I—and probably Adrienne as well—that whatever was offered would go to Adrienne; I think she felt unable to accept anything for herself in the context of our exclusion. She would not stand for our being window dressing. . . . We knew how rare we were, all three being honored at the same time; we also knew most women poets and artists were still being unread and unhonored."

MORE CONFOUNDING to Alice than the response her triumphs generated at *Essence* was the resentment directed toward her by Muriel Rukeyser upon her return to New York. In 1970, Rukeyser had moved to Westbeth, an artists' community near the Hudson River docks (photographer Diane Arbus and dancer Merce Cunningham were among the eclectic mix who also lived in the building). It was fine, evidently, for Alice's work to garner favor, even for her to obtain a plum editorial job. But Rukeyser had never imagined that her own literary light might be outshone by the impoverished black woman from Georgia whom she had taken "under her wing." Alas, that was the scenario she could feel looming on the horizon in the wake of Alice's National Book Award nomination for *Revolutionary Petunias*. And the accolades would continue to pour in, reaching a crescendo with the March 1975 release (in *Ms.*) of Alice's article about Zora Neale Hurston, later to be lauded in *The Best American Essays of the Century* (2000).

Miffed by a television interview in which she felt Alice had failed to acknowledge the whites who had assisted Hurston, not to mention those who had nurtured her own writing career, Rukeyser dispatched a note to her former student. Peppered with the fragmented phrases and stylistic quirks that characterized the poet's work, the May 1975 letter read, in part:

Dear Alice,
Turned on TV, and suddenly saw you talking about Zora. I'm glad you're hunting her. . . . I have always regretted that I couldn't take up her invitation to go south with her. . . . At any rate, that was not the unhelped story you were telling. Zora was helped. . . . In interest and seeing her value and with money. By white women. It's much more interesting, the truth. More true people, more the way it happens, and deep in the story of us all. You were helped at Sarah Lawrence in comparable ways. . . .

Then, turning to what Rukeyser perceived to be Alice's slight of Monica McCall, she continued:

Monica, who brought you to Langston Hughes as well as to Hiram [Haydn], and fought for you—and whom you left saying that you "could not talk" to her—although you didn't even say that to her face, and never tried to talk to her, and went down the hall to another agent in the same firm. That's a very painful scene to me, and it's been what has been standing between us.

To see it repeated about Zora is a kind of rhyming in life, and I hope you can go over both of them and do what you can to correct them. Although the harm is done. Tell me what you think.

In a three-page, single-spaced letter dated May 19, 1975, Alice shared her thoughts:

Dear Muriel,

. . . As far as I'm concerned, what has stood between us was never Monica. Or how I reacted to Monica, or she to me. We were simply not compatible and I did not feel strong enough at the time to deal with her. I was, when I broke with her, living a precarious existence in many ways in Mississippi, with its own pressures . . . that she actually frightened me I cannot explain . . . some people are born with a superior air, I think, and it has been a fact of my life that I could never bear to be around someone who seemed to have one. . . . I have tried in every way I can honorably do so to show how much you've [both] meant to me. . . .

This is what I see as standing between us: 1. The role you played early on at Sarah Lawrence was such a deep one, bound up with the absolute nadir of my moral and physical life (or so I thought then) that it was necessary to put as much distance between us as possible because you brought to mind . . . all those feelings I did not like to recall. 2. When Mel and I saw you at Langston's funeral we wanted so much to talk to and be with you . . . but you continually looked over our heads. . . . I guessed we were not important enough for you to waste your time on but we were both very hurt. . . . And, there is in me— for better or worse—an absolute hatred of having to feel beholden to anyone. What is given should be given and for- gotten the next day, I think. Have you ever considered how like a beggar I felt those days when all of you were "helping" me? How it felt to have absolutely nothing? To have to depend on people who had no concept of poverty that they did not get from visits to it? . . .

It was through Rukeyser's letter that Alice discovered that the poet had actually *known* Zora Neale Hurston. This news prompted her to wonder why Rukeyser had never mentioned, let alone taught, *Their Eyes Were Watching God* in her class on Southern writers. On a syllabus groaning with Carson McCullers, Eudora Welty, and enough of Faulkner's Snopeses to last a lifetime, surely there was room for a self-loving Southern black woman like Janie Crawford, Alice thought. And for all the talk at Sarah Lawrence about giving students free rein to pursue their passions, Alice couldn't fathom why Muriel, at a minimum, hadn't encouraged her to seek out Hurston's work independently. The letter continued:

> What I want you to understand is this: when I spoke of "helping" and of Zora being "helped" or not "helped" <u>I mean by her own people.</u> The reason Langston Hughes became so quickly a part of me was that he was black. And for me that meant that black people could and would help and support each other. . . . I know you felt I consciously overlooked you in the whole thing, and you're right. I did, publicly, at least some of the time. Because I wanted everyone to know that a black person had helped me. White people have helped and our literary history is full [of them], but it is not full of black people who helped each other. When I first noticed this I felt myself shrinking. Because I know we are endangered as much by our indifference and cruelty to each other as by outside murderers. . . .
>
> You ask what I think. I think I always expected your letter. It was like waiting for the other shoe to fall. . . . I think that whenever I have felt "Harm" done by you I have explained it to myself in ways that made sense, without calling you a coward or a liar. I think I just assumed you would "correct" your own omissions. . . .
>
> If you taught Southern Writers and the South now, you would teach Zora, wouldn't you? And Toomer? And Margaret Walker perhaps? That is growth, or would be.

Alice continued with thoughts along a similar vein before signing her name, sans salutation.

Rukeyser responded with a short letter to Alice in which she declared "my wishes and love for you and for your work are unchanged." The most revealing portion of the letter was its post-script: "Do you remember my part in the abortion—that abortion that proved to be so fertile? You say . . . that you were alone, and I know you felt alone, but what about the rest of it?"

The letter—attached to an envelope addressed to Alice and bearing a ten-cent postage stamp—was found unmailed after Rukeyser's death.

32

We Were a Part of It

IN THE opening scene of the movie *Faithless*, filmmaker Ingmar Bergman quotes German playwright Botho Strauss on the disintegration of a marriage: "No common failure, whether it be sickness or bankruptcy, or professional misfortune, will reverberate so cruelly and deeply in the unconscious as a divorce. It penetrates the seat of all anguish, forcing it to life. With one cut, it slices more deeply than life can ever reach."

Alice had left Mississippi, uncertain about the direction of her marriage, with a complete draft of her second novel, *Meridian*. But before submitting it to Harcourt, she made minor revisions and started other work at Yaddo, a prestigious writer's retreat in Saratoga Springs, New York, where she'd been granted a residency in August 1975. Another writer-in-residence at the time remembered being enthralled by the author, who, in the midst of the flailing egotism at Yaddo, exuded a rare combination of confidence and calm.

"I thought Alice was sensational and the prettiest woman there, by far," said John Leggett, a novelist and biographer of William Saroyan. "Yaddo had a reputation for being a place where, you know, sparks flew, so I definitely wanted to know her better."

To that end, Leggett said he one day steeled his nerves and asked Alice if she'd care to join him for an afternoon at the racetrack (Saratoga Springs is a horse-racing center). She declined. Instead, Leggett recalled, Alice told him about her plans to attend a B.B. King concert the next night. To which he said he replied, "Who is B.B. King?"

"She looked at me like I was the sorriest, most pathetic white man on earth," Leggett remembered. "She said, 'You mean to tell me you've never heard of B.B. King?' When I confessed that I hadn't, she said, 'O.K. I'm taking you to see him.' "

About the soulful blues extravaganza he watched, sitting next to Alice on a blanket in an open field, Leggett later said, matter-of-factly, "People were really into it. I thought the guitar-playing was good."

He went on to admit that the famed singer of such blues classics as "The Thrill Is Gone" had not commanded his full attention because throughout the concert, Leggett had been plotting how to steal a kiss.

"Hoping to show Alice how much I liked her, and that I really wanted to go out again, I leaned down and kissed her when we got back to Yaddo," he explained. "She reared back with her entire body and let me know that what I thought was a 'date' wasn't going anywhere."

MEL AND Alice had hoped that their departure from Mississippi would ease the tensions in their marriage and rekindle the excitement they had felt when they first met. With the demands of renovating "the ruin," arranging schooling for Rebecca, and getting settled in their new jobs, they were realistic, neither expecting a return to wedded bliss overnight. But after a year in New York, they were still struggling to regain the sense of purpose and passion that had fueled their love, both as intimate partners and as political allies. Difficult though it was to accept, they had to face the grim truth that Mississippi, with all its hatreds and hardships, had worn them out. While Alice had rebuffed the overture at Yaddo, she knew that her marriage was faltering badly and feared it would not survive. It was not lost on her that she had misplaced five wedding rings since Mel had placed the first one on her finger in 1967. Nor that she was increasingly drawn to the haunting ballads of singers such as Phoebe Snow and Roberta Flack, whose mournful "Killing Me Softly" seemed to speak directly to her heart.

Echoing the concerns she had shared with Diana Young prior to her trip to California, Alice now wrote to another friend: "I am slowly being pulled in two. Frankly, I think I'm unsuited for marriage. . . . The problem is that Mel is magnificent and leaving him will take just about every ounce of gumption I can muster. And there is the pull of Rebecca, her happiness and so on."

Alice's natural inclination toward mysticism now began to loom larger in her life. As she continued to assess her marriage, she opened herself to spiritual guidance and welcomed the special talents of a Bunting Institute colleague, the poet Fanny Howe. Author of more than twenty books including *O'Clock* (1995), *Forged* (1999), and the award-winning *Selected Poems* (2000), Howe had embraced Alice as a trusted friend and confidant.

"As a white woman who'd married a black man, I'd been crossed out by a lot of white people," remembered Howe, whose daughter, Danzy Senna, would pen the haunting 1998 novel *Caucasia*. "I was thrilled to meet Alice at Radcliffe because we were both in mixed-race situations. It was a time of great struggle for me and she really listened as I poured out my heart."

Like Alice, Howe was drawn to the metaphysical. Searching for insight after her marriage ended, she said she studied tarot cards, numerology, and kabbalah, the Jewish mystical tradition. "In my lonely nights with a glass of wine while the children were asleep, I'd teach myself these things," Howe remembered. "I got so good, I was scaring myself."

Alice was fascinated. Forging an alliance the women would maintain for several years, Howe, beginning in the mid-1970s, became Alice's tarot card reader. While the precise origins of the tarot remain unknown, its ideas and imagery took form in medieval

Europe and may be linked, through trade routes, to occult traditions in northern Africa, Asia, and India, asserts Karen Vogel, cocreator of the popular Motherpeace Tarot cards.

Allowing for public skepticism about the practice, Howe said her readings with Alice revealed "a conflict between work-driven forces and an equally powerful sensuality."

"The dynamic went back and forth all the time," Howe explained, adding that she had a photograph of Alice that she'd sometimes put underneath her deck so the women could "communicate long-distance with her input coming through."

"I was always surprised by how much romance Alice, as a serious writer, was actually able to generate," Howe continued. "Most artists can't cope with the stress of competing passions. But with Alice, both sides fought to survive. It created a lot of chaos and confusion."

MEL, TOO, felt the strain that their new life in New York seemed unable to assuage. But as a man whose father had walked out on his family, the prospect of divorce was difficult to countenance. "We had mustered up the courage to fall in love, but something was happening in the 1970s that made it impossible," said Mel, who had dutifully replaced each lost wedding ring. "We drifted apart, and I think a lot of it had to do with race. As Alice became better known, I think the negativity about our marriage did make her feel like a traitor. As strong as she was, I believe the criticism took a toll."

That Alice had renewed her friendship with Robert Allen in the midst of their marital strife was evidence enough, to Mel's mind, that race was indeed a factor in the growing estrangement between him and his wife. Still living in the San Francisco Bay area where he was now an editor for the academic journal *The Black Scholar*, Allen, by the mid-1970s, was also undergoing a crisis in his marriage—a union that had, in the parlance of the era, been "open" from the start, he later explained. Mindful that Alice had no such arrangement, Allen was quick to note that while he'd always enjoyed their intermittent visits, he'd also made sure to "sublimate any lingering feelings" from the past. "Neither of us was trying to seduce the other or anything like that," he maintained.

Then one day, when he was in New York to interview *Roots* author Alex Haley, Allen said Alice stunned him with unexpected news. "We'd just had dinner and as Alice was leaving, she quietly said that she and Mel had decided to separate," Allen recalled. "I was surprised because I hadn't been aware of that level of unhappiness." Still, not wanting, in his words, "to miss an opportunity," Allen immediately invited Alice to join him and Haley the next day and "hang out."

"So, Alice met us at my hotel and we all had a great time laughing and talking," Allen remembered. "After Alex left, Alice and I chatted a bit and embraced, but that's as far as it went. I think Mel might have suspected we slept together then, but we didn't."

But it was just a matter of time. The separation marked by sadness but no visible rancor, Alice soon moved with Rebecca to a small apartment opposite Brooklyn's Prospect Park while Mel remained in the Midwood house. "I never saw my parents fight, not once," remembered Rebecca, noting that her bond with her father remained intact. "And there was no sense of one blaming the other for what went wrong."

Alice put it this way: "As long as you exist, you are changing. I cared for Mel, but I didn't want to live with him anymore. I needed to be free."

As neither Alice nor Mel had envisioned a reconciliation, by 1976 the couple had officially filed for divorce. "We were running on empty," Alice recalled. In the interim, Mel had reconnected with Judith Goldsmith, a woman he'd previously dated and would marry in 1978. Continuing a journey that had started in Howard Zinn's Russian history class, Robert and Alice had become lovers. Although with three thousand miles between them and Allen's unorthodox marital life, the early stage of the relationship had a nebulous quality that was best expressed in verse by Anna Akhmatova.

I will tend these rich, black beds,
With spring water I will sprinkle them;
The flowers of the field are free,
There's no need to touch or pick them.

Allen elaborated: "It's important to say here that Alice and I began our affair while *I* was married, *she* was disengaged. Since we were both speaking and participating in various cultural events around the country, we'd try to arrange a rendezvous whenever we could. I was deliriously in love with Alice, but the romance had its stresses because I was also confused."

As it happened, Allen was visiting Alice in New York at the close of the divorce proceedings and, remarkably, accompanied Mel as he dealt with the legalities of ending a union that had itself once been "illegal" (ruling in *Loving v. Virginia*, the U.S. Supreme Court had outlawed state bans on interracial marriage in June 1967, three months after Alice and Mel wed).

"We were all just sitting around when Mel mentioned that he needed to get some divorce papers notarized," Allen remembered. "So Alice stayed at home while Mel and I took off and got the papers signed. If Mel was upset and angry, he kept his feelings to himself. He's a very nice man who doesn't show much emotion."

During the nearly ten years of their marriage, Alice had seen Mel—a passionate defender of freedom—open, vulnerable, and unveiled. It was those memories that would mingle, as in a mosaic, with his cold, stony-faced rejection of her invitation to a cup of tea on the day their divorce became final. "We fought for the same issues, life on this planet," Alice declared.

"It really did seem at times as if our love made us bulletproof, or perhaps invisible," Alice would write decades later to her "young husband" in a poignant meditation on their marriage, *The Way Forward Is with a Broken Heart* (2000). "When we walked down the street together the bullets that were the glances of the racist onlookers seemed turned back and sent hurtling off into outer space. The days passed in a blur of hard work, constant awareness of violence, and unutterable tenderness between ourselves. At the end of the long afternoons listening to the sorrows of your clients . . . we read poetry to each other. Yeats, Walt Whitman, cummings. We spent the humid evenings learning to give pleasure to each other. . . . One day we made love during a rousing afternoon thunderstorm. Torrents of rain cascaded down the streets; the air was blue with it. Lightning streaked our bodies with silver. . . . We were a part of it, no questions asked."

PART THREE

Life Is the Award

33

Meridian

WRITING SHORTLY before his death, James Baldwin evoked "the price of the ticket" as the term that embodied the fierce psychological cleansing without which, he believed, blacks would forever be burdened by the paralyzing effects of racism: "The black American must find a way to keep faith with, and excavate, a reality much older than Europe. Europe has never been, and cannot be, a useful or valid touchstone for the American experience because America is not, and never can be, white."

In *Meridian,* her second novel and sixth book, Alice examined, even before Baldwin's exhortation, the price blacks (and whites) paid as they struggled to achieve a common humanity during the civil rights era. Colored by her experiences at Spelman and the tumultuous years she'd spent with Mel in Mississippi, *Meridian* addressed not only the battles that had been waged over bus seats and voting ballots, but also the conflicts that erupted between blacks as well. Among the most incendiary complaints was that of black women who had given their lifeblood to the movement only to be forsaken by black men.

The hard facts of this struggle would be brought into sharp

relief by white feminist writer Robin Morgan in her 1989 nonfiction work, *The Demon Lover*. The scene is a tense meeting of CORE (Congress of Racial Equality) and SNCC members during the disappearance, in Mississippi, of the civil rights workers Chaney, Goodman, and Schwerner. An intense search is underway for the men, who were later found dead.

A movement activist, Morgan wrote, "I am one of seven women . . . three of us white. More than twenty men, black and white, are running the meeting. During the search [for Chaney et al.], the mutilated parts of an estimated seventeen different human bodies are found. . . . As word filters in about the difficulty of identifying mutilated bodies long decomposed, we also learn that all but one of the unidentified bodies are female. A male CORE leader mutters, in a state of fury, 'There's been a whole goddamned lynching we never even *knew* about. There's been some brother disappeared who never even got *reported*.' "

Morgan continued, "My head goes spinning. Have I heard correctly? Finally I hazard a question. Why *one* lynching? What about the sixteen unidentified female bodies? . . . Absolute silence. . . . Then the answer comes, in a tone of impatience, as if I were politically retarded, 'Those were obviously *sex* murders. Those weren't *political*.' "

In interviews upon the novel's release in 1976, Alice said that the major themes in *Meridian* had been inspired by legendary activist Ruby Doris Smith (later Robinson), a Spelman graduate and "backbone member" of SNCC. "*Meridian* . . . is a sort of corner of [Ruby's] life that I saw in passing," Alice explained. "I didn't know her all that well, but she stayed in my mind. I knew that she gave all her energy to SNCC and was really treated shabbily."

Though eclipsed in memory and monument by such SNCC leaders as Stokely Carmichael, Robinson was a galvanizing force within the organization from its earliest years. A brilliant tactician, it was Robinson who had masterminded the "jail no bail" policy by which SNCC leaders would descend en masse to any city where students were being held for their participation in lunch counter sit-ins or the harrowing journeys on segregated buses that came to be known as "Freedom Rides."

The media-savvy SNCC cadre would purposefully get arrested, thereby ensuring the public scrutiny that whites in repressive Southern towns abhorred. And in 1964, alerted that a SNCC delegation en route to Africa from New York would not be boarded because the plane was "overbooked," Robinson (sensing government harassment) sat down in the jetway and refused to move. Thrown into a panic by her behavior, airline clerks quickly managed to find seats for the group, which included Fannie Lou Hamer, a civil rights icon, who, as Robinson well knew, need only sing one note of her trademark, "This Little Light of Mine," to attract the likes of Walter Cronkite, who'd shame the nation during his nightly newscast.

But Robinson was soon depleted, body and soul, by the jealous rivalries, gender conflicts, and endless infighting (over the role of whites) that would eventually tear SNCC asunder. After a long decline, she was diagnosed with terminal cancer and died in October 1967, at age twenty-five.

Weaving her story from the intertwining threads of the Ruby Robinsons of the movement and personal reflection, Alice explored, in provocative detail, the charged dynamics between the three main characters of the novel: Meridian Hill, an activist banished from a black radical group after refusing to swear that she would kill whites; her lover, Truman Held; and Lynne Rabinowitz, a Jewish woman who Truman (black) has married, having once boasted to Meridian that he preferred white women because "they read *The New York Times*."

Coiling back and forth in time from the age of the ancient Cherokee to the murder of Martin Luther King Jr., the narrative unfolds within a forceful meditation on the relationship between Meridian and her mother. Mrs. Hill is a former schoolteacher whom her contemplative daughter feels has forfeited her independence on the twin altars of Christianity and maternal devotion. Angered by what she perceives to be her mother's blind acceptance of tradition, Meridian is also guilt-ridden, feeling as she does, that her very *birth* is one of the bricks in the wall that has imprisoned Mrs. Hill.

Alice writes, "It was for stealing her mother's serenity, for shattering her mother's emerging self, that Meridian felt guilty from the very first, though she was unable to understand how this could possibly be her fault. . . . When her mother asked, without glancing at her, 'Have you stolen anything?' a stillness fell over Meridian and for seconds she could not move. The question literally stopped her in her tracks."

With scant information from her parents about the perils of adolescence ("Keep your panties up and your dress down"), Meridian becomes pregnant by Eddie, her high school sweetheart. She drops out of school and they wed. Ironically, Meridian finds a certain sanctuary in the union. "Mainly, it saved her from the strain of responding to other boys or even noting the whole category of Men. This was worth a great deal. . . . It was resting from pursuit."

But Meridian soon feels suffocated by her marriage and is relieved when Eddie walks out ("Why did his pants and shirts have to be starched and ironed after every second wearing?"). Given a second chance to blossom, Meridian, age seventeen, is determined to escape the plight of her mother, who, depleted by domestic chores, has only one artistic outlet—the crafting of paper flowers and prayer pillows "too small for kneeling." In a telling symbol, Alice reveals that the pillows only fit one knee.

Meanwhile, Meridian craves freedom. To that end, she offers her son for adoption ("the thought of murdering her own child eventually frightened her"), joins the civil rights struggle, and enrolls in Saxon College (read: Spelman). It is in her reclaiming of self that Meridian begins to probe the deep contours of race and responsibility. Unlike black women of her mother's generation, she lives in an era of expanded *choice*.

And so it is that while at Saxon (repressive, bureaucratic) Meridian chooses as her lover Truman Held, a dashiki-clad "revolutionary" committed, like her, to the fight for justice. Through their pained relationship, Meridian experiences the contradictions of "black power," for Truman leaves her for Lynne, a white civil rights activist he both desires and mistrusts.

As a militant, Truman deems Lynne "guilty of whiteness." At the same time, she represents a "treasure" historically denied Southern black men on the penalty of death. Thus, in Truman's mind, Lynne affirms his social status and masculinity. In the battle between gender and race, Alice suggests that his male ego stoops to conquer. She writes:

How marvelous it was to find that . . . [Lynne] read everything. That she thought, deeply. That she longed to put her body on the line for his freedom. How her idealism had warmed him, brought him into the world, made him eager to tuck her under his wing, under himself, sheltering her. . . . Her awareness of wrong, her indignant political response to whatever caused him to suffer, was a definite part of her charm.

Eschewing the "off whitey" riffs that then predominated in much black writing, Alice renders the novel from unanticipated angles, as when Lynne confronts Truman about his "change of heart." Regretful that he has dumped Meridian and confident ("black prince" that he is) that she'll welcome him back, Truman one day informs Lynne that he can no longer countenance their relationship and, by turn, their mixed-race child.

"'You only married me because you were too much of a coward to throw a bomb at all the crackers who make you sick,' " Lynne rages at Truman. " 'You're like the rest of those nigger zombies. No life of your own at all unless it's something against white folks. You can't even enjoy a good fuck without hoping some cracker is somewhere grinding his teeth.' " Their eyes off the prize of social justice, Truman and Lynne sink deeper into the quagmire of "pussy politics."

By contrast, having survived the self-negating psychoses of blacks during her student years at Saxon, Meridian holds firm in her quest for wholeness. Dressed in her trademark overalls and train engineer's cap (read: Harriet Tubman), Meridian continues her civil rights crusades. In finely honed tableaux (as opposed to conventional chapters) such as "The Wild Child," Alice chronicles Meridian's defense of an ill-kempt homeless girl who's been shunned by "respectable" blacks. "Wile Chile upset her tablemates with the uncouthness of her manners. . . . She farted, as if to music, raising a thigh."

In "The Last Return," Meridian is angered by the Jim Crow policy that restricts admission to a carnival attraction a group of black children wish to visit at whim. To wit, she stands in front of a tank (painted white and decked with red, white, and blue ribbons), her courageous act bringing the demise of "Negro Day." In a pointed commentary, the "attraction" is a mummified white woman: "Marilene O'Shay, One of the Twelve Human Wonders of the World: Dead for Twenty-Five Years Preserved in Life-Like Condition." Redolent of Scarlett O'Hara, O'Shay is a clear condemnation of the moonlight and magnolia *Gone with the Wind* plantation mythology.

In her embrace of the carnival motif, Alice also evoked *Letter from a Birmingham Jail* and King's rending passages about his torment as a father who'd been forced to tell his daughter that "Funtown is closed to colored children, and see the depressing clouds of inferiority begin to form in her little mental sky."

But after each confrontation, contrary to the cliched image of the "invincible" black woman, Meridian succumbs to a debilitating collapse. Her pain stems, in large part, from ongoing tensions with a mother who looks askance at her civil rights work. That Meridian has refused to "accept Jesus" makes Mrs. Hill all the more wary of her daughter's efforts to vanquish segregation, a system she tolerates as "the Lord's will."

Here Mrs. Hill admonishes Meridian:

As far as I'm concerned, you've wasted a year of your life, fooling around with [civil rights activists]. The papers say they're crazy. God separated the sheeps from the goats and the black folks from the white. And me from anybody that acts as foolish as they do. It never bothered *me* to sit in the back of the bus, you get just as good a view and you don't have all those nasty white asses passing you.

Central to Meridian's vision is the celebration of a rich black heritage that, as she sees it, has gone unappreciated by both the "don't rock the boat" older generation and the "burn baby burn" firebrands. By novel's end, Meridian, weary but still thirsting for freedom, visits a rural black church, the consummate symbol of civil rights battles. There, she discovers that the time-honored stained-glass image of a "pale Christ with stray lamb" has been replaced by a broad-shouldered black man, "B.B., With Sword."

"His face was thrown back, contorted in song, and sweat, like glowing diamonds, fell from his head," Alice writes in a masterful counterpoint to both "Jesus of Nazareth" and "Marilene O'Shay." "In one hand he held a guitar that was attached to a golden strap that ran over his shoulder. . . . The other arm was raised above his head and it held a long shiny object the end of which was dripping with blood."

In her elevation of Riley "B.B." King, the Mississippi-born blues singer who'd risen to fame during her parents' generation, Alice offered a provocative contrast to black nationalists who'd proffered "Mother Africa" as the most righteous path to black liberation. For the elders, Alice suggested that the gospel could be found in *home-grown music and art* just as readily as in Bible verse. Or as she later put it: "We are led and guided by people we don't even know. How many of us, personally, know Jeremiah?"

After *Meridian*'s publication, Alice said, "I believe in [immediate] generations," asserting her loyalty to the flesh-and-blood people who had nurtured her in Wards Chapel as opposed to the vaunted "black nobility of the Nile." "We have turned from those shining faces and what they meant. Part of our legacy is to maintain [their] values so that our children will be able to see the beauty of their ancestors' faces." Understanding that the elders, under segregation, had been taught to devalue their natural spirits, Alice had labored to help them reclaim their beauty too.

With her work informed by nature, the daring black voice of Zora Neale Hurston, and the observation skills she'd honed as a child, Alice's writing process had become increasingly organic. Thus, the trajectory of *Meridian* had veered from the description she'd put forth in her Radcliffe application. As promised, she'd examined the impact of a "misplaced nostalgia and romanticism," but there was infinitely more mystery in the text. And in crafting, like *Cane*, a work of kaleidoscopic patterns narrated from varying perspectives, Alice had also kept faith with Jean Toomer, whose lengthy 1936 lyric "Blue Meridian" would find an obvious echo in the title of her book. A fervent plea for the unity of all people, the poem read, in part:

> *I would give my life to see inscribed*
> *Upon the arch of our consciousness*
> *These aims: Growth, Transformation, Love . . .*

Writing in the *New Yorker*, Greil Marcus would fault Alice for sometimes "high-flown language," but still hail *Meridian* for its luminous evocation of the philosophical conundrums debated in Albert Camus' *The Rebel* (1954), a book in which it is argued, in the context of justice, "There is a limit beyond which you shall not go."

"The questions [Camus] raises are at the heart of *Meridian*, a . . . spiritual and political biography of a black woman who determines to live out the [civil rights] movement long after it has faded away," Marcus observed. "[It] is beautifully presented and utterly convincing; each incident is memorable, shaped as a story in itself."

By contrast, Gordon Burnside, a reviewer for *Commonweal*, argued that *Meridian* lacked a tangible center and questioned whether the book worked as a novel. "But if *Meridian* is a failure as a novel—and I think it is—it is also an extremely interesting historical document," he declared.

Underscoring the explosiveness of the novel, *Newsweek* critic Margo Jefferson praised Alice for even broaching a subject "as complicated as the era it examines and elegizes." "Walker documents the turning toward radical violence in the movement: the wearing psychological and sexual confrontations between black and white co-workers that often revealed them to be as much enemies as comrades. . . . Both ruthless and tender . . . [Walker's] eye for hypocrisy is painfully sharp." Twenty years later, Jefferson, a black woman, would win a Pulitzer Prize for her searing arts criticism in the *New York Times*, an achievement that could scarcely have been imagined by the fictional Truman Held.

Beyond the critics, general readers noted that with *Meridian* Alice had emerged as a writer who, increasingly, demonstrated talents that separated her from her peers. "Even with all the permutations, the storytelling in *Meridian* was accessible," observed Tammy Sanders, a resident of Northern California and avid reader of Alice's work. "I was extremely impressed with her ability to write about sex and sexuality in a non-loaded way. Most writers provide so much build-up to sex that you already know it's coming by the time it gets there. In *Meridian*, sex was just another function that would appear unexpectedly on the page. A character would be cooking one minute and having sex the next. Stylistically, that was such a nice change."

As for Alice, the release of *Meridian* would trigger a shift in her relationship with editors and the whole machinery of commercial publishing. Following the 1973 death of Hiram Haydn, she found herself paired with Harcourt editor Tony Godwin. Promoting book sales in pubs and gas stations, Godwin had become a legend in his native England before arriving in New York. Alice had not been overly impressed with a man then trumpeted as among the most talented in the industry.

"Tony Godwin took over as my editor, but I think I met with him only once or twice," Alice recalled. "This story tells it all: After reading *Meridian* he wanted to correct my description of a straightened-out wire clothes hanger to which Mrs. Hill attached pieces of crepe paper in order to make paper flowers. He was unfamiliar with wire clothes hangers, so he assumed they didn't exist."

Long reluctant to discuss her work-in-progress, Alice, in the aftermath of *Meridian*, took an unorthodox stance with regard to editors and publishing executives. It is a position she still maintains. "I never tell them, in advance, what I'm working on," Alice said. "When I finish a manuscript, I send it. Generations of people have suffered and died so that I could be this free. And with that always in my heart, I write whatever I feel needs to be written. I work for the ancestors. Period."

34

Refuge

ACCOLADES NOTWITHSTANDING, the daring thrust of *Meridian* would not sit well with some readers who had known Alice in Mississippi and were crushed to discover what they perceived to be thinly veiled portraits of their lives in her narrative. What critics had declared as "bold" and "courageous" seemed to them a betrayal of trust. Twenty-five years later, a white woman, convinced that Alice had cast Lynne Rabinowitz from her persona, dissolved into tears when discussing the pain she'd suffered while reading the book.

"I got physically ill and went into a complete state of shock," said the woman, who had been married to a black man and worked on desegregation efforts in Jackson. "I felt that Alice had stripped me naked. I didn't want to go down in history that way."

Noting that she'd always had a penchant for long, dangling earrings, the woman said she'd stopped wearing such jewelry after the release of *Meridian* because "Lynne wore them, too." "At the time, there was already so much venom going around with people making white women the scapegoat for 'stealing' black men that the book just kind of pushed me over the edge," she lamented. "On the one hand, the black nationalists who I'd busted my ass for had started telling me I wasn't shit. And on the other, I'd get shit from the feminists when I called them on their racism. As much as I love Alice, I was hurt by *Meridian*. But I didn't have the strength to refute it, so I chose to remain silent."

In coming years, Alice would be increasingly criticized by people who would take personal offense at her work on the basis of its language ("crude"), images ("negative"), and overall themes ("antiblack"). In their inability or unwillingness to grant her artistic license, she could not help but feel that there was a double standard at play. After all, Flannery O'Connor had put forth a veritable library of less-than-noble figures, the reward for which was a National Book Award, conferred even after her death. In the year that *Meridian* had raised eyebrows, the black writer Ishmael Reed had published *Flight to Canada* (1976), a novel chockablock with material poised to aggrieve, not the least of which was a black servant named "Mammy the Barracuda."

And while she didn't discuss the practice publicly, Alice, as a matter of principle, would sometimes share "sensitive" work on select subjects prior to publication. For example, she'd given Mamie advance notice of "For My Sister Molly."

That is not to say that Alice ever changed a syllable that might discomfort. But she was not inclined to inflict intentional harm. "I don't set out to upset people, but I've never been afraid to speak my truth," Alice explained. "In my life and in my art, I've been loyal to myself. And that distresses folks. It's their task, not mine, to understand why."

As for *Meridian,* people seeking "certificates of innocence" to exempt them from the tinderbox that was race and sex in the South could stick with *Gone with the Wind.* Better yet, Alice thought, they could write their own novels, recite their own poems, paint their own canvasses, or direct their own plays. Until then, readers dismayed by Alice's depiction of Lynne Rabinowitz could take solace in a response she'd written to a friend: "P. thinks Lynne is her! All my white women friends see themselves, isn't that interesting?"

. . .

OF THE mind that joint custody would be the least disruptive for their child, Alice and Mel had decided, amicably, on an arrangement by which Rebecca would spend two years with each parent. Thus Rebecca would remain with her mother from 1976 to 1978. She would then spend the next two years with her father, who was soon to relocate to Washington, D.C., with his new wife. Such was the plan.

"Our intention was for Rebecca to grow up with both of us and to have as much stability as possible, given the circumstances," Alice later explained. "The decision was made out of total love."

Rebecca never doubted that she was loved by her parents. Still, the adjustment was hard. Two decades later, over lunch in a restaurant not far from her home in Northern California, she revisited the challenges of her childhood. As the thirtyish Yale graduate began her reflections, the opening strains of Roberta Flack's "Killing Me Softly" wafted through the room. "My parents played that song all the time," she noted, wistfully.

"Moving every two years, I was completely fragmented," continued Rebecca, author of the 2000 memoir *Black, White, and Jewish*. "Like slivers from a mirror, I've had to struggle to see myself. But when my parents divorced, I became a little trooper. I did whatever was necessary so as not to add to their pain."

Although outwardly composed, Rebecca said that she was often rattled by circumstances that compelled her to grow up quickly and straddle two worlds. By way of example, she cited the night that Alice, not long after she and Mel parted, suddenly dictated plans for her funeral. Ever the dutiful daughter, Rebecca grabbed a legal pad and scribbled, to her mother's specifications, the "do's and don'ts" of the affair. She was not quite ten years old.

Rebecca recalled, "We were sitting in bed and very matter-of-factly, my mother announced that she wanted to be buried in a beautiful pine box. After the funeral, she said there was to be a party with lots of food, dancing, and Stevie Wonder music. I felt proud that my mother trusted me, you know, to take care of business. But it was terrifying to hear her talk about dying. I kept thinking, 'What about me?' "

As much as Alice steered her daughter toward independence, Mel's new wife encouraged her in "typical girl things." "My father remarried a traditional woman who didn't have a problem with ballet lessons and who took me shopping and taught me how to cook," Rebecca maintained. "So I had two completely different models of the mother-daughter relationship. When I was with my mother, I'd feel guilty about enjoying a life with my 'white family' that was like a suburban fairy tale. Then I'd return to my father and feel like the embodiment of all the black stuff from the civil rights movement that he'd loved and lost. I began to feel part alien to both my parents."

In her memoir, Rebecca described the impact, on her psyche, of the "zigzag years":

> Black-on-black love is the new recipe for revolution, mulatto half-breeds are tainted with the blood of the oppressor. . . . My father, once an ally, is, overnight, recast as an interloper. My mother, having once found refuge in a love that is unfashionable, may no longer have been willing to make the sacrifice. . . . The only problem, of course, is me. My little copper-colored body that held so much promise and broke so many rules. I no longer make sense. I am a remnant, a throwaway, a painful reminder of a happier and more optimistic but ultimately unsustainable time. Who am I if not a Movement Child?

To be sure, Alice grieved the loss of a companion for whom she said her respect and admiration remained undiminished. That Rebecca was suffering (albeit quietly) only added to the penetrating pain of divorce Bergman depicted in *Faithless*. As Rebecca noted in *Black, White, and Jewish*, Alice did her best to comfort. She deepened the bond with her daughter through books ("on Sojourner Truth and by Louisa May Alcott"), music ("Come Together" by the Beatles), and a Willie Lee Walker-inspired "magic soup" made from "whatever vegetables we have in the fridge tossed into chicken broth."

Still, as a newly single mother, Alice understood her vulnerability to the kind of crushing despair she'd suffered after her eye injury and during the tortuous months at Sarah Lawrence. Besieged with sadness, confusion, and debilitating onslaughts of insomnia that left her dazed, Alice began to practice Transcendental Meditation. Her hope was that by sitting, daily, in silent meditation, she could restore her wounded spirit and regain the serenity that had vanished in the wake of her parting from Mel. By turn, she'd be a stronger presence for Rebecca, who, insecure at her new school and longing for acceptance, had begun showering her friends with toys and candy purchased with money pilfered from Alice's purse. "I feel safer, older, bigger, knowing that [friends] look to me as some kind of provider," Rebecca noted, poignantly, in her memoir.

Directed to a Transcendental Meditation teacher by a friend, Alice took a few classes. Inner peace was not immediate. "I remember sitting on my cushion and thinking, 'This will never work,' " she later noted. "Then gradually . . . I wasn't quite so jumpy, and mornings no longer made me want to draw the covers over my head."

Over time, Alice discovered that with meditation, she could transport herself back to the restful and soothing days of her childhood in Wards Chapel, to the afternoons when she'd meander through meadows or sit under a tree "gazing out into the landscape, merging with it and disappearing."

"I was surprised to find how many and how varied one's transitory states can be," she continued. "There were sittings that were amazingly sexual. . . . There were times when I wept copiously as old sorrows from the past put in their final bids. . . . There were times of pure joy, as I felt the lightness of heart that comes from knowing you've found something truly reliable and helpful. . . . It was a time when ancestors sometimes appeared." Alice would be a devoted seeker of meditative practices for the rest of her life.

FILLING A void that had exacerbated her sense of isolation in Jackson, after the divorce Alice also found refuge in The Sisterhood. Organized by Alice and June Jordan (in whose Brooklyn home the group met), the group was composed of black women who gathered, informally, to socialize, share their creative work, and debate the political issues of the day. In addition to Alice ("I brought gumbo in a large red pot to the first meeting") and Jordan, regular participants included Toni Morrison, playwright Ntozake Shange, food writer Verta Mae Grosvenor, and editor Audrey Edwards. And with no membership requirement beyond the loosely defined sobriquet of "artist," many other black women attended Sisterhood soirees as the spirit moved them.

"I remember wanting us black women writers not to be strangers to each other and felt after a couple of gatherings that we weren't," Alice said. "It was like a council. Being together was the medicine."

In her 1985 essay "A Knowing So Deep," Toni Morrison would write of the solace that drew black women (then as now) to support groups like The Sisterhood:

> I think about us, Black women, a lot. How many of us are battered and how many are champions. I note the strides that have replaced the tiptoe. . . . If each hour of every day brings fresh reasons to weep, the same hour is full of cause for congratulations. . . . And all along the way you had the best of company—others, we others, just like you.

That there was a coterie of lively black women who had fashioned their own "consciousness-raising group" was especially important to Ntozake Shange. Born Paulette Williams in 1948 to an affluent family with a consuming passion for the arts, Williams assumed the Zulu name that means "she who walks with her own things" and "she who walks like a lion," in tribute to the civil rights struggles of the 1960s, she later explained.

In 1976, *For Colored Girls,* Shange's searing collage of choreographed poems about the oppression of black women, was produced on Broadway to a thunderous response. Not since the 1959 opening of Lorraine Hansberry's *A Raisin in the Sun* had a play by a black woman appeared on "the great white way." And in an unprecedented affirmation of her achievement, Shange would be deluged with honors, among them nominations for Tony, Grammy, and Emmy Awards. But the praise would not come without a swift and virulent condemnation by those who felt that in its dramatization of the anguish of black women, *For Colored Girls* had also publicly maligned black men. Especially galling to Shange's detractors were scenes in the play about a black Vietnam veteran who flings his children out of a window to avenge his rejection by his abused wife, and "Sorry," in which the all-female cast recited, to pointed effect, a litany of excuses men give for their mistreatment of women.

Blindsided by both her meteoric rise and the harsh criticism she endured in the aftermath of her success, Shange descended into a tailspin of depression and self-acknowledged substance abuse. Nearly thirty years later, she said it was the support of The Sisterhood, most notably the compassionate concern of Alice, that buttressed her as she struggled to reclaim herself.

"I never understood why my telling truthful stories about black women's lives enraged so many people," said Shange, who in *For Colored Girls* had launched the anthem *I found god in myself and loved her / loved her / fiercely.* "Alice had already been hit with the slings and arrows. So in her I could see I needed to move forward and ignore the negativity. Sometimes just thinking about Alice would give me enough strength to get up and face the attacks another day."

A dedicated and inspired artist, Shange would continue to create plays, poems, novels, essays, ensemble pieces with musicians, even a cookbook. But scar tissue from *For Colored Girls* would remain. "I try not to focus on that period of my life because it was so hurtful and vicious," she said, as her voice trailed off into a fuzzy haze. "I'm still trying to heal."

35

Correct Relationship

ALICE'S ROMANCE with Robert Allen remained a long-distance affair. For despite the incessant blaring of taxis and miles of concrete, New York was where she wanted to be. As a teeming arts center, the city was the perfect antidote to the cultural blight that had marked her sojourn in Mississippi. And having answered the call of conscience that had triggered her departure in 1966, Alice could now immerse herself in the city without mental distraction. Decades later, she'd still revel in memories of attending a New York screening of *Jesus Christ Superstar*. Adapted from the hippie-filled Broadway production and featuring a black Judas, the film had not been released with the moviegoing habits of Jackson residents in mind.

While she had no regrets about leaving the South, Alice's birthplace would never be far from her heart. In keeping with cherished customs from her heritage, Alice, now in her mid-thirties, planted a patch of collard greens among the hundred-year-old roses already in her Brooklyn garden. She upheld this tradition in all of her homes. Likewise, her guests (then as now) could count on being greeted with an overflowing basket of fresh pecans, dispatched to her regularly from kinfolk in Georgia. Alice held tight in New York to her loving homeland. Of the South's hurt, ignorance, and hatred, she'd had her fill.

As for Robert, the "openness" of his marriage notwithstanding, the fact was that he had a legal spouse with whom he lived in San Francisco. They had a child, born in 1975. He wrestled to reconcile his family obligations with his passion for Alice. "My wife knew all about the relationship," Allen said. "But Alice was firmly settled in New York and I was basically happy in San Francisco. It was the sexual revolution and people were acting that out with greater or lesser disasters." Presumably more disaster from her perspective, the woman Allen married declined to comment.

Thirty years later, Allen noted the links between his marital strife and wounding childhood memories. Intrigued by technology, Allen's father had imbued his only son with a love of science that had led him to a double major in math and physics at Morehouse (he'd also entered the college at age fifteen on an early admissions scholarship). But Mr. Allen's ambition had been thwarted by racism and private demons. Anguished, he presented his son a troubling model of manhood. Robert Allen said that as he struggled to walk "upright," his turbulent family history often caused him to stumble.

"My father loved to tinker and wanted to have his own mechanic's shop," Allen remembered. "Instead he worked as a maintenance man in the housing projects across the street from Morehouse and Spelman. The failure was a symbol of his life."

His voice quieting, Allen continued: "He was also an alcoholic and very violent. I remember when I was five or six and he came home late. I must have left my toys on the walkway to the house because he tripped and fell and got a big gash in his upper arm. He charged into my bedroom and shook me awake. Pointing at his bloody arm, he started screaming, 'Look what you did to me.' My mother stayed with him until the children were educated. Then she left. My father died at age fifty-two."

Alice was not unaware of Robert's tumultuous upbringing nor of its impact on his self-esteem. She said that despite his outward success, Robert feared that, like his father, he might be destined for failure. And at the start of the romance he, too, had a "a quiet drinking problem" and a temper that easily flared out of control. "Robert was very angry," Alice remembered. "And out of that anger, he could sometimes act in cowardly ways. At night, if we'd return to the car and someone had parked too close, he'd grab a stick and bash out the headlights. Then he'd turn to me and say, 'I'm hurting. I know that if I'm with you, I'll get my health back.' "

In that, Robert understood the message from artist Yoko Ono in her poem "Reincarnation":

> *Mirror becomes a razor when it's broken*
> *A stick becomes a flute when it's loved.*

But still reeling from the emotions that punctuated the end of her marriage, Alice, even in her yearning for Robert, could withstand only so much more turmoil. As a philosophical concept, perhaps "free love" had its merits. But as a practical matter, Alice's sense of honor and empathy for Robert's wife made it difficult for her to commit fully to the relationship. Furthermore, she later noted, she had not left Mississippi and endured the anguish of divorce only to fling herself into the heated drama of a love triangle. This was territory she'd already probed in *Meridian* and had no desire to reprise personally.

Confident that her relationship with Robert would sort itself out (or not), Alice trained her focus, even more intently, on the one passion that had always sustained: writing. The poem "Janie Crawford" would reflect her sentiments as she began a new phase of her life.

> *i love the way Janie Crawford*
>
> *left her husbands the one who wanted*
> *to change her into a mule*
> *and the other who tried to interest her*

in being a queen
a woman unless she submits is neither a mule
nor a queen
though like a mule she may suffer
and like a queen pace
the floor

As befitted her expertise, Alice had taken the lead in evaluating the piles of poetry and fiction manuscripts that poured into *Ms.* magazine. In addition to women writers from Africa, she championed other authors whose artistry was routinely ignored. For example, in a characteristic counterpoint to the media frenzy that accompanied the 1974 release of such books as *Jaws* and *All the President's Men*, Alice, in a rave review, directed *Ms.* readers to *Cruelty*, a debut volume of poems by a writer of African American and Japanese descent born as Florence Anthony and later known as Ai (which means love in Japanese). Bedazzled by the release, which included the poem "Forty-Three-Year-Old Woman, Masturbating," Alice later declared to a friend, "The book is so raw and cuttingly honest it makes me feel women (including myself) have frittered away centuries speaking in euphemisms." Ai would win the 1999 National Book Award in poetry for her collection *Vice*.

Trumped by Watergate and the killer sharks in Peter Benchley's saga, *Faith and the Good Thing*, an impressive 1974 novel about a black woman's quest for wholeness, also searched for an audience ("Listen. The Devil was beating his wife on the day Faith's mother, Lavidia, died her second death"). Like Ai, the book's author, Charles Johnson, would go on to receive a National Book Award (in 1990) for *Middle Passage*.

To be sure, any doubts that Alice might have harbored about the impact of her writing were countered, increasingly, by her confidence in her stylistic precision and the fearlessness of her content. Writing for *Ms.* in April 1975, she had taken dead aim at a topic about which the black male critic Frank Lamont Phillips had angrily proclaimed, "This bullshit should not be encouraged." The object of his wrath? *Loving Her*, a groundbreaking novel by Ann Allen Shockley, a librarian at historically black Fisk University.

"To my knowledge, *Loving Her* is the first novel about an interracial lesbian relationship written by a black woman," Alice observed, matter-of-factly, in a review of Shockley's controversial 1974 book. "Viewed as an artistic work, I think the novel fails. But in its exploration of a daring subject boldly shared . . . I think it has immense value. It enables us to see and understand . . . the choices certain women have made about how they will live their lives, and allows us glimpses at physical intimacies between women that have been, in the past, deliberately ridiculed or obscured."

In later correspondence Alice applauded Shockley for her courage and revealed that she'd dispatched *Loving Her* to a relative in Georgia, who, after falling in love with a white woman, had divorced her husband ("who is a nice guy except that my cousin discovered she simply cannot relate sexually to men"). In another letter, foreshadowing difficulties to come, Alice shared her dismay at the resistance she'd met from *Ms.* staffers after presenting *Loving Her* for review. "I have had three fights so far with the book committee and one was over your book," Alice confided to Shockley. "People are very chicken-hearted everywhere. . . . I hadn't expected to do the review at all and had assigned it to two other people who just couldn't seem to come to grips with it. But I'm glad you liked [the review] overall and I think it is important that *Ms.* covered it."

At Alice's direction, *Ms.* also published "The Thorn," a debut story by Mary Gordon about a heart-sick girl grieving the death of her father. As such, the tale held resonance for a woman who'd recently laid her father to rest. "I was completely unknown and unpublished when Alice Walker bought the story," remembered Gordon, who'd go on to write the highly acclaimed novels *Final Payments* (1978) and *The Company of Women* (1980). "It made me feel legitimated, anointed, and set me on my way. I was over the moon." Then attesting to the down-to-earth nature of the new *Ms.* hire, Gordon added that she'd had very little contact with Alice, "except that she told me I needed a new typewriter ribbon."

Contrary to those who'd later deride *Ms.* as a hotbed of bra-burning, Sappho-worshipping "feminazis," Steinem noted that the magazine, in its initial conception, was never as extremist as depicted by the media. About Alice's editorial contributions, she said, "There was blatant rebelliousness, in Alice's own work and in that of other writers she brought to the magazine. She saw rebellion as key to the freedom and empowerment of women. She was far more radical than most of us in that regard."

ALICE FELT that a psychic burden had been lifted when, in 1978, Robert Allen separated from his wife. Two more years would pass before the couple officially divorced. From the outset, Alice had made it plain to Robert that she would never again utter marriage vows. "I am more committed to learning to speak Spanish than I am to the institution of marriage," she'd later declare. Still, she was heartened by a decision that put an end to the limbo status of a relationship that, even with its challenges, she felt was a vital part of her journey.

For there was no denying the depth of her attraction to Robert. Like Mel, he was a crusader for justice. He was also intelligent, creative, and adventurous. The fact that he'd spent childhood summers visiting kinfolk near Wards Chapel cast, to Alice's thinking, a fated glow on their bond. "It was a deep connection," she later observed.

With Robert finally freed from his domestic crisis, Alice was thrilled to discover the ease with which he fully embraced the gentle and nurturing aspects of his being. In an era that proffered slick "superfly" movie images of "John Shaft" and "Sweet Sweetback" as the epitome of black manhood, Robert, through his writing and activism, would dedicate himself to battling sexism. On the personal front, he'd tackle his substance abuse issues and commit to sobriety. And it didn't hurt that Robert, reared primarily in a household of women, had learned to make, *from scratch*, a delectable sweet potato pie.

Mindful of the intimate conversations the two women had shared at Sarah Lawrence, Diana Young remembered the sense of anticipation she felt upon hearing of Alice's new love. To her eager questions about the special attributes of Robert Allen, Young said that Alice had a ready reply:

"Well, last night, for starters, Robert painted my toenails," Alice told Diana, detailing a recent rendezvous. Then she let go with a cascade of rapturous laughter that might have come from Janie Crawford flush in her bliss with Tea Cake.

36

Country People

DETERMINED TO cultivate the most authentic setting for her work, Alice decided to leave New York for San Francisco. She was the first to admit that her romance with Robert was a motivating factor in her move, at the end of 1978, to the city of sensuous hills and sweeping ocean vistas. But the main spark was her dedication to art. Like Zora Neale Hurston, Alice was driven to offer readers a vision of (primarily) black folk life that was rendered unapologetic and *whole*. And if, like Hurston, she sometimes found herself "doubting the good sense" of the recipients of her labor, that was a risk she was willing to take. For there was now an audacious cast of characters clamoring for her attention with the fervor of a jackleg preacher trying to snatch his flock from Satan's grip. To their mind, that hell was New York.

Truth be told, aside from the now-predictable complaints about her "lifestyle" (read: liberated) from the usual critics, Alice's work was, more often than not, well received. However, her advances had never topped ten thousand dollars, even with a publication list that included, by decade's end, two novels, three poetry volumes, a collection of short stories, and a 1974 children's biography of Langston

Hughes so intelligently written that it defied the singsong "picture book" categorizing by the publishing marketers.

And on that note, what could be said (really) about the marketing forces that had catapulted, in 1976, Agatha Christie's *Sleeping Murder* to the top of the *New York Times* Best-Seller List while sales of *Meridian* languished? For those who cared to know, the Miss Marple mystery actually had been written *in 1946*, then stored in a vault for thirty years. The book's release was timed to coincide with its author's death in order to maximize sales.

Its veracity later questioned, *Roots*, Alex Haley's blockbuster work on slavery, was also released in 1976. And thus was Alice's effort and extraordinary works like *Eva's Man* by Gayl Jones and *Coming Through Slaughter* (the debut novel by Michael Ondaatje) eclipsed that year. Writing in the *New York Review of Books* long after the novel's publication, critic Robert Towers would bemoan the nation's inattention to *Meridian*, hailing it as "the most impressive fictional treatment of the 'Movement' that I have yet read."

As a black woman writing in the 1970s, Alice knew that to measure herself by mainstream literary standards was to court despair. Indeed, Gwendolyn Brooks, disaffected with the "major houses," had abandoned commercial publishing altogether by the mid-1960s. She would go to her death with such shimmering works as *A Street in Bronzeville* (1945), *Maud Martha*, and the Pulitzer Prize–winning *Annie Allen* (all released by Harper & Row) barely known to the majority of American readers. Never prone to self-pity, Brooks was clear-eyed about her plight: "Once, I considered *burying* my precious manuscripts in the back yard so that in the future—at some time in the hundreds of years to come—they would be discovered and loved," she revealed in *Report from Part One*, the 1972 autobiography she published with the black-owned Broadside Press.

Raised by a mother who planted flowers and preserved fruit to create beautiful tapestries out of the only artist's "tools" available to her, Alice took heart, nonetheless, in the belief that her novels and poems, if not profitable, were at least useful and uplifting to the "common folk" whose opinions she most valued. Her talents had also been affirmed, since the prize-winning essay for *American Scholar*, with several other prestigious awards, among them a Guggenheim Fellowship (about $13,000) she'd received in 1977. As Rebecca was to be with her father until 1980, it was the Guggenheim money (dwindling) and a $300 monthly retainer from *Ms.* that Alice planned to live on in California as she worked on a new novel whose characters had set up house in her imagination.

"Alice had always worked independently at *Ms.*," remembered Joanne Edgar. "Call us ahead of the curve on telecommuting, in any event, we supported her completely. It wasn't necessary for Alice to be in New York, physically, to continue her work with the magazine."

This was welcome news. For the collard greens in Alice's Brooklyn backyard notwithstanding, the characters (Southern, full of spunk) in her new novel had made clear their displeasure with screeching subways and towering skyscrapers that, to their mind, seemed to block God's view. About California's infamous earthquakes, Alice's characters told her they were "iffy" but willing to take their chances, having survived many a bottle-slinging, chair-tossing, table-upending, jook joint rumble.

As she headed for San Francisco, Alice, age thirty-four, was mindful of Lucy Hurston's exhortation to her daughter Zora: "Jump at the sun." That Zora had jumped high, there could be no question. It was the landing on one's feet that Alice was called to test by a bodacious quartet named Shug, Celie, Nettie, and Sofia.

Led by Ms. Shug (a flashy blues singer), the characters in Alice's new novel were so feisty that they jabbered on, with additional "helpful hints," even after she'd spirited them out of New York. They found the picturesque ferries and cable cars of San Francisco to be a heap more tolerable than the frenzied madness of Times Square. Nettie thrilled to the proliferation of bookstores, Sofia to the lusty aroma of sourdough bread. But the apartment that Alice shared with Robert, while sunny and bright, had a major drawback. It was right smack in the middle of San Francisco, near the city's bustling downtown area. And therefore would not do.

"They didn't like seeing buses, cars, or other people whenever they attempted to look out," Alice later noted, recounting the "directives" she received from her characters (a wearisome man named Mr. _____ and his son Harpo were now on the scene).

"That was when I knew for sure these were country people. . . . So [Robert] and I started driving around the state looking for a country house to rent. Eventually we found a place . . . that my characters liked. And no wonder: it looked a lot like the town in Georgia most of them were from, only it was more beautiful and the local swimming hole was not segregated."

About a three-hour drive north of San Francisco, the area to which Alice's characters gave their approval was originally settled in the 1880s by an independent-minded group of loggers and sheep ranchers. Today, the community (Boonville) is an iconoclastic mix of artisans, small farmers, vintners, and "free radicals" of every stripe. And their rebelliousness is worn with pride.

The community even had its own language, Boontling, which was still understood, if not widely spoken, when Alice arrived in the late 1970s. Dating back nearly a century, the colorful patois had been developed with the express purpose of excluding "bright lighters" (city people) and preventing them from meddling in local affairs.

For example, taking their inspiration from the appearance of livestock that had recently been sheared, the residents used the term *croppie* for sheep. Recast from "sky pilot" (itself slang), *skipe* meant preacher. When making reference to a black person, Boontling demanded *booker*, as in Booker T. Washington, whose portrait Alice had coveted at Ma Jessie's. As for bookers, well, compared to New York City, their ranks were thin in this stretch of Northern California, but the area was not completely bereft of black families. Alice and her characters (partial themselves to an earthy folk language) took the presence of minorities as a powerful message that she should make the community her new home.

"Robert and I had just visited a town a little farther north but found it too artificial and touristy," Alice later recalled. "On the drive back, we passed a little black boy walking along the side of the road in Boonville and he looked really happy. So, we stopped, bought the local newspaper, checked out the listings, and rented a house. I figured that any place where a black child looked that happy and carefree was probably a good place to live." Admiring of Alice's writing and activism, Bootlingers welcomed her with open arms. "It's as if the goddess herself had arrived," remembered Sue Sellars, a local artist.

As Robert still had job responsibilities in the city, he and Alice agreed that he'd keep an apartment in San Francisco and come to the country as his schedule permitted. And her plans? Before leaving Brooklyn, Alice had given herself five years to complete the novel that would become *The Color Purple*. Now comfortably settled in the midst of a redwood forest, she bought cascades of fabric in brilliant hues and started stitching a quilt pattern called (aptly) "Sister's Choice." Alice also gardened. She took walks. She cooked okra. She played Bessie Smith records, and when Robert visited, they took pleasure in each other's company with a fair amount of *burlapping*, the local lingo for . . . an activity Bessie tended to praise in her musical repertoire.

Writing in the *Village Voice* about the 1920s-era photographer Tina Modotti (1896–1942), critic Katherine Dieckman noted that the politically engaged and sexually uninhibited artist had been disdained by cultural standard-bearers outraged that a woman had "dared to create, agitate, and make love all at once in the same lifetime."

By contrast, content that they'd found the kindred spirit (finally!) with whom they could share their story, Alice's characters rejoiced. That is, all of them except for Mr. _____, who, sensing trouble, headed for the nearest jook joint.

37

An Ugly One at That

THE BUCOLIC life Alice had created in the countryside was disrupted in January 1979 when *Ms.* featured a young black woman named Michele Wallace on its cover. Then in her midtwenties, Wallace (daughter of celebrated quilt artist Faith Ringgold) had set off a firestorm of controversy with the release of her debut book, *Black Macho and the Myth of the Superwoman.*

In it Wallace chronicled her upbringing against the backdrop of what she cast as "the growing distrust, even hatred" between black men and black women. Chief among the markers of such "hatred" she cited in her impassioned but largely anecdotal book was the sexist treatment of black women during the civil rights era and a subsequent "grand coming-out of black male/white female couples" that Wallace faulted for plunging black women of her generation into near-suicidal despair.

She lashed out at a remark made by black comedian Redd Foxx that had been widely circulated at the time. Asked about the aspirations of a pioneering black woman politician, Foxx had brayed, to the resounding cheers of many, that black men would rather have "a Raquel Welch in the bedroom than a Shirley Chisholm in the White House." Campaigning under the banner "Unbought and

Unbossed," Chisholm (D-Brooklyn) made political history when, in 1968, she became the first black woman to win a House seat. She failed in a 1972 bid for the presidential nomination.

"Black men often could not separate their interest in white women from the hostility toward black women," Wallace observed in her scathing assessment of black gender relations at the end of the 1970s. " 'I can't stand that black bitch,' was the way it was usually put. Other black men argued that white women gave them money, didn't put them down, made them feel like men. . . . And some black women would laugh low in their throats when they saw a black man with a white woman and make cracks about his high-water pants or his flat head: 'Only the rejects crawl for white pussy.' "

Like Ntozake Shange, Wallace was swiftly rebuked by many blacks who were outraged not only by the thematic thrust of her book, but perhaps even more so by her uncensored airing of black gender conflicts in the full glare of white society. First *For Colored Girls* on Broadway. Now a cover story about *Black Macho* (replete with chapter excerpts) in *Ms.*! That the magazine had pronounced Wallace's rambling work "the book that will shape the 1980s" only fueled suspicions that white feminists were plotting the advance of their movement by exploiting tensions in a black community that many felt had more pressing problems (i.e., racism) than the offhand "jokes" of black men.

An essay in the March–April 1979 issue of the *Black Scholar* in which black sociologist Robert Staples from the University of California at San Francisco denounced Wallace and Shange *and* offered his own theories as to why interracial relationships often appealed to "the best and brightest of black men" likewise drew national attention and ensured that the controversy raged on. Alice, by virtue of her affiliation with *Ms.*, was generally believed to have "conspired with Gloria Steinem" to promote *Black Macho* (and thereby elevate its legitimacy), according to writer hattie gossett. "People thought of Alice as the gatekeeper for anything black at *Ms.*," she explained.

"Since white feminists could not marshal an all-out attack on black males . . . how could they be put in their place," fumed

Staples in "The Myth of Black Macho: A Response to Angry Black Feminists." "Enter Ntozake Shange and Michele Wallace. While other black writers have trouble finding a forum to discuss the persistence of racist conditions, Shange's play . . . has drawn sell-out audiences . . . composed mostly of black women and whites . . . Wallace can be found on the cover of *Ms.* Magazine. . . . There are, as always, two sides to the story—which is an ugly one at that."

"Black women like to dismiss the interracially involved black male as a classic example of the brainwashed idiot who is seduced by whiteness," Staples continued, revisiting a subject that seemed to have no end. "Yet, we never question how such a large proportion of black men who can lead our organizations, publish our magazines, star in our films, sing our songs and write our books, can be so gullible as to be seduced by nothing more than white skin. . . . It could be that the most successful black men have values and lifestyles most in tune with white society. Among those values will exist the one that women should be supportive and subordinate. . . . Many black men, including those involved with black women, do not believe black women fit that model very well."

Anticipating the deluge of letters that the Staples article provoked, the next issue of the *Black Scholar* (May–June 1979) featured a forum that continued the heated debate about *Black Macho*. Michele Wallace did not respond. But damned if she'd apologize for urging black women to "love themselves fiercely," Ntozake Shange rose up and fired off a poem about rape. It was printed in the *Black Scholar* exchange:

> *women shd go everywhere in 2's after dark*
> *women who don't have roommates or friends or want to*
>   *take a walk alone*
> *have to stay in or getta police dog.*
> *also women walking alone or in 2's after dark*
> *must counter rumors that the only thing two women wd*
>   *want to do without a man is fuck each other*
> *in this case*
> *they are still preventing rape.*

As for her part, Alice would later reveal that she had been happy to assist when Wallace, prior to the release of *Black Macho*, contacted her, seeking comments on the manuscript, though Wallace apparently ignored Alice's suggestions. A detailed memo she crafted for the forum in the *Black Scholar* was similarly dismissed after Alice refused to "revise" comments deemed "too hysterical" to be included in the exchange. Thus, her public response to the controversy would not appear until four years later when the memo was published in *In Search of Our Mothers' Gardens*. (An editor at the *Black Scholar*, Robert had recused himself from the entire affair.)

Allowing that she found flaws in their work, Alice nonetheless applauded Wallace and Shange for "affirming themselves and remarking on the general condition of black life as they know it, which they are entitled to do." To the free-floating allegation that she had parlayed her *Ms.* ties into an explosive cover story ruthlessly calculated to malign black men, Alice replied, matter-of-factly, "I was not the editor of the Wallace piece." (It had been acquired and edited by Robin Morgan, then on staff at the magazine.)

"Instead of arguing . . . about whether there is or is not sexism in the black community (and how could our community possibly be different from every other one in that respect), look around you," Alice continued. "Look at the black men and women that you know. Look at your family. . . . Look at what we actually *do* to each other. Look at what we actually *say*. . . . In Michele Wallace's book, there are many good things that (though not as original as she thinks) can be very helpful to us, if we will *hear* them. . . . While not sound or visionary or even honest enough to 'shape the eighties' [*Black Macho*] can still help us shape our thinking."

The comments about her book did not come soon enough for Wallace, who, twenty years later, said she felt ambushed by a cover story that, to her mind, had Alice's blessing, inadvertent (or equivocal) though it might have been. She added that her feelings were colored by a "hatchet job" review of *Black Macho* authored by June Jordan. Wallace said she felt certain, given the friendship between the two women, that Alice had been apprised of Jordan's harsh critique prior to its publication in the *New York Times* on March 18, 1979. "You do have to concede championship qualities to Miss Wallace's capacity for the unsubstantiated, self-demeaning, ahistorical pronouncement," Jordan sneered, in an overall slam of the book. She was especially offended, as were many readers of *Black Macho*, by Wallace's assertion that black women, because of a long legacy of mental anguish, considered themselves to be "exempt from human responsibility." For Alice, the argument was beyond comprehension.

"I am delighted when another black woman speaks her mind and offers her own opinion, but this—even in context—is a stunner," she noted in her memo. "In what way have we not been responsible? How have we been exempt? . . . There is nothing one can think of to which [the statement] actually applies."

During a telephone interview, Wallace did not rebut charges that she'd produced an ill-conceived book riddled with poorly wrought ideas. "The book was written in innocence and ignorance," Wallace explained. "There's no question but that the book had problems that would prevent it from being published today. . . . But the big publicity spread in *Ms.* was backed with the full machinery of the magazine. When things got hot, everybody on the masthead ducked for cover and I was treated like the plague." Still, *Black Macho* appeared briefly on the best-seller list of the *Washington Post* and generated sixty thousand hardcover sales, she said.

Firm in her memory of having been an ally to Wallace throughout the *Black Macho* ordeal, Alice said that she found the author's recollection of events "profoundly weird." "I remember being one of several women who helped launch Michele's book in New York," she countered. "I thought [*Black Macho*] was bold and brilliant and I'm sure I said so. I didn't agree with everything, of course, but that's never a necessity when something useful is being offered.

"And June was never in the habit of sharing what she wrote with me before it was published. We didn't have that kind of relationship. . . . I've felt so sad for Michele over the years because I think she was deeply wounded by the criticism and she was so young."

Added Robin Morgan: "I think Michele Wallace's apparently

to-this-day defensiveness arises from the attacks that she was anti-Black-male, a man-hater, all the usual, I fear. . . . She was totally unprepared for the level of vituperation. . . . As for all of *Ms.*—including Alice and me—treating Michele like 'the plague' . . . that's simply not true. *Black Macho* made many folks at the magazine nervous, but Alice remained her serene and courteous self. As for me, I continued to see Michele now and then socially, as well as at political events, for years thereafter."

During the phone interview, Wallace also revealed that she has yet to fully recover from the anger that was directed toward her in the aftermath of the release of her debut book. "I had a nervous breakdown," she declared, unashamedly. Hoping to put distance between herself and the controversy, she later took a teaching job in Oklahoma where, with the state's negligible black population, she said she felt less likely to be condemned for her work. "It was a refuge," she said. "There was this sense that . . . there wasn't much you could do to get in any trouble. Everybody was so relaxed, so unjudgemental, so laid back."

Wallace would also present her account of events relating to *Black Macho* in the essay, "To Hell and Back." If she felt betrayed by Alice or *Ms.* magazine, she also seemed willing to say *mea culpa* for the conflict.

"I went from obscurity to celebrity to notoriety overnight," Wallace notes in the piece, which appears in the 1998 collection, *The Feminist Memoir Project*. Writing with candor about her confused mental state when she crafted *Black Macho*, she continues, "The result of an unhappy alliance between a perfectionist unfeminist aesthete and a young, nihilistic, black, feminist, militant half-crazed and sexually frustrated maniac, the text could only hope to crash and burn, which it promptly did after first driving a lot of people crazy, including me. . . . Just because I gave it birth doesn't mean I understand it."

In 1990, Verso publishers reissued *Black Macho* in connection with the company's release of Wallace's book *Invisibility Blues*. A decade later, Alice offered reflections on the entire affair as it related to strengthening alliances between black women: "Sisterhood is hard work. Yet I believe it has only been good for us not to let any of these disappointments keep us from seeing that we must uphold, as much as possible, for this time or for that time, which was so treacherous, a united front. It has always pleased me enormously that for the most part you could not get one black woman writer to 'kill' another one for the cheers of the crowd. Though I suppose June came close with her review of *Black Macho*."

ALICE MARKED the end of the 1970s with the release of two works that expanded her reputation as a writer with a penchant for distinctive titles: A new volume of poems, *Good Night, Willie Lee, I'll See You in the Morning* and *I Love Myself When I Am Laughing . . . And Then Again When I Am Looking Mean and Impressive*, a collection of autobiography, folklore, essays, articles, and fiction by Zora Neale Hurston. The title of the Hurston anthology was borrowed from a 1934 letter the author had written to photographer Carl Van Vechten (1880–1964) in reference to a series of portraits he'd taken of her. Many of the works in the collection had previously been out of print or difficult to find.

"Financial dependency is the thread that sewed a cloud over Hurston's life, from the time she left home to work as a maid at fourteen to the day of her death," Alice wrote in the opening pages of the landmark reader she edited for the Feminist Press.

"It is ironic that *this* woman, who many claimed sold her soul to record the sources of authentic, black American folk art (whereas it is apparently cool to sell your soul for a university job, say, or a new car) and who was made of some of the universe's most naturally free stuff . . . was denied even a steady pittance, free from strings, that would have kept her secure enough to do her best work. . . . Only after she died penniless . . . still following *her* vision and *her* road, did it begin to seem to some that yes, perhaps this woman *was* a serious artist after all. But you're up against a hard game if you have to die to win it, and we must insist that dying in poverty is an unacceptable extreme."

The reader also featured a stirring introduction ("Zora Neale

Hurston: A Woman Half in Shadow") by Mary Helen Washington. "What Hurston left us is only a fraction of what she might have accomplished," she ventured, in the essay. She later recalled her work on the project: "Alice asked me to write the introduction to the Hurston reader. It turned out to be a wonderful collaboration. Alice has a fine sense of literature and is not encumbered by academia which causes most scholars to be cut off from themselves. Alice is in community and brings herself to the text. Through Zora, Alice brought us back to our roots."

In a review for the *New York Times*, Randall Kennedy declared *I Love Myself* an extraordinary collection that helped to resurrect Hurston's life and work "from unmerited oblivion." Emphasizing the book's larger scope, Kennedy said that it reflected an emerging black feminism and, in its sophisticated analysis, set new standards for the study of black literature. "The eclipse of Hurston's reputation was due in part to black critics who angrily dismissed her work because they disagreed with her politics," Kennedy asserted. "Miss Walker, however, demands that her heroine's writing be considered on its own terms. 'We are better off,' she counsels, 'if we think of Zora Neale Hurston as an artist, period—rather than as the artist/politician most black writers have been required to be.' "

Kennedy hailed Alice as a worthy interpreter of Hurston's talents, noting that both writers celebrated the complexity of black people, "reveling in their squalor as well as their beauty" without apology.

Insistent themes declare themselves in *I Love Myself*. One involves the struggle of black women to achieve the liberation of self-awareness. . . . In marked contrast to the leading tendency of her time, Hurston [also] confined the menace of white intrusion to the periphery of her fiction. Well aware of bigotry, she chose to portray the manner in which, in the midst of white oppression, blacks work to create their own way of life. . . .

Indeed, Hurston displayed without inhibition the underside of black society. . . . Her openness was predicated upon an assurance of her people's humanity. The [collection] is edited with similar assurance, for Alice Walker also evinces a willingness to present her subject in full.

In the notes that preceded each section, Alice was forthright in discussing Hurston's literary failings, most notably the "frustrating generalities" about love in her autobiography, *Dust Tracks on a Road*. "However, we have far too few records—even evasive ones—of what black women have thought about the two most important human drives: the need to work and the need to love," Alice maintained.

As is evident in excerpts Alice selected, even in its evasiveness, Hurston's prose sparkled: "A man may lose interest in me and go where his fancy leads him, and we can still meet as friends. But if I get tired and let on about it, he is certain to become an enemy of mine. That forces me to lie like the cross-ties from New York to Key West. . . . I have a strong suspicion, but I can't be sure, that much that passes for constant love is a golded-up moment walking in its sleep."

ALICE EXAMINED the nitty-gritty intimacies of black life in *Good Night, Willie Lee*. Composed of poems written during the end of her marriage and the early stages of her liaison with Robert Allen, the collection eschewed "moon, June, swoon" rhapsodizing for hard-hitting testimonies that demystified romantic love. Indeed, in an unvarnished "anti-valentine," the volume opened with "Did This Happen to Your Mother? Did Your Sister Throw up a Lot?" in which Alice declared:

> *Love has made me sick.*
>
> *Did your sister throw up a lot?*
> *Did your cousin complain*
> *of a painful knot*
> *in her back?*

Did your aunt always
seem to have something else
troubling her mind? . . .

Such needful love has to be chopped out
or forced to wilt back,
poisoned by disapproval
from its own soil.

This is bad news, for the conservationist.

In equally candid poems about Africa and the assassinations of Malcolm X and Martin Luther King Jr. ("they gave us rebellion as pure love"), Alice revisited the cataclysmic political uprisings of the 1960s. Dedicated to South African writer Bessie Head (1937–1986), "Having Eaten Two Pillows" heralded Alice's progress from a despairing young student who'd once mimed slashing her wrists to a fearless artist determined to save her soul, if not society.

Having eaten two pillows
in the middle of the night
having stumbled from bullets
my close friends have fired
having loved all those fully
that I love
and still not loving
all those to whom time
has not brought grace
ambition raises itself:
to survive my life
"just anyone"
                hello
though I know quite well
the words to say goodbye.

In a note at the end of the text, Alice explained that Head, whose fiction she'd published in *Ms.*, often created characters who aspired not to greatness but rather to become "just anyone." "Which is perceived as the correct relationship to other people and to the world," Alice wrote. "I feel this is also a correct alternative to despair, or, in some cases, suicide."

In the title poem, "Good Night, Willie Lee," Alice stands as witness to the ritual reconciliation between her mother and a father in whose torment she'd soon discover a healing talisman. Her artistry fueled by the intertwined gifts of succor and sorrow, Alice trained her eyes on redemption, as reflected in the forcefully rendered poem "On Stripping Bark from Myself."

> *because women are expected to keep silent about*
> *their close escapes I will not keep silent*
> *and if I am destroyed (naked tree!) someone will*
> *   please*
> *mark the spot*
> *where I fall and know I could not live*
> *silent in my own lies*
> *hearing their "how* nice *she is!"*
> *whose adoration of the retouched image*
> *I so despise.*
>
> *No. I am finished with living*
> *for what my mother believes*
> *for what my brother and father defend*
> *for what my lover elevates*
> *for what my sister, blushing, denies or rushes*
> *to embrace.*
>
> *I find my own*
> *small person*
> *a standing self*
> *against the world*
> *an equality of wills*
> *I finally understand.*

Besides:

*My struggle was always against
an inner darkness: I carry within myself
the only known keys
to my death—to unlock life, or close it shut
forever. A woman who loves wood grains, the color
    yellow
and the sun, I am happy to fight
all outside murderers
as I see I must.*

Writing in *Publishers Weekly,* Genevieve Stuttaford praised the collection as "forthright, spare, antithetical, and eloquent of spirit." "[Walker] speaks for . . . a new asceticism wherein women are holy and alone. . . . If there is one thing that unifies these poems, sometimes harsh but never strident, frequently exultant and always quiet, it is the beating of a fine poet's heart."

Less impressed, Alan Williamson, a reviewer for the journal *Poetry,* discerned a predilection for "theatrical" line-breaking and a "preachy" tone in *Good Night, Willie Lee.* Still, he noted that Alice "has a gift for the luminous image which makes the entire poem coalesce around it." He cited as one of her finest examples "Early Losses: a Requiem," in which Alice traces the history of an African girl stolen from her homeland and sold into slavery. The girl holds fast to a memory that unspeakable in its inhumanity still sustains.

*A sound like a small wind
finding the door of a
hollow reed
my mother's farewell
glocked up from the back
to her throat*

The sound itself is all

Offering comments that appeared on the paperback edition, poet Denise Levertov said about *Good Night, Willie Lee*, "I always await new work by Alice Walker with eagerness, and this volume is no disappointment. In these poems there's the power of a mind's concentrated passion. . . . Nothing here is facile or verbose. . . . There's a compassion in the poems that is not only painfully earned but has, each time, to be earned over again—and it is this that gives [the collection] its authenticity."

38

A Room to Move Into

ANNOYING. TIRESOME. The hue and cry over *Black Macho* had been all that, but the controversy had not stopped Alice from moving forward with her writing. In 1981, she released a second volume of short stories heralded with a book party announcement that read:

Your Grandmama Survived
Taft
Your Mama Survived
Hoover
You've Already Survived
Nixon
and
One Hundred and Forty Days
of
Reagan
Why?
Because
YOU CAN'T KEEP A GOOD WOMAN DOWN
Celebrate
the
Tradition!

Held at the San Francisco Women's Building, the party was a celebration of a book in which Alice offered fourteen provocative tales about black women struggling, but not defeated. Women like the protagonist who, in the story "How Did I Get Away with Killing One of the Biggest Lawyers in the State? It Was Easy," finds herself sitting in bed savoring fried chicken prepared by the wife of the man who has stolen her youth. Or Elethia, a "salad girl" at a café (segregated) who liberates a waxen replica of a docile black man that has been placed, by the restaurant's white owners, in a window display to attract customers. And then there was Gracie Mae Still, a talented songwriter who watched in disgust, but not despair, as a swivel-hipped white boy (read: Elvis Presley) made hit records off of her artistry.

"He had followed every turning of my voice, side streets, avenues, red lights, train crossings and all," Alice wrote, describing Gracie Mae's response to the theft of her music in the story "Nineteen Fifty-five." "It give me a chill. Everywhere I went I heard [him] singing my song, and all the little white girls just eating it up. I never had so many ponytails switched across my line of vision in my life. They was so *proud*. He was a *genius.*"

With Tony Godwin dead of a heart attack in March 1976, Alice was now working with, in her words, a "meticulous and persistent" third Harcourt editor, John Ferrone. The former head of the company's paperback division, Ferrone was instantly impressed with *You Can't Keep a Good Woman Down*, which also included graphic stories about rape, abortion, and perhaps most notably, pornography. That Alice had embraced such taboo subject matter came as no surprise to Maryam Lowen, an old friend she had invited, before leaving New York, to a screening of *Deep Throat*. The story of a woman who, with a "clitoris in her throat," can only reach orgasm through fellatio, the 1972 release was the first X-rated movie to be marketed to a general audience. "Not to have seen it," mused Nora Ephron, writing for *Esquire* as the film racked up profits topping $600 million, "seemed somehow . . . derelict."

However, the profits (production costs were reputedly $40,000) held little meaning for the film's star, with whom the money was never shared. Revealing that her performance had been coerced under the threat of violence, Linda Lovelace later emerged as an outspoken critic of the sex industry, which she condemned as "legalized rape." She died in April 2002, at age fifty-three, from injuries sustained in a car accident.

"With all the hype about *Deep Throat*, Alice called me up one day and said we needed to go see it," recalled Lowen, a civil rights colleague from Jackson who had also moved to New York. "It was hard to watch. But in hindsight, I've appreciated Alice's foresight and courage in realizing that it was a movie we shouldn't ignore. And this was long before anybody knew that Linda Lovelace had been drugged and beaten into looking like she was enjoying herself. It wasn't sexy at all."

Hard-pressed to discover what proponents praised as the "eroticism" in pornography, in "Coming Part" Alice offered a glimpse of the industry through the eyes of a woman whose husband has a penchant for smut magazines. Presented as a fable, the story opens with the man's arrival home after work. Ignoring, momentarily, the elaborate meal his wife has prepared, the man visits the bathroom. "Sitting on the commode, he opens up the *Jiveboy* magazine he has brought home in his briefcase. There are a couple of jivemate poses that particularly arouse him. He studies the young women . . . and strokes his penis. . . . He emerges spent, relaxed—hungry for dinner. His wife, using the bathroom later, comes upon the slightly damp magazine." Unwilling to accept the dismissive "boys will be boys" quip her husband offers in response to her objections to porn ("you're the only black woman in the world that worries about any of this stuff"), she fights back with a treasure trove of her own that prompts him to question his sexuality.

In an introductory author's note about the piece, Alice revealed that it had been deemed pornographic and "banned temporarily by at least one school district in the United States." "[But] I believe it is only by writing stories in which pornography is confronted openly and explicitly that writers can make a contribution, in their own medium, to a necessary fight."

Writing in the *San Francisco Chronicle and Examiner*, author

Alice Adams applauded the daring of the collection: "[Walker] is exceptionally brave. She takes on subjects at which most writers would flinch and quail, and probably fail. She shrinks from no moral or emotional complexity and she writes consummately skillful short stories."

But notwithstanding the "edge and sparkle" to be found in some of the stories, another reviewer pronounced the overall collection uninspiring. "As Miss Walker aims for more, she achieves less," lamented Katha Pollitt in the *New York Times*. The stories are "too partisan (the black woman is always the most sympathetic character)." Especially critical of the experimental techniques Alice employed in the volume, Pollitt went on to declare, "[They call] our attention to the author as inventor and manipulator of every aspect of what we are reading."

She pointed to "Advancing Luna—and Ida B. Wells," a story in which Alice explores the rape of a white civil rights worker (Luna) by a black freedom fighter in Georgia. The unnamed black woman narrator is Luna's best friend. Now roommates in New York, Luna confides to the narrator that she acquiesced to her assailant (a minor media "star" named Freddie Pye) rather than scream and leave him prey to a lynch mob.

The narrator's response: "It is hard for me . . . to relate my feeling of horror and incredulity. . . . Suddenly I was embarrassed. Then angry. . . . *How dare she tell me this!* I thought. Who knows what the black woman thinks of rape? Who has asked her? Who *cares*? Who has even properly acknowledged that *she* and not the white woman in this story is the most likely victim of rape?"

In a scenario nearly impossible to imagine, Luna, apparently plagued by white liberal guilt, reconciles with her attacker. Again, the narrator: "One night . . . I noticed a man's blue denim jacket [in the apartment]. The next morning, out of Luna's bedroom walked Freddie Pye. He barely spoke to me—possibly because as a black woman I was expected to be hostile toward his presence in a white woman's bedroom. I was too surprised to exhibit hostility, however, which is only a part of what I felt. . . . Luna and I did not discuss this. . . . It was as if he was never there."

In a series of afterwords, Alice presents "discarded notes" and an alternate ending to the story. In the new ending, Luna informs the narrator that Pye was stranded in New York after speaking at a fund-raising event. She arms herself with a knife before permitting him to enter the apartment and the pair talk through the night about the racially charged politics of rape.

Not without merit, Pollitt argued that the story was burdened by weak character development and a "quasi-fictional" plot device. "I never believed for a minute . . . that the black woman narrator was really the best friend of poor Luna," she complained. "A friend would have felt some human sympathy, along with however much political angst, or if not, would have had to confront this lack. Instead, Luna, the person, is quickly bundled offstage. . . . Why? So that Miss Walker can spend the rest of the story on disjointed sections . . . that put forward a confused welter of thoughts and feelings about interracial rape."

Similarly, the *Kirkus Review* argued that the collection was largely propaganda, dismissing it as "ragged, often superficial work . . . with more sociological interest (the black/feminist intersection) than literary."

The charges leveled against *You Can't Keep a Good Woman Down* seemed to be batted about selectively. After all, what could be more "inventive" than *The Covenant* (1980), a best-selling James Michener novel released during the same publishing cycle that chronicled fifteen thousand years of South African history from the vantage of an Afrikaner championing apartheid? In passages about the country's mining industry, Michener's narrator opines, "No black was ever assigned to a job more treacherous than that what the white overseer was willing to do. . . . It took the white overseers only a few weeks to promote Jonathan [black] as the best. . . . They designated him to work . . . more than ten thousand feet down in a constant temperature of 114 degrees. . . . Jonathan's job was an exciting one."

Alice would later ponder said "excitement" in her poem "The Diamonds on Liz's Bosom."

The diamonds on Liz's bosom
are not as bright
as his eyes
the morning they took him
to work in the mines
The rubies in Nancy's
jewel box (Oh, how he
loves red!)
not as vivid
as the despair
in his children's
frowns.

Oh, those Africans!

Everywhere you look
they're bleeding
and crying
Crying and bleeding
on some of the whitest necks
in your town.

Those who would cast as unfair a comparison to a commercial writer like Michener were free to assess Alice in the glimmer of William Styron, winner of the 1968 Pulitzer Prize in fiction for *The Confessions of Nat Turner.* Writing in the persona of the leader of a notorious 1831 Virginia slave revolt, Styron presents a lasciviously savage portrait of Turner as a man driven less by a desire for freedom than a lust for white women denied black men under slavery.

In Styron's hands, Turner, captured and condemned to death, is consumed by masturbatory fantasies even as he is being led to the gallows:

And as I think of her . . . beyond my fear, beyond my dread . . . I feel the warmth flow into my loins and my legs tingle with desire. I tremble and I search for her face in my mind, seek the young body, yearning for her suddenly, with a craving beyond pain. . . . With tender stroking motions I pour out my love within her; pulsing flood; she arches against me, cries out, and the twain-black and white-are one. . . . Footsteps outside the door jar me from my reverie.

Thirty years later, Styron, unrepentant, continued to mock critics and scholars who'd been enraged by a work some had denounced as "The Second Crucifixion of Nat Turner." Defending himself in a 1998 speech at the Library of Congress, the author sneered, "Basically [*The Confessions*] is a very politically incorrect book written by a white man trying to seize his own interpretation and put it into the soul and heart of a black man."

As for the prevailing literary voices when critics such as Pollitt decried Alice's work as "too partisan," well, they could hardly have been less diverse. Already a 1969 Pulitzer Prize winner for *The Armies of the Night*, Norman Mailer was awarded the 1980 Pulitzer in fiction for *The Executioner's Song*. In a triumvirate of white male acclamation, William Wharton (*Birdy*) would join William Styron (*Sophie's Choice*) and John Irving (*The World According to Garp*) as winners (all!) of the 1980 National Book Award for fiction. Two first-rate novels by black authors released during the era have yet to reach the masses: *The Salt Eaters* (1980) by Toni Cade Bambara and *Kindred* (1979) by the pioneering black science fiction writer Octavia Butler.

But as Langston Hughes noted in his poem "I Dream a World" ("where all / will know sweet freedom's way"), Alice had literary aspirations that she'd never expected to be embraced by the establishment. In a 1979 interview with Alice, Mary Helen Washington observed that the author had explored two cycles in the sociocultural history of black women: The first, Alice told Washington, was the "suspended black woman," as detailed in her essay "In Search of Our Mothers' Gardens." Next came a generation of women, who, with more freedoms than their enslaved foremothers, remained battle-scarred by Jim Crow and the conflicts of the civil rights era.

Describing the plight of such women, Alice told Washington, "They were . . . in a time in history where the options for Black women were severely limited. . . . And they either kill themselves or they are used up by the man, or by the children, or by . . . whatever pressures against them. And they cannot go anywhere. I mean, you can't just move, until there is room for you to move *into*. And that's the way I see many of the women I have created [thus far]."

"My women, in the future, will not burn themselves up," she continued, alluding to the literary lineage of characters like Mem, Myrna, Roselily, and Gracie Mae Still. "Now I am ready to look at women who have made the room larger for others to move in. . . . The Movement of the Sixties, Black Power, the Muslims, the Panthers . . . have changed the options of Black people generally and of Black Women in particular. So that my women characters won't all end the way they have been. . . . We have made a place to move on."

And with that said, proceeding from *You Can't Keep a Good Woman Down*, Alice returned to a narrative inspired by a black woman asking another for her silk panties.

39

Radically Brilliant

WHO COULD have predicted, Ruth later said, that a memory shared with the natural ease of a "country cook rolling out pie crust" would lead her baby sister to write *The Color Purple*?

As Ruth recalled, the fateful exchange with Alice took place in the late 1970s, not too long after the death of their paternal grandfather, Henry Clay Walker. Alice returned to Wards Chapel to honor the memory of a once-brutal man who had softened in his elder years. The transformation was shaped, in large part, by the love Pa-Pa had shared with Shug Perry throughout his marriage to Rachel, the young girl he had reluctantly wed after the murder of his first wife, Kate. Although she'd moved to Cleveland, Shug journeyed back to Georgia regularly to visit family and friends. In fact, Shug had two children by Henry Walker. Thus, they remained bound not only by the passion that lingered from the courtship of their youth, but by their "outside" (out-of-wedlock) children as well.

Simply put, Henry adored Shug Perry and would have married her gladly had his father not pressured him to pursue a more "respectable" wife. And as much as it hurt to be mistreated by a man whose children (Willie Lee Walker) and grandchildren (Alice et al.) she had loved and nurtured as her own, Rachel understood why Shug held an eternal place in her husband's heart. You'd have to be wearing smoked glasses and a blindfold, as the saying went, not to notice Shug's dazzle and spark.

"It was just a given that whenever Miss Shug came to Georgia, she would spend a few nights with Pa-Pa," Ruth explained. "In the beginning, this was hard on my grandmother because she essentially had 'the other woman' up under her roof. But over time, Ma-Ma started liking the arrangement because Pa-Pa would treat her better when Miss Shug came to visit. The family ate better, the conversations were livelier, and best of all, my grandfather wasn't as mean. Seeing how much the atmosphere improved, Ma-Ma made peace with the situation. Eventually she and Miss Shug became good friends."

And from that friendship came the underwear story. One Sunday, in the early 1940s, during one of Miss Shug's visits to Putnam County, she and Rachel walked home from church together. About age five at the time, Ruth had accompanied the two women. Some sixty years later, she recalled, "We were near about home when all three of us realized we needed to go to the bathroom. So, we cut across the field and headed for the outhouse. With me being a child, I naturally waited my turn. So, I was standing right there when Miss Shug started to pull up her underwear. My grandmother looked over and said, 'Ooh, give me them pretty pink panties you got on.' Just as quick as that, Miss Shug turned 'em loose, let 'em drop to the ground, and, with her foot, flipped the panties over to Ma-Ma, who put them in her pocket.

"You see, my grandmother never had any of those soft, frilly things," Ruth continued. "Knowing how Pa-Pa abused her, Miss Shug, maybe out of guilt, but mostly out of kindness, tried to make up for some of the hardships in Ma-Ma's life. She'd send her nice robes, slippers, and nightgowns from Cleveland. And it was just by chance that I was there that Sunday when Miss Shug gave my grandmother her pink panties. Walking through the woods with Alice after Pa-Pa died, I mentioned the incident in passing. Needless to say, it was an image I never forgot."

Ever welcoming of "spiritual forces" to guide her work, Alice knew that in Ruth's reminiscence she'd found the affirmation for the story she'd been plotting, in her head, about a lover's triangle. "I carried my sister's comment delicately balanced in the center of the novel's construction," Alice later revealed. She said it made her laugh to imagine what critics might one day say about the impetus for the book. "My 'history' starts not with the taking of lands, or the births, battles, and deaths of Great Men, but with one woman asking another for her underwear. Oh well, I thought, one function of critics is to be appalled by such behavior. But what woman (or sensuous man) could avoid being intrigued?"

The black lesbian activist and writer Barbara Smith was not only intrigued, but also enchanted by the novel she received from Harcourt for review. Like Barbara Christian and Mary Helen Washington, Smith had followed Alice's career for many years. As a doctoral student in the 1970s, she'd also audited the landmark black women's literature class that Alice taught at Wellesley and then at the University of Massachusetts, Boston, where Smith joined the class. And writing for *Ms.* in February 1974, Smith had reviewed *In Love & Trouble*, deeming Alice's honest exploration of the "textures and terrors" of black women's lives a major break-through in American letters.

"For every one of Walker's fictional characters I knew or had heard of a real woman whose fate was all too similar," wrote Smith, who, in her stirring 1977 essay "Toward A Black Feminist Criticism," had expressed the need for "one book . . . that would tell me something specific about my life."

Well versed though she might have been in the creativity and consciousness of Alice Walker, Smith said that nothing could have prepared her for the magnificence to come. Describing her thoughts upon receiving the new novel, she recalled, "I read *The Color Purple* in galleys [proof pages] and understood immediately that we were dealing with a book that was going to rock the publishing world. A black girl? Incest? Lesbianism? Letters to God? In black English? It was from another planet. Without question, it was the most radically brilliant book I'd ever read."

An epistolary novel composed of ninety letters, *The Color Purple* tells the story of Celie, an impoverished black girl in rural Georgia who struggles to free herself from crushing physical and emotional abuse. As the novel opens in the early 1900s, Celie is raped repeatedly by Fonso, a man she believes to be her father. Defenseless, she turns to the only source of comfort she can divine:

Dear God,
I am fourteen years old. ~~I am~~. I have always been a good girl. Maybe you can give me a sign letting me know what is happening to me . . . First he put his thing up gainst my hip. . . . Then he grab hold my titties. Then he push his thing inside my pussy. When that hurt, I cry.

Fonso takes the two infants Celie bears in the aftermath of his rapes and offers them for adoption, a transaction for which readers assume he gets paid. The children are embraced by a family of dedicated missionaries who lived nearby. Afraid that her sister Nettie might become Fonso's victim too, Celie has urged her to leave home and work with the family.

Having gratified his needs, Fonso marries Celie off ("she ain't fresh tho, I spect you know that") to a brutish widower with four children. This man Celie calls Mr._____. It is an appellation that reflects both her silenced condition and his insistence that she afford him the respect historically denied Southern black men. This he demands despite the fact that he beats Celie at whim and mounts her, like an animal, with no regard for her feelings: "I make myself wood. I say to myself, Celie, you a tree. That's how come I know trees fear men."

As the novel unfolds, readers learn, through Celie's letters, that Mr._____ is himself tormented by a lifelong passion for a vivacious singer named Shug Avery, who visits periodically. In her ebullience, Mr._____ is less abusive to Celie. Unfettered on every front, Shug initiates a sexual relationship with the battered young woman at the same time she carries on a romance with Mr._____ (whose birth name is Albert). It is through Shug's caress that Celie, experiencing tenderness for the first time, gains the strength to reject the shattering mistreatment she has endured and becomes whole. Shouting at Mr.____ that his dead body is "just the welcome mat I need," she confronts him about her discovery (with Shug's help) of his theft of the letters her sister Nettie has mailed over the years. From these letters, she is able to piece together a past that does not include incest, having learned that Fonso is not her real father. More importantly, the letters enable her to see that even in her anguish, she was always loved by her sister. Empowered, she begins to write to Nettie instead of God. Celie also grows stronger through her friendship with Sofia, a feisty black woman who is married to Mr.____'s son Harpo and who refuses to be dominated by anyone.

As Mr.____ comes to understand the roots of his emotional pain, he also undergoes a transformation that inspires him to help Celie reunite with her children. By the novel's end, the lover's triangle that was Shug, Celie, and Mr.____ has become a circle of compassion in which the characters in *The Color Purple* (and by turn the readers) learn that it is possible to heal from the hurts and humiliations of the past.

Gloria Steinem had also received an advance copy of Alice's new novel. She read the book on a flight back to New York from Utah, where her help had been solicited by Mormon women fighting for equal rights. In an October 25, 1981, letter that she wrote in transit, Steinem, like Barbara Smith, raved about *The Color Purple*:

> Dearest Alice,
> It is wonderful—I mean, full of wonder. You bring people straight off the page . . . who seem full of hate and irredeemable (like Mr.____) and then allow them to redeem themselves—which gives us faith in the possibilities of changing everything, even ourselves . . . . The lenses of somebody's race or somebody's sex that we are used to viewing everything through suddenly melt away, and there's a person there, whose race or sex is only one cherished part of them. That means that love and injustice and anger and just plain silliness or whatever cross all the barriers because they just aren't barriers anymore.

. . . How you make all this happen without ever selling short on telling the truth about people's habit of humiliating and torturing and breaking each other's spirits—precisely because they feel only boundaries and no empathy—is the real miracle. . . .

My pleasure by the end was so great that it couldn't even be ruined by some asshole anthropologist (tall, red-haired + a beard, who I thought was good-looking until he opened his mouth) who walked back in the plane to tell me that my remarks about god having once been in women + nature were ridiculous, that any pre-historical matriarchal or more equal society was hogwash. I argued and got my stomach all in a turmoil—but it settled right down again the moment I turned back to Celie's reunion with Nettie.

After signing off, Steinem scribbled another thought in the left margin of the lined notepaper. "And your novel is also the best + most human description of the injustice of colonialism—worth a dozen dry textbooks."

40

At a Double Remove

Writing for *Ms.* following the death of Anais Nin in January 1977, Alice paid tribute to an author whose praise for *In Love & Trouble* she had warmly received. She noted that in Nin's work (especially *Delta of Venus*, 1969) she had found much to admire, despite an elitist "insularity" that, to her mind, had diluted the writer's power and undermined her overall career. "Anais's apolitical nature was self-indulgent and escapist . . . her analysis of poverty [a] mere romantic construction," Alice asserted in the April 1977 piece. "But throughout her life she . . . made of her own mind and body a perpetually *new* frontier. . . . Her readers travel with less fear through those strange countries inside ourselves, which [Anais] in herself was unafraid to explore."

As the Harcourt editor for Anais and Alice, John Ferrone was awed by the daring of both women and pleased that they found value in each other's work (the exchange of which he facilitated). He could only imagine how Nin might have responded to *The Color Purple*, a work so compelling in its blend of art and politics that he was prepared to publish the narrative verbatim, if need be. "Alice had taken an enormous risk by writing a book in 'dialect' and presenting it in letter form," Ferrone remembered. "I thought the language in the 'Nettie sections' could be stronger and suggested some changes. Alice and I went back and forth on that. But the basic editorial stance was that we were willing to publish the novel as delivered, and hope for the best."

In his concern about the epistolary style of Alice's new novel, Ferrone reflected a sentiment that was widespread in the publishing industry. For the technique had long been considered an anachronism with little appeal to modern readers. The first notable example in English was a translation from French in 1678 of *Letters of a Portuguese Nun*. The most notorious example was generally agreed to be *Pamela*, Samuel Richardson's 1741 novel about a virtuous servant girl who resists her master's advances and is ultimately rewarded by winning his hand.

One of the century's best sellers, the novel sparked fiery debate between those who denounced Pamela as a scheming vixen and others who upheld her as a paragon of morality. In the former camp with a vengeance was Henry Fielding, who immediately ridiculed both *Pamela* and its author with his satire, *Shamela* (1741). While Jane Austen and others experimented with the form, the epistolary novel eventually fell out of favor.

However, Alice never wavered in her thinking that ancestral forces had guided her to the perfect stylistic device for the book. She pointed to the woeful lament of abolitionist Sojourner Truth ("none but God heard me") after her children were sold into slavery. "The letter method seemed best on a number of levels, including the historical," Alice explained. "When [Sojourner Truth] cried out in a mother's grief . . . that, in a way, is the precursor of a letter to God."

Continuing, Alice said that the legacy had thus been established for Celie to write: "Dear God, this has happened to me and I have to tell somebody and so I write to you."

Concerns about the letter writing notwithstanding, by early 1982 the insider buzz about *The Color Purple* was palpable. "There was talk about Alice Walker having delivered a 'big book,'" remembered veteran New York editor Joyce Engleson. Still, longtime friends and supporters of Alice feared that a publishing industry poised to release, that year, *Jane Fonda's Workout Book* might give short shrift to an effort by a black woman author, written in black folk language about a poor, black girl in the South. Not to mention the graphic allusions to incest and the passages in which Shug and Celie "kiss and kiss till us can't kiss no more."

It was against such a backdrop that Gloria Steinem and Mary Helen Washington—both having read advance copies of *The Color Purple*—prepared the first full-length cover story on the literary career of Alice Walker. To their minds, such exposure was long overdue for a dedicated author-activist who, published since 1968, now had ten books to her credit and who had almost single-handedly resurrected the life and art of Zora Neale Hurston.

"I had this ritual where I would go into bookstores and ask if they carried Alice's work and more often than not, the answer was 'no,' " Steinem remembered. "It just made me so mad that her contributions weren't valued."

In a layout bearing the caption "Alice Walker: A Major American Writer," Alice's photo graced the cover of a special June 1982 issue of *Ms.* devoted to fiction.

"Traveling and listening over the years, I've noticed that the readers of Alice Walker's work tend to speak of her as a friend: someone who has rescued them from passivity or anger; someone who has taught them sensuality or self-respect, humor or redemption," Steinem wrote in a profile entitled "Do You Know This Woman? She Knows You." "[Still] her visibility . . . has been obscured by a familiar bias that assumes white male writers and the literature they create to be the norm. That puts black women (and all women of color) at a double remove."

"Authority. Generational continuity. The presence of the ancestor. Historical awareness," Washington added in "Her Mother's Gifts," a companion piece that detailed Alice's bond with a woman who had transformed the indignities she suffered in white women's kitchens into a typewriter with which her youngest child could soar. "One thing Alice Walker has convinced me of is that the long chain of presences that inhabit the literature of black women did not convey any sense of inferiority, submissive femininity or intellectual powerlessness."

Even in their belief that *The Color Purple* would shatter publishing biases and reach a mass audience, neither Washington nor Steinem could have imagined how Alice would transform the American literary landscape with a novel that opened with a heart-rending letter to God.

However, the most immediate impact of the *Ms.* cover story was not on Alice's career, but rather on her self-esteem. For in readying herself for the photography session, she confronted wounds that still lingered from her eye injury. Since the initial surgery in 1958, she'd undergone other procedures to minimize the "wandering" to which blind eyes are prone. Still, she worried that in the absence of a restful night's sleep, her right eye might "drift out of orbit," giving rise to an "unflattering" image for the magazine.

Describing her apprehension in "Beauty: When the Other Dancer Is the Self," Alice later wrote, "At night in bed with my lover I think up reasons why I should not appear on the cover of a magazine. 'My meanest critics will say I've sold out,' I say. 'My family will now realize I write scandalous books.'

"But what's the real reason you don't want to do this?' he asks. 'Because in all probability,' I say in a rush, 'my eye won't be straight.' "

Alice went on to write that in the ensuing exchange with her lover (Robert), her anxiety was assuaged by her memory of a gift she had received from her child. She recalled Rebecca's delight, at about age three, with "Big Blue Marble," an educational television program that opened with a picture of the earth, "bluish, a little battered-looking, but full of light."

"One day when I am putting Rebecca down for her nap, she suddenly focuses on my eye," Alice continued in the essay, noting that she had always feared how her child would respond to her injury. "Something inside me cringes, gets ready to protect myself. All children are cruel about physical differences, I know from experience, and that they don't always mean to be is another matter. I assume Rebecca will be the same.

"But no-o-o-o. She studies my face intently . . . even holds [it] maternally between her dimpled hands. Then, looking every bit as serious and lawyerlike as her father, she says, as if it may just possibly have slipped my attention: 'Mommy, there's a *world* in your eye . . . Where did you *get* that world in your eye?'"

Stunned by the loving truth of Rebecca's observation, Alice wrote that she ran (crying and laughing) to a mirror and gazed anew at a reflection that she had considered "flawed," even with the scar tissue removed: "There *was* a world in my eye. And I saw that it was possible to love it: that in fact, for all it had taught me of shame and anger and inner vision, I *did* love it."

Like many others over the years, Steinem was astounded to learn that Alice felt insecure about her appearance. "It was a classic case of how our perceptions of people are often so different from how they perceive themselves," said a woman who has never rested easy with the "glamorous" image ascribed to her by the media. "I was surprised by Alice's vulnerability because she is, of course, so very beautiful to me."

In addition to Jane Fonda's "go for the burn" exercise treatise, there were several other books released in 1982 that, given publishing industry history, seemed sure bets to outdistance *The Color Purple.* From the 1976 Nobel laureate Saul Bellow there was *The Dean's December*; from Gabriel García Márquez, *Chronicle of a Death Foretold.* The critically acclaimed Anne Tyler offered *Dinner at the Homesick Restaurant* and John Updike, seemingly indefatigable, published *Bech is Back.* But having completed the novel (written by hand in a spiral notebook) as her "spirit guides" directed, Alice wasn't concerned with such matters. She did, however, weigh in on the dust jacket for *The Color Purple,* a book that would retail at $11.95 in hardcover. At first blush, she'd been dismayed by the unadorned pencil drawing of a small wood-frame house on a background of gray. "It is square and cliché," Alice lamented to editor Ferrone. "I suggest a round patchwork quilt design . . . *roundness, complexity, something made by women, please.*" However, a few weeks later, even before Ferrone could ponder her request, Alice had a change of heart. "Keep the house," she wrote again. "It looks almost exactly like the church I attended as a child."

In correspondence with Ferrone before the release of *The Color Purple*, Alice shared her thoughts about a novel that would change her life forevermore:

> It was a decided high, for me, while I was writing it. I worried (a little) that the language . . . would be an impediment. Though obviously, I didn't feel that it should. Your feeling of wanting to rush through Nettie's letters to get back to Celie is what I want the reader to feel . . . only by feeling that will s/he understand how beautiful Celie's language can be, and how entirely suitable for her expression of her experience. . . . Our struggle as a people (one of many) is not to be swallowed up and erased by the bland majority. And in this struggle, language is crucial.

Alice closed the letter with "Peace," before signing her name.

41

God Love All Them Feelings

Approaching town, you couldn't miss the huge welcome sign heralding "Historic Eatonton" as the proud birthplace of Joel Chandler Harris. And the way Ruth saw it, that was exactly the problem. It peeved her that Putnam County celebrated *only* the creator of the *Uncle Remus* stories. To her mind, the reason was clear: In his role as "ventriloquist" to a docile plantation-era character ("Dis sho' am good" read a popular advertisement for Uncle Remus brand syrup), Harris had perpetuated a blissful master-slave mythology. *Song of the South*, the 1946 Disney film adaptation of Harris's fiction, took the damning images even deeper into the culture. Rendered like a happy soundtrack for slavery, the movie's hit tune, "Zip a Dee Doo Dah," even won an Oscar for best song.

By contrast, Alice's work revealed the South through a prism of hypocrisy and violence that, given the reality of *Mister Charlie*, hardly inspired rhapsodies about "Mister Bluebird on my shoulder." Hers was a portrait that the Eatonton establishment refused to acknowledge, let alone trumpet on billboards.

"Joel Chandler Harris had been dead for more than fifty years when Alice started writing and they were still shoving Brer Rabbit and Tar Baby down our throats," Ruth said. "He was idolized because he was white. I'd sell Alice's books out of the trunk of my car because you couldn't find them anywhere else in town."

Eatonton's power brokers might have ignored Alice, but as they'd soon come to know, she'd scrutinized them. She shared thoughts about her hometown's obsession in a 1981 speech, "The Dummy in the Window: Joel Chandler Harris and the Invention of Uncle Remus." Delivered at the Atlanta Historical Society, the address would later be published in her essay collection, *Living by the Word.*

> Uncle Remus told the stories of Br'er Rabbit and Br'er Fox, all the classic folk tales that came from Africa and that, even now in Africa, are still being told. We too, my brothers and sisters and I, listened to them. But after we saw *Song of the South*, we no longer listened to them. They were killed for us. . . .

> In Eatonton . . . to this day, there is a large iron rabbit on the courthouse lawn in honor of Joel Chandler Harris. . . . There is now and has been for several years an Uncle Remus museum. There was also, until a few years ago, an Uncle Remus restaurant. There used to be a dummy of a black man, an elderly, kindly cottony-haired darkie, seated in a rocking chair in the restaurant window. In fantasy, I frequently liberated him, using army tanks and guns. Blacks, of course, were not allowed in this restaurant.

> As far as I'm concerned [Joel Chandler Harris] stole a good part of my heritage. How did he steal it? By making me feel ashamed of it. In creating Uncle Remus, he placed an effective barrier between me and the stories that meant so much to me, the stories that could have meant so much to all of our children, the stories that they would have heard from their own people and not from Walt Disney.

Compared to the glorification of Joel Chandler Harris, the local response to Alice's literary achievements had been, as the saying went, "as quiet as a church mouse pissin' on cotton." Ruth was now primed for a roar. She was convinced that *The Color Purple* would prompt a retreat on Uncle Remus and force Eatonton to claim a home-grown daughter whose writing offered a redemptive path for all.

"Alice let me read the novel before it was published and when I finished, I said to myself, 'This is it,' " Ruth recalled. "She'd done such a beautiful job. I knew that with *The Color Purple* Alice would finally get the recognition in Eatonton that she deserved. It was a book that couldn't be ignored."

Such was the sentiment of Peter S. Prescott, who, writing for *Newsweek*, pronounced the novel a work of "permanent importance." "Alice Walker excels at making difficulties for herself and then transcending them," Prescott raved, his view soon to be echoed by book critics from Alaska to Alabama. "Her story begins at about the point that a respectable Greek tragedy reserves for its climax . . . then works its way toward acceptance, serenity and joy. . . . Her narrative advances entirely by means of letters that are either never delivered or are delivered too late for a response, and most of these are written in a black English that Walker appears to have modified artfully for general consumption."

Rita Mae Brown, author of the lesbian classic *Rubyfruit Jungle* (1973), was similarly awed by Alice's choice of narrative style. "Language . . . a difficult task under simple circumstances is raised to the level of genius in this book," wrote Brown in a review for the *San Francisco Chronicle and Examiner*. "When you close [*The Color Purple*] you will be left with your own heartbeat. . . . It is a work to stand beside literature from any time and any place. It needs no category other than the fact that it is superb."

Writing for the *New York Times*, Mel Watkins called Alice "a lavishly gifted writer," noting that with *The Color Purple* she'd brought together all the themes of her past work.

> Most prominent is the estrangement and violence that mark the relationships between . . . black men and women. Although

this subject has been raised in the fiction of earlier American writers, such as Zora Neale Hurston and in comic caricatures of the Frankie and Johnny variety, it was largely ignored by most black writers until the 1960s. . . . Walker explores the estrangement of her men and women through a triangular love affair. It is Shug Avery who forces Albert to stop brutalizing Celie, and it is Shug with whom Celie first consummates a satisfying and reciprocally loving relationship. . . . The cumulative effect is a novel that is convincing because of the authenticity of its folk voice. . . . Walker's . . . handling of the epistolary style has enabled her to tell a poignant tale of women's struggle for equality and independence. . . .

Interestingly, the black poet Lucille Clifton offered an early critique of *The Color Purple* that was noteworthy for its dissent. The author of such works as *Blessing the Boats* (2000) and *The Terrible Stories* (1990), Clifton, writing for the *Baltimore Sun*, found fault with Alice's depiction of male characters and with the novel's folk speech, lamenting that it appealed to the ear, but in letter form was incompatible to the eye. By that, one presumes that Clifton found *The Color Purple* cumbersome to read as printed text, although she neglected to include passages that might have supported her remarks. Still, she went on to conclude that in its exploration of "female bonding and the redemptive power of love," the novel "should further enhance Alice Walker's considerable reputation as a serious American author of major intent."

From the outset, *The Color Purple* had wide appeal among international readers, insisted Norah Mellor, a Latina community activist who had immigrated to the United States from Mexico in the early 1980s. As she tells it, the novel was the first she ever read in English. "I bought the book because everybody was talking about it," remembered Mellor, fifty-four, now an early education teacher in Northern California. "I'd only read books in Spanish before because I was insecure about my English. But I could understand everything Alice Walker wrote."

"I come from a family of thirteen children and there were many similarities between my life and the black women in *The Color Purple*," Mellor explained. "I had a brother who was terribly mean to me and a younger sister with whom I was very close. Men not being very loyal to women, it is the same all over the world."

Tokyo resident Yumiko Yanagisawa was in the United States conducting research on the feminist movement shortly after *The Color Purple* was released. Like Mellor, she said the novel was the center of debate among friends and associates she met from Boston to Long Beach. "Everywhere I went, people were discussing *The Color Purple*, so I had to read it," recalled Yanagisawa, who'd later become the translator of Japanese-language editions of the book. "I immediately understood the excitement. In Japan, the text is now used in universities as a model for standing up against obstacles. *The Color Purple* is taken quite seriously as a code of resistance."

And Alice's response? By the time readers were cheering Celie's transformed relationship with Mr. _____ ("Us sew . . . Make idle conversation."), Alice had already turned her attention to the essays that would appear in her eleventh book, *In Search of Our Mothers' Gardens*. Perhaps the best indicator of her feelings about the success of *The Color Purple* could be found in a short profile that accompanied the Prescott review. "It is my happiest book," Alice told *Newsweek*. "I had to do all the other writing to get to this point. I had to live a lot and . . . much of it was hurt. But I learned that you can get a lot out of whatever happens to you."

Asked if she considered the novel a triumph, Alice demurred as she had a decade before when June Jordan spoke of her future as "a big-time writer." "It's hard for me to say, you know. Here I am trying to get my characters in a house they like, in a country where they can feel at home. Maybe one day I'll think this was an artistic leap for me. But right now I'm thinking, 'Did I do it in a way they wanted me to do it? Did I give them to the world in a way they wanted to be presented?' Let's hope people can hear Celie's voice."

IN THE latter part of *The Color Purple*, Celie writes to Nettie explaining that Shug has brought her a new vision of a God that she once believed had forsaken her: "Here's the thing, say Shug . . . God is inside you and inside everybody else. You come into the world with God. But only them that search for it inside find it. And sometimes it just manifest itself even if you not looking, or don't know what you looking for."

About her fears that God might frown on the sexual relationship that has helped her to heal from her abuse, Celie tells Nettie that the spirited nightclub singer ("grinning and rubbing high up on my thigh") has equally novel ideas: "Oh, she say. God love all them feelings. That's some of the best stuff God did. And when you know God loves 'em you enjoys 'em a lot more. . . . God love everything you love—and a mess of stuff you don't. But more than anything else, God love admiration. . . . I think it pisses God off if you walk by the color purple in a field somewhere and don't notice it."

Any lingering doubt in Alice about whether she'd kept faith with her characters was lost in the whirlwind when, on Monday, April 18, 1983, she became the first black woman to win a Pulitzer Prize in fiction.

42

The Balance Had Begun to Tilt

CONFERRED ANNUALLY since 1917 as stipulated in the will of newspaper mogul Joseph Pulitzer (1847–1911) to works of unparalleled excellence, the Pulitzer Prize is widely viewed as the most distinguished award in American journalism, arts, and letters. In keeping with their luster as one of the country's most sought-after accolades, the awards have long generated spirited debate before, during, and after winners are announced each spring by the trustees of Columbia University in New York. *The Color Purple* triggered a battle royal.

The events that culminated in Alice receiving a historic phone call in April 1983 had begun the previous summer when Peter S. Prescott was asked to join the group of three (all white) that would compose the Pulitzer fiction jury. Then the senior book critic for *Newsweek*, Prescott had prior experience as a juror and was honored that Pulitzer officials found value in the rigor with which he surveyed the American literary landscape. He was pleased to be invited to serve again.

That is, until he learned that the appointed chair of the jury was neither a fiction writer nor a literary critic; Midge Decter was, to his mind, an ill-considered choice to oversee what he hoped would be informed discussion about the nation's most compelling novels and stories (Pulitzer fiction jurors were charged with recommending three titles, in rank order, preferably on an American theme). Dismayed by the conflicts he envisioned with the conservative political pundit and author of such works as *The New Chastity and Other Arguments Against Women's Liberation* (1972), Prescott then declined a juror's slot. He detailed his decision in a letter to the Pulitzer administration:

> My difficulty is with Midge Decter as chairwoman of the fiction jury. . . . I have never met her, but feel I know her through her published work, which shows her plainly to be anti-feminist, anti-liberal, anti-homosexual and unsympathetic to blacks. . . . Miss Decter's writing shows something else: that she is unaccustomed to evaluating a book on its merits. The question with her is always: which side are you on?

> There's no reason why Pulitzer jurors should enjoy their colleagues' company. But each should feel that [we] are grappling with a common task in a spirit of disinterested inquiry, that reason and persuasion may prevail. Because I'm rather gloomy about such a prospect this year, I feel I must stand aside. I am sorry.

However, before dispatching his regrets, Prescott reconsidered. Raised in a home where, he later noted, "books were talked about as something serious, not just entertainment" (his father was former *New York Times* book critic Orville Prescott), he stashed the letter in a file and signed on for the jury, which also included the esteemed writer John Clellon Holmes (1926–1988). In joining the jury, Prescott was also mindful of the notorious behind-the-scenes machinations and politicking that had, in the past, derailed Pulitzer Prize nominees in fiction.

For example, in 1977 a jury had put forth for the honor Norman Maclean's widely heralded *A River Runs Through It*. But unimpressed, the Pulitzer Board of newspaper executives (vested with sweeping powers, including the right to confer awards to works not even submitted for review) vetoed the selection and made no fiction award. In his mid-seventies at the time, Maclean made headlines when he protested that his book (set in Montana) had been rejected because the board, top heavy with Easterners, shunned stories that "had trees in them." In his determination to fight for the integrity of the 1983 fiction prize, Prescott, writing in his personal journal about the proceedings, noted that he was motivated by a sentiment Maclean surely would have appreciated: "Why should I let a bigot carry the day?"

And fight he did. Reminding the chairwoman that a nearly thirty-year-old book was a bit wide of Pulitzer guidelines for demonstrated excellence in the previous year, Prescott immediately challenged Decter's first nominee: *The Issa Valley*, a 1955 novel by Czeslaw Milosz about a village boy's upbringing in Lithuania (a paperback reprint had been released in 1982). Decter was angered by his opposition to her choice, "but realized this cause was a nonstarter," Prescott recalled.

In the next round of deliberations, the chairwoman put forth another slate: *Rabbis and Wives* by Chaim Grade and *The Best-Loved Short Stories of Jesse Stuart*. She bemoaned her inability to come up with a third. Prescott found both choices "meritorious" but said that neither he nor Holmes felt that Decter's new recommendations bested other eligible works. Further teeth gnashing ensued.

As the wrangling continued, Prescott said that Decter insisted that she could not abide the selections both he and Holmes considered to be most deserving: *The Color Purple*, Anne Tyler's *Dinner at the Homesick Restaurant*, and Cynthia Ozick's *Levitation*. To that end, as chair, she drafted a report to the Pulitzer Board in which she posited, Prescott said, that the only book on which the three could agree was *Rabbis and Wives*. How she came to such a conclusion remained a mystery to Prescott more than twenty years later.

"It was a masterpiece of obfuscation," he noted in another journal entry describing Decter's rendering of the jury's proceedings. "I wrote her a stiffly judicious letter saying this won't do. I read it over the phone to John Holmes."

Challenged yet again, the chairwoman finally desisted. By January 1983, she had submitted a revised report, which included the award citation Prescott had crafted for *The Color Purple*:

> A majority of the 1983 Fiction Jury (Peter S. Prescott and John Clellon Holmes) believes Alice Walker's novel *The Color Purple* to be far superior to any other American fiction published this year. We enthusiastically and emphatically recommend that this extraordinary novel be awarded the Pulitzer Prize in Fiction.
>
> Covering thirty years in the life of an impoverished black family in rural Georgia, Walker's story revivifies the form of the epistolary novel. . . . The narrative's exceptional strength derives from its guarded optimism about the possibility of becoming fully human under the most appalling circumstances. Writing with pathos, but without a hint of sentimentality, Walker shows us a young woman gaining control of her life. . . . Love redeems, meanness kills—that is this novel's principal theme, as it has been the theme of most of the world's great fiction.
>
> Walker had written good fiction before that has gone largely unnoticed. With *The Color Purple* . . . we will honor ourselves by honoring her.

Thus ended the novel's journey to a landmark Pulitzer Prize.

NOT SURPRISINGLY, Decter did not depart quietly. After all, this was a woman who, in an infamous rant, "Boys at the Beach," had blasted gays for ruining her annual summer sojourn on New York's Fire Island. Decter wrote, "The balance between the homosexuals and the straights had clearly begun to tilt. . . . Our once friendly neighbors were beginning to indicate to us in all sorts of ways—

from a new shrillness of voice to the appearance of drag costumes in the afternoon to a provocative display of social interest in our teen-age children—that the place was getting too small to contain the tastes and wishes of both communities."

In the aftermath of the April 18 announcement about *The Color Purple*, Decter let loose with an equally defiant salvo. Writing in his journal, Prescott said that he received a note from her that read, "If you can honestly say you remember this book three years from now, I'll buy you lunch at Lutece." Although he was assured of the novel's enduring power and much admiring of the renowned New York restaurant, he declined the wager. "What a blend of sensations!" Prescott confided to his journal. "The world's best food savored with the world's worst company."

And in a perfunctory response to a query from this author about her tenure as chair of the jury that awarded the first Pulitzer Prize to an African American novelist, Decter made clear her distaste with the entire affair. In a letter dated September 18, 1997, she lamented that fiction jurors were compelled to read dozens of books, most "submitted by their publishers simply to please the authors." "In the end, the three of us disagreed and could not reconcile our differences," Decter proclaimed. "It was growing late, and Alice Walker, as must often happen in this process, was the compromise candidate. Lucky for her."

It was a remark that prompted another swift and uncompromising rebuttal from Peter S. Prescott. Having reviewed the novel upon publication, Prescott said, as noted in *Newsweek*, that he was wildly impressed with *The Color Purple*, but "couldn't possibly know at that point that there wouldn't be something better coming down the road by the end of the year."

"There were strong books," he continued. "But nothing appeared that could best the Walker novel for the Pulitzer Prize. In that realm, Alice Walker had no competition. Over time, *The Color Purple* has achieved a status few books ever attain. It is one of the few books that is read by most students in the country. It has become a rite of passage.

"It is also one of the few literary books to capture the popular imagination and leave a permanent imprint on our society. There are some commercial books that did that, like *The Godfather* and *Jaws*. But *The Color Purple* is literature of the highest form. If an author has anything to show you, she'll show it on the first page. Alice Walker met the mark and then continued to soar.

"I've asked myself, did the fact that this was a black woman have anything to do with me casting my ballot. And I can honestly say that it did not enter my decision to award the prize. I fulfilled my duty, as charged, to find the most distinguished American novel. In that sense, I am proud to have been a part of history."

43

Some of Our Work

ALICE'S IMMEDIATE response to the news that she'd won the Pulitzer Prize was colored by two factors: Oblivious to the particulars of the publishing industry, she was unaware that the award was granted to writers other than journalists. And contrary to Decter's innuendo, she did not and would not have lobbied Harcourt to submit *The Color Purple* to the Pulitzer jury had she known. Nor had she sought the novel's nomination for the 1983 American Book Award in fiction, which it had also won the previous week. With regard to prizes, Alice was satisfied that she'd served, with openness and admiration, as a medium for her characters. And so deep was her gratitude for their presence as she crafted *The Color Purple* that she'd wept in Robert's arms after writing the last page. That she'd rendered the lives of Shug, Celie, and Mr._____with authenticity and compassion was all the reward she needed. Like Zora Neale Hurston, she knew that in death she could meet her ancestors without shame.

Given her disinterest in prizes, Alice responded with both shock and annoyance to the reporter who phoned her at about 10:00 A.M. seeking a comment about her milestone achievement. "I thought it was a joke and a mean-spirited one at that," she remembered. "I was completely stunned."

No sooner had she put down the receiver than the phone rang again. This time the call was from a friend who let out a congratulatory cheer. It was no prank. No trick. No crank call. Fifteen years after the release of a poetry book in which she'd paid tribute to Camus' thoughts about the richness that could be found between "misery and the sun," she'd been honored for a novel about an abused black woman who embodied such truth.

As the flood of phone calls continued, Alice offered a response that would subsequently be quoted in newspapers nationwide: "I feel really happy for the people in *The Color Purple*. They'll really like this. The characters are 'composites' of people I love from my childhood—my grandmothers and my really stylish aunts, the ones who would visit from up north wearing those furs with animal heads and little beady eyes.

"Actually, I think life is the award. I love being a black Southern woman. All three add incredible enlargements to being a writer."

But by midafternoon, Alice had discovered just how much the Pulitzer Prize had enlarged her reputation and catapulted her, unwittingly, out of her much-cherished solitude into celebrity. Overwhelmed by the attention, she drew the curtains in the small San Francisco co-op on Galilee Lane in which she had bought a share to provide a city home for Rebecca, who was entering her teen years. And unique among her friends at the time, Alice had neither answering machine nor message service. Having reached her limit with the praise that was pouring in, she'd unplugged the phone. Such was the scenario—curtains drawn, lights dimmed, phone disconnected—when a friend arrived at around 6 P.M. to accompany Alice to a lecture by Gloria Steinem, who just happened to be in town.

"She was her usual warm, composed self," remembered Belvie Rooks, who had first met Alice through activist work on Cuba and South Africa in the late 1970s. "The lighting was a bit subdued, but knowing that Alice practiced meditation, I didn't think anything of it.

"She was in the kitchen preparing tea and I was sitting in the rocking chair when she said, almost in a whisper, 'You haven't heard?'

" 'No, what?' " I answered.

"Alice sighed and said, 'Well . . . I just won the Pulitzer for *The Color Purple*. The phone's been ringing all day and good news can be just as stressful as bad.'"

Unable to contain her excitement, Rooks said that she leapt out of the rocker and began screaming while Alice, nonplussed, poured tea and then excused herself to change clothes. "I was ecstatic," Rooks recalled. "It was so wonderful to shout and holler and just run around the room in complete glee. I also knew that I'd have to reel myself in and hold the consciousness of calm that Alice would need to get through the evening. It was a really big moment in her life and I didn't want to ruin it by acting a fool."

Upon their arrival at the event, held in downtown San Francisco, Rooks said that Steinem walked onto the stage, delivered news of the award, and beseeched Alice (knowing she was in the audience) to stand. The packed crowd let out a thunderous roar. As if in a trance, Alice rose slowly and stood motionless for several moments as the cheers washed over her like a waterfall. Then she sat down.

"My sense was that Alice was in a deep, transcendent place of connectedness and prayer," Rooks said nearly twenty years later, as tears welled in her eyes. "I knew what the Pulitzer Prize meant for all of us as her friends. But I could only imagine how it must have felt for Alice, knowing where she'd come from; the writing on scraps of papers; her commitment to expressing her truth and never knowing what obstacles she'd have to overcome.

"I felt that wherever she was, mentally, in the midst of all the celebration, she was as much with her people in Georgia. With her mother. Her father. Her teachers. The land. Had I won the Pulitzer and you came to my house, you wouldn't have had a chance to sit in a rocking chair and sip tea before I told you. I would have met you at the door and your ears would still be ringing, today, from my screams."

Steinem would later remember the evening as "an incredible moment" for a beloved friend and colleague who'd expanded her understanding of rebellion; who'd chosen action—leaving Spelman, ending her marriage, moving to San Francisco—over endless consciousness-raising debates about the liberation of women.

It was the teacher who'd welcomed Alice within hours of her birth who understood, perhaps better than anyone, the significance of the day. Apprised of Alice's triumph by a neighbor, Miss Reynolds said she made her way to the front porch, where she stood and stared out at the wildflowers that had begun to blossom all over Wards Chapel. "I remembered Miss Minnie Lou asking if Alice could come to school. I couldn't say 'no.' Her mother wanted to keep her out of the cotton fields. And then Alice went on out into the world, but she never forgot us. I was so proud to have hung on long enough to see the big city people recognize some of our work."

44

Through It All

WITHIN DAYS of the Pulitzer Prize announcement, *The Color Purple* appeared on the *New York Times* Best-Seller List, where it stayed for more than a year. The already scheduled paperback release was rushed to production with its print run increased exponentially, remembered Susan Ginsburg, the editor at Pocket Books who'd negotiated the deal with Harcourt before Alice made literary history.

"I'd had a huge argument with my boss, who told me that I was nuts for pursuing *The Color Purple*," Ginsburg said, adding that the publishing house paid about $30,000 for paperback rights. "We'd done the paperback release of *Meridian* and it had sold very few copies. So now I'm showing up with another Alice Walker novel. This one's in dialect and written in letter form. I do my pitch in the editorial meeting and jaws drop. I basically bully them into it."

"I knew *The Color Purple* was important from the very beginning," she continued. "But after the Pulitzer, it became a phenomenon beyond belief. We marked the milestones. One million copies sold. Five million copies. I stopped counting, personally, at six million."

True to form, Alice declined to travel to New York for the Pulitzer festivities—a lavish luncheon and presentation of a $1,000 award. "I didn't have to show up and the check arrived in the mail," she happily remembered.

The prestige of the Pulitzer Prize sparked new interest in a novel that many had overlooked upon its initial release, winning reviews notwithstanding. Such was the case for Gwendolyn Brooks, who said she was delighted, after thirty-three years, to be unburdened of her status as the only black woman to have received the award. (Playwright Charles Gordone was the first black man to be so honored—in 1970, for his drama *No Place to Be Somebody*.)

"Alice is a real adventurer," Brooks said. "And *The Color Purple* certainly deserved the prize. I was grateful for her company."

But unable to see beyond Alice's graphic depictions of Mr.____'s brutality or her positive treatment of sexual relationships between women, others began to rail against a novel that they believed denigrated black men. The book was the last straw in what they viewed as a near decade-long assault against black men that began with *For Color Girls*, crested with *Black Macho*, and now, with the critical and commercial success of *The Color Purple*, was creeping into the mainstream.

At the outset *The Color Purple* controversy was contained, for the most part, within the black community. Voicing their concern at informal gatherings, those who found fault with the novel leaned toward narrow interpretations. Their basic problem with the text? *The Color Purple* lacked "strong black male role models" and failed to address the white oppression that caused black men like Mr.____ to abuse black women. There was no *context* for his cruelty, they complained. Rarely mentioned was Alice's depiction of the transformation of Mr.____, seen here through Celie's eyes: "The old devil put his arms around me and just stood there on the porch with me real quiet. . . . Here us is, I thought, two old fools left over from love, keeping each other company under the stars."

The antipathy toward the novel was compounded by its publication during the administration of President Ronald Reagan. Almost immediately after he was sworn into office in January 1981,

Reagan began to cut funding to federal programs (affirmative action, Aid to Families with Dependent Children) that had historically supported minorities. At a time when the black community was perceived to be under siege, critics feared that *The Color Purple* played into the hands of conservative forces plotting to dismantle civil rights gains.

Adding to the already racially charged atmosphere of the early 1980s were the highly publicized murders of nearly thirty black children in Atlanta. For more than two years, local black activists had pressured Atlanta police to intensify what many perceived to be a lax investigation of rumored Klan involvement in the crimes. Then, in 1982, a black man, Wayne Bertram Williams, was convicted of the murders. That a black woman had dared, against such a backdrop, to publish a novel that revealed discord in black families was, for many, a bitter pill. *The Color Purple* made no mention of slave ships, iron shackles, vicious overseers, or burning crosses. There was no finger-pointing at "whitey."

Author of such works as *Mumbo Jumbo* (1972) and *The Terrible Twos* (1982), Oakland, California, writer Ishmael Reed would emerge as one of the most impassioned opponents of *The Color Purple*. Speaking in press interviews and in public forums, he denounced the novel as a destructive force. "It was like a sentinel book, exposing the depth and intensity of hatred of black men in this country," he later said. "White feminists and white men took the fictional character [Mr.____] and used him to represent all black men, something they would never do with a book written by a white."

Reed reserved a special disdain for a woman he believed to have had undue influence in the ascent of *The Color Purple* and its clearly unrepentant author: "Gloria Steinem was a modern-day Dracula [in] the way that she would manipulate black divas and then look for fresh blood when the former ones had served their purpose," he recalled to an interviewer.

SEEKING REFUGE from media requests, angry critics, and worshipful readers who were mailing her fan letters by the thousands,

Alice departed for China with a group of women writers in June 1983. The three-week cultural exchange was organized by the black writer Paule Marshall. Nellie Wong, Lisa Alther, Blanche Boyd, and Tillie Olsen were among the other writers included in the delegation. As a traveling companion, Alice invited Susan Kirschner—a devoted friend and professor of English at Lewis and Clark College in Oregon.

It was Kirschner who, in the mid-1970s, had facilitated one of the first meetings between Alice and Olsen, admirers of each other's work who had corresponded for several years. She brought both authors to her Portland campus as featured speakers for a program on women's writing.

Born in 1912 (the same year as Alice's mother), Olsen was best known, at the time, for "Tell Me a Riddle," a tragicomic story about an elderly Jewish couple and winner of a 1961 O. Henry Prize. In 1978, she published *Silences*, a highly praised analysis of the barriers to women's creativity.

A San Francisco resident, Olsen had welcomed Alice warmly when she first moved to the Bay area. And when the city later proclaimed an official "Tillie Olsen Day," in honor of the author's achievements as a community activist, Alice (aided by Rebecca) presented her with a "Revolutionary Petunia Award" ("I am more cynical, I think, than Tillie. She is more tolerant and committed to a belief in the goodness of human beings," Alice noted, as Rebecca came forward with a small vase and flower). But according to Kirschner, Olsen soon began to feel threatened by the younger writer who was making literary strides on her home turf. The sense of rivalry reached a flash point when Alice won the Pulitzer Prize. By contrast, the 1980 film adaptation of "Tell Me a Riddle" (starring Melvyn Douglas) had been released to lackluster reviews.

"Tillie was jealous of the accolades Alice received from the establishment," Kirschner explained. "I wouldn't be surprised if Tillie said something offensive to Alice, who has a part of her, as a person and as a writer, that does not allow slights."

Admitting that she and Alice had suffered a breach, Olsen later attributed the conflict to Alice's "lack of grace," not career envy.

She recalled, "I was out of town when I heard the news about the Pulitzer Prize and *The Color Purple*. As soon as I got home, I rushed over to bring Alice flowers. For some reason, she thought I was insincere in my happiness over her sudden success. I asked, 'Are you mixing me up with Muriel Rukeyser?'

"I was terribly hurt and from then on decided that my relationship would be with her books. We were respectful to each other in China. But I will go to my grave believing Alice Walker owes me an apology."

Olsen's reference to Rukeyser was telling. The poet never witnessed the triumph of *The Color Purple*, which was published after her death. But during a West Coast trip during her waning years, Rukeyser had visited briefly with Alice and attempted a reconciliation. And years later, a writer who'd attended, in the late 1970s, a Rukeyser workshop in Upstate New York, remembered the poet's wistful comments about the probing student she'd taught in a gardener's cottage. The writer, Mona Vold, said that Rukeyser, then impaired by a stroke, had discovered a rip in the dress she planned to wear for a reading. She beseeched workshop organizers for aid before taking the stage. Skilled with needle and thread, Vold volunteered.

"When I got to her hotel room, Muriel told me that the garment needed a 'French seam,' " Vold recalled. "I didn't know exactly what that was, but I did the best that I could. As I was sewing, Muriel started talking about poetry and writers. Calling her 'the hope of the future,' she said I should read Alice Walker. I got her books the next day."

And finally, perhaps hoping to gain perspective on her feelings, Rukeyser dedicated to Alice one of her last published works, "An Unborn Poet." Printed in the *American Poetry Review*, the poem read, in part:

> *A young woman stands at the door of my small room,*
> *a marvelous young woman, the daughter I never had,*
> *no poems yet, only the digging questions . . .*

Alice, landscaper of grief, love, anger, bring me to birth,
bring back my poems. No. Bring me my next poem!
Here it is, to give to all of you.
To do what we mean, in poetry and sex,
to give each other what we really are.

End of a time of intercepted music.

About Rukeyser's efforts to make amends, Alice later said, "I don't know what Muriel meant by the poem. I was surprised to see it. I think she, on some level, still wanted to control, if not me, then our connection to each other. She wanted credit, more than I offered, for what I'd become, the work I'd done. . . . [Muriel] was formidable and stubborn and caring. I loved and respected her. However, the moment I felt a twinge of nonfreedom in the friendship, I removed myself."

Alice would affirm the gifts received in "Pagan," a poem dedicated to Rukeyser and published a decade after her death.

At home
in the countryside
I make the decision
to leave your book
—overdue at the library—
face up, "promiscuous"
out in the sun.

Pagan.

I laugh to see
this was our religion
all along . . .

And the breach with Olsen? "She had offended me. At one point, she'd said that my mother's three gifts sent a mixed message, implying that she was happy to send me away. The older white women who'd helped me seemed, finally, angered to find themselves in competition with my 'humble' mother and furious that I never forgot to put her first. I also think they found it difficult to learn about my mother's success as a human being since she'd been denied the various privileges they'd enjoyed. Such as just being white."

THANKFULLY, PAINS from the past and the growing furor over *The Color Purple* receded from Alice's consciousness (for the most part) upon her arrival in China. Her spirit was renewed by the generosity of the people. And as always, she found sanctuary in the natural landscape, marveling over Beijing's broad boulevards of trees. "They are a kind of magic," Alice noted. "They seem modest and young, and one thinks of them in future tense. How grand they will look at eighty. . . . One feels irresistibly drawn to people who would plant and care for so many millions of trees . . . because, for one thing, the planting of trees demonstrates a clear intention to have a future and a definite disinterest in war."

Rivaling the trees in beauty was the legendary Chinese writer Ding Ling, who, as it happened, was nearly eighty years old at the time. The author of numerous works, among them a celebrated novel about the struggle of peasants against rich farmers (*The Sun Shines over the Sangkan River*, 1949), Ding Ling impressed Alice with her optimism despite a life of punishing travails.

"She is short and brown and round," Alice noted, describing her joyful meeting with the author. "Imprisoned by reactionaries and radicals . . . her husband executed by firing squad . . . herself locked in solitary confinement . . . this 'old' woman . . . has through everything, simply continued to write. . . . She holds no bitterness, only saying . . . 'I lost time. Oh, to be sixty-seven again!' "

Alice was also cheered by a chance encounter with the editor of a Shanghai literary magazine who stunned her with news of a forthcoming translation of *The Color Purple* in Chinese (such was the pace after the Pulitzer Prize that Alice could barely keep up with developments in her own career). Unable to fathom the novel's appeal to a people so removed from the pained history of blacks in the American South, Alice found affirmation in the editor's response: "But Alice, it is a very *Chinese* story."

Indeed, it was during her sojourn in China that Alice was reminded again of the universality of human struggle. She experienced anew the feeling that had prompted her to declare, at age twenty-three, her desire to write novels with the passion and power of Victor Hugo. As she visited such sites as the Great Wall ("folly") and Tiananmen Square, Alice also remembered the fighting spirit she'd encountered when she joined the conga line at the youth festival in Helsinki and later during her first trip to Fidel Castro's Cuba in the late 1970s.

Traveling with a group of black artists in open defiance of the U.S. blockade against Cuba, Alice had spent two weeks in the country touring schools, hospitals, and child care centers. During the flurry of meetings (and casual conversations with everyday people) she had not backed down from asking pointed questions about dissident voices in Cuba ("Just what is it about homosexuals that threatens the revolution?"), or in expressing her concern that black Cubans, disinclined culturally to focus on difference, took no special pride in being black ("The more we insisted on calling ourselves *black* Americans the more confused and distant they grew").

Allowing that her understanding of Castro's vision was "neither definitive nor complete," she offered comments that she continued to refine, after many visits to Cuba, in subsequent years.

"How could I not identify with Fidel and his hearty band of peasants?" Alice responded to those who challenged her solidarity with Cuba. "In 1959, when Fidel came to power, I was living in the brutally racist, completely segregated state of Georgia. Fascism was a way of life, so entrenched there seemed no other possibility.

"As long as there are poor people, exploited people, downhearted, stolen-from people, Fidel will have an audience. The Cuban Revolution gave me hope."

45

I Try to Make Sense

IT MIGHT have seemed as if Alice had a master plan for her meteoric rise in the publishing world. As it happened, her eleventh book, *In Search of Our Mothers' Gardens*, was ready for release six months after she won the Pulitzer Prize. Thanks to *The Color Purple* (translations were slated in twenty languages), the audience for her work now spanned the globe. But it was a young woman, close at hand, who'd been foremost in her thinking when she began to sort material for the collection that carried the subtitle *Womanist Prose*.

"This [book] is my legacy to Rebecca," Alice declared in an October 1981 letter to her editor, John Ferrone. "So it must be as right as we can make it." She'd go on to dedicate the text to her daughter:

> *Who saw in me*
> *what I considered*
> *a scar*
> *And redefined it*
> *as*
> *a world.*

The reference was to Rebecca's remark, as a toddler, about the "big blue marble" of a world in Alice's wounded eye.

Twenty years later, Rebecca shared her feelings about the poignant tribute: "I have always been proud of my ability to help my mother see herself as more beautiful, more whole, more perfect. That my words and in fact my love for her affected her so deeply during a period when she was still feeling deep ambivalence about the project of motherhood means a great deal to me. When I read that dedication I feel trusted, loved, and that my intentions to take care of and honor her have been understood and received."

Alice had labored on *In Search* (with the aid of Susan Kirschner) throughout the period she was writing *The Color Purple*. Guided by the voices of Shug, Celie, Mr.____, Nettie, and Sofia ("I'm gitting tired of Harpo"), the "divining" of the novel had been filled with joy. But the compilation of her first nonfiction collection often evoked anguish. For in selecting the pieces to be included in the book, Alice was haunted by doubts and vulnerabilities from the past.

"I am aware that the state of this manuscript is poor, and I ask you to help me work on it in a way that was not needed with the other books," Alice confided to Ferrone in a letter dated January 26, 1982. "It is messy because I find it so hard to work with such . . . personal and revealing pieces."

By way of example, she cited the 1973 O'Brien interview in which she'd spoken candidly on subjects ranging from her suicidal depression to misgivings about poems she later deemed flawed ("Johann" in *Once* and "Nothing Is Right" in *Revolutionary Petunias*). While she made no specific mention of other works in the letter, she was mindful of such essays as "*One* Child of One's Own," in which she'd discussed her reservations about motherhood. Initially published in *Ms.* in August 1979, Alice revealed, "For me, there has been conflict, struggle, occasional defeat—not only in affirming the life of my own child . . . but also in seeing in that affirmation a fond acceptance and confirmation of myself in a world that would deny me the untrampled blossoming of my own existence."

In a passage that gave rise to the essay's title, Alice recalled having once been asked if women artists should have children, noting pointedly, "This question is never asked artists who are men." She'd replied in the affirmative. "But only one," she told her interviewer. "Because with one [child] you can move. With more than one you're a sitting duck."

Alice went on to explain that her view had been shaped by her own mother's craftily rendered advice about family planning. Not yet twenty-five when her fifth child (Ruth) was born, Minnie Lou Walker, shortly after Rebecca's birth, had urged Alice to have another child quickly ("So you can get it all over with faster"). This was the same woman, Alice observed in the essay, who had a ready response for women wanting children, but who'd been unable to conceive: "If the Lord sets you free, be free indeed."

As with other thorny social issues, Alice was ahead of the debate in her determined questioning of motherhood as the most exalted role and responsibility for women. "*One* Child" had a profound impact on readers like Allison Sampson-Anthony, who later said that the essay prompted her to examine decisions she'd made about family and career. Married, Anthony was in the early stages of a second pregnancy when she read the piece. Today, a registered nurse and graduate student in anthropology, the forty-seven-year-old resident of Santa Cruz, California, recalled:

> It was a very active period in both my creative and political life. I was writing like crazy thanks in large part to the example of Alice Walker. Then I read the essay in which she said that the energy and focus necessary for writing wasn't possible with more than one child.

> I wrote Alice and said that in making such a disparaging statement she'd done a disservice to all the sisters who had more than one child and who aspired to write. In purple ink, she wrote back and said that in her experience she'd found it helpful to listen to what was useful and ignore the rest. "Have you tried this?" Her advice was something that would have come

straight out of my mother's mouth and that was unnerving. . . .
I now have three children and of course, Alice Walker was
right.

In Search would also include "Coretta King: Revisited," in
which Alice shared her embarrassment at having once queried the
wife of Martin Luther King Jr. (and a freedom fighter in her own
right) about her horoscope sign and proficiency at "dancing the
bougaloo." Alice had, in fact, been more interested in the dance
habits of the slain civil rights leader, she later explained. Allowing
that people might be curious about such matters, Mrs. King (a
Taurus) had dismissed the questions as irrelevant.

"I interviewed Coretta after Martin's assassination," Alice said.
"He was rumored to be quite a good dancer and I thought this was
important. I still do. I wish Coretta had let me explore that part of
Martin's personality in my article. I thought it meant he was alive,
vital, down with the vibes of good music, and in touch with his
erotic soul. No wonder so many of us were following him, I
thought. He wasn't your usual two-left-feet-and-no-juice sort of
preacher. I'm sure I was after his horoscope as well. He was a classic Capricorn."

Hopeful that Rebecca (then thirteen) would find in the collection observations, personal revelations, family history, even missteps from which she might benefit, Alice went forward with
In Search, including an excerpt from the O'Brien interview, "*One
Child*," and her musings about Coretta King among the book's
thirty-six offerings.

Released in the fall of 1983, the volume was instantly praised
for its nuanced exploration of black women in relation to their families, to their communities, to each other, and most importantly, to
themselves. Not only did *In Search* sell briskly in the historically
lackluster genre of essay collections but the title piece, "In Search of
Our Mothers' Gardens," quickly emerged as a cornerstone of black
women's literary theory, a discipline Alice had helped to initiate in
the 1970s with her course at Wellesley. Today, the expanded field of
study commands respect at major universities with such scholars as

Hazel Carby, Ann duCille, Farah Jasmine Griffin, Beverly Guy-Sheftall, Evelynn M. Hammonds, Akasha Hull, Deborah McDowell, Nellie McKay, Nell Irvin Painter, Lowery Stokes Sims, Valerie Smith, Hortense Spillers, and Ula Taylor garnering international recognition for their distinguished work on black women's writing, art, health, history, and politics.

Time has not diminished the eloquent power of "In Search," which Alice introduced with the poem "Motheroot" by Cherokee-Appalachian writer Marilou Awiakta.

> *Creation often*
> *needs two hearts*
> *one to root*
> *and one to flower*
> *One to sustain . . .*
> *the fragile bloom*
> *that in the glory*
> *of its hour*
> *affirms a heart*
> *unsung, unseen.*

In this, her opening tribute to an indigenous writer, Alice honored the alliances between women as she laid claim to the interlocking nature of creativity. Proceeding to the historical constraints on the artistry of black women, Alice posed a question that, courageous in its call, warrants repeating: *What did it mean for a black woman to be an artist in our grandmothers' time? In our great-grandmothers' day? It is a question with an answer cruel enough to stop the blood.*

Beginning in the 1800s, the repression of black women had been examined in diverse nonfiction works ranging from Maria Stewart's 1831 "Religion and the Pure Principles of Morality, the Sure Foundation on Which We Must Build" ("O, ye daughters of Africa, awake!") to the 1977 Combahee River Collective "Black Feminist Statement" ("As black feminists and lesbians we know that we have a very definite revolutionary task to perform . . .").

Building *on the tradition*, Alice broke new ground in her fearless assessment of the status of black women from the vantage of never-begun or abandoned novels, murals, plays, symphonies, paintings, essays, and poems.

In a chilling analogy, Alice delineated the impact of slavery and segregation on black women's creative expression. "Consider, if you can bear to imagine it, what might have been the result if singing, too had been forbidden. . . . Listen to the voices of Bessie Smith, Billie Holiday, Nina Simone, Roberta Flack, and Aretha Franklin, among others, and imagine those voices muzzled for life. . . . Then you may begin to comprehend the lives of . . . our mothers and grandmothers. . . . The agony of women . . . who died with their real gifts stifled within them."

It was thus, in her public mourning of the breadth of black women's art, that Alice shattered a long-standing silence. Still, the dirge was sung to an uplifting harmony. For now praising *unacknowledged* splendor, Alice went on to affirm quilt-making, canning, storytelling, and gardening as sublime art forms in which black women had exhibited unparalleled genius despite their subjugation. She described a quilt she'd seen at the Smithsonian Institute in Washington, D.C.

> In fanciful, inspired, and yet simple and identifiable figures, it portrayed the story of the Crucifixion. It is considered rare, beyond price. Though it follows no known pattern of quilt-making, and though it is made of bits and pieces of worthless rags, it is obviously the work of a person of powerful imagination and deep spiritual feeling. . . . It was made by "an anonymous Black woman in Alabama, a hundred years ago." If we could locate [her], she would turn out to be one of our grandmothers—an artist who left her mark . . . in the only medium her position in society allowed her to use.

Then, circling back to her opening, Alice underscored the message in Awiakta's poem: "Our mothers and grandmothers have, more often than not anonymously, handed on the creative spark, the seed of the flower they themselves never hoped to see: or like a sealed letter they could not plainly read."

A milestone in black and feminist writing, "In Search of Our Mothers' Gardens" elevated, as had been Alice's intention, the unsung talents of the Minnie Lou Walkers of the world. "Alice Walker helped people to understand the cultural significance of quilting," asserted Rachel D. K. Clark, a Watsonville, California, fabric artist who creates widely coveted quilted garments she calls "talking clothes." "Since the early 1980s, there's been an explosion in quilt exhibits, classes, and collecting. Quilting gained prestige as an art form and Alice's writing definitely contributed to that trend."

Similarly, critics cheered the collection Alice had first presented to Harcourt with concerns about its quality. "This womanist of intelligence, memory, will, humor and energy encourages us to speak out against offenses to human dignity as she reminds us of what is essential to survival," wrote Julian Bach in a glowing *Publishers Weekly* review. Writing for the Louisville, Kentucky, *Courier-Journal*, Lucretia B. Ward praised Alice as a "tough, enchanted and wise writer." She noted that with *In Search*, Alice had delivered a work "singing" not only of contradictions and cruelties, but of revelation and transformation as well. "This is one of the healthiest collections of essays I have come across in a long time," added Ben Okri in the *New Statesman*. "You seldom get writers writing so personally, so feelingly about the need to be saved, about the ways in which their personal salvation can be achieved. What she says about the black woman she says from the depths of oppression. What is said from the depths of oppression illuminates all other oppressions."

But in a review for the *Nation*, Patricia Vigderman offered a dissent. Pronouncing much in the volume "disappointing" and "irritating," she charged that Alice avoided "larger and much more difficult issues in favor of much smaller, flashy assertions." Far from a masterpiece, Vigderman pooh-poohed the title essay with its allusions to quilts and gardens as tangential and "somewhat contrived." Apparently warming to the platform afforded her by

the *Nation*, Vigerdman also took a belated swipe at *The Color
Purple*: "I stopped believing in both the book and the main character, Celie, every time I felt I was seeing . . . road signs. When . . .
Celie becomes a mouthpiece for Walker's opinions she becomes a
foolish character."

To be sure, Alice's recasting of feminism in language reflective
of the history and traditions of black women was celebrated by
many as one of the most significant contributions of *In Search of
Our Mothers' Gardens*. In the opening pages of the collection, Alice
defined *womanism* as a term that comprised several elements:

1. From *womanish*. (Opp. Of "girlish," i.e. frivolous, irresponsible, not serious.) A black feminist or feminist of color.
From the black folk expression of mothers to female children,
"You acting womanish," i.e. like a woman. Usually referring to
outrageous, audacious, courageous, or *willful* behavior. . . .

2. *Also*: A woman who loves other women, sexually and/or
nonsexually. Appreciates and prefers women's culture,
women's emotional flexibility (values tears as natural counter-
balance of laughter). . . . Sometimes loves individual men, sexually and/or nonsexually. Committed to survival and
wholeness of entire people, male *and* female. . . .

3. Loves music. Loves dance. Loves the moon. *Loves* the
Spirit. . . . Loves herself. *Regardless*.

4. Womanist is to feminist as purple to lavender.

The term resonated profoundly with black and other minority
women for whom identification with the "white" feminist movement had become highly charged, if not anathema. The debate
about feminism and its relevance to black women was by definition
complex, demanding as it did (then as now) both race and gender
analysis of economics, reproductive rights, sexual orientation, and
religion, among other issues. Still, as Paula Giddings had argued,

how could black women not feel alienated by such standard bearers of mainstream feminism as Betty Friedan? She who, in a 1972 initiative with the National Women's Political Caucus, reputedly announced her plans to appear in Harlem with a "Traveling Watermelon Feast" to distribute to residents. Of that brand of "feminism," women of color wanted no part.

" 'Womanist,' with its emphasis on independence and unity, came directly out of black women's culture," explained Barbara Christian, who, in her essay "Alice Walker: The Black Woman Artist as Wayward," records the womanist themes in the author's work. "The word had a monumental impact in shaping a consciousness that allowed black women to dialogue and organize separate from white feminists who had proven themselves to be insensitive to our concerns."

With *womanist* in the lexicon, many black women felt more comfortable speaking about their experiences as survivors of rape, child abuse, or domestic violence. Gone was their fear of being labeled "man-hater" or lesbian, the routine "slurs" directed at women identified as feminists, regardless of their sexuality. By the same turn, many black lesbians took refuge in a word they could readily link to their mothers, grandmothers, and aunts. In short, *womanist* was devoid of the damning social stigmas affiliated with women's liberation.

The term was embraced with a special vigor by a growing group of black women theologians who asserted that in womanism they found affirmation of their religious beliefs. "Because Walker emphasizes African-American women's love for the Spirit [black] Christian women have used 'womanist' to articulate their witness and participation in God's power and presence in the world," noted the Rev. Irene Monroe, a black minister and writer in Boston. Indeed, with womanism came a proliferation of religious scholarship published by black women, including *Black Womanist Ethics* (1988) by Katie G. Cannon; *Sisters in the Wilderness: The Challenges of Womanist God-Talk* (1993) by Delores S. Williams; and the pointedly titled *White Women's Christ and Black Women's Jesus: Feminist Christology and*

Womanist Response (1989), in which the Rev. Jacquelyn Grant argued that womanism was key to developing faith practices that met black community needs. This was no idle observation for black clergy who, increasingly, looked down from pulpits to discover pews occupied almost exclusively by black women. That the black male church-going population was vanishing could not be denied.

As with all her writing, Alice hoped that *In Search* would empower black women (and others) to claim their heritage. She also felt it was important for readers to know that her preference for *womanist* was prompted as much by art as politics. "As a poet, I can't have a word that requires an adjective to impart meaning," she said, explaining her disdain for the phrase "black feminist." "*Womanist* needs no qualification. Just the word itself stands for doing something that might get you in trouble."

Such was the scenario for Georgette Mosbacher, a major Republican Party fund-raiser who, in an apparent burst of enthusiasm, adopted the term to market a line of beauty products. "What we need is [cosmetics] developed by women for women," Mosbacher told the *New York Times*. "We are womanists today . . . not feminists." Alerted to the comment by friends, Alice dispatched a note to Mosbacher in which she apprised her of the word's roots in black women's culture. Confiding that she'd been unclear on the concept, Mosbacher, in a return letter, thanked Alice for enlightenment. Her advertising campaign for "womanist" blush and mascara did not come to pass.

Interestingly, a respected black woman poet found the term wanting. Writing in *Callaloo*, a prestigious African American literary journal, Elizabeth Alexander explained her ambivalence. "I like the word 'feminist,'" Alexander declared in her 1994 essay, "Memory, Community, Voice." " 'Womanist' makes sense to me as Alice Walker defines it, but in my mouth it feels too round and warm and lovely; feminism has a bit of flint to it, a spine in the lack of round vowels, and seems also not to exclude me as a black woman, so that's what I like."

.   .   .

NO ONE could remember the last time they'd seen it. And if they could, the experience had receded from memory. So rare were cover stories about black women in the esteemed Sunday *New York Times Magazine* that the image of Alice, holding a walking stick and nestled against a rail fence, was still fresh to some readers, nearly twenty years later. "Oh, it was major," said Suzanne Murphy, a Seattle writer who was in graduate school in New York at the time. "After *The Color Purple*, folks were ravenous for information about Alice Walker. The phone lines were burning up that day with people talking about her being on the cover of the magazine."

Published January 8, 1984, "Novelist Alice Walker: Telling the Black Woman's Story" was written by David Bradley. An academic, Bradley was also author of *The Chaneysville Incident*, a much-praised 1981 novel that drew on a historical account of thirteen runaway slaves who chose death over recapture. In crafting the profile, Bradley, perhaps still enamored of techniques he'd utilized in his novel, devoted a good portion of the seven thousand-word piece to self-reflective analysis. To wit, readers were regaled with *his* personal response to Alice's success; *his* memories of a luncheon with Alice ("she was given to artless touching"); *his* deduction that influential black women (i.e., poet Sonia Sanchez) were displeased by *The Color Purple* but disinclined to say so publicly. And finally, readers, on about page thirteen, were left to ponder *his* conclusion that Alice, "afflicted" with an "artificial eye," could not help but have distorted vision, the subtext there being that her anger at Curtis Walker flowed as river to ocean, inevitably, to all black men.

In passages about the "excesses" in her writing, Bradley elaborated: "It seems . . . Alice Walker has a high level of enmity toward black men. . . . Her acidity flows beyond black male writers. It pours over men who are attracted to light-skinned women. . . . It spatters, in general, men she considers fundamentally illiterate. . . . There *is* a world in . . . her eye. It is etched there by pain and sacrifice, and it is probably too much to expect that anything so violently created would be free of some distortion."

Discussion of Alice's artistry could be found but not without a rigorous wading through the life and times of David Bradley ("I had had some taste of what it is like to scribble in obscurity and then suddenly have people ripping manuscripts out of your hands").

"Alone in my hotel room, I try to make sense of Alice Walker or, more correctly, of my feelings about her," Bradley ventured, as he approached the close of a soul-searching ramble in which he also deduced that her preference for *womanist* was skewed. "I'm not sure that I like her as much as I once did, or that she sees as deeply and as clearly as I once thought. Yet, I am sure that there is no one I like more as a writer. . . . I would like to forget about 30 percent of what she has written and said. And yet the remaining 70 percent is so powerful that, even in this quandary, I am . . . looking for answers."

His request was fulfilled. "I regret that David Bradley found me less likeable after discerning my feet of clay," Alice replied in a letter printed in the February 12, 1984, issue of the magazine. "However, it may help him to know that my blind eye, also perceived by him as artificial, is in fact flesh and blood. . . . The perception that something that no longer functions normally is therefore false is also a 'distortion.' . . . In any event, most of thinking humankind, even the totally blind, can now see quite clearly the oppression of women by sexist men, customs and laws, and I believe it is the prerogative of women to write freely (and as much) about their oppression by men (and to the same purpose) as men of color have written of their oppression by whites. 'Who would be free must . . . strike the blow,' said our grandfather, Frederick Douglass. If he thought only his grandsons would act on this, he was mistaken."

On the other hand, in a dispatch from Brooklyn, letter writer G. Kirkpatrick expressed his admiration for Bradley's widely read and heatedly debated profile. In so doing, he set the stage for a battle that would rage, as few could have imagined, through the black community for years to come.

"By waging her 'womanish' [*sic*] quest, however genuine, Alice Walker deepens the wounds of equally oppressed black men . . . her voice emasculating those who have already been tried. . . . The deconstructive and often point-blank tone of her prose has taken a heavier toll on black male writers who have already lost literary ground. Miss Walker and other womanists have, perhaps unconsciously, yet irresponsibly, architected a place right above them, hindering their access. . . . The history between black men and women is not a complimentary one; however, this should not preclude [their] co-existence—womanists and machoists alike."

46

The Glimpse of Life beyond the Words

PERHAPS THEY were angered by her open criticism of *Essence*. Shaken by her stance on mothering (long touted as *holiness itself* in Black America). Envious of her publishing acclaim. Who knew? But increasingly, Alice began to rile black women too.

Apparently less enamored with the sisterly spirit that had prompted her to join Alice and Adrienne Rich in drafting a statement of solidarity for the National Book Awards, poet Audre Lorde did not hesitate to convey her mixed feelings about Alice's appearance on the cover of the *New York Times Magazine*. Beginning in the late 1970s, Lorde had emerged as a prominent black lesbian literary figure. Speaking in March 1984 with a writer for *Blacklight*, a magazine for black gays, she said, "When I saw her picture on the cover of [the magazine] I thought, 'Well, good for you Alice! I wish it had been me but if it wasn't me, I'm really glad it's you.'"

Suggesting that Alice was less threatening to powerful media brokers, Lorde continued, "I really can't see a picture of a black dyke on the cover of *The New York Times*. I'd start to get real worried. . . . I'd begin to ask myself what that meant as a black Lesbian feminist committed to radical social change. . . . Alice Walker is not a Lesbian . . . and I think that's a real factor in her acceptability."

In a newspaper column headlined, "There has to be a chance for love in a middle ground," the black writer Pearl Cleage also questioned the celebration of Alice and her work. However, in a counter to Lorde, Cleage attributed the success of *The Color Purple*, in part, to its positive portrait of love between women. Writing for the *Atlanta Journal-Constitution*, she complained, "Although it is unfair to summarize, suffice it to say that the book suggests that black women can best find sexual and emotional fulfillment with other black women and that the best they can hope for from black men is purely platonic comradeship and this only under the strictest controls. . . .

"The fact that *The Color Purple* is being hailed from *Ms.* magazine to *The New York Times* . . . raises for me the question of whose vision of black life I am being prompted to accept and why."

About David Bradley and his casting of her as a quiet critic of Alice, with whom she'd admittedly disagreed during the Black Nationalist years, Sonia Sanchez explained, "Because of my politics, I never expected anyone to pay me for what I had to say. Nobody was going to jump up and say, 'Sonia, here's a million dollars, sit down and write.' I never had that kind of protection. . . . Perpetrators picked up on that and said Sanchez hated *The Color Purple*. I finally had to tell people to stop evoking my name in opposition to Alice Walker. I didn't report back to her, but I did put folks in check."

Noting that she'd read Alice's work and attended many of her readings, another black woman contended, bluntly, that the reason for the author's triumph was clear. "I always had the sense that Alice went out of her way to make herself likeable to white people," said Mary Hoover, a San Francisco–area teacher, during an interview. "Though I will give her credit for *Meridian*."

And in one of the most scathing assessments of *The Color Purple*, black feminist scholar Trudier Harris, echoing Cleage, decried the "canonization" of a book that "reads like a political shopping list of all the IOUs Walker felt it was time to repay."

"Sadly, a book that might have been ignored if it had been published ten years earlier or later has now become *the* classic by a black woman . . .," Harris lamented in *Black American Literature Forum*. "Alice Walker had been waiting in the wings of the feminist movement and the power it had generated long enough for her curtain call to come."

UNLIKE SOME critics, Donna Green had no personal history with Alice. Nor had the African American resident of Oakland, California, read any of her work. Green's sole connection to Alice was her daughter, a tenth-grade student who'd been assigned *The Color Purple* in her English class at the city's Far West High School. Aggrieved by what she viewed as the indecent themes of the novel, Green, in May 1984, lobbied the local Board of Education to ban the novel from public schools.

In a formal complaint, she reeled off the purported offenses of *The Color Purple*: it was sexually explicit, sacrilegious, exceedingly violent, biased toward lesbianism, and degrading to black people through its use of an "embarrassing" folk dialect. Exhorting officials to "determine whether this material is suitable for children," Green then took it upon herself to read excerpts from the novel during school board meetings (i.e., "First time I got full sight of Shug Avery long black body with it black plum nipples . . . I thought I had turned into a man.").

"I wouldn't want my child reading this garbage," fumed a director, in response to the outraged mother's campaign. "I don't care if it did receive a Pulitzer. As a black person I'm offended."

"If taken out of context, I can see how [Green] might be upset," said another. "I just think you have to read the whole book. It's beautiful."

The controversy swirled for months, offering others, such as Ishmael Reed, a chance to enter the fray. In a lengthy dispatch to the letters page of the *Oakland Tribune*, printed on July 2, 1984, he offered his perspective:

> Ms. Donna Green's reservations about . . . *The Color Purple* reflect those voiced by a considerable section of the Afro-American media. . . . Their responses to this book were over-shadowed by the media hype . . . orchestrated by Gloria Steinem, a feminist ideologue. . . .

> A solution to the [conflict] might be for *The Color Purple* to be taught in conjunction with books by . . . authors like Sonia Sanchez and Lucille Clifton, both of whom have been critical of Alice Walker's outlook. . . .

> Ms. Green is to be commended for exercising independent judgment when many readers, writers and scholars merely salivate over the latest literary cabbage patch doll. She weakens her case, however, by insisting that the book be banned.

In an effort to resolve the dispute, the school district convened a panel of literary experts (among them future U.S. poet laureate Robert Hass) who ultimately endorsed *The Color Purple* as appropriate for high school curriculum. But Green's attempt would give rise to other censorship campaigns. Explaining their actions with such statements as "what is said on the first page is all we need to hear," officials in locales from Kenna, West Virginia, to Eugene, Oregon, initiated procedures to ban the novel from libraries and classrooms.

As such, *The Color Purple* joined an illustrious list of books by American authors that had been challenged in the past. Among them: Harper Lee's *To Kill a Mockingbird* (1960), Mark Twain's *Huckleberry Finn* (1884), Madeleine L'Engle's *A Wrinkle in Time* (1962), and John Steinbeck's *The Grapes of Wrath*. Indeed, making clear his displeasure with what he viewed as Steinbeck's false portrait of the "Okie situation," a politician damned the 1939 classic, calling the novel "a lie, a black, infernal creation of a twisted, distorted mind."

And in a case rife with meaning with regard to Alice and *The Color Purple*, a Boston teacher was fired, in 1967, for reading a poem to his fourth-grade class. The piece? "Ballad of the Landlord" by Langston Hughes. At the time, Boston was in the midst of a pitched battle over school integration, with whites fearful that the poem ("Landlord, landlord / My roof has sprung a leak / Don't you 'member I told you about it / Way last week?") would increase racial strife.

Writing in his provocatively prescient 1926 essay "The Negro Artist and the Racial Mountain," Hughes had, in fact, examined many of the issues that later emerged in *The Color Purple* debate about freedom of expression and the "accountability" of black authors. His work steeped in black culture ("I am the darker brother / They send me to the kitchen to eat") and a love for the common folk ("Put on yo' red silk stockings / Black gal"), Hughes was revered by readers who felt his deep appreciation for the everyday highs and lows of black life. But protesting his frequent use of dialect and blues rhythms, others criticized Hughes for a raw eroticism that they charged "demeaned" blacks in the eyes of whites. And so it was that he declared in perhaps the premier manifesto of the Harlem Renaissance, "Let the blare of Negro jazz bands and the bellowing voice of Bessie Smith singing Blues penetrate the closed ears of the colored near-intellectuals until they listen and hear. . . . We younger Negro artists who create now intend to express our individual dark-skinned selves without fear or shame. . . . We know we are beautiful. And ugly too."

NONPLUSSED, ALICE took Green's crusade against *The Color Purple* in stride. The Oakland mother was not the first, nor would she be the last, Alice suspected, to denounce her work as "unseemly." She had already endured an attempt by antiporn factions to suppress her story "Coming Apart," itself a critique (to her mind, at least) of pornography.

"Certain forms of censorship of a writer's work can be seen as honoring the writer," Alice later mused about efforts to ban *The Color Purple*. "I have come to understand that it is 'the glimpse of life beyond the words' that those who censor writers are seeking to blot out."

. . .

HOPING THAT Alice might craft a life that had been denied her in the Jim Crow South, Minnie Lou Walker had dispatched her youngest child from Eatonton with a suitcase, sewing machine, and typewriter. She'd chosen her gifts wisely. Shaped by gratitude and tradition, Alice, attacks on her artistry notwithstanding, started a small publishing firm in 1984.

She christened the enterprise Wild Trees Press, setting up office and living quarters on a forty-acre retreat in Mendocino County that she'd purchased with some of her earnings from *The Color Purple*. Reared in a sharecropping family that had been uprooted at whim, Alice was determined not to suffer the same fate. Her name on the deed, she began landscaping the property with one hundred fruit trees (pear, persimmon, and peach among them) and several luxuriant gardens.

In launching a publishing company (Robert Allen and friend Belvie Rooks joined her as partners), Alice had in mind Virginia Woolf's success in a similar venture. Working with her husband, Leonard, Woolf started the Hogarth Press in 1917, releasing such classics as *The Waste Land* (1922) by T. S. Eliot. However, positioned to acquire *Ulysses* by James Joyce, Woolf passed, wrongly deducing that the "distasteful" novel was destined for oblivion.

"Of course, I knew about Hogarth," Alice said. "It was part of my thinking. But mostly, Robert and I needed a project we could do in the country, having fallen in love with living there. I suddenly had money to do publishing and Belvie was game. We loved doing things together!"

Thus inspired, Alice went forth with a simple credo for Wild Trees Press: "We publish only what we love." She and her partners were unanimous in their choice for the company's debut release, in November 1984: *A Piece of Mine*, a collection of short stories by J. California Cooper.

"In its strong folk flavor, Cooper's work reminds us of Langston Hughes and Zora Neale Hurston," Alice noted in her foreword. "Like theirs, her style is deceptively simple and direct, and the vale of tears in which some of her characters reside is never so deep that a rich chuckle at a foolish person's foolishness cannot be heard."

Cooper could not believe her good fortune when she was asked directly by Alice to submit a manuscript for review. At the time, she was known primarily as a dramatist and had never been published in any other genre. "Alice attended one of my plays and afterward asked if I could recast the text as short stories," remembered Cooper, whose subsequent work was contracted by major publishing houses. "You better believe I went home and started writing."

"I was consulted on the design of the book, its distribution, everything," she continued. "People were riding Alice pretty rough because of *The Color Purple*. But from what I could see, she just concentrated on Wild Trees and her own writing."

Cooper was on point. For in addition to her publishing venture, Alice, at the close of 1984, released her twelfth book, the poetry collection *Horses Make a Landscape Look More Beautiful* (the title was taken from the writings of Lakota Holy Man, Lame Deer). In a series of short poems about Mississippi, Alice gave quiet voice to her tumultuous years in Jackson. "When you remember me, my child / be sure to recall that Mama was a sinner / . . . She was not happy with fences."

The theme of transgression would also infuse "Love Is Not Concerned," a poem later adopted as credo by gay liberation and peace activists.

love is not concerned
with whom you pray
or where you slept
the night you ran away
from home
love is concerned
that the beating of your heart
should kill no one.

Reflecting her solidarity with Native American struggles (and the Cherokee lineage of Minnie Lou Walker), other poems tackled the destruction of the cosmos and offered strategies to help protect the natural world. "When they torture your mother / plant a tree / When they . . . cut down the forest / . . . start another."

In the poem "Representing the Universe" Alice admonished a long-winded speaker: "It is not enough to be interminable; / one must also be precise."

Horses Make a Landscape garnered favorable reviews from critics who extolled Alice's melding of personal and political themes. "In the tradition of Whitman, Walker sings, celebrates and agonizes over vicissitudes that link and separate all of humankind," noted Sonia Gernes in *America* magazine.

Proponents of traditional poetics were less enthused by her subject matter and imagery. Writing for the *New York Times Book Review*, L. M. Rosenberg grumbled, "Whatever else the book may be—often touching, sometimes irritating; a little stiff; a touch preacherly, with gems of wisdom inserted parenthetically—it is almost never poetry." Still, Rosenberg acknowledged Alice's verve and musicality.

And those looking for a more spirited response to detractors of *The Color Purple* would find it in Alice's poem "Each One, Pull One (Thinking of Lorraine Hansberry)."

> *We must say it all, and as clearly*
> *as we can. For, even before we are dead,*
> *they are busy*
> *trying to bury us.*
>
> *Were we black? Were we women? Were we gay?*
> *Were we the wrong shade of black? Were we yellow?*
> *Did we, God forbid, love the wrong person, country*
> *or politics? . . .*
>
> *But most of all, did we write exactly what we saw,*
> *as clearly as we could? Were we unsophisticated*
> *enough to cry and scream? . . .*

Lately you have begun to help them
bury us . . .

I look into your eyes;
you are throwing dirt.
You, standing in the grave with me.

And like Hansberry, who had weighed her options when, in 1961, Hollywood came calling about *A Raisin in the Sun*, Alice took a hard look at the man who now appeared at her door and introduced himself as Steven Spielberg.

47

Something to Lift Spirits

BORN DECEMBER 18, 1946, in Cincinnati, Ohio, Steven Spielberg, by his mid-thirties, had distinguished himself as the most successful director in American film. His unprecedented string of triumphs—*Jaws, Close Encounters of the Third Kind, Raiders of the Lost Ark, E.T.*—gave rise to the very concept of a "blockbuster" hit. The now-routine merchandising of movies (lunch boxes, toys), hyperbolic advertising campaigns (THE SUMMER'S SMASH SENSATION!), and stampede of pre-release celebrity interviews emerged as industry standards after Spielberg's *Jaws* became the first Hollywood film to reap a domestic gross of more than $100 million, breaking the record of $86 million set by *The Godfather*. Released in 1982, *E.T.*—a story about a boy's love for an extraterrestrial stranded on Earth—raked in a reported $400 million and charmed critics and viewers alike.

That an American alive in the mid-1980s might be unacquainted with Steven Spielberg was a notion so far-fetched (for most people) as to strain belief. But such was the case for Alice. Her fascination minimal for ferocious sharks, outer space creatures, and swashbuckling adventurers in the style of Indiana Jones, Alice was the first to admit that Spielberg's celebrity had escaped her completely. Simply put, it was not her habit to track the ever-changing constellation of Hollywood stars.

"I'd never heard of Steven," she said, with a cheerful laugh. "I hadn't seen *E.T.* or any other Spielberg movies. His name didn't mean a thing to me."

But for composer and black icon Quincy Jones, the famed director was the premier choice for a project he was determined to bring to the silver screen. A long-time admirer of Alice's work, Jones said he tossed a copy of *The Color Purple* ("the shortest book I had") into his luggage as he departed for a vacation in the early 1980s. In what he later described as "a mystical confluence of events," Jones was contacted, upon his return, by Hollywood producer Peter Guber, who, for $65,000, had optioned film rights to the novel after it won the Pulitzer Prize.

A lawyer and financier of such films as *Shampoo*, *Flashdance*, and *Midnight Express*, Guber was led to *The Color Purple* by a then-aspiring producer named Carole Isenberg. Enthralled by Shug, Celie, Mr.____, and Nettie, Isenberg said she "felt it was my personal responsibility to help the novel become a film." "The book put me on fire," she later exclaimed.

But unproven in the industry, Isenberg knew she needed "heavy hitters" to advance her idea. Before approaching Guber, she said she pitched *The Color Purple* to other Hollywood producers, power brokers, and sundry studio heads. "At the time, Richard Pryor had a deal at Columbia for doing movies," recalled Isenberg, speaking of the well-known black comedian and actor. "I thought his people might be interested, but they rejected it out flat. Nobody wanted to step up to the plate."

The few who listened to her proposal ventured that *The Color Purple* might fly as a film, but not without changes in the story line. To wit: Mr.____ would be cast as a woman. Shug as a man. Celie would remain as crafted by Alice. With the "love triangle" thus reconfigured, Mr.____ (now female) and Celie (herself) would then vie for the affection of Shug (now envisioned, perhaps, as a studly John Shaft).

"I was warned that any hint of a sexual relationship between Shug and Celie was out of the question," Isenberg recalled. "But Peter was different. Already a commercial success, he was willing to take a chance on a movie of real quality and substance." And to that end, Guber contacted Quincy Delightt Jones Jr.

The composer of numerous film scores (*The Pawnbroker*, *In the Heat of the Night*, *In Cold Blood*), Jones was (then as now) one of the most respected figures in the entertainment industry. As producer of *Thriller* by Michael Jackson, he had masterminded the most successful album (26 times platinum) ever released. Wowed by the genius of Jones as a conductor, arranger, and all-around impresario, Guber hoped he might work a similar magic with a Warner Bros. film production of *The Color Purple*.

"When she agreed to the option, Alice was very firm in her standards should a movie come to pass," remembered Guber, who, coincidentally, had been in the same NYU law school class as Mel Leventhal. "Quincy and I went way back. I definitely wanted him involved."

But with his name already engraved on nearly thirty Grammies, Jones was not inclined to score another film. Instead, he asked for a hand in the entire project: as coproducer. "It would be my first time out, so I made it clear to Peter that I'd step aside if I proved to be out of my element," Jones explained. "But I loved *The Color Purple* and believed that it could make a powerful movie. Peter was very generous and said yes."

Encouraged by Guber, Jones said he immediately placed a call to Spielberg. Professional colleagues, the men had become better acquainted in 1982 when Jones visited the set of *E.T.* and Spielberg observed the production of *Thriller*. Now the rumor mills went wild with speculation that the "boy genius" (as Spielberg was called) was poised to take his first crack at a *real* film. For no matter their commercial success, his previous efforts had often been dismissed as lightweight, escapist fare. As director of *The Color Purple*, Spielberg would tackle a serious subject—about black people, no less. Hollywood was mesmerized.

"From day one, people started complaining that the blackness of *The Color Purple* would be 'diluted' if a white person directed the film," Jones recalled. "I resented such thinking and took it as an insult to Alice and all artists.

"I respected Steven, so I moved straight ahead," he added, steely-eyed nearly twenty years later. "I'd been watching the man closely and knew he was not afraid to experiment or stretch out."

Not surprising for the movie industry, there are multiple story lines as to exactly how *The Color Purple* was brought to Spielberg's attention. The director would later assert that he also read the novel at the suggestion of *E.T.* coproducer Kathleen Kennedy.

JONES AND Spielberg. A dynamic duo, no doubt. But the men were not the first to show interest in adapting Alice's work for the screen. That distinction was held by Julie Dash, a black woman director who became well known for her 1991 film *Daughters of the Dust*. In 1977, Dash had developed *The Diary of an African Nun*, a thirteen-minute movie based on Alice's story of the same title. Then a graduate film student at the University of California at Los Angeles, Dash said she was drawn to the work because it gave her an opportunity to "redefine how black women are depicted cinematically."

"When I first read the story, I cried," said Dash, about Alice's portrait of a nun whose faith is shaken by worldly desires. "The text was extremely visual in its detail.

"Young filmmakers often attempt to write their own first films in addition to directing them, and I think that's a mistake," she continued. "When you are struggling to learn, you need to work with a good, solid story. For me, 'The Diary of an African Nun' was an excellent choice."

Using her own funds, Dash shot the black-and-white film on a budget of nine hundred dollars, in about five weeks. In the title role, she cast Barbara O. Jones, who, dropping her surname, would later appear in *Daughters of the Dust* as Yellow-Mary. Exhibited in film festivals in the United States and abroad, *The Diary of an African*

Nun garnered glowing reviews and a Directors Guild Award for student films. Indeed, Dash said it was her student status that prompted a lapse in her thinking—she neglected to contact Alice before the cameras rolled.

"In hindsight, I know I should have asked her permission," Dash later explained. "But because it was a class project, never meant for distribution, I didn't. I think I was also afraid that Alice Walker would say no. I'd tried to adapt the work of other black writers. Each time I was denied."

Dash did send Alice a copy of the film, "with my apologies." Her response? She thought the sound quality could stand improvement. Still, she offered praise for the fledgling filmmaker in a letter dated May 7, 1980.

> Dear Julie Dash,
> I enjoyed the visuals of the film immensely. It is beautifully done. However, I would urge you to do the sound over. . . . I think I was the only one who knew what was being said. It is *such* a lovely film and the actress is so compelling. . . . Be well. It was a fun experience for me.

Fun. The history of black women in film leading up to the mid-1980s had been shaped by many forces, with hardship tending to overshadow delight. Nurturing mammy. Tragic mulatto. Sepia siren. Long-suffering matriarch. In keeping with the racism of an industry that had released *The Birth of a Nation,* such were the roles typically offered to black women. And all too often the bias reflected on the Hollywood screen was mirrored in the real lives of black women actors, aspiring movie directors, and screenwriters (rare though they were). They endured a maddening existence, perhaps best exemplified by Hattie McDaniel, who, barred from attending the 1939 premiere of *Gone with the Wind* in Jim Crow Atlanta, then won an Oscar for best supporting actress (the first ever given to a black actor) for her role as Mammy.

Pressured by civil rights and black nationalist protests, the film industry changed in the 1960s to reflect a shifting political climate in American society. Thus came a deluge of so-called blaxploitation movies in which black women were still stereotyped, most often as sex-hungry appendages to "bad ass" militant black men.

The 1970s showcased the talents of black women in such films as *Sounder* (Cecily Tyson) and *Claudine* (Diahann Carroll). *The Landlord*, a frustrating 1966 novel by black writer Kristin Hunter, reappeared as a frustrating 1970 movie starring Pearl Bailey, Diana Sands, and a rhythm-impaired Beau Bridges. Perhaps the most anticipated film of the era featuring a black female lead was *Lady Sings the Blues*, in which Diana Ross reprised (to tepid reviews) the tortured life of Billie Holiday. While less likely to encounter overt discrimination in the 1980s, black actresses had yet to see themselves fully realized in, arguably, the culture's most powerful medium.

And clearly, black men in Hollywood had been forced to battle for their dignity too. For example, Bill (Bojangles) Robinson had died bankrupt and broken despite his pairing with Shirley Temple in numerous 1930s-era smash hits. With yearly earnings of $300,000 to $400,000, the ringlet-haired child was the nation's highest-paid film star during the Depression—the "shift-for-self" years when Willie Lee Walker labored to feed eight children on twelve dollars a month.

To BE sure, Alice had misgivings about the film industry. As a politically conscious black woman, how could she not? Still, there was no denying her lifelong love for the movies. Neither the Jim Crow seating nor the racially dispiriting *Song of the South* had dimmed her passion for outings at the Pex Theater during her youth. Even in her doubts about the industry, Alice understood the power of film. In that, she and Guber were aligned. She later noted that it was Guber's boyish exuberance about movies ("his little child is so apparent") that gave her faith he could deliver a film that reflected the rich cultural heritage of her forebears.

As for Quincy Jones, Alice had been impressed with his musical score for *Roots*, the epic television miniseries based on Alex

Haley's book. That his middle name was Delightt evoked in her a womanish glee.

And the proposed director? Well, encouraged by Jones's enthusiasm, she was willing, although other options emerged. According to Guber, the much-praised English director Roland Joffe (*The Killing Fields*) expressed interest in *The Color Purple*. But uncertain of his command of the text, he eventually bowed out. Euzhan Palcy was similarly intrigued with the idea of bringing Alice's characters to life. However, by the time the two women met, negotiations with Spielberg were too far advanced to consider the young director, born in Martinique, whose debut film (*Sugar Cane Alley*) had been released to stunning reviews.

"In order to get financing, *The Color Purple* needed a director with a big name," Palcy said. "I wanted to do the movie, but the deal was already in the works. When I met with Alice, I told her to go ahead and see what Steven could do."

Appreciative of Palcy's support, Alice later said, "It was a wonderful gift Euzhan gave me. Her saying, 'Let Steven do it and if he fails . . .' followed by a mirthful grin and great, expressive, gallic shrug."

But before giving her blessing to a film adaptation of *The Color Purple*, Alice consulted her friends. Was she setting herself up for betrayal? Would she have to beg the forgiveness of her ancestors? Call on the conjuring spirit of Zora Neale Hurston for protective voodoo spells?

The overall consensus was that Alice should go forward in hope of transforming the demeaning images of blacks that had prevailed in Hollywood for generations. Only then did she agree to "take a meeting" with Jones and Spielberg—in San Francisco. Worn out by all the hubbub surrounding *The Color Purple*, Celie had insisted on staying home. Show business? As long as her name was on the agenda, Shug didn't care where her movie star future got hashed out.

Arriving in San Francisco from Los Angeles on a Warner Bros. jet, Jones and Spielberg dined with Alice at Ernie's, one of the city's poshest restaurants. Spielberg, in what he'd later describe as an "audition" for the director's slot, let Jones steer most of the conversation, though it was obvious he'd done a close reading of the novel and, after his initial shyness passed, he readily shared his ideas for the film.

Alice chronicled the meeting in a journal entry: "Quincy had talked so positively about [Spielberg] I was almost dreading his appearance—but then after a moment of uneasiness . . . he [made] really intelligent comments. . . . We went out for dinner where Quincy and Steven and I got slightly tipsy and energetic in our thoughts about Celie and Shug and Nettie. After three hours . . . they rode off into the night.

"It is agreed that Steven and I will work together on the screenplay. I will write it and confer. I feel some panic. I want so much for this to be good. Something to lift spirits and encourage people."

48

Guide and Protect

IN HER desire to lift spirits with a film version of *The Color Purple*, Alice had one particular person in mind: Minnie Lou Walker. Beginning in the late 1970s, Mrs. Walker had suffered a series of strokes that had left her increasingly impaired. But Mrs. Walker mustered her strength and, in early 1982, made one triumphant trip from Eatonton to experience the life her youngest child had carved out for herself in Northern California. There, leaning on Alice's arm, she reveled in the majesty of the redwood trees, the mighty roar of the ocean, and the exotic bird-of-paradise flower that, such was her passion for gardening, she was certain she could nurture into bloom in the red clay of Georgia.

Ever devout and now a Jehovah's Witness, Mrs. Walker, nearly seventy, gave thanks to the Creator that she'd lived to see Alice rise victorious over hardships that had vanquished so many. That her daughter tended to "trespass" in her writing only confirmed for Mrs. Walker that Alice remained the "little mess" who'd sashayed past jook joints to deliver eggs as a child.

Illness prevented Mrs. Walker from reading more than a few pages of *The Color Purple*. Her decline had catapulted Alice (who'd named the character Nettie in honor of her maternal grandmother) into a wrenching despair. But she kept her anguish concealed from the public eye. "From the moment I realized my mother would never again be the woman I knew, something fell inside of me," Alice later wrote of her life beyond the shimmer of the Pulitzer Prize. "There was a strong green cord connecting me to this great, simple-seeming but complicated woman, who was herself rooted in the earth. I felt this cord weakening, becoming a thread. . . . There was not a day . . . that I did not feel the emptiness left by my mother's absence, particularly as she gradually lost the ability to talk, beyond a slurred greeting, which, true to her spirit, she slurred cheerfully."

Alice hoped the movie would help her mother recapture memories (reimagined on the palette of art) of her early life as a young black woman in Putnam County. Although Mr. Walker had passed on, Alice envisioned a film that would likewise ennoble his spirit, which she'd put forth with poignant touches in the character Harpo. And of course, there was the language—its vibrancy, rhythm, poetry, and flair. As Alice had written Ferrone about her novel, she was certain that a well-cast adaptation of *The Color Purple* could reconnect moviegoers of all hues to the language of their hearts.

"I loved the way my mother talked, which was always fresh, honest, straight as an arrow," Alice mused, describing the rich folk language many of her critics had rejected as "insulting" to black people. "In a movie she could hear her voice and know that it was authentic, sturdy and strong."

As it happened, it was a voice that grabbed the attention of an actress later cast in a lead role of "*Moonsong*," the decoy title used by Spielberg to avert the masses now wild to appear in the first major black film to be released by Hollywood in years. Born Caryn Johnson in New York City, the actress exhibited early talent, performing in community arts workshops. The divorced mother of a young daughter, Johnson moved to California in the mid-1970s, where she joined local theater troupes and honed comedy routines infused with social satire (i.e., "Blee T.," a black version of *E.T.* in which a space creature lands in a ghetto rather than in the suburbs).

To pay the bills, she took odd jobs (bricklayer, cosmetologist for a funeral parlor). When there was no work to be found, Johnson signed up for welfare.

In 1984, after an acclaimed one-woman show about black comic Jackie "Moms" Mabley, the actress, now rising with an adopted stage name, opened in *Whoopi Goldberg: Direct from Broadway*. It was a name fated for stardom. But before she achieved international celebrity, Goldberg was driving near her Berkeley home when, enthralled by a voice on the car radio, she pulled to the side of the road.

"It was Alice Walker reading from *The Color Purple*," Goldberg remembered. "What I heard was so moving, I just stopped and listened. When the program ended, I drove right to a bookstore and bought the novel. I wrote her a letter begging for a part if a movie was ever made. I was ready to play the dust on the floor, the lint on a sweater, the grease in a skillet, anything."

More reserved in tone, Goldberg's dispatch read, in part:

Dear Alice Walker,
I would like to begin by telling you that I think *The Color Purple* is amazing. I've just read it to my daughter. . . . My mom just received it . . . again, it is wonderful. . . .

I called your publisher to ask about [the movie]. Well, the name Whoopi Goldberg sounds like a joke and I don't think they realized I was not a crank caller. . . .

If you think I fit any of the folks in your book perhaps you would let me know whom I should [contact] about auditioning. . . . I don't know what else to say except thank you for your time.

Already familiar with Goldberg's work, Alice alerted Spielberg and casting director Reuben Cannon, who, after a screen test, knew they'd found in the driven, dreadlocked actress the perfect Celie ("I was beyond the beyond," Goldberg recalled).

One of the premier casting directors in the industry, Cannon called on his credentials, shrewd eye, and international ties with actors ("as a black man, I have to outwork everybody") as he continued to contract the best talent for the ensemble performance that would be *The Color Purple*. For example, originally from the Virgin Islands, Desreta Jackson (young Celie) wowed Cannon at an open casting he held at a Los Angeles high school. "There were at least three hundred girls there," Jackson recalled.

With his film career on the ascent in the early 1980s, Danny Glover (*Places in the Heart, Witness, Silverado*) had scant competition for the role of Mr._____, Cannon said. Ghana native Akosua Busia had arrived in Hollywood determined to make her mark "either in a Spielberg movie or on *The Tonight Show* with Johnny Carson." A bus rider, Busia "splurged on a taxi" after learning, while shopping, that she'd been cast as Nettie. (Her agent had tracked her down.) Willard Pugh, primarily a television actor (*Hill Street Blues*), endured five nerve-wracking screen tests before he landed the role of Harpo. "I blacked out for a minute," he said, describing his elation.

Besting singers Chaka Khan, Patti LaBelle, and Phyllis Hyman, licensed realtor Margaret Avery ("there was so little dignified work for black actors preceding *The Color Purple*") won the part of Shug, but only after the much-desired Tina Turner declined. Then in Los Angeles to record "We Are the World," the star-studded Africa famine relief extravaganza produced by Quincy Jones, Turner had agreed to a meeting about the film.

Jones recalled, "Everybody was all excited, thinking we'd have our first choice for Shug. But when we started to talk, Tina said forget *The Color Purple*. After twenty years of abuse, she said, the only role she wanted to play was Indiana Jones!"

By contrast, the woman cast as Sofia felt destined to play the feisty character who went tit for tat with Harpo ("I try to beat her, she black my eyes"). Born January 29, 1954, in Mississippi, Oprah Gail Winfrey braved a life of poverty and childhood molestation to emerge, in her thirties, as a widely hailed television personality. In the early 1980s, Winfrey arrived in Chicago, where, in a few months, ratings for her local program surpassed that of the silver-haired talk-show king, Phil Donahue.

Winfrey said she bought *The Color Purple* after reading an early review and became obsessed with the novel, buying copies by the dozens and handing them out "like holy water" to friends. "I was *gone* with the book," she remembered. "I always had several copies on me. For two years, I steered every conversation toward *The Color Purple*. If there was a movie, I knew in my heart that I'd be in it."

With her talk show drawing in unprecedented millions of viewers (and advertising revenues), Winfrey was in negotiations for national syndication when she received a call from Cannon about an upcoming movie, "*Moonsong*." By chance, Quincy Jones had been in Chicago and seen Winfrey on television. Taken by her down-home style, he'd stopped in his tracks and peered at the screen. "It just slapped me in the face that I was staring at Sofia," he remembered. "I didn't know if Oprah could act or not, but I immediately called Reuben. He arranged an audition."

Certain though she was about her movie future, Winfrey had never performed on film. But her lack of acting experience didn't deter her from pursuing her dream. "They were using this fake title, but it didn't fool me," Winfrey recalled, with a laugh. "I told Reuben, 'I know these people. This ain't no *Moonsong*. This is *The Color Purple*. Sofia is married to Harpo. The name Harpo is Oprah spelled backwards. This is my destiny.' "

Well, Alfre Woodard felt the same. Indeed, Winfrey's heart sank upon learning that her competition was the accomplished Oklahoma-born actress who'd garnered a 1983 Oscar nomination for her role as Geechee in *Cross Creek*. "When Reuben told me that Alfre had also auditioned for Sofia, I knew I would never get the part," Winfrey said. "I mean, how could I beat Alfre? So, to free myself, I prayed to Jesus and asked to be released from the desire to be in *The Color Purple*. That way, I could get on with my life."

Winfrey began her "detox" while at a "fat farm" (her words) in Wisconsin, having made a public bet with entertainer Joan Rivers to shed fifteen pounds. ("I really needed to lose fifty-five," she shrugged.) She'd just finished an exercise session when she received a phone call from Cannon, admonishing her to abandon her weight-loss regimen. "Reuben said that Steven wanted me for Sofia and I needed to stay the same size," Winfrey happily remembered. "Girl, I packed up and went directly to Dairy Queen."

THE MAJOR roles cast, *The Color Purple* was now poised for production at a projected cost of $14 million, decidedly low budget in 1980s Hollywood. But there was a detail that had yet to be resolved: the script.

Spielberg had determined that the screenplay Alice drafted, while useful as a foundation, did not mesh with his overall vision of the film. According to Cannon, the director then approached more than twenty writers (among them South African playwright Athol Fugard) before signing on Menno Meyjes.

"At the time, I was living in San Francisco and *The Color Purple* was very much in the air," recalled Meyjes, a Dutch writer who'd just completed the screenplay for *Lionheart*, a movie based on the medieval children's crusade. "Apparently other writers had been afraid of the letters, which I felt were the strength of the narrative. I presented myself as an artisan who could perform the practical task of distilling the magnificent material that was already there."

"In about three weeks, I drafted a 170-page screenplay, which I gave to Steven to mold," he continued. "Unbeknownst to me, the script was then mailed to Alice. I nearly had a heart attack."

Meyjes's fears that Alice might be miffed by his treatment of *The Color Purple* were put to rest when he soon received, by letter, her "vote of confidence." That Spielberg preferred Meyjes's script, she accepted with equanimity. "I had completed [one] to my own satisfaction," she said about her shelved screenplay. "It was, however, not the script that Steven loved."

On the other hand, Alice had reserved the right to evaluate (with vigor) all major casting decisions. While Tina Turner was grand, she'd always preferred Margaret Avery as Shug. By contract, she had also stipulated that fifty percent of the crew (apart from the actors) be composed of women and minorities. About the unprecedented diversity of *The Color Purple* production staff, some joked that the film warranted a new title: Steven Spielberg's *Close Encounters of the Third World.*

"There had never before been that many black folks involved in every aspect of a major release," Whoopi Goldberg later declared. "Not taking anything away from it, but *Roots* aired on television. *The Color Purple* would be on the big screen."

With cast, crew, and script in place, Spielberg began shooting in July 1985 in rural Monroe, North Carolina—a locale chosen because of the state's much-heralded film infrastructure. Scenes would also be filmed in Kenya and in a Burbank studio.

In keeping with her conscience, Alice, age forty-one, lent her name to the project, officially, only as a consultant. "No matter how good his intentions, I feared that Steven's version of *The Color Purple* might not be worthy," she explained. "I wanted it to be clear to the ancestors that I'd tried to honor them as best I could. Beyond that, the movie was out of my realm."

That said, Alice was happy to visit the sets in Burbank and Monroe as the spirits guided. Sitting in a director's chair and wearing a wide-brimmed straw hat, she made every effort to assist—as a dialogue coach, script doctor to Meyjes ("she'd take a legal pad and suggest a fix for a scene that wasn't working"), and tarot card reader.

During lulls in the shooting schedule, cast and crew (Jones and Spielberg included) lined up to hear Alice analyze the images they'd divined from her treasured deck of Motherpeace tarot cards. To be sure, it was a first in the annals of the Hollywood film industry.

That there was such harmony bolstered Alice when confronted, during visits to the set, with incidents that gave her pause. First there was Goldberg's revelation, well into production, that she'd never read the script for *The Color Purple*. Then another shocker: the announcement by Spielberg (delivered ever so cavalierly) that he considered *Gone with the Wind* "the greatest movie ever made." In a May 1989 *Architectural Digest* feature about his Pacific Palisades estate, Spielberg noted that he'd been drawn to the property because a previous owner had ties to the film.

"The history of the house attracted me instinctively," Spielberg told writer Harry Hurt III. "It was important for me to know that David Selznick lived there during the time he produced *Gone with the Wind*."

Alice said she had embarked on *The Color Purple* film project aware that Spielberg, sheltered in Hollywood, had "yet to come to consciousness" on sociopolitical matters that were her lifeblood. "Like many people in our culture, he had huge gaps in his education," she maintained. Yet she was shocked that the director, apparently dazzled by the grandeur of *Gone with the Wind*, had failed to consider its racial implications. She found release through cosmic forces. "I meditated and sang Bob Marley songs," she said.

Alice faced other challenges during the filming of *The Color Purple* that compounded the stress caused by her mother's illness. Negotiating the demands of her writing with the needs of her daughter had become increasingly complex. At age fourteen, Rebecca Walker (now in San Francisco year-round) found herself in need of an abortion. In a scenario worlds apart from Alice's experience, she escorted her child to a local clinic to terminate the pregnancy.

"I was extremely precocious," Rebecca later said. "And my mother was very open about my sexuality. Most parents are just not willing to face young peoples' need to explore and this is a serious problem. It probably would have been better had I not spent so much time alone. But my mother gave me space, almost as if I were a peer or a sister. It was a mixed-blessing, as blessings tend to be."

In the evocative opening passages of her memoir, Rebecca elaborates on the freedoms she experienced as a child. Read in the context of the childhood rhyme about her Mississippi birthplace ("What has four eyes and can't see?"), her reflections speak volumes about the gains and *costs* of the civil rights movement.

> Growing up I did not, ever, feel contained. I never felt the four walls of my room or my apartment or my house or my town or my culture close around me; I never knew the feeling of the extended womb. My parents did not hold me tight, but encouraged me to go. They did not buffer, protect, watch out for, or

look after me. I was watered, fed, admired, stroked and expected to grow. I was mostly left alone to discover the world and my place in it. From the houses and apartments in which I lived, I remember most of all the doors and how they opened for me.

Having grown frustrated by the complications of her mixed-race status in the suburban enclave where she lived with her father (she tells friends that she's "Spanish, like from Spain"), Rebecca writes in the memoir that she became impregnated in San Francisco by an older teen with whom she'd become smitten during her "zigzag" years between the East and West Coasts.

> When my mother is away, Michael spends the night and we try out every sexual position we can think of. We suck and lick and taste every single part of each other. . . . When I tell my mother I am pregnant I am calm, sad, and tearful maybe, but not because I expect she's going to be mad. I walk into her bed-room after she's been meditating and the air around her is all quiet and still. . . . Find a doctor to get a test she says. . . . She doesn't lecture me, she doesn't say How did this happen, aren't you using birth control, she doesn't say much of anything except to call [Robert Allen] a few hours later and tell him. . . . I hear her sighing as she speaks, the same sigh I hear when she worries about money, when she's feeling overwhelmed . . . .

At her suggestion, Rebecca writes, she, Alice, Robert, and Michael attended a screening of the Prince film *Purple Rain* after her proce-dure. "I don't really think about the abortion again, except to stop Michael from trying to have sex too soon afterward," she notes. "I know that my mother had an abortion before they were legal and so I know to be grateful that I didn't have a baby way before I was old enough to take care of it."

Such expressions of thanks are countered by other portraits Rebecca presents of her mother as a negligent, self-absorbed artist who jetted off to readings, leaving her alone with an empty refrigerator. She writes that Michael's lamentations ("Damn, you don't have no food") made her feel "embarrassed, like I am naked, maybe poor."

Alice's response? "I was right there ninety-five percent of the time. At first, I was hurt by Rebecca's book, but now, I'm completely over it. I told her, 'I will always be your mother and always love you.' Mel and I were a lot for Rebecca, but maybe one day, she'll understand the gifts she received."

In sharing her burdens as the child of a celebrity, Rebecca (who at age seventeen traded the anonymity of her surname with a legal name change to Rebecca Leventhal Walker), was far from unique. Writing in *Lives of Mothers & Daughters* (2001), Sheila Munro chronicled her struggles as the child of Alice Munro, a writer who, like Alice Walker, also achieved international acclaim. About the Canadian author heralded for her mastery of the short story, Munro declared, "There is something so out-of-proportion about having *Alice Munro* as my mother. She is the gold standard by which everything is compared. I understand why. I don't disagree. [Still] I don't suppose anyone wants their mother, or their father for that matter, to become an icon. What is there to do with an icon besides worshipping it, or ignoring it, or smashing it to pieces?"

At the conclusion of *Black, White, and Jewish*, a similar theme lingers. Rebecca writes, "I do not mind being my mother's daughter, I like it even. I like the attention, the way people who love my mother's writing make me feel like I am special, too. Standing by my mother's elbow at the head of a long line of people, I make myself available to them and drink in all of their adoration. . . . Am I proud of my mother? This question is harder to answer. . . . Isn't she supposed to be proud of me?"

Alice's tremendous success also triggered conflicts in Robert Allen. As *The Color Purple* began production, he confessed that he'd betrayed their monogamous relationship and pursued an affair with an old flame. Admittedly prone to mood swings that diminished her ardor, Alice was nevertheless astonished by Robert's rationale for the liaison: He charged that she'd been "sexually inattentive and distracted" by her work.

In the age of AIDS (first detected in the United States in the early 1980s), Robert's behavior sent Alice reeling. Since her return from China, she'd suffered a debilitating fatigue—one that she felt extended beyond worries for her mother. The malady would later be self-diagnosed as Lyme disease.

But at the time of Robert's confession, Alice feared that her exhaustion might be related to his infidelity. After all, actor Rock Hudson had shocked the nation in July 1985 with news that he was infected with AIDS, alerting the public to a health crisis that had been largely ignored. Alice's anxiety was captured in *Visions of the Spirit*, a 1989 documentary by San Francisco filmmaker Elena Featherston that included "behind-the-scenes" footage filmed on *The Color Purple* set in Monroe. The documentary later aired on many public television stations.

Seated next to Alice, Allen recounted, in quivering fits and starts, his mixed emotions about her triumph: "I was very pleased and happy for her. . . . At the same time there was a period when I felt some envy. I was ashamed to admit that I felt that way and tried to push it down. But [my feelings] came out in negative and under-mining behavior. It was only after I discussed it with Alice and told her hey, 'I'm having a hard time with this,' that I could free myself."

Alice later noted that she'd been caught off-guard by Robert's candor with Featherston's film crew. Close viewers can easily detect the vulnerability and discomfort in her otherwise stoic face. "I am studying [Robert] as he speaks with a look of horror, for I am fearful he will speak of his affair as an example of his undermining behavior, and I feel trapped to still be trying to stay with him and not be ashamed. This is the feeling of being deep in the messy stuff of women's secret lives, that place from which unscathed survivors are so rare."

Still, Alice found compassion for Robert. Mindful that he was a man who'd boldly confronted his flaws and whose "sweetness, intelligence, love of the moon and refusal to be inducted into the Vietnam War" she cherished, Alice remained in the relationship. Since her arrival in San Francisco, she'd also identified publicly as a "homospiritual," meaning, as she'd later write, that she rejoiced "in the sight of two people (whatever they are, and even if they're more than two!) brazenly expressing love."

Such leanings did not come as a surprise to her friends. In early (pre-rift) correspondence with Tillie Olsen, Alice had written of her admiration of an Adrienne Rich essay, " 'It Is The Lesbian In Us . . . .'" Reprinted in her 1979 collection, *On Lies, Secrets, and Silence*, Rich noted that she had come to understand lesbianism as "nothing so simple and dismissible as the fact that two women might go to bed together. It was a sense of desiring oneself; above all, of choosing oneself; it was also a primary intensity between women, an intensity which in the world at large was trivialized, caricatured, or invested with evil."

Sharing her response to the essay with Olsen, Alice wrote, "I keep feeling that clearly I should be with a woman and not with a man—so what does it mean?" In another letter, she continued the train of thought: "I suppose I feel lesbianism is the only way a self-respecting woman would go. . . . My one major problem, however, is that I am thoroughly in love with and love Robert. It is almost a humorous predicament. In my heart I feel lesbian. . . . [We] discuss this 'condition' of mine. That I love women and I love him."

Fanny Howe would recall Alice grappling with the topic in the early 1970s. For example, in her story "Really, *Doesn't* Crime Pay?," Mordechai Rich regales Myrna with an "anecdote" about a man who arrives home to discover his wife in the arms of another woman. "Even when he makes me laugh I know that nobody ought to look on other people's confusion with that cold an eye," Myrna responds, tellingly.

"Back then, most of the progressive, ostensibly heterosexual women were focused on race," Howe said. "But Alice was dealing with the lesbian issue as well. My perception is that Alice knew, intuitively, that as with the writing of *The Color Purple*, she'd be 'received' and free to explore all of herself in California. Everytime we'd talk, she'd say, 'Come out. This is the only place to live.' "

In addition to her defense of Ann Shockley ("Alice was a lone voice," the author later said), Alice had also publicly aligned herself with lesbians in "Breaking Chains and Encouraging Life," a 1980 *Ms.* review of *Conditions Five: The Black Women's Issue.*

Published from 1977 to 1989, *Conditions* was a pioneering feminist literary journal. The widely hailed *Black Women's Issue* included the artistry of several open and politically active black lesbians, among them Cheryl Clarke, Becky Birtha, and Pat Parker. As guest editors Barbara Smith and Lorraine Bethel stated in their introduction, *Conditions Five* disapproved "the 'non-existence' of Black feminist and Black lesbian writers and challenges forever our invisibility, particularly in the feminist press. . . ."

Alice began her review with a series of personal vignettes aimed to illustrate the daunting challenges faced by black lesbians. She recounted her conversation with a white lesbian separatist who had lamented her inability to organize with black women because they "always seem connected to some man."

In another, she recorded an exchange with a black lesbian acquaintance who bemoaned a "split in the ranks" over black lesbians with white lovers. "We only have so much time and money to spend getting our own shit together, and we end up wasting it discussing them [white women]," the friend complained. Alice shared her response: "Two thoughts come to mind. A swaggering one first: Black women are notorious for loving anybody they want to love and some of those they don't. And, less swaggering: Black women love those who love them."

Then turning her attention to the prose and poetry in *Conditions Five*, Alice declared, "One of the most exciting and healthiest things to happen lately in the black community is the coming out of black lesbians. . . . Reading [*The Black Women's Issue*] is not unlike seeing women breaking chains with their bare hands."

Taking on a black icon, Alice referenced a 1970s-era quote from boxing champion Muhammad Ali, who, in response to a reporter's question about women's equality, had replied, "Some professions shouldn't be open to women because they can't handle certain jobs, like construction work. Lesbians, maybe, but not women."

"In this one comment Ali undermines [black women]," Alice insisted. "As surely as if he clamped a chain on her body, he has clamped a chain on her spirit. And by our silence, our fear of being labeled lesbian, we help hold it there. *And this is inexcusable.* Because we know, whatever else we don't know and are afraid to guess, black lesbians *are* women. It is in our power to say that the days of intimidating black women with impunity are over."

She continued: "Perhaps black women writers and nonwriters should say, simply, whenever black lesbians are being put down, held up, messed over, and generally told their lives should not be encouraged, *We are all lesbians.* For surely it is better to be thought a lesbian, and to say and write your life exactly as you experience it, than to be a token 'pet' black woman for those whose contempt of our autonomous existence makes them a menace to human life."

Barbara Smith said that at a time when few others stood in solidarity with black lesbians, Alice's assessment of *The Black Women's Issue* carried tremendous weight. "Alice was highly visible and influential, so her support meant a lot," Smith noted. "To be a black feminist in the early 1970s meant you were visionary, some people haven't gotten there yet. Alice's gender analysis was always rigorous and out front. Black lesbians knew we had a friend in Alice."

Come what may with Robert, Alice knew that her love for women was leading her, increasingly, to embrace her bisexuality. "I have the support of the Universe," she said about the ever-shifting contours of her life.

The way she saw it, affirmation came in the form of an item she discovered while shopping in a local boutique. Delighted, Alice purchased the magic wand, made of black walnut with a two-inch crystal on the end. She took to waving it, with a flourish, as she readied herself for the premiere of *The Color Purple.*

SHE WOULD need all the affirmation she could muster. Forces claiming to "uphold black cultural standards" had mobilized upon hearing of the movie's planned release. As with the novel, debates raged in churches, in schools, at sporting events and parties. Such were the tensions that Willard Pugh said he was denounced before he'd uttered a line. "When my friends found out I'd been cast in *The Color Purple*, they were really upset," he recalled. "They said, 'Didn't that shit make you mad?' Black folks didn't want to see any spousal abuse on the screen. And lesbianism? Well, forget that. Finally, I just had to tell people that these issues were real and that *The Color Purple* didn't start it."

Indeed, as one of the few female leaders of the Black Panther Party, Elaine Brown had spent many years among the most radical of black men. About the sexual depictions in *The Color Purple*, she offered a perspective not commonly heard: "Any sister who's been with one of the militant brothers knows one thing: It's just a matter of time before he rolls over and asks, 'Don't you have a girlfriend who can come over and help us get it on?' "

That was not the stance of the Coalition Against Black Exploitation, a group in Compton, California, that came together for the express purpose of offering "feedback" on the film. Starting in the spring of 1985, the coalition had called for meetings with Warner Bros., demanding that the movie be "carefully packaged to uplift rather than degrade black people." Their request for input denied, the group then unleashed a barrage of "action bulletins" designed to spark national protest against *The Color Purple*.

Distributed to media outlets, a typical dispatch read, "One must suspect a movie portrayal will focus on the dramatic visuals of homosexual play revealed in the book. One must also suspect this affectionate feminine display will be contrasted with an unfulfilling exchange between a Black man and a Black woman. Such contrast, presented on top of the music of a Quincy Jones . . . could be quite persuasive in pushing homosexuality as an attractive alternative to the Black woman's frustration with Black men. . . . What lyrics will Shug Avery and others be singing? Will there be any positive male images in the movie?

"At stake are the minds of young Black women and men who may still have the will and desire to struggle for love, male/female style. . . . In the spirit of collective welfare we suggest the movie *The Color Purple* be critically scrutinized. . . . We also recommend a boycott of this project unless assurances are given in advance that homosexuality is not projected to the masses as a solution to the problems Black men and women face with each other."

Voicing similar complaints, officials from the Hollywood chapter of the NAACP also issued edicts against the film. As a black man who'd labored for more than two years on a project to which he'd proudly attached his name and reputation, Quincy Jones let it be known that he was not amused.

"They did not have the expertise to evaluate what we were doing," Jones insisted, speaking of the coalition and the NAACP. "It would have been like me telling Bill Gates how to run Microsoft. I made it clear that I'd fight to the death before I let anybody try to control the artistic vision of *The Color Purple*. Moreover, I did everything in my power to protect Alice and Steven from those people because they were ignorant, ridiculous, and insane."

Ironically, for all their outrage about *The Color Purple*, the self-appointed keepers of the culture never mentioned another work that featured a black sharecropper who, in the words of its author, "took both his wife and his daughter." Writing in graphic detail in the second chapter of the 1952 novel, the author told the story of Jim Trueblood and the plight he suffered after the discovery, by his wife, Kate, that he'd impregnated their daughter Matty Lou.

" 'Goddamn yo' soul to hell! Git up offa my chile!' " the distraught mother screamed, as she grabbed a double-barrel shotgun. " '. . . You done *fouled*!' "

Describing Trueblood's response, the author continued: "'The nigguhs up at the school come down to chase me off and that made me mad. I went to see the white folks then and they gave me help. . . . Except that my wife and daughter won't speak to me, I'm better off than I ever been before. . . . But what I don't understand is how I done the worse thing a man can do in his own family and 'stead of things gittin' bad, they got better. The nigguhs up at the school don't like me, but the white folks treats me fine.' "

The novel? Celebrated by the masses and multitudes of black male literary scholars as one of the most dazzling works of the twentieth century: *Invisible Man* by Ralph Ellison.

49

More Than Many Hoped

IN THE spirit of "save the best for last," Hollywood studios customarily release in late December films they wish to position for Oscar contention. With expectations high for several Academy Award nominations, Warner Bros. scheduled *The Color Purple* for release on December 18, 1985 (the date marked Spielberg's thirty-ninth birthday). To qualify for Oscar consideration, a movie must run in a general theater, open to the public, for at least one week during the year. Before the official opening, Alice, accompanied by Robert Allen and Belvie Rooks, saw the movie at a private screening in San Francisco. Although Alice was frequently present on the set, she had not participated in the film's editing or final stages of production.

"There was major tension because the risk Alice had taken would be up there for God and everybody to see," Rooks recalled. "I was so nervous, I could barely breathe."

Added Allen: "There was a whole lot on the line."

As the movie began, Alice let out a deep sigh. Rooks took her hand. It was only after Alice laughed ("about ten minutes in") that Rooks felt she could relax "because I knew her heart was O.K."

It was true, Alice felt no need to apologize to the ancestors for what she'd watched unfold on the screen. But ecstatic she was not. On the contrary, by the end of the movie, she had a pounding headache. "Peter Guber had warned me that I might be shocked the first time I saw it," Alice remembered, "and I definitely was."

"It wasn't that the movie was a total disaster, but there was so much about it that struck me as wrong."

To Alice's mind, the missteps began with the film's opening score, which she thought "sounded like it belonged in *Oklahoma*." Next came Celie's statement that she'd been "raped by her father." As written in the novel, the abuser was her stepfather (Fonso). Thus, the remark, as rendered by Celie on the screen, undermined the fact that "her biological father was forcefully heroic," Alice explained.

Alice regretted that Mr.____, in an implausible scene for a man of his station, didn't know how to start a fire or where the butter was stored in his own house. His spiritual transformation, central to the novel, was minimized in the film.

Why Harpo kept falling through ceilings was a mystery she could not fathom. Sofia's straightened hair? The rain *inside* the jook joint? Ditto.

But the biggest blunder in the Spielberg version of *The Color Purple* was the veil that had been drawn over the romantic relationship between Shug and Celie. As crafted in the novel, the women were lovers. Likewise in Alice's screenplay and the Menno Meyjes script she'd ultimately approved. However, a fully erotic union was reduced, in the movie, to a single physical encounter (a moderately steamy kiss, at that).

Jones had cautioned Alice that Spielberg, concerned about narrative "distractions," had decided to downplay the sexual passion between Celie and Shug. "The kiss on the lips to me is so suggestive of the bringing together of those two characters . . . I just didn't feel I had to beat the audience over the head by showing anything beyond that bonding," Spielberg later explained. Contrary to the views of the Coalition Against Black Exploitation, Alice had never fashioned her novel, nor its film adaptation, as a lesbian polemic.

Still, Spielberg's soft-pedaling of the issue hit her hard. "I mourned the movie's lack of eroticism," she lamented. "It looked slick, sanitized, and apolitical to me."

More annoyed and frustrated than angered, Alice joined multitudes of writers who'd struggled to reconcile their art with that which a filmmaker later crafted for the screen. A particularly pertinent example could be found in Vladimir Nabokov. Contracted to write the screenplay for his 1955 novel about the obsession of an aging professor with a twelve-year-old "nymphet," the author delivered a script that director Stanley Kubrick rejected in its entirety. Although Nabokov later warmed to the 1962 film release, nothing could temper his first impression of Kubrick's adaptation of *Lolita*, which he likened to "a scenic drive as perceived by the horizontal passenger of an ambulance."

Shaken though she was by Spielberg's rendering of *The Color Purple*, Alice remained upright. After the screening, she held fast to her magic wand and braced herself for the response from the public. Drawn by the controversy, the cast, the Pulitzer Prize, and "the boy genius," audiences lined up in droves.

THE NEW York premiere of *The Color Purple* was a glittering affair attended by such luminaries as Ruby Dee and Ossie Davis, Bill and Camille Cosby, Arthur and Jeanne Moutoussamy-Ashe, and Toni Morrison. Busy with her own writing (*Tar Baby* had been published in 1981, *Beloved* was forthcoming), Morrison had been disinclined to participate in public debates about the novel or the film. In subsequent years, however, she would share her thoughts about allegations that Alice had received "special help" from Gloria Steinem in the promotion of *The Color Purple* and that she had sought the favor of whites throughout her career.

"I know Alice Walker doesn't do it, as far as white men are concerned, but you are suggesting that she plays to white women?" Morrison said in an interview with black writer Cecil Brown. ". . . I don't believe it, and the evidence that you have is that Gloria Steinem has been very serious in promoting her. They were colleagues because Alice was her consulting editor on *Ms.* magazine. What magazine was in a position to do that? *Essence* didn't do it."

And writing in his book, *The Sexual Mountain and Black Women Writers* (1987), black scholar Calvin C. Hernton would add his perspective: "Quite a few of the black writer machos of the 1960s rubbed shoulders with Norman Mailer, Leonard Bernstein, Jean Genet, Marlon Brando, and others of the so-called white liberal revolutionary *chic*. But when a black woman writer . . . is rumored to be associating with Gloria Steinem or Adrienne Rich, or even Grace Paley—black male writers feel 'threatened.' They fear that a 'conspiracy' is being concocted not just against black men writers, but against the entire black race."

As much as Alice appreciated the support of celebrities who rejected the coalition's campaign for a boycott of the film, it was the response of the "common folk" that best helped her to understand the cultural impact of *The Color Purple*. By Alice's directive, the New York premiere was a benefit for Reading Is Fundamental, a local literacy group. Many of the agency's low-income clients were in attendance. Sitting in the theater this time, unlike at the private screening, Alice realized that Spielberg's film was "more than many hoped or had seen on a movie screen before."

"I was finally able to see *it*, and to let go of the scenes that were *not* there," noted Alice, remembering the pleasure of watching *The Color Purple* with a full audience. "It is far more conventional than the novel, especially in terms of religion vs. spirituality and Shug and Celie's relationship, and even Celie and Mr. _____'s relationship and Harpo and Sofia's, too."

"But I still felt a lot of the soul of the people," she continued, "and that was lovely."

His *Oklahoma*-tinged overture notwithstanding, Alice was heartened by the joyful response of Quincy Jones and likewise that of the ever-maligned Gloria Steinem, both of whom attended the gala event. They had taken substantive heat for their unapologetic support of *The Color Purple* ("Without Quincy, it's doubtful the movie would have ever been made," Guber later said). Yet such was the integrity of Jones and Steinem that Alice had no doubt but that they would have held to their conscience and told her if they thought the movie had failed. Neither of them did. "I trust both of them because of what I feel is a deep, abiding, *innate* decency," Alice said. "And both of them are models of love."

And of all the people who attended the New York premiere of *The Color Purple*, Alice was especially happy that the film had not disappointed a viewer who had cheered every step of her career. "I was elated," remembered Ruth Walker Hood. "As I watched the movie, I was flooded with memories of my grandparents, of growing up in the country, of all the good times and the bad. Alice had brought it all back and put it up on the screen. Being up there in New York with all those famous people, I tried to keep hold of my emotions. But after a while, I just cried."

Alice had made peace with Spielberg's effort ("Imperfections aside, I think he can be proud of his film"). Many friends, family members, and film professionals found the movie worthy ("I think he tried to be respectful of the culture," noted Julie Dash). But the controversy over Alice grew like an ever-creeping field of kudzu after the release of *The Color Purple*. People who'd never read the novel, tracked Pulitzer Prizes, or cared which of Alice's supporters was being likened to Dracula could now, for the price of a movie ticket (average cost $3.55), enter the fray. With reviews running the gamut, those new to the long-running saga could fortify their positions with opinions from movie critics on either side. That Whoopi Goldberg, in interviews about the movie, had announced that she didn't consider herself black ("I see myself as colorless and sexless") only fanned the flames.

Writing in the *Macon Telegraph and News*, Jeffrey Day reflected the sentiments of anti-Spielberg factions who'd never believed that the director could rise above Tinseltown "feel-good" traditions to produce a serious film. "*The Color Purple* buries a literary masterpiece beneath 400 tons of sugar," scoffed Day in a bruising slam. "You wonder who has given director Steven Spielberg the right to gut a deep story. . . . An old argument is one shouldn't compare a film to the book on which it is based. . . . But

The Color Purple is such a hatchet job . . . outrage must be expressed."

Newsweek reviewer David Ansen put it this way: "Early on I had the disorienting sensation that I was watching the first Disney movie about incest."

Not so, said Judy Stone, a critic with the *San Francisco Chronicle*. In a review headlined "Many Shades of Purple," Stone exhorted readers to rush out and see Spielberg's "change-of-pace-movie"—one that presented many reasons to shout "Whoopee," she raved.

"Not only does Whoopi Goldberg emerge as a performer of considerable stature, but she is joined by a formidable array of talented black actors, ready, willing, and able to add zest and strength to the Hollywood scene," Stone wrote. ". . . Spielberg shows that he can create as wonderfully intuitive a drama for adults as the perilous razzle-dazzle he invents for the adolescents and the kiddie trade. . . . Overall, this is a stunning movie."

But Spielberg had played too hard for emotion, countered Janet Maslin who, writing for the *New York Times,* said the director had produced "a grand, multi-hanky entertainment that is as lavish as the book is plain." "Some parts of it are rapturous and stirring, others hugely improbable, and the film moves unpredictably from one mode to another," Maslin declared.

It was precisely the uneven quality of *The Color Purple* that prompted *Time* magazine critic Richard Corliss to offer his review under a banner that read, "The Three Faces of Steve." Corliss complained that for every inspired scene in the movie, three others struck him as "too noble." "It's all very pretty, but it's cinematography, not cinema," he concluded about a film he effectively dismissed as "golden fairy dust."

Pretty? That was not the thinking of Vernon Jarrett, an influential African American columnist for the *Chicago Sun-Times*. Echoing detractors of the novel, he ventured that Spielberg's adaptation of *The Color Purple* would help 1980s-era lawmakers justify cutbacks on social programs. "Mr. Reagan, and his Attorney General, Mr. Meese, have decided that they are going to turn back the clock on us," Jarrett warned. "The purpose of movies like this is to make it acceptable to you."

Joining Jarrett in his denunciation of the film was another Chicago-based force born Louis Eugene Walcott. In the mid-1950s, Walcott was befriended by Black Muslim leader Malcolm X, who persuaded the former nightclub singer to drop his "slave name" and convert to Islam. By the 1980s, rising on a platform of black self-reliance and direct confrontation with racism, the man now known as Minister Louis Farrakhan had become a national figure both celebrated and condemned. Speaking before a group of followers shortly after the opening of *The Color Purple*, he delivered a videotaped message unparalleled, if not in its logic, surely in its originality.

"Our people's hunger to be seen, to be famous, to have fun is like a trap because the Jews who control Hollywood recognize that your rise is the fall of their world," Farrakhan thundered as the packed, all-black audience nodded approvingly during the rambling address billed as "Farrakhan on *The Color Purple*." "Until we make the movies with resurrected minds, we will always be prey to the gravitational pull of the white people."

Deriding them as "freaks" with woefully unresurrected minds, Farrakhan then segued into a rant against musicians Prince, Rick James, and Bootsy Collins for putting forth what he damned as effeminate images of black men. "And you're such freaks, you pay to see the freaks perform," he bellowed, sending the audience into riotous laughter. "You want yourself. That's why lesbianism is growing."

Now at full pitch, Farrakhan blasted Stevie Wonder for "walking around in braids and what not," during a national television appearance. "It made me throw up," he fumed, in disgust. "It's *The Color Purple*. It's a sickness. All of this is death for you. We must destroy *The Color Purple*. It can be done."

50

She Liked Everything She Saw

FARRAKHAN'S BIZARRE coupling of *The Color Purple* and the braided hairstyle of Stevie Wonder proved to be ironic, for Alice had, in fact, opened the novel with an epigram taken from the musician's 1980 song "Do Like You." The lyrics ("Show me how to do like you / Show me how to do it") reflected her belief that spiritual forces respond to all who seek their powers. Wonder's artistry was in keeping with her mantra, "The universe provides."

With her work now offered worldwide on both the page and the screen, Alice, happily in the glow of the ancestors, was poised to complete the spiritual journey that had begun when Ruth shared the story about Shug Perry's pink panties. And Ruth would play a pivotal role in the next stage of *The Color Purple* odyssey. For she now envisioned a splashy hometown premiere that would forever stand as a symbol of her baby sister's triumph and enable Minnie Lou Walker to bask in the glory of it all.

"After I finished reading the novel, I knew that people would finally take notice of Alice, and I had a real strong feeling that the book would be made into a movie," Ruth explained. "Seeing as

Mama was an invalid, the movie would have to come to Eatonton for her to see it."

After attending the New York opening, Ruth pitched the idea of a local premiere to John Peck, owner of Eatonton's Pex Theater, the only picture show in town. As it happened, the 1940s-era cinema had been closed for several years, having lost business to nearby multiplexes built on plots that had been dairy farms and cotton fields when Alice was a child. Still, Peck contacted movie suppliers, who insisted it was impossible for him to obtain *The Color Purple*, which would rake in gross receipts of nearly $200 million even as picket lines formed under marquees where the film was being shown.

They put it this way: Given the economics, why would Hollywood screen the movie in a town of 5,000, when there was an audience of 20,000 in Milledgeville, many of them film industry–targeted college students at that? Down the road a bit in Macon, the population was upward of 100,000. To say nothing of the nearly half a million residents of Atlanta with cash to spend on popcorn and Coca-Cola.

The suppliers said that should a print become available, Peck shouldn't expect to receive it until after *The Color Purple* had completed its run in major market venues. To Peck's query as to when that might be, they ventured April 1986. But in all their calculations, the movie suppliers had neglected to consider one factor: Ruth was not of a mind to wait.

"I was thinking about the young folk and them constantly being force-fed Joel Chandler Harris as the only somebody Eatonton had ever produced," Ruth said. "I wanted them to see that a sharecropper's daughter from Wards Chapel had come up from nothing and done well. And besides, Mama needed to see the movie. Period."

Determined that *The Color Purple* would play (sooner, not later) in the exact same theater where her family, neighbors, and other blacks had suffered discrimination, Ruth circumvented the movie suppliers and spoke directly to officials at Warner Bros., who agreed to an Eatonton premiere on Saturday, January 18, 1986. Their only stipulation was that proceeds be donated to charity. Aware of the nearly lost legacy of Zora Neale Hurston, Ruth had long wanted to create a "living memorial" to Alice. Prompted by Warner Bros., she established The Color Purple Scholarship Fund for high school students of the arts. The ten-dollar-per-ticket fee provided the seed money for dozens of scholarships that would be awarded to Georgia youth in ensuing years.

The date set and a charitable foundation incorporated, Ruth busied herself with the launching of an event that had now blossomed into two screenings at the 360-seat Pex Theater and a reception for 1,500 (at the National Guard Armory). Caught up in the rapture, local civic groups (said by Ruth to have once been "sometimey" toward Alice) joined Warner Bros. in covering the costs for flowers, refreshments, cartons of purple crepe-paper streamers, and the time-honored red carpet.

Ruth forbade Alice from lifting a finger in preparation for the festivities. On the other hand, she took manifest satisfaction in watching John Peck reopen and then spitshine and polish the moviehouse that blacks had once been forced to enter through a grimy door marked "Colored" before climbing to the balcony.

WEARING HIGH heels and a pale-green evening gown, bejeweled, and with her hair done just so, Mrs. Walker arrived at the Pex Theater in a specially equipped *ambulance* that facilitated her transport, allowing her to recline as if Cleopatra on the Nile (had there been a telegram it would have read: Eatonton to Vladimir Nabokov!). For her added comfort, a favored chair—plush and beautifully upholstered—had been borrowed from Mrs. Walker's home and installed (by Pex management) in a prime viewing spot for the premiere. Surrounded by an adoring entourage of family and friends, Mrs. Walker, age seventy-four, smiled expectantly as the theater darkened and Celie and Nettie appeared on the movie screen.

For Alice, who'd come to treasure the movie as a mystically inspired and uniquely wrapped gift to her mother, the Eatonton premiere was rife with sentiment. She was hopeful that her mother would be uplifted by Spielberg's rendering of *The Color Purple*, but there were no guarantees. After all, even in her illness Mrs. Walker did not hesitate to convey her displeasure with a mealy peach or a soap opera with a tiresome story line. Would she still be smiling at movie's end? Sitting in the front of the theater flanked by Rebecca and Robert Allen, Alice could not help but fret.

"I didn't want her to be embarrassed, offended, or disappointed," Alice later said of her mother. "I wanted so much for her to see something on screen worth her time. Can you imagine a lifetime of only watching white people? Doing really violent, culturally puzzling, or irrelevant things? And that you'd had to watch them order you around all of your life?"

"I risked a lot to have Steven make the movie," she added. "But I would have risked even more to wipe away the assault on my mother's dignity moviegoing had represented in the past."

But Alice need not have worried. "Mama enjoyed every minute," Ruth remembered, "she liked everything that she saw."

"Mama knew that Alice would never do anything that went against her upbringing," she continued. "She took pride in all of Alice's achievements, but the movie was extra special because she could relate to the characters personally."

The premiere was the talk of the town. Writing in the weekly *Eatonton Messenger*, reporter Sloan Gregory recounted the gala proceedings for the crowd who'd been unable to obtain a ticket. "If you missed out on the excitement Saturday at the homecoming of Alice Walker's movie, then you lost the chance to enjoy a celebration of love and pride. . . . Observers could sense the hushed silence . . . and occasionally hear someone trying to stifle tears. Roars of laughter would follow as this movie led the audience from deep drama to tender humor."

Among the excited crush of well-wishers at the premiere ("people calling out to me that I hadn't seen since I was an infant," Alice remembered) was Doris Reid. In her elation about the movie, Reid had only one regret—that the portrait of Booker T. Washington promised to Alice by Ma Jessie had somehow vanished over the years. As Reid constructed the chain of events, her grandmother had been placed in a nursing facility and her home rented to a tenant who announced plans to "redecorate and stuff." Upon Ma Jessie's death in the mid-1970s, Reid was ready to crate and ship the portrait to Alice when she discovered another art work where the beautifully framed image had once hung. The renter was long gone.

"Talk about having a fit," Reid remembered. "I was praying that the tenant might have put the portrait in storage, so I tore through all the rent receipts trying to find her. But I never did. Knowing how much Ma Jessie had wanted Alice to have that picture, I was extremely upset."

Although Alice accepted the news with understanding, Reid couldn't forgive herself for failing to deliver the portrait of Booker T. Washington. And so it was that Reid said she was especially delighted to hear the news that came not long after the Eatonton premiere. On February 5, 1986, *The Color Purple* was nominated for eleven Academy Awards.

"I said to myself, 'Well, Alice can just put an Oscar where Booker T. should have been,' " Reid recalled, laughing. "Because everybody knew that *The Color Purple* was going to clean up."

51

The World Is Held Together

THE NOVEL. The Pulitzer Prize. The Spielberg-directed movie. The prospect of eleven Oscars. Far from diminishing, the frenzy surrounding *The Color Purple* (now entering its fourth year) seemed to have no end. And the Academy Award nominations brought new trends: The attacks against Alice and her work became more pointed ("Most Dangerous Film since 'Birth of a Nation,'" blared the headline in the New York *Guardian*). At the same time, celebrity-seekers abandoned all decorum in their efforts to "befriend" the woman then widely considered to be the most influential black writer in the United States.

"There'd always been folks trying to get next to Alice, but after the movie and the Oscar nominations people went wild," remembered Daphne Muse, an Oakland, California, writer who, through her sideline as an events planner, had helped Alice herald the 1982 release of *The Color Purple* with a book party held on a yacht that cruised San Francisco Bay. "I'd get calls at all hours from people demanding that I hook them up with Alice. I'd get cursed out for not sharing her address or telephone number. Everybody wanted a piece of her fame."

That factions were now scrambling for "insider" status with Alice did not surprise those who'd followed her career. In addition to her Hollywood ties and publishing clout (her next novel would command more than $3.5 million in today's dollars), Alice had established a reputation as a free and principled artist with a penchant for breathtakingly memorable repartee. For example, approached (during *The Color Purple* furor) by the president of Sarah Lawrence about a reading at her alma mater, Alice pondered the proposed date (April 20) and then quietly replied, "I will not read on Hitler's birthday." "It was an amazing moment," remembered New York writer Catherine McKinley, who was then a student at the college and witnessed the exchange.

"Alice had become a cultural force back when it was rare for black writers to have that kind of power," said Judy Dothard Simmons, a long-time editor and seasoned observer of the 1980s publishing world. "People were hungry for her attention, but Alice also bred resentment because she was not subject to control. Her stance was that of a woman of the world, and that baffled a lot of black people. Then there were folks who were just plain jealous of her material success."

An influential New York literary agent offered a vivid analogy: "In terms of earning power and status, Alice Walker was like the Rosa Parks of publishing. Not only did *The Color Purple* move her to the front of the bus, it put her in the driver's seat. A lot of writers coming up right after Alice wanted the same kind of power. But it wasn't going to happen for them."

As a prominent but unassuming political figure who'd been elevated to iconic status, Angela Y. Davis empathized with the "love-hate" dynamic that intensified around Alice as the Academy Awards drew near. Once placed on the Federal Bureau of Investigation's ten-most-wanted list for her alleged role in a 1970 courtroom shooting involving black prisoners in California, Davis spent more than a year in jail before a jury acquitted her of all charges. "She's a black woman who wants freedom for all black people," proclaimed Aretha Franklin, who had offered to help pay Davis's bail.

Like the Queen of Soul, Alice was an ardent supporter of the

"Free Angela" movement that erupted during Davis's ordeal. The women who'd never met at the youth festival in Helsinki had become allies after sharing the stage at a San Francisco area rally (circa 1985) for South African leader Winnie Mandela. "*The Color Purple* was extremely important in that I can't think of any other book or film or cultural product that immersed the community in issues about which we had learned to remain silent," said Davis, today a professor of history of consciousness at the University of California, Santa Cruz. "Because of her courage in breaking taboos, people projected their expectations on Alice. It was a difficult position. I could definitely relate."

Burdened, in his own words, by a predilection to "do things crooked," a man who went back to Alice's beginnings said that the incessant debate about *The Color Purple* inspired him to examine the pain he had caused in her life. "Looking at all she'd accomplished, I felt bad that I'd never told Alice that I was sorry for what happened that day with the BB gun," confessed Curtis Walker, who, by the mid-1980s, had spent substantive time behind bars for drug-related offenses. "I knew she felt so alone."

"I really haven't been able to hold a decent conversation with her because of all the hurt from the past," he continued. "But what I learned from *The Color Purple* is that peace can be made."

PEACE WAS not the objective of the demonstrators who arrived at the Dorothy Chandler Pavilion to protest *The Color Purple*—tied with *Out of Africa* as the most heavily nominated movie of the Fifty-eighth Annual Academy Awards, held March 24, 1986. But unlike Sydney Pollack, director of the romantic adventure (adapted from the Isak Dinesen memoir), Steven Spielberg was not included in the slate of best director nominees. People could only speculate as to why his name was not to be found on the impressive list of accolades for *The Color Purple*: Oscar nominations for best picture, best cinematography, best screenplay, best costume design, best art direction, best makeup, best song ("Miss Celie's Blues/Sister"), best original score, best supporting actress (Margaret Avery *and* Oprah

Winfrey), and best actress (Whoopi Goldberg). The nominations for Winfrey and Goldberg were especially remarkable in that *The Color Purple* marked their debut screen performances. Indeed, the opening credits read, "Introducing Whoopi Goldberg."

As counseled by Jones, Spielberg steered clear of the fracas about his movie, which was increasingly dominated by men such as Tony Brown, host of the black issues–oriented talk show *Tony Brown's Journal* (a mainstay on public television stations in "urban" venues). Writing in a widely circulated article, Brown declared that he hadn't seen *The Color Purple* and never intended to see *The Color Purple*—then proceeded to condemn what he summarily rejected as "a white man's movie focusing only on [black men's] failures." "Lesbian affairs will never replace the passion and beauty of a free black man and a free black woman," he huffed. "That's not the real world, as some black women, out of frustration, seem to want to believe."

The movie also rankled an emerging filmmaker whose debut feature about a promiscuous black woman (*She's Gotta Have It*) would itself draw criticism for "unflattering" portraits of black life. "I dislike the movie," said a not-yet-famous Spike Lee in televised comments about the controversy. "But we can't rely on Hollywood or we're going to deserve all *The Color Purples* in the world."

For the special effects wizard who had aspired, with *The Color Purple*, to be embraced as a serious director if not a cinema auteur ("I thought that was my art film"), the uproar was difficult to grasp. "I never saw the movie in any way as reinforcing [negative] stereo-types," Spielberg said, in a measured response that Jones felt belied his profound disappointment at not being nominated for an Oscar. "This is a movie about the triumph of the spirit—and spirit and soul never had any racial boundaries."

THE SENSE of triumph that had infused the cast and crew in the making of *The Color Purple* ("Celie's story paralleled the life of my grandmother," noted Danny Glover) was not shared by the voting members of the Academy of Motion Picture Arts and Sciences, who deemed the film unworthy of a single Oscar. Blanked, *The Color Purple* joined ranks with *The Turning Point* as the only films to ever garner eleven nominations and no wins. Casting director Reuben Cannon said it was excruciating to sit through the evening and hear *The Color Purple* announced in nearly every category, only to have no one ascend to the stage to receive an award. "After a while, it became laughable," remembered Cannon, who escorted Oprah Winfrey to the festivities. "The dislike of Steven was obvious. Everyone understood that the backlash was about him."

"I was disappointed for the film, but not for myself because the whole experience had been a marvelous dream," added Winfrey, who lost the Oscar to Anjelica Huston (*Prizzi's Honor*). "I had on the tightest dress of my life. So even if they had called my name, I wouldn't have been able to get up out of the seat. I was just happy to go home and cut the dress off my body."

As a producer, Peter Guber was privy to the inner machinations of Hollywood powerbrokers. Like Cannon, he agreed that the Academy was sending Spielberg a message that he yet had dues to pay, a message they aimed to temper by honoring him, the next year, with the Irving G. Thalberg Memorial Award (for "creative producers whose bodies of work reflect a consistently high quality of motion picture production"). Guber was certain that Spielberg would have preferred an Oscar, which, for all his blockbuster clout, the director had never received. Instead, *Out of Africa* dominated the evening, winning seven Oscars, including those for best picture, best director, and best musical score. Ironically, Lionel Richie, who'd helped compose "Miss Celie's Blues/Sister," won the Oscar for best song for another tune—"Say You, Say Me" from the film *White Nights*.

"As the person who also bought the movie rights to *Out of Africa*, I can tell you that *The Color Purple* was a much more daring and audacious film," Guber declared. "Steven brought the white light of celebrity in getting the movie made and became a lightning rod of liability when it was released. *The Color Purple* deserved Oscars. But for whatever reasons, the Academy deduced that it wasn't Steven's time."

Never one to hold her tongue, Whoopi Goldberg said that Oscar prospects for *The Color Purple* were damaged by critics who diverted attention from the film's artistic merits with a "pissy political fight."

"The Hollywood NAACP cost us every one of the Academy Awards," insisted Goldberg, bested by Geraldine Page for *The Trip to Bountiful*. "They killed the chances for me, Oprah, Margaret Avery, Quincy, everybody—I truly believe that. And blacks in Hollywood paid a price for years to come. Because after all the hell that was raised, the studios didn't want to do any more black movies for fear of the picket lines and boycotts."

While sympathetic to the frustration of the cast and crew, Alice said she considered the Academy's snub of *The Color Purple* a "blessing" that preserved the purity of intention with which the film was made. The way she saw it, everyone from Spielberg to the impish black child in the movie who warned Harpo, "It's gonna rain on your head," deserved more than an Oscar for "their loving radiance as a healing beam for our communities and the world."

"Because we had so many nominations, I thought someone on the jury understood the impetus of the movie, which was love," Alice explained. "But when I realized they had understanding, but no courage, I lost interest in winning. We were freed from the corruption that prizes often bring."

But the experience brought other benefits. Ever the curious artist, Alice said she was grateful for "the adventure" of attending an Academy Awards show. The naysayers protesting the movie ("*The Color Purple* Destroys The Color Black!" read a placard) only added to the stockpile of fabric for her future writing. "It was a lot less sophisticated up close than it appears on television," she remembered. "With people outside on bleachers yelling and screaming, it was like entering a high school gym."

"I'd never crossed a picket line before," she continued. "I never thought that I would. But I wasn't going to let my people, either in the movie or the book, go into such hostile territory alone. My characters had gotten me from New York to San Francisco. Now really, how could I leave them amidst bleacher seats in Beverly Hills?"

. . .

DESPITE THE demonstrations, *The Color Purple* was never abandoned by audiences, who continued to pack theaters screening the film. The overwhelmingly positive response from the public was mirrored by many in the entertainment industry. For example, appearing on *The Tonight Show* with Johnny Carson the evening after the Oscars, singer Willie Nelson wore a purple baseball cap emblazoned with the words "The Color Purple" (a souvenir item from the film shoot). Although Nelson never mentioned the controversy, his gesture was widely interpreted as an expression of solidarity with the cast and crew. It was not lost on him that tens of millions of viewers tuned in to watch the Carson show.

And asked during an appearance on *The Phil Donahue Show* about the absence of "redeeming" black male characters in the movie, the actor then celebrated as America's "favorite dad" weighed in, saying "there doesn't need to be any." "I feel that it is one of the silliest controversies ever made up," continued Bill Cosby, who, as Dr. Cliff Huxtable, had charmed the nation with his hit program *The Cosby Show*.

To be sure, in addition to the outpouring of affection Alice had received after the release of the novel ("I will not give up on love," wrote a struggling student from American Samoa), she was now besieged by admirers of the film. "It was absolutely staggering," said Joan Miura, a former arts administrator Alice hired to help with the deluge of fan mail, speaking invitations, fund-raising pitches, and inquiries about Wild Trees Press. "What we'd envisioned as a one-day-a-week job quickly expanded into a full-time enterprise. Alice received cartons of gifts and bouquets of flowers. You name it, it came through the door."

More than adept at assisting Alice with the crush of celebrity, Miura could not quell the depression that descended on her after the Academy Awards. Alice had been publicly scorned and castigated over the years, never revealing the impact of the abuse on her spirit ("I accepted it with all the grace and humor I possessed"). But contrary to stereotypes about the enduring strength of black women, she was not made of steel. Like Ntozake Shange and

Michele Wallace before her, Alice was upset and confounded by the attacks—against not only her art, but also her integrity.

How was it, she wondered, that she who'd helped bring the vote to exploited sharecroppers, who'd created curriculum for Head Start teachers, who'd funded a literary award at Tougaloo College had come to find herself vilified as a "deep-down hater of blacks"? What was she to make of the fact that the *first and only* picket line she'd ever crossed was one organized by blacks protesting her movie—a movie for which she'd secured substantive positions for women and minorities? And how was she to interpret the behavior of Hollywood NAACP director Willis Edwards, who, after damning *The Color Purple*, then denounced the Academy for not honoring the movie with Oscars? The contradiction brought to his attention, Edwards effectively shrugged.

But Alice could not shrug off the ordeal. "If the attacks against *The Color Purple* had happened earlier, I would not have survived," she confided. "As an artist, you're really just opening up your veins and bleeding for people. To have your gift distorted and flung back into your face as 'garbage' is traumatic. At a younger age, I wouldn't have had the coping skills to continue to write."

To those enraged by her depictions of black men as "brutal," she responded, "There is a section in my novel where Mister starts to bring Celie seashells. He and Celie sew together. They have long discussions and embrace under the stars. People need to ask themselves why they are blind to that as male behavior. Why it is that when a man can sit with a woman and interact with her like a human being, he becomes invisible as a man?"

And thus Alice retreated to her home in the undulating hills of Mendocino County to sit in silence and reflection after one of the most contentious debates about sex relations in black American culture. It was from there, a decade later, that she recounted a story infused with the faith in transformation that had prevailed since she'd written in *Once*, "A silent lake / Bone strewn banks / Luminous / In the sun."

As Alice told it, not too long after she recused herself from the public, she received word that James Baldwin, twenty years her senior, was to make an appearance in San Francisco. He'd made a single request to the organizers of the event: That Alice Walker introduce him to the community where Shug, Celie, Mr.___, Sofia, and the others had come to voice. "Baldwin and I never met, had never spoke, never wrote," Alice said. "I have no idea what he thought about *The Color Purple* or the controversy. Though the fact that he wanted me to introduce him speaks to his solidarity, which I treasure."

Baldwin had read Alice's work and rejoiced in her literary career, maintained a friend and former student with whom he kept close ties. "He rather adored her," said Alexa Birdsong, who studied with the author during Baldwin's tenure, in the mid-1980s, at Mount Holyoke College in Massachusetts. "He understood they were cut from the same cloth."

As Alice pondered Baldwin's request, she remembered the inspiration she'd found, as a fledging writer, in his first novel, *Go Tell It on the Mountain* (1953). She thought of Baldwin's courage, during the McCarthy era, in publishing *Giovanni's Room* (1956) with its daring theme of gay love. She exulted in the ferocity of *Blues for Mister Charlie* (1964), the elevation of black culture in *The Amen Corner* (1955), Baldwin's lamentation for the murdered children of Atlanta in *The Evidence of Things Not Seen* (1985). And understanding the gift, she carried Baldwin's posthumous tribute to Lorraine Hansberry, always in her heart: "With strength dictated by absolutely impersonal ambition, she was not trying to 'make it'— she was trying to keep the faith."

"Just as I loved Langston Hughes as a spiritual father, I loved James Baldwin as a spiritual brother," Alice said. "He was so beautiful, wise, gentle, committed, and strong."

But as much as she longed to share Baldwin's embrace, she was weary of the derisive taunts and jeers ("You Should Be Ashamed!") that had dogged her throughout *The Color Purple* imbroglio. Loathe that her presence might disrupt Baldwin's much-anticipated appearance, she declined to introduce him. Moreover, she determined it best not to even attend the presentation of the legendary writer, who, in detailing the consequences of oppression, had warned with chilling foresight, "There will be bloody actions all over the world for years to come; but the Western party is over, and the white man's sun has set. Period."

"Knowing that Baldwin had specifically asked for Alice, I got on the phone and tried to convince her to come," remembered Gus Newport, then the mayor of Berkeley, California, and a close observer of *The Color Purple* debate. "But she was really down and said she didn't want to be a distraction; that she couldn't face another protest."

He continued: "As a black man, I was shocked and dismayed by the attacks against Alice. I'd witnessed everything in *The Color Purple*. Every scene in the movie rang true. I offered her all of my support. Because as a people, I felt we owed her an apology."

Although she was grateful for Newport's allegiance and that of other black men who'd risen to her defense over the years ("Black women writers are telling it like it is, and often not telling all of it," asserted scholar Calvin Hernton), Alice, depleted, stood firm in her decision to stay home. Like its impetus, the significance of her decision was profound.

"The next thing I knew, James Baldwin was dead," Alice said, as tears trickled down her cheeks. "I never got a chance to tell him how much I loved him. But I was exhausted by then."

There is no public record of Baldwin's views about *The Color Purple*. Whatever he might have felt about the book, the movie, or Alice's pained response to his speaking invitation was lost to history when, on November 30, 1987, he made his transition to ancestor at his home in the south of France. But there's little doubt that he understood the price she'd paid for her artistry. After all, discussing the demons he'd confronted as a pioneering black, gay, and ferociously political writer, Baldwin had once proclaimed, "Love has never been a popular movement. The world is held together, really it is held together by the love and passion of a very few people."

52

They Saw the Airplane Coming

AT A healthy distance of eight thousand miles from San Francisco, Bali was just the place for Alice to restore her spirit and heal from the sorrow of the Baldwin affair. Accompanied by Robert and Rebecca, she traveled to the South Pacific island, where, calmed by the scent of plumeria and the spectacular vista of waterfalls outside her rented house, she celebrated her forty-third birthday. She'd chronicle the adventure in *Living by the Word*, the 1988 essay collection that, as Alice wrote in the introduction, reflected her hope for "a new age of heightened global consciousness."

> I set out on a journey to find my old planet; to gaze at its moon, to swim in its waters, to eat its fruits, to rediscover and admire its creatures; to purify myself in its wind and its sun. To my inexpressible joy I found it still there, though battered as an unwanted dog. But still beautiful, still mysterious . . . still profound.

In addition to her musings on Bali ("Just *be* . . . Being is All"), Alice addressed such topics as Native American rights, nuclear peril, respect for elders, her admiration of reggae legend Bob Marley ("a free spirit if there ever was one"), and determined commitment to vegetarianism despite occasional lapses ("There is the stray drumstick or slice of prosciutto that somehow finds its way into my mouth").

In the essay "My Daughter Smokes," Alice bemoaned Rebecca's cigarette habit. Far from an antismoking diatribe, she instead shared her compassion for tobacco as a sacred plant that had become poisoned with carcinogens and peddled for profit. "For thousands of years [tobacco] has been venerated by Native Americans," Alice observed. "They have used it extensively . . . to heal wounds and cure diseases, and in ceremonies of prayer and peace. . . . It's true nature suppressed no wonder it has become deadly. Maybe by sowing a few seeds of tobacco in our gardens and treating the plant with the reverence it deserves, we can redeem the tobacco's soul and restore its self-respect."

Similarly, in "Everything Is a Human Being," Alice detailed her efforts to welcome the snakes in her country garden as "kinfolk" rather than "dangerous and repulsive" creatures society had taught her to fear. Indeed, she'd dedicate the collection to "Susie and her Children," a snake "family" that regularly sunned itself near the entrance to Alice's writing studio.

Calling *Living by the Word* a shining example of Alice's "abiding obsession with the oneness of the universe," the *Chicago Tribune* cheered the volume's expansive tone. "Each essay paints a picture and draws a lesson from it, combining at their most successful the pristine imagery of haiku with the allegorical meanderings of the black pulpit. Taken together they project a voice and style unique among current American writers."

But comparing the book to Alice's previous offerings, *Washington Post* writer Jill Nelson maintained that the collection disappointed, in form and content. "In her fiction . . . Walker demonstrates that she is capable of bringing out the magical in language. . . . Walker the essayist offers, at best, small enlightenments. Far too often . . . her subject and her observations are merely pedestrian."

In a brief journal entry included in *Living by the Word*, Alice offered a personal assessment of her literary accomplishments since the release of *Once*. She'd always staked her claim with spiritual forces. By *their* measure, she was satisfied that the little girl who'd once "scribbled" in the Sears and Roebuck catalog had fulfilled her destiny.

> In some ways, I feel my early life's work is done, and done completely. The books that I have produced already carry forward the thoughts that I feel the ancestors were trying to help me pass on. In every generation someone (or two or three) is chosen for this work. . . . Great spirit, I thank you for the length of my days and fullness of my work. If you wanted me to move on, come home, or whatever is next, I would try to bear it joyfully.

HER ROOTEDNESS in the South everlasting, Alice, after an absence of more than twenty years, soon returned to Spelman as the honored speaker at Sisters Chapel, where she'd suffered through compulsory services as a student. She'd agreed to the April 1987 invitation because the college had appointed, that year, its first black woman president, the distinguished anthropologist Dr. Johnnetta Cole. Paying homage to the artists she revered as "literary parents," she also established, at the college, an annual $5,000 Zora Neale Hurston–Langston Hughes Award in Creative Writing. To be sure, Alice wanted to support an aspiring writer at Spelman (such as she'd been). But her action was also prompted by a desire to reunite Zora and Langston, who'd quarreled over the authorship of a play (*Mule Bone*) and gone to their graves without reconciling the breach. "Each was to the other an affirming example of what black people could be like: wild, crazy, creative, spontaneous, at ease with who they are, and funny . . . ," Alice insisted. "And I have never felt that they were fundamentally at odds."

Mindful of the significance of her appearance at Spelman, Alice chose as her topic a black cultural issue then rarely discussed in public forums, one that surely would have tickled Hughes and

Hurston: in her words, "oppressed hair." Meaning the practice, common among many black women, of straightening their naturally kinky, curly, wiry, or wavy hair with hot combs or chemical "relaxers."

"You can imagine how *that* went over," said Beverly Guy-Sheftall, recalling the masses of straightened-haired Spelman students (and staff) who jammed the chapel unknowing that the college's most celebrated "daughter" had been moved to extol the beauty of black hair free from "domination or control."

"Don't give a thought to the state of yours at the moment," cautioned Alice, attempting to calm the uneasy audience. "Don't be at all alarmed. This is not an appraisal. I simply want to share with you some of my own experiences."

Alice went on to reveal that she'd worn many hairstyles, adding that, like most black women of her generation, she'd too fallen prey to the hot comb. She told the crowd (a little less tense now) that her hair odyssey had included an Afro, braided extensions (from the hair of Korean women), natural twists, and ultimately, dreadlocks. "Eventually I knew *precisely* what hair wanted: it wanted to grow, to be itself, to attract lint, if that was its destiny, but to be left alone by anyone, including me, who did not love it as it was," Alice declared. The speech, "Oppressed Hair Puts a Ceiling on the Brain," also appears in *Living by the Word*.

Allowing that Alice's candor could be unsettling, Dr. Cole applauded her dedication, in life and in art, to "unveiling the complexity of African-American sisters." "Most people think they can know everything about black women in three words," Dr. Cole ventured. "But you can't just go up or down, good or bad, black or white with Alice. She's not simplistic."

The observation even applied to Alice's love life, as Dr. Cole would note. "Certainly Alice's refusal to be defined with respect to her sexuality has been an enduring contribution to black women. She's always pushing against boundaries."

By the end of the decade, Alice had, in fact, ended her sexual liaison with Robert and embraced female lovers. Her action never meant as a disavowal of men, Alice still kept close ties with the companion with whom she'd weathered so much over the years. "She caught me with my humanity showing," Robert later said, appreciatively, of Alice's reasoned response to his infidelity. Apparently unaccustomed to such congenial break-up scenarios among heterosexuals, a lesbian acquaintance was surprised by Alice's continued relationship with her former paramour. The woman remembered, "I told Alice that I'd thought it was only lesbians who could end a romance but remain close friends. Without missing a beat, she said about herself and Robert: 'We are lesbians.'"

Lesbian. Bisexual. Queer. "Homospirtual." The nomenclature was irrelevant to Jean Weisinger, a San Francisco area photographer who found herself attracted to Alice in the late 1980s. Weisinger said that she first felt the rumblings of desire after Alice complimented her hair at a local literary gathering both women attended. "I had just started to dreadlock my hair and friends were complaining because I didn't control the way it was growing," Weisinger recalled. "Wild would be a good way to describe my hair. But Alice liked it and she got right up out of her seat to tell me so. I felt validated and appreciated."

Not long after the encounter, Weisinger took a photo of Alice during a celebration for South African leader Nelson Mandela, who, released from prison after a nearly thirty-year stay, visited Northern California in 1990. (Alice had donated a portion of royalties from *The Color Purple* to the African National Congress and had blocked distribution of the movie in South Africa until Mandela was freed.) At the click of the shutter, Alice, signing a book for a fan, raised her eyes and, as Weisinger remembered, "locked into my gaze." "I felt something pass between us. It was so powerful, I ran back to my car."

The women next met at a Bay area party for a black lesbian poet, where, remarkably, Weisinger said, Alice was seated at a huge table "all alone." "When I walked in, Alice got up and embraced me, laughing. She invited me back to the table where we talked and talked. The following weekend we became lovers."

Weisinger was passionate about music, art, politics, and gardening. She was also a devoted grandmother to two inquisitive boys. As such, Weisinger's appeal to Alice wasn't difficult to grasp. She'd always been drawn to fighters and Weisinger—a former special education teacher and self-taught at photography—was certainly that.

"I connected with Jean's grit," Alice later said. "I liked that she was making her own way." Discussing her shifting sexuality, Alice recalled her enchantment with another woman who had similar attributes: "Once, during a trip to Nicaragua, I met a Sandinista woman who'd taken over an entire city. I fell in love with her completely! I'm always attracted to revolutionaries; people who are just fighting so hard and standing up for themselves."

Given Alice's celebrity, it wasn't long before her relationship with Weisinger became a hot topic among lesbians from Syracuse to Santa Cruz. Her sense of self firm, Weisinger said she ignored the nattering chatter about how Alice, presumably with access to the "lesbian elite," had taken up with an "unknown." "I knew where I stood," Weisinger maintained.

Further, calling herself "out of the loop," Weisinger said she hadn't been privy to the swirl of gossip that had trailed Alice ever since she'd brought Shug and Celie together in a lusty romance. "Like most lesbians who'd read *The Color Purple*, I'd hoped that Alice herself had had the pleasure of a woman's touch and passion. When I discovered that she'd been with a man before we met, I realized that Alice and I were alike in that we were both most attracted to the spirit of people. Sometimes that spirit is housed in a male, other times in a woman."

That was precisely the message Alice hoped to impart at a gathering of the National Coalition of Black Gays and Lesbians later held in Long Beach, California. There, in a keynote address before a standing room–only crowd, she presented herself as "two-spirited." "I get a thrill out of Bob Marley *and* Tina Turner," Alice happily proclaimed. Having expected her to announce her homosexuality, many in the audience were miffed at what they interpreted as Alice's refusal to come out of the closet. "She could have left that at home," sneered an obviously disgruntled gay black man.

The disaffection with Alice among certain gay factions didn't surprise self-described queer folksinger Ani DiFranco, whose song "In or Out" has been cheered as an anthem by the bisexual community ("I just want more than one membership to more than one club, because I owe my life to the people that I love"). Her maverick stance propelling her to near iconic status in the early 1990s, DiFranco outraged many of her lesbian fans when, in 1998, she married, as she put it, "a boy creature." That her beloved turned out to be the sound man for Righteous Babe Records (the wildly successful record company DiFranco owns) only added to the uproar.

"I was vilified as a sell-out and a traitor to the tribe that first made me a 'star,'" recalled DiFranco, wearily, before a recent concert in Oakland, California. "But my relationship with my male partner is as queer as any other that I've ever had. Alice Walker gets slammed for not hoisting the 'gay banner' because persecuted people are so desperate to see themselves reflected in the culture. So they miss out on her really powerful messages about freedom, integrity, and being true to your soul."

Be that as it may, another prominent queer activist said that he did not move easily from a stance he described as "bitterly antibisexual." "I had no patience for those children whatsoever," scoffed Ibrahim Farajaje-Jones, dean of the Starr-King School for Ministry in Berkeley, California. "To my mind, bisexuals were 'fence sitters' who diluted the gay movement. They didn't want to give up their heterosexual privilege. Bi-politics? Please . . ."

Today the parent of a young son and partner, in his words, with a "mixed-race bi-dyke," Farajaje-Jones credited *The Color Purple* and, especially, Alice's womanist philosophy with ushering him to "new models of erotic practices." "It was liberatory to have this black woman say out loud that we didn't have to continue to be suffocated by our choices, that we could experience a sexuality that is fluid. Alice forces gays to look at how we've colonized our bodies and enacted a kind of slavery on desire. The way I see it, all this drama about Alice Walker and her sex life is fueled by an alienation from the body as a divinely unshackled entity."

Anastasia Higginbotham, a bisexual writer in Brooklyn, New York, also claimed Alice as a heroine for, as she put it, "sex outlaws": "There's an extravagance to bisexuality. To a lot people it seems greedy. To them, being bisexual says: 'I want everything.' I must be one of millions who felt something ignite when Shug talked to Celie about how good sex once felt with Albert and in the next breath leaned in to kiss Celie full on the mouth. When I heard rumors about Alice's private life what it revealed to me was that her sexuality fit with what my imagination had already made up about her after reading her stories and poems. I figured she'd be drawn to pleasure and connection in all its forms."

BESIDES CURIOSITY about Alice's love life ("I'm bisexual. I don't think I have to phone in and tell everybody," she'd ultimately declare), another topic now consumed many of her readers: What kind of novel would Alice publish next?

The Pulitzer Prize is a notoriously difficult act to follow. Many winning writers fail to meet expectations for a smash encore. Awarded the 1975 fiction prize for his civil war epic *The Killer Angels*, Michael Shaara's next novel, *The Herald* (1981), barely found an audience. Winner in 1961 for the time-honored classic *To Kill a Mockingbird*, Harper Lee never published another book.

But there was more fiction yet from the author of *The Color Purple*. As befits a writer who'd always marched to a different drummer, Alice's next novel was inspired, in part, by a vanilla-bean pod. Not surprisingly, many readers were jolted by her dramatic departure from Celie's letters to God. They'd waited seven years and *The Temple of My Familiar* did not ring familiar at all.

"They'd been given to me by a dear friend in Latin America," Alice told the *San Francisco Chronicle*, speaking of the aromatic vanilla beans that had helped to spark her eagerly anticipated 1989 release. "One day when I looked at [a pod], I thought, this is like a boat. Then there was just no stopping it . . . then you find people for it, and you ask yourself where a boat like this might be."

There was globetrotting aplenty in the mystical narrative Alice described as a "romance of the last 500,000 years" and which she dedicated to Robert, "in whom the Goddess shines." The story of three couples struggling to achieve cosmic harmony, *The Temple* moves through Europe, Africa, and the Americas and features bold strokes of fantasy in which animals, plants, and humans, unrestricted by genus or species, emerge as symbols of a universal family.

The protagonists of the novel (history professor, rock musician, masseuse, psychic, to name a few) are guided on their journeys of self-discovery by Miss Lissie, an elderly black woman who, having lived in multiple incarnations (witch, white man, pygmy, lion), emphasizes the kinship of all things. Rife with ancestral wisdom, Lissie delivers the overarching message of the novel when she declares, "When you love someone, you want to share yourself, or, in my case . . . you want to share *yourselves*. . . . One of the people I most appreciated . . . was Janis Joplin. She knew Bessie Smith was her momma, and she sang her guts out trying to tear open that closed door between them."

Their bond still strong, Celie and Shug also appear in *The Temple*, the latter now a charismatic preacher who offers a womanist gospel to those seeking enlightenment: "Helped are those who receive only to give; always in their house will be the circular energy of generosity and in their hearts a beginning of a new age on Earth. . . . Helped are those who *know*."

As Alice later told it, she aimed, with her fourth novel, to render a total reinterpretation of history. "I wondered what it means that there is a human *family* on this Earth. I wanted to make this idea real to people in a society that is constantly trying to make you think you are separate—not only from other people but from animals and trees and everything. . . . What was hard to bear, and very insulting to me, was that my whole existence, as told to me by other people, had been a lie. . . . I realized *I* had to remember . . . and that my notion of what was true is just as good as anybody else's— anyway it made me a hell of a lot happier. So I just threw caution to the wind."

Her writing steeped in magical realism, fantasy, and myth, science fiction master Ursula K. Le Guin was wowed by Alice's abandonment of traditional plotting and constructs of reality. Writing for the *San Francisco Review of Books*, the author of such celebrated works as *The Left Hand of Darkness* and *The Dispossessed* exclaimed, "The richness of Alice Walker's new novel is amazing, overwhelming. A hundred themes and subjects spin through it . . . a whirl of times and places. None is touched superficially. . . . Every character in the book bears witness that if we don't change, we perish."

Change or perish? If *that* was Alice's message, another critic pleaded for the process to begin with *The Temple of My Familiar.* Exasperated by a novel he decried as a "hootchie-cootchie dance to castration," James Wolcott, in a review for the *New Republic,* ridiculed the book as so much flaky, faddish, New Age starshine. It was absurd, he insisted, for Alice to suggest that animals and humans had once coexisted, peacefully, in a matriarchal Eden; that mankind would do well to reimagine the penis as an "elongated clitoris"; that whites could find salvation if they'd only dare to claim the African-ness within their souls.

"Cover to cover *The Temple of My Familiar* is the nuttiest novel I've ever read . . . ," Wolcott railed. "Walker carries on as if she were Mother Africa's flower-power favorite. Her hippie prose is a form of handicrafts, tie-dyed and dated." Writing for the *Washington Post,* David Nicholson likewise dismissed *The Temple* as a "catalogue of goofy California enthusiasms." Meanwhile, the *New York Times,* employing a policy unique among newspapers in the United States, weighed in with two reviews. "*The Temple* has the same feeling of over-ambition about it that one sees in a batter so determined to hit a home run that she swings before the ball is pitched," wrote Christopher Lehmann-Haupt, adding that in the novel there was "something to irritate everyone." Three days later, South African writer and future Nobel laureate J. M. Coetzee sought to temper the blow: "Cliché-ridden prose is not representative of the best of *The Temple* . . . but there is enough of it to give one pause."

"The Sunday *Book Review* and the daily operate independently, that is, and without consulting each other; and so it happens fairly often that we will each review the same book, especially when (as in the case of Walker) it's by a well-known author . . . ," explained Charles McGrath, book editor at the *New York Times.* "I think it's healthy that some books get a second chance, and it's a reminder that reviews are opinions, not verdicts."

Having never embraced reviews as "gospel," Alice was not undone by the harsh critiques *The Temple* received. Moreover, she noted that during an era when black women's literary criticism was in full blossom, she found it odd that her novel had been assigned, for the most part, to a coterie of white male reviewers. By contrast, she added, the mainstream press rarely (if ever) afforded black women writers a platform to assess the literary talents of white men. Had Paule Marshall, she ventured, ever been assigned to review Phillip Roth? Adrienne Kennedy to ponder Arthur Miller? Sonia Sanchez to evaluate Robert Frost? Celie had put it this way: "If God ever listened to poor colored women the world would be a different place. I can tell you."

"I think I'm being reviewed by the defenders of the patriarchy, the white male patriarchy, the really hard-core establishment," Alice told the *Boston Globe* when queried about the lackluster response to her fourth novel. "So I must say that I don't feel totally concerned because I don't feel they are really qualified to judge me. I am so entirely different from them."

Interestingly, *The Temple* found an unexpected admirer in Ishmael Reed. Reed's support was all the more surprising because in 1986 he'd published *Reckless Eyeballing*, a satirical novel about a famous black feminist playwright accused of "blood libel" against black men. A scathing send-up of 1980s gender battles, the novel's allusions to *The Color Purple* controversy were barely veiled. But for *The Temple*, Reed had only raves.

"It is a formidable achievement," he concluded. "I bought thirty copies of the novel for my warehouse of books written by black authors, which I think will be regarded as classics down the line. The problem is that Alice blames white males for the terrible state of the planet. And so the same white males who frothed over *The Color Purple* put her down."

The critics could pontificate (pro or con) however much they wanted. Now tempered by the fire of her literary life, Alice had moved on. To those for whom *The Temple* signaled a tarnishing of her Pulitzer Prize crown, she replied, matter-of-factly: "It's like any other thing you create. If I make shoes, then I'll make shoes and put them out there. My part will have been done."

NEARLY A hundred years before Alice evoked shoes as a symbol of her artistic independence, another author had made vivid use of a similar metaphor. Such imagery holds special resonance in African American culture where the adage "All god's children got traveling shoes" signifies a determination to live free and unfettered despite the challenges imposed in an unwelcoming society.

As Valerie Boyd recounts the story in *Wrapped in Rainbows*, Zora Neale Hurston, when she was about nine years old, fantasized about walking into the horizon to explore "the end of the world." Unfazed by Jim Crow restrictions on the minds, bodies, and spirits of blacks, young Zora further imagined herself in shoes with "sky-blue bottoms" as she set off to discover whether the horizon "tucked under like the hem of a dress," or dropped off into an airy nothingness, at the "belly band of the world."

And while Hurston *did* travel vast distances from her home in Eatonville, Florida, her many jaunts (literary and real) might well have remained in the shadows had Alice not placed a marker on the mound of weed-choked earth she deduced to be Zora's grave. By the same token, without Zora as the bodacious sister spirit who penned *Their Eyes Were Watching God*, Alice might have had less of an artistic foundation from which to build on Ruth's memory of swapped silk panties. But enthralled by Hurston's novel, Alice was primed to receive the voices that insisted she ditch Brooklyn and settle in Boonville.

In the opening pages of *In Search of Our Mothers' Gardens*, Alice describes the magical cycle of giving and receiving that would prove to be the hallmark of her years.

> In my development as a human being and as a writer I have been . . . extremely blessed, even while complaining. Wherever I have knocked, a door has opened. Wherever I have wan-

dered, a path has appeared. I have been helped, supported, encouraged, and nurtured by people of all races, creeds, colors, and dreams; and I have, to the best of my ability, returned help, support, encouragement, and nurture. This receiving, returning or passing on has been one of the most amazing, joyous, and continuous experiences of my life.

The circle's flow would be in full evidence when, nearly three decades after Alice championed disenfranchised sharecroppers in the South, she lent her voice to a voter registration program at the Colleges of the City University of New York. Linked to a national campaign to increase voter education (especially among college-age students) the 1991 effort was funded, in part, by the bookstore company Barnes & Noble. The brochures for the New York drive featured a photo of Alice and a statement she released in support of the project: "Voting Is One Way to Say Hello to Your Grandchildren."

"I was very moved by Alice's remark and her willingness to participate in the project," remembered Len Riggio, founder of Barnes & Noble. "Her generosity of heart stayed with me."

And so Riggio was happy to intervene when, in 2002, the Spence School in New York selected Alice as graduation speaker. A member of the graduating class at the private secondary school, Stephanie Riggio gave her father added impetus to extend the invitation.

Alice has historically reserved the summer months for festive dance parties, gardening, swimming, and prolonged meditation at her country retreat (which she christened "Temple Jook House," as a symbol of revelry and spiritual replenishment). Given the security measures enacted after the attacks on September 11, 2001, she was even less disposed to air travel and respectfully declined the invitation. Hoping Alice might reconsider, Riggio offered to send, at his private expense, a corporate jet so as to minimize her stress and inconvenience. Impressed by his tenacity, she agreed to deliver the commencement address.

Alice was joined on the trip by her companion at the time, William Poy Lee, a former attorney she met at a 1999 Northern

California meditation retreat for people of color. In the interim between her relationships with Weisinger and Lee, Alice had two other significant liaisons. "We created a net, a place of true safety where we could rest in each other's love," remembered Zelie Kuliaikanuu'u Duvauchelle, a native Hawaiian singer with whom Alice was involved in the mid-1990s. Venturing to such places as Scotland (in homage to Alice's Scottish roots) and to the Amazon jungle, where the couple participated in traditional healing rituals, Duvauchelle said that for two years, she and Alice "had one experience after another of saying 'Yes' to life."

Alice was also linked, romantically, with Grammy Award–winning musician Tracy Chapman. Famously private, Chapman declined to comment on the relationship. As with all her intimate companions, Alice said she remains opened-hearted toward a woman who once gifted her with an elegant green bicycle and whose beauty, she wrote, "reminds me always of the liberating power of that which is free, natural and whole."

Alice would also allude to the relationship in "Poem for Aneta Chapman on Her 33rd Birthday," which appears in her poetry collection *Absolute Trust in the Goodness of the Earth* (2003). Aneta is Tracy Chapman's older sister and personal assistant.

The liaison between Alice and Chapman, two of the most celebrated contemporary black women creative artists, was a source of intrigue for many. "I don't think that I attended a party, barbecue, poetry reading, academic affair or any other 1990s social gathering of well-known and so-called ordinary Black lesbians where the relationship between Alice and Tracy was not discussed with certainty and some semblance of pride almost," remembered Chana Kai Lee, a history professor at the University of Georgia and author of *For Freedom's Sake*, a masterful 1999 biography of Fannie Lou Hamer. "Although very few of us could claim to know either personally, all that mattered was that we could imagine and speculate on a 'real thing' that charmed us, because we held both women in such high esteem. We could claim and hold up these two strong, wonderfully beautiful black women together."

"This imagined reality of Alice's private life made us hold on to her just a little tighter, a little closer," Lee continued. "Alice has that way of helping us honor our own truths and to clarify our own aspiration for wholeness, even when we are just imagining or speculating about how she lives and how she loves."

Elaborating on her love interests, Alice said, "For me it has never been about color or any other external characteristics. . . . The quality I look for [in a partner] is a sense of readiness. If I'm in a setting where there are really conscious people, I look around to see who is ready to go with me on the next journey, for however long that might be. . . . People present themselves to us in as many forms as there are in nature. I really like the young masculine, whether in male or female, in young or old. It is a special quality and always means adventure, irreverence and fun."

Not her first trip on a corporate plane, Alice had traveled on a Warner Bros. jet to attend the 1985 New York premiere of *The Color Purple*. Still, she reveled in her unplanned air escapade with William Lee to New York. "It was like traveling in my living room and being served by my cousins," Alice said, adding that one of the pilots was of African descent.

The Spence graduation ceremony was held at a nearby parish, The Church of the Heavenly Rest at East 90th Street and Fifth Avenue. To the suggestion that Zora Neale Hurston, buried at the Garden of Heavenly Rest, might have had a "cosmic" hand in the event, Alice, replied, "Yes. Sometimes the Universe gives a double underscore. One Heavenly Rest in poorest black Florida, the other in richest white New York. Yet the path a single track from one to the other."

SHORTLY AFTER Alice returned from New York, she recounted her experience to a group of close friends. Aware of the circumstances surrounding Alice's eye injury, one woman later reminded her of the hard-hearted motorist who, in 1952, had rebuffed Willie Lee Walker's desperate plea for a ride. Wasn't it incredible, the friend marveled, that another white man had just dispatched for Alice a private plane?

"I hadn't thought of the connection," Alice responded, first pensive and then happily amused. "How right and what a chuckle for the ancestors for whom fifty years isn't even a flash. They saw the airplane coming for me as the car in Milledgeville sped away."

To be sure, Alice defied Dickie Stribling's vile curse about the "futility" of treating her wounded eye. In "Expect Nothing," a poem published in *Revolutionary Petunias*, Alice Walker, healed and healer, expresses a sentiment that, perhaps more than any, embodies her victory.

> *Expect nothing. Live frugally*
> *On surprise.*
> *Become a stranger*
> *To need of pity*
> *Or, if compassion be freely*
> *Given out*
> *Take only enough*
> *Stop short of urge to plead*
> *Then purge away the need.*
> *Wish for nothing larger*
> *Than your own small heart*
> *Or greater than a star;*
> *Tame wild disappointment*
> *With caress unmoved and cold*
> *Make of it a parka*
> *For your soul.*
> *Discover the reason why*
> *So tiny human giant*
> *Exists at all*
> *So scared unwise*
> *But expect nothing. Live frugally*
> *On surprise.*

Epilogue

It's All Love

WHEN PULITZER PRIZE juror Peter Prescott declared *The Color Purple* a work of "permanent importance," it's doubtful that he could have envisioned the novel's reach. Opening a space for other artists to enter, Alice's portrait of Shug, Celie, and Mr. _____ moved previously taboo subject matter from the margins into the full glare of American society. Their eyes opened to both the cultural and the commercial value of such work, literary agents, editors, publishers, and moviemakers followed in kind.

For example, *Thereafter Johnnie* (1991) by Carolivia Herron, the wrenching *Gal* (1994) by Ruthie Bolton, *The Serpent's Gift* (1994) by Helen Elaine Lee, and Sapphire's *Push* (1996) all touched on themes of family abuse and violence that Alice had explored. Published the same year as *The Color Purple* and winner of the 1983 American Book Award for first fiction, Gloria Naylor's *The Women of Brewster Place* featured a struggling black lesbian couple and in 1989 was adapted for television by Oprah Winfrey.

In film, the scintillating *Eve's Bayou* (1997) hinted at an incestuous relationship involving a philandering country doctor played by black actor Samuel L. Jackson. With a subplot that presented singer Erykah Badu as the sexually abused daughter of a black migrant worker, *The Cider House Rules*, a 1999 movie based on the novel by John Irving, also called to mind tensions between Celie and Mr. _____. That an established white male author would dare to wade in such waters could hardly be imagined before Alice established the precedent. The storyline would also emerge in *Monsoon Wedding*, a film about an upper-class family in India during which a woman confronts the male relative who molested her as a child. None of the works sparked the rancor that greeted *The Color Purple*, which hit its forty-second printing in the year 2000. At the time of this writing, a Broadway musical production of *The Color Purple* was also in development.

Author of *Whose Song? and Other Stories* (2000) an acclaimed debut fiction collection that features a womanist-infused title story about rape, Thomas Glave elaborated on Alice's artistic impact. "In being transgressive, Alice Walker inspired many writers of my generation to examine what we could do to fight misogyny," said Glave, a black and openly gay professor of English at the State University of New York at Binghamton who is in his late thirties. "Many of us are interested in the well-being of black women and want to give voice, in our art, to black women's reality. We understand that we can learn a lot about humanity when we listen closely to women's voices."

Calvin Hernton had emphasized the same point in his essay "Who's Afraid of Alice Walker?" The title alluded to the famed Edward Albee play *Who's Afraid of Virginia Woolf?* and, like the highly charged drama (later adapted for film), the essay addressed age-old gender battles. "Alice Walker [was denounced] as a subversive for daring to make public the barbarity of black men," Hernton wrote in the piece, which appears in *The Sexual Mountain and Black Women Writers*. "But what about the substance of *The Color Purple* and its developmental process?" Reflecting on her writing twenty years after the publication of the book that made her a household name, Alice maintained that she wanted only to produce work that "helps to heal." For influential *New York Times* critic Michiko Kakutani there was no such medicine to be found in *Now Is the Time to Open Your Heart*, Alice's 2004 novel about Kate Talkingtree, a woman faltering in her Buddhist practice. "*Now Is the Time* is a remarkably awful compendium of inanities," Kakutani scoffed. "Whereas the heroine of *The Color Purple* was struggling to free herself from a controlling and abusive husband . . . Kate is simply looking for some fuzzy New Age affirmation of herself." Perhaps anticipating such criticsm, Alice wrote in the acknowledgments page of the novel: "*With this writing, whatever its faults, I express my gratitude to all the devas, angels, and bodhisattvas who accompany, watch over, and protect explorers, pioneers, and artists.*"

Dedicated to the development of marginalized writers, Alice published six books under the imprimatur of Wild Trees Press, among them a novel set in Columbia (*Condor and Hummingbird* by Charlotte Mendez); *The Spirit Journey*, a collection of folktales and paintings by Balinese artist Madi Kertonegoro; and *As Wonderful as All That?*, a memoir by 1920s-era black musician Henry Crowder about his seven-year affair with white shipping heiress Nancy Cunard. But overwhelmed by the deluge of manuscripts, Alice closed the press in 1988. "We became too successful and we really didn't want to turn it over to other people because it was our vision," she explained.

Those who criticized Alice for "going light" on white folks in *The Color Purple* would find a counterpoint in *Behind God's Back*, a 1989 film adaptation of her story "How Did I Get Away with Killing One of the Biggest Lawyers in the State? It Was Easy" (published in *You Can't Keep a Good Woman Down*). Featuring actor Beau Bridges in the role of a sleazy Southern attorney who is having an affair with his family's teen-age black maid, the thirty-two-minute project (shot in five days for $5,000) was conceived and directed by actress Judyann Elder for the Directing Workshop for Women at the American Film Institute. *Behind God's Back* generated enthusiastic response at the 1989 Los Angeles Women in Film Festival and may become available on cable television, said Elder, a founding member of the Negro Ensemble Company.

"I'd read Alice's work since the 1970s and became fascinated with the theatricality of her stories," Elder continued. "She gets to the underside of huge topics in a very compelling way."

As for weighty subjects, Steven Spielberg later said that his experience with *The Color Purple* helped to shape his vision for the 1993 Holocaust epic that delivered his first Academy Award for best director. "I wouldn't have had the interest in an adult story like *Schindler's List* unless *The Color Purple* had come along," Spielberg told *Vibe* magazine. "When I made *The Color Purple*, that was my first dose of real life. . . . So if I began growing up, if I began taking myself seriously as a Jew, it's really because of that."

Lost in the controversy surrounding the film release of *The Color Purple*, Alice would later attribute her campaign to end female genital mutilation (FGM) to deeper insights she gained about the practice during the movie's production. FGM, forced excision of the clitoris and other parts of female genitalia, is performed on an estimated 100 million girls and women in areas of the Middle East, the Far East, and Africa and has historically been defended by proponents as "tribal custom."

Alice said she first came to know of FGM during her sojourn in East Africa in the summer of 1965. But unaware of the cultural significance or myriad health dangers of the practice (hemorrhaging, HIV transmission, emotional trauma, chronic infections), Alice said she failed to grasp its full impact. Her troubled memories of girls in Kenya walking painfully after their "bath" were reawakened when she met Lillian Njoki Distefano, the African actress playing the role of Tashi, who meets Celie's family at the end of *The Color Purple*. Also a minor character in *The Temple of My Familiar*, Tashi emerged full-flesh as the protagonist of *Possessing the Secret of Joy*, Alice's 1992 novel about an African woman who is spared FGM as a child. Caught in a clash of cultures, Tashi succumbs to "tradition" and undergoes the procedure voluntarily. She then descends into madness.

Writing for the *Los Angeles Times*, Tina McElroy Ansa extolled the novel Alice dedicated "with tenderness and respect to the blameless vulva." "Alice Walker [again] takes her readers into formerly taboo territory. . . . She insists that we look at what we would rather pretend doesn't exist."

Determined to further expose the ritual and its harmful effects, Alice joined forces with British-Indian filmmaker Pratibha Parmar to produce the 1993 documentary *Warrior Marks*—released with a companion book that bears the same title. Parmar is an unapologetically political artist whose documentaries address topics ranging from South Asian activism in England to actress Jodie Foster as an icon for lesbians. Screened primarily at film festivals and at fundraising events, *Warrior Marks* was repudiated, in the United States and abroad, by a cadre of activists who branded Alice a "cultural imperialist" for bringing attention to a practice they asserted was a "private affair" best left to Africans.

Protesting that there were more important social ills for Alice to address, an influential black woman reporter huffed, "I wish Alice Walker would leave the African pussy alone."

Alice's response? "As far as I'm concerned, I am speaking for my great-great-great-great-grandmother who came here with all this pain in her body. In addition to having been captured, put in the hull of a ship, packed like sardines, put on the auction block, in addition to her children being sold, she being raped, in addition to all this, she might have been genitally mutilated. I would go nuts if this part of her story weren't factored in. Imagine if men came from Africa with their penises removed. Believe me, we would have many a tale about it."

While Alice was not the first to tackle the issue (she'd duly noted the pioneering work of others in the pages of *Warrior Marks*), her advocacy turned a global spotlight on FGM as a tool of oppression with horrific consequences for its victims. Indeed, her consciousness raised by Alice's efforts, Stephanie Welsh, then a twenty-two-year-old American journalist, left for a village near Nairobi. There, she took a series of photos about female circumcision that garnered her the 1996 Pulitzer Prize for feature photography. "Alice Walker planted the seed in me," said Welsh, who, inspired to improve conditions for women and children after documenting FGM, later became a midwife.

"A culture that subjects me to go under the knife needs to be criticized," added Fauziya Kassindja, author of *Do They Hear You When You Cry?* (1998), in which she chronicled her harrowing escape from Togo to avoid FGM. "Alice speaks up, not necessarily for us, but about our pain. When she stepped forward, the debate reached another level."

Subsequent developments seemed to support Kassindja's claim. For in July 2001, prompted by the ongoing outcry about the procedure, officials from nearly two hundred countries pledged, in a landmark United Nations resolution, to "respect women's right to control their own sexuality and reject the harmful custom of female genital mutilation."

Beginning in the 1990s, Alice also championed the cause of Mumia Abu-Jamal, a black journalist serving a death sentence for the alleged murder of a white police officer in Philadelphia. After visiting Abu-Jamal (twice) in prison and studying his case, Alice lent her voice to his legal defense. "We passed the hat and because of Alice's participation, we took in more than $6,000," recalled the organizer of a "Free Mumia" benefit at which Alice asserted that Abu-Jamal embodied a "gentle, masculine beauty" that his jailers were unable to honor within themselves.

As with Mumia, Alice stood squarely with Black Panther activist Assata Shakur, sentenced to life in prison for her purported role in a 1973 shoot-out that left a New Jersey state patrolman dead. Shakur eventually escaped from confinement and was granted political asylum in Cuba, where she has lived for more than twenty years. "I take Assata's word when she says she didn't kill the man," said Alice, in response to a recent reward offered by New Jersey officials for Shakur's return to the United States. "Cuba permitted Assata to have a life, but she is still unable to be with her family and friends. To put a bounty on her head is evil."

"She is righteous," said Shakur of Alice during an interview in Havana. "Her belief in the people is profound." Indeed, invited to visit the White House during the administration of President Bill Clinton, Alice, upset by a U.S. government policy that, to her mind, punishes Cuban people, declined to attend. "Would you want

Chelsea to have no milk?" Alice wrote to Clinton, referring to the long-standing embargo against Cuba. "You are a large man, how would you yourself survive?"

Alice would also weigh in on Supreme Court Justice Clarence Thomas, whose 1991 Senate confirmation hearing revealed allegations of sexual harassment. Likening the accusation to a "high-tech lynching," Thomas denied the complaint that was leveled against him by a respected black woman attorney, Anita Hill. "I wonder what Clarence would do if you just locked him in a room for five days with Bernice Johnson Reagon," Alice mused, referring to the founder of the internationally acclaimed singing group Sweet Honey in the Rock. "He is one of those people who has turned against his roots and Sweet Honey works constantly to affirm and uplift us. I bet Bernice could bring Clarence around."

As much as Alice was admired for her activism, some felt that, immersed in her political passions, she could sometimes be inattentive to personal relationships closer to home. Mary Helen Washington would later remember the sting of Alice's charge that she had surreptitiously copied a draft version of *Meridian* (presumably to circulate among friends and colleagues). "Given our friendship, I couldn't believe she would accuse me of such a thing," Washington recalled. "I immediately phoned her and we got past it, but the experience was hurtful." Similarly, John Ferrone said that he was stunned to be informed, after the release of *The Temple of My Familiar*, that Harcourt management had honored Alice's request for a new editor. "We'd worked together for several years, so it came as quite a blow," he remarked. "And I felt sad that she didn't see fit to tell me personally."

Allowing for the stress of the Mississippi years during which she wrote *Meridian*, Alice said she could not recall the conflict with Washington. While she appreciated Ferrone's craft, she confided that she'd felt mismatched, increasingly, with the white male editors she'd been assigned at Harcourt since 1968. She said she'd been rocked when Ferrone, apparently puzzled by her epigraph in *The Color Purple*, one day asked her, "Who is Stevie Wonder?"

"When I began working on *Possessing*, I knew I'd need an editor who was more culturally attuned," Alice said. "Everyone brings different gifts at different times."

Over the years, it's been difficult for some people to reconcile the calm and contemplative Alice with the woman who often discomforts with her candor and who can be testy, blunt, and uncompromising in her commitment to justice. She has never claimed to be without idiosyncrasy or human flaw. "Life is not bright, cheerful, and sunny all the time," Alice said. "The wise ones know this. . . . Sometimes things go wrong to teach you what is right. And if you harm some folks along the way, well, that's why the apology is born. The way I see it, life is about growth, struggle, and trying to expand your love of self and of other people. . . . This is likely to take all your energy for your entire life."

On September 10, 1993, Alice was confronted with the not unexpected but still shattering news that her long-ailing mother, age eighty, had passed away. She took comfort in the throngs of mourners who came to pay their respects to a woman whose devotion to family and friends was immortalized in a headstone that read, "Loving Soul, Great Spirit."

Alice was also bolstered by the batch of sympathy cards she received from children at an early learning center in Eatonton whose schooling she helped to finance. Reading their crayon-scrawled notes of condolence, she knew that Shug, Celie, Mr. _____, Nettie, Sofia, and Harpo still lived.

> Dear Ms. Walker,
> I am very sore that yer Mom died. Ms. Walker she up wite God and as long as she in heven she safe. So you don't have nuting to worey about.
> Love,
> Keith Pruett

Alice paid special tribute to her mother and paternal grandmother when, on her fiftieth birthday, she officially changed her middle name from Malsenior to Tallulah-Kate. "Whatever the word Tallulah means in itself, to me it means 'restored' in me," Alice said at the ceremony held February 9, 1994, at a Thai restaurant in San Francisco. "The word Kate means 'remembered' in me." Among the friends, old and new, who attended the festivities was former Cherokee chief Wilma Mankiller, who said in acknowledgement, "Alice taught me that pain can be a gift."

Alice would later put it this way: "Love is big. Love can hold anger, love can hold pain, love can even hold hatred. It's all about love."

Chronology

1944 Born Alice Malsenior Walker under sign of Aquarius on February 9 in Eatonton, Georgia.

1952 Loses sight in right eye as a result of BB gun incident.

1961 Graduates valedictorian from Butler-Baker High School. Enrolls at Spelman College.

1962 Serves as delegate to World Festival of Youth and Students in Helsinki, Finland.

1964 Transfers to Sarah Lawrence College.

1965 Works with voter registration in Georgia. Travels to Africa.

1966 Graduates from Sarah Lawrence. Moves to New York City and works for welfare office. Leaves for Mississippi.

1967 Marries civil rights attorney Melvyn Rosenman Leventhal. Returns to Mississippi.

1968 *Once* published. Becomes writer-in-residence at Jackson State College.

1969 Daughter, Rebecca Grant, born November 17.

1970 *The Third Life of Grange Copeland* published. Becomes writer-in-residence at Tougaloo College. Awarded Radcliffe Institute Fellowship.

1972 Becomes lecturer at Wellesley College and the University of Massachusetts, Boston.

1973 *Revolutionary Petunias* and *In Love & Trouble* published. Father, Willie Lee Walker, dies. Places marker at grave of Zora Neale Hurston.

1974 Moves to New York City. Becomes editor at *Ms.* magazine. *Langston Hughes: American Poet* published.

1976 Divorces Mel Leventhal. *Meridian* published.

1978 Moves to San Francisco, California; embraces the pastoral landscape of Mendocino County.

1979 *Goodnight, Willie Lee, I'll See You in the Morning* and *I Love Myself When I Am Laughing . . . and Then Again When I Am Looking Mean and Impressive* published.

1981 *You Can't Keep a Good Woman Down* published.

1982 *The Color Purple* published.

1983 Pulitzer Prize awarded for *The Color Purple*. *In Search of Our Mothers' Gardens* published.

1984 Launches Wild Trees Press.
Horses Make a Landscape Look More Beautiful published.

1985 Release of film version of *The Color Purple*.

1986 Attends Eatonton premiere of *The Color Purple*. Nominated for eleven Oscars, the film does not receive a single award.

1988 *To Hell with Dying* and *Living by the Word* published.

1989 *The Temple of My Familiar* published.

1991 *Finding the Green Stone* and collected poems *Her Blue Body Everything We Know* published.

1992 *Possessing the Secret of Joy* published.

1993 *Warrior Marks* (film/companion book) released. Mother, Minnie Lou Walker, dies.

1994 *Alice Walker: The Complete Stories* published. Changes name to Alice Tallulah-Kate Walker.

1996 *The Same River Twice* published. Brother William (Bill) Walker dies.

1997 *Anything We Love Can Be Saved* published. Alice Walker Literary Society chartered at Spelman College.

1998 *By the Light of My Father's Smile* published.

2000 *The Way Forward Is with a Broken Heart* published.

2001 *Sent by Earth* published.

2002 Brother James (Jimmy) Walker dies.

2003 *Absolute Trust in the Goodness of the Earth* and *A Poem Traveled down My Arm* published.

2004 *Now Is the Time to Open Your Heart* published. Broadway-bound musical production of *The Color Purple* premieres in Atlanta. Brother Curtis Walker dies.

Publications List

Once; Poems (1968)

The Third Life of Grange Copeland (1970)

In Love & Trouble: Stories of Black Women (1973)

Revolutionary Petunias & Other Poems (1973)

Langston Hughes, American Poet (1974 and 2002)

Meridian (1976)

Good Night, Willie Lee, I'll See You in the Morning: Poems (1979)

I Love Myself When I Am Laughing . . . and Then Again When I Am Looking Mean and Impressive: A Zora Neale Hurston Reader (editor) (1979)

You Can't Keep a Good Woman Down: Stories (1981)

The Color Purple: A Novel (1982)

In Search of Our Mothers' Gardens: Womanist Prose (1983)

Horses Make a Landscape Look More Beautiful: Poems (1984)

Living by the Word: Selected Writings, 1973–1987 (1988)

To Hell with Dying (1988)

The Temple of My Familiar (1989)

Finding the Green Stone (1991)

Her Blue Body Everything We Know: Earthling Poems, 1965–1990 Complete (1991*)*

Possessing the Secret of Joy (1992*)*

Warrior Marks: Female Genital Mutilation and the Sexual Blinding of Women (with Pratibha Parmar) (1993)

Alice Walker: The Complete Stories (1994)

The Same River Twice: Honoring the Difficult: A Meditation on Life, Spirit, Art, and the Making of the Film, The Color Purple, Ten Years Later (1996)

Anything We Love Can Be Saved: A Writer's Activism (1997)

By the Light of My Father's Smile: A Novel (1998)

The Way Forward Is with a Broken Heart (2000)

*Sent by Earth: A Message from the Grandmother Spirit (*after the attacks on the World Trade Center and Pentagon*)* (2001)

Absolute Trust in the Goodness of the Earth: New Poems (2003)

A Poem Traveled down My Arm: Poems & Drawings (2003)

Now Is the Time to Open Your Heart: A Novel (2004)

Wild Trees Press, 1984-1988
Publisher, Alice Walker
Navarro, California

A Piece of Mine (1984) by J. California Cooper

Escape from Billy's Bar-B-Que (1985) by JoAnne Brasil

Ready from Within: Septima Clark and the Civil Rights Movement (1986), edited by Cynthia Stokes Brown

Condor and Hummingbird (1986) by Charlotte Méndez

As Wonderful as All That?: Henry Crowder's Memoir of His Affair with Nancy Cunard 1928–1935 (1987) by Henry Crowder (with Hugo Speck)

The Spirit Journey: Stories and Paintings of Bali (1988) by Madi Kertonegoro

Acknowledgments

"I do my work and I try not to blunder."
—Toni Cade Bambara

When I began this project nearly a decade ago, I knew that the task would not be completed alone. Still, I've been humbled and amazed by the degree to which people extended themselves during the course of my labor. It's a testament to the life and legacy of Alice Walker that nearly everyone I contacted was eager to assist. My sincere thanks to all.

From its inception, this work has been in the embrace of Mills College in Oakland, California. I thank: Janet L. Holmgren, president of Mills College; Elizabeth Potter, professor of women's studies; Women's Studies program assistant Lynne Jerome; and Mary Enos of the Mills Mail Center. For expert and unfailing support, I am indebted to the staff of the F. W. Olin Library at Mills, *especially* Carol Jarvis.

I am also grateful for the research assistance of Mills graduates Jennifer Hoofard, Robin Mitchell, and Tammy Sanders. Thanks to Patricia E. Mullan at the Berkeley Public Library, as well as to the staff at the Howard University Library; the Library of Congress; the Mississippi Department of Archives and History; the New York Public Library; the Schomburg Center for Research in Black

Culture, New York City; and the Stanford University Library. I am indebted to the following individuals and institutions for their support: Andrew Cassel, the *Philadelphia Inquirer*; Mike Gray, the *Baltimore Sun*; Renee Michael, the *New York Times*; Brenda Payton, the *Oakland Tribune*; Kathleen Rhodes, the *San Francisco Chronicle*; and Sheila Rule, the *New York Times*.

This book is graced with the superb transcription and research skills of Amelia K. Smith. Thanks to Laura Merlo and Mary N. Babcock for excellent copyediting. For much appreciated artistry, I thank: Allan Bealy, Gina Gayle, Phiz Mezey, Sue Sellars, Jean Weisinger, and Kevin Woodson.

For sustaining love, friendship, wisdom, hospitality, and culinary support, I thank: Judith Barrington, Gerarda and John Bealy, Helen Berggruen, Candace Coughlin, Nikky Finney, Leah Garchik, Jane Gottesman, Catherine Gund, Ruth Gundle, Melanie Hope, Elaine Lee, Ursula K. Le Guin, Wendy Levy, Carolyn Lochhead, Catherine A. S. Lyons, Holly Morris, Sean Reynolds, Moira Roth, Kathy Simas, Jerry Thompson, Mona Vold, Rosalie Walls, Don Weise, Angelo L. White Sr., Phyllis Denise White, and, especially, my council sisters.

I want to acknowledge the extraordinary kindnesses of the extended Jadene Lim/Darry Louie family (especially daughter Daryl Anais Toy), as well as that of Larry Bensky, Lisa Brock, Dr. Greta F. Clarke, Joyce Engleson, John Ferrone, Daphne Muse, Adrienne Rich, William Rukeyser, Frankie Walton White, and Yumiko Yanagisawa. Special thanks to Mary Anne Adams, who volunteered to be my personal guide in Mississippi; also to Carol Christiansen, Susan Ito, Judi Kincaid, Gilbey Strub, Wendy Weil, Johnny Carson Productions, Vanguard Public Foundation, Women Make Movies, and John Rockwell of the Norman Rockwell Family Agency.

Most sincere gratitude for the bigheartedness of Julie Dash, Catherine Deeter, Ani DiFranco, Whoopi Goldberg, Quincy Jones, Toni Morrison, Yoko Ono, Fran Ravel, Oprah Winfrey, and Howard Zinn. A sisterly salute to Brian Lanker for his exquisite cover portrait of Alice.

As for Gloria Steinem: Let the church say, *"Amen!"*

Special thanks to Joan Miura for steadfast integrity, professionalism, humor, and love.

Honoring those—now ancestors—who encouraged my efforts, I pay tribute to the memory of Gwendolyn Brooks, Barbara Christian, John Henrik Clarke, Faith Gabelnick, Calvin Hernton, June Jordan, Mary Lou Lee, Peter S. Prescott, Helen Sonthoff, Bill Walker, Curtis Walker, Jimmy Walker, Michael Walker, and Margaret Walker.

For much appreciated writing residencies, I am grateful to Hedgebrook Cottages for Women, the Mesa Refuge, and Soapstone Writing Retreat for Women. Thanks to Helen LaKelly Hunt and the Sister Fund in New York.

This work has benefited from the support of several contemporary black women biographers who've journeyed with me on this path: Valerie Boyd, A'Lelia Bundles, and Alexis DeVeaux. For her unparalleled scholarship, righteousness, and unsparing humor, I give all praises to Chana Kai Lee, author of *For Freedom's Sake*, a stirring biography of Fannie Lou Hamer.

I thank Jill Bialosky, executive editor and vice president at W. W. Norton, for her patience and understanding of the higher calling that this work represented to me. I am most appreciative of the cheerful support of her editorial assistants (past and present), Evan Carver, Deirdre O'Dwyer, and Sarah Moriarty. Thanks also to Norton publicist Winfrida Mbewe and all the production staff.

A toast to Jane Rule in British Columbia, Canada, for a rigorous reading of the manuscript and an activist life that inspires.

I am deeply grateful for the candor and affection of: Robert Allen, Bobby Walker, Denise Walker, Fred Walker, Gaynell Joyner-Walker, Mamie Walker, Melvyn Leventhal, and Rebecca Leventhal Walker.

This book is infused with the love and devotion of Ruth Walker Hood, who *never faltered*. I am indebted to the enduring spirits of Minnie Lou and Willie Lee Walker.

I am honored to be represented by Faith Hampton Childs, whose distinguished New York literary agency bears her name. The consummate professional, Faith attended to every aspect of this project with her trademark diligence, intelligence, and flair. Thank you.

For poetry, passion, laughter, adventure, swing dancing, Ping Pong, computer genius, and levelheadedness (when most needed), I thank my outrageous fortune, Joanne Bealy.

With supreme trust, patience, optimism, and love, Alice Walker gave me free and unfettered access to her life. The refrain from an old gospel song comes to mind: "You didn't have to do what you did, but you did it, anyhow." Eternal blessings.

I lay claim to all blunders and thank the ancestors for every lesson learned.

Source Notes

Unless otherwise noted, quotes from Alice Walker are drawn from in-person, telephone, letter, and electronic exchanges between Evelyn C. White (ECW) and Alice Walker (AW), during the period 1995 to 2003.

First brought to my attention by poet Lucinda Roy, the quote "purple is black blooming" is a common variation of a line in *Jubilate Agno (Rejoice in the Lamb)* by eighteenth-century British poet Christopher Smart.

Prologue: In Service

xiii   Confiding that whenever: Alice would not be apprised of the incident until after her speech, but a woman did collapse during her remarks at the college event.

Chapter 1: Georgia, the Whole Day Through

The account in this chapter of the circumstances relating to Alice Walker's eye injury is drawn primarily from ECW interviews with William (Bill) and James (Jimmy) Walker conducted in Dorchester, MA, on April 6, 1995.

5   "England will grow rich": Webb Garrison, *Oglethorpe's Folly: The Birth of Georgia* (Lakemont, GA: Copple House Books,

1982), p. 53. Subsequent quotes about Oglethorpe and Georgia are from this source.

7   On a cool, crisp: ECW interview with Ruth Walker Hood, Atlanta, GA, September 28, 1995.

Chapter 2: Babies and Stumps

The reflections on Alice's birth are drawn primarily from ECW interviews with Ruth Walker Hood conducted in Atlanta, GA, September–October 1995.

9   "Few blacks spent": AW, "Choosing to Stay at Home," in *In Search of Our Mothers' Gardens: Womanist Prose* (New York: Harcourt, 1983), p. 162.

10   "White people": ECW interview with Lucy Montgomery, Chicago, IL, April 1997.

10   "I was completely unaware": Douglas Martin, "Emily W. Reed, 89, Librarian in '59 Alabama Racial Dispute," *New York Times,* May 29, 2000, p. 17.

12   "These colorful individuals": Gary Goldschneider and Joost Elffers, *The Secret Language of Birthdays* (New York: Penguin Studio, 1994), p. 730.

13   "Mr. Willie Lee": ECW interview with Birda Reynolds, Eatonton, GA, September 30, 1995. Subsequent quotes from Reynolds in this chapter are from this interview.

13   "Three Dollars Cash": AW, *Revolutionary Petunias & Other Poems* (New York: Harcourt, 1973), p. 6.

15   Alice's success: Donald L. Grant, *The Way It Was in the South: The Black Experience in Georgia* (New York: Birch Lane Press, 1993), p. 233.

Chapter 3: Roots

Information on Alice's forebears is based on cemetery records and ECW interviews with Ruth Walker Hood and Bill Walker, 1995.

17   "Running in and out": Alice Walker bio. Random House Press Packet, September 1998.

22   "I grew up believing": "Minnie Grant Walker," *San Francisco Chronicle*, September 15, 1993, p. A22.

Chapter 4: "Shift for Self"

Information in this chapter is based on ECW interviews with Ruth Walker Hood and Bill Walker, 1995.

24   "Applications are not": John A. Garrity and Peter Gay,

eds., *The Columbia History of the World* (New York: Harper & Row, 1972) p. 1012.

25　Between 1890 and 1940: Kenneth Coleman, ed., *A History of Georgia* (Athens: University of Georgia Press, 1977), p. 286.

25　"If it requires": *The New Georgia Guide* (Athens: University of Georgia Press, 1996), p. 35. See also Laura Wexler, *Fire in a Canebrake: The Last Mass Lynching in America* (New York: Scribner, 2003).

25　"How to God": William Faulkner, *Go Down, Moses* (New York: Library of America Literary Classics, 1994), p. 46.

26　The Klan re-emerged: Coleman, *History of Georgia*, p. 292.

26　Woodrow Wilson: Wilson, after viewing *The Birth of a Nation*, famously remarked that the film was "like writing history with lightning and my only regret is that it is all so terribly true." See TurnerClassicMovies.com.

28　"She automatically raised": AW, "Saving the Life That Is Your Own," in *In Search*, pp. 9–10.

Chapter 5: Booker T.

Information in this chapter is based on ECW interviews with Bill Walker in Dorchester, MA, in 1995 and with Doris Reid in Decatur, GA, in 1995.

Chapter 6: "I Been Cryin' . . ."

Information in this chapter is based on ECW interviews with Doris Reid, Bill Walker, Curtis Walker, and Ruth Walker Hood, 1995.

35　"I can see it": ECW phone interview with Bobby Walker, January 16, 1996.

35　"I was given": Religious & Spiritualities Forum, 1998, www.Talkcity.com/religious/daily. Accessed April 7, 1998.

36　"It seemed": AW, "The Flowers," in *In Love & Trouble: Stories of Black Women* (New York: Harcourt, 1973), p. 119.

38　"Eyes are sympathetic": See AW, "Beauty: When the Other Dancer Is the Self," in *In Search*, p. 384.

38　"Now when I stare": Ibid.

Chapter 7: Knights in Shining Armor

Information in this chapter is based on ECW interviews with Bill Walker and Ruth Walker Hood, 1995.

42　"Remember?": AW, *Horses Make a Landscape Look More*

Beautiful: Poems (New York: Harcourt, 1984), p. 1.

42 "In a dark time": Theodore Roethke, *The Collected Poems* (New York: Doubleday, 1966), p. 239.

42 "solitary, lonely": AW, "From an Interview," in *In Search*, p. 244.

42 "I daydreamed": AW, as quoted in John O'Brien, ed., *Interviews with Black Writers* (New York: Liveright, 1973), p. 186.

43 "While we never": ECW phone interview with Trellie Jeffers, February 4, 1998.

45 Medical records: Dept. of Medical Records, Massachusetts General Hospital, Boston, MA.

47 "What I remember": ECW interview with Morriss Henry, MD, Fayetteville, AR, October 13, 1995.

Chapter 8: A Long Walk

Information in this chapter is based on ECW interviews with Bill Walker and Doris Reid, 1995.

51 "How Poems Are Made": AW, *Horses Make a Landscape*, p. 17.

52 "Our parents": ECW phone interview with Porter Sanford III, October 10, 1995.

53 "Eagle Rock": AW, *Revolutionary Petunias*, p. 20.

53 "Alice never accepted": ECW phone interview with Bobby Baines, January 25, 1996.

54 "I'm tired": *Black Collegian*, February 1997, p. 156. For a lyrical incantation on events relating to the Montgomery bus boycott, see the title sequence in Rita Dove, *On the Bus with Rosa Parks* (New York: Norton, 1999).

Chapter 9: Order My Steps

56 "gave away": ECW interview with Ruth Walker Hood, Atlanta, GA, September 23, 1995.

58 "the impact of": ECW interview with Mamie Walker, Atlanta, GA, September 29, 1995.

58 "I could go": Mary Helen Washington, "Alice Walker: Her Mother's Gifts," *Ms.*, June 1982, p. 38.

60 "He [King] had": AW, "Choice: A Tribute to Martin Luther King, Jr.," in *In Search*, p. 144.

61 "Alice's staging": ECW interview with Doris Reid, Decatur, GA, September 28, 1995.

63 "and the way": AW as quoted in O'Brien, *Interviews*, p. 210.

63   "When I saw the first": ECW phone interview with Mamie Walker, May 1, 2002.

64   "three things she": Mary Helen Washington, "Alice Walker."

64   "A white woman": O'Brien, *Interviews*, p. 194. Also AW, "Choosing to Stay at Home," in *In Search*, p. 163.

Chapter 10: Nobody in Atlanta

A rich overview of the history of Spelman College, leading up to the 1980s, can be found in *Spelman: A Centennial Celebration* (1981) by Beverly Guy-Sheftall and Jo Moore Stewart (available from Spelman College, 350 Spelman Lane, SW, Atlanta, GA 30314).

68   moonshine-drinkin' "crackers": There are multiple theories about the origins of the term *cracker*. According to the *New Georgia Guide*, *cracker* was the appellation given to people of Scots-Irish descent who enjoyed a "mutually disdainful relationship with their Anglican detractors." The term is also believed to be derived from the "whip-cracking" of herders who drove their livestock through antebellum Georgia and Florida. Among blacks, the term came to denote poor whites (i.e., "white trash") who held fast to plantation ideals.

68   "The manager": Howard Zinn, unpublished paper, 1990, Howard Zinn files.

69   "I remember": Howard Zinn, *You Can't Be Neutral on a Moving Train: A Personal History of Our Times* (Boston: Beacon Press, 1994), p. 44.

69   "Around campus": ECW phone interview with Sadie Allen, circa 1996.

70   "bright-eyed, slim": AW, "Coretta King: Revisited," in *In Search*, p. 146.

71   Davis writes: Angela Y. Davis, *An Autobiography* (New York: Random House, 1974), pp. 123–124.

71   "Compared to some": ECW phone interview with Julius Coles, May 5, 1999.

71   "Finished with lies": Yevgeny Yevtushenko as quoted in Charles Merrill, *The Walled Garden: The Story of a School* (Boston: Rowan Tree Press, 1982), p. 23.

72   "I was so": AW, "My Father's Country Is the Poor," in *In Search*, p. 201.

72   "I thought I'd": ECW interview with Howard Zinn, Berkeley, CA, January 19, 1996.

73   "Parting": Judith Hemschemeyer, trans., *The Complete Poems of Anna Akhmatova* (Boston: Zephyr Press, 1992), p. 401.

73 "I read all": O'Brien, *Interviews*, p. 198.

74 "beyond their Friday": ECW phone interview with Constance Nabwire, April 18, 2000.

74 "Fred Astaire": AW letter to Howard Zinn, Fall 1963, Howard Zinn files.

75 "I'd done a year": ECW interview with Robert Allen, Oakland, CA, May 24, 1996.

75 "The feeling I got": ECW interview with David DeMoss, Sharon, MA, November 22, 1996.

76 "As the only": ECW electronic correspondence with Howard Zinn, March 17, 2002.

77 "I don't think": ECW phone interview with Porter Sanford III, October 10, 1995.

Chapter 11: Forbidden Things

78 "We preach freedom": Lerone Bennett Jr., *Before the Mayflower* (New York: Penguin, 1986), pp. 403–404.

79 "Why aren't you": Zinn, *You Can't Be*, pp. 40–41.

79 "To be perfectly": AW letter to Howard Zinn, Howard Zinn personal files.

80 "Well, I must": AW letter to Howard Zinn, Howard Zinn personal files.

80 "Contemplation": Howard Zinn personal files.

80 "clearly disappointed": ECW interview with David DeMoss, Sharon, MA, November 22, 1996. Subsequent quotes from DeMoss are from this interview.

81 "It seemed to me": ECW phone interview with Bobby Walker, April 26, 1999.

82 "I didn't have": ECW interview with Bill Walker, Dorchester, MA, April 6, 1995.

83 "the opportunity": John Hope Franklin, *From Slavery to Freedom* (New York: Knopf, 1980), p. 469.

83 "I Have a Dream": King's speech has rightly been hailed as one of the most stirring orations of the twentieth century. He had delivered variations of the speech prior to the 1963 march on Washington. Gospel singer Mahalia Jackson, also a featured artist at the march that day, had heard King give the speech before. Sitting on the dais and sensing that the civil rights leader needed to "pump up the volume," Jackson reputedly urged the civil rights leader to "tell them about the *dream,* Martin." King then switched gears and went on to deliver his landmark address. See John Lewis, *Walking with the Wind: A Memoir of the Movement* (New York: Simon & Schuster, 1998), p. 225.

83   "Martin King was": AW, "Choosing to Stay at Home," in *In Search*, pp. 159–160.

84   "You are on": Phyllis Rose, *Jazz Cleopatra: Josephine Baker in Her Time* (New York: Doubleday, 1989), p. 242.

Chapter 12: Fit for Myself to Know

85   "When I flew": ECW interview with David DeMoss, Sharon, MA, November 12, 1996. Subsequent quotes from DeMoss in this chapter are from this interview.

86   "I'm pinned": AW letter to Howard Zinn, Howard Zinn personal files.

86   "I feel sort of lost": AW letter to Howard Zinn, Howard Zinn personal files.

86   "Dear Editor": Howard Zinn personal files.

88   "It was heartening": ECW electronic correspondence with Howard Zinn, March 17, 2002.

88   "Alice, Alice": Howard Zinn personal files.

88   "Folks were truly": ECW interview with Beverly Guy-Sheftall, Palo Alto, CA, June 24, 1998.

88   "the most distinguished member": ECW phone interview with Staughton Lynd, August 7, 1996.

89   "My one concern": Howard Zinn personal files.

89   "The crooked dogwood": Howard Zinn personal files.

90   "Here's one we": Charles Merrill letter to ECW, April 23, 1996.

91   "memorialization of my arrogance": Charles Merrill letter to ECW, November 28, 1999.

91   "unwanted though": AW letter to Howard Zinn, Fall 1963, Howard Zinn personal files.

91   "And so I had": AW, "Choosing to Stay at Home," in *In Search*, p. 159.

92   "There is nothing": Howard Zinn personal files.

92   In yet another: Howard Zinn personal files.

93   "She was a little": ECW phone interview with Marilyn Pryce Hoytt, May 5, 1999.

93   "Chic Freedom's Reflection": AW, *Once: Poems* (New York: Harcourt, 1968), p. 37.

94   "Compulsory Chapel": Ibid., p. 47.

95   "I owe the world": Guy-Sheftall, *Spelman: A Centennial Celebration*, p. 97.

Chapter 13: Make Yourself Useful

99   "break down the": Helen Lynd, *Field Work in College Education* (New York: Columbia University Press, 1945), pp. vii–viii.

99   "Nobody in the family": ECW phone interview with Ruth Walker Hood, April 29, 2002.

100   "educated human": Sarah Lawrence College catalogue, circa 1996.

100   "She was the first": AW, "A Talk: Convocation 1972," in *In Search*, p. 38.

102   "There was a dress": ECW interview with Samuel Seigle, Bronxville, NY, July 29, 1996.

102   "If I hadn't": ECW interview with Helen Berggruen, Oakland, CA, March 1, 1998.

104   "What's different": ECW interview with Jane Cooper, New York, NY, April 24, 1995.

105   "phallic joke": Pauline Kael, *For Keeps: Thirty Years at the Movies* (New York: Dutton, 1994), p. 713.

105   "The Suicide": AW personal archives.

106   "[They] are well": O'Brien, *Interviews*, p. 193.

107   Interestingly, a one-act: LeRoi Jones and Larry Neal, eds., *Black Fire* (New York: William Morrow, 1968), p. 631.

107   "technical perfection": "The Suicide," AW personal files.

107   "Nothing Has Been": Jane Cooper, *Scaffolding* (Gardiner, ME: Tilbury House Publishers, 1993), p. 19.

107   "I'd rather be": Muriel Rukeyser, "Not To Be Printed, Not To Be Said, Not To Be Thought," in *The Collected Poems of Muriel Rukeyser* (New York: McGraw-Hill, 1978), p. 558.

Chapter 14: Reclaimed

Information in this chapter is based on ECW interview with David DeMoss in Sharon, MA, November 22, 1996.

109   "Pied Beauty": Robert Bridges, ed., *Poems of Gerard Manley Hopkins* (London: Oxford University Press, 1930), p. 30.

109   "Many times": Sarah Lawrence College faculty report for AW, June 10, 1964, AW personal archives.

109   "Muriel whom I": ECW interview with Grace Paley, Eugene, OR, June 23, 1995.

111   "The pill had just become available": It was not until 1970 that the Food and Drug Administration (FDA) required the first package insert with information about how to correctly use oral contraceptive pills.

113 "with lots of": ECW interview with Diana Young, Oakland, CA, December 19, 1996.

114 "stopped the killing": For a comprehensive overview of the pro-choice movement, see Faye Wattleton, *Life on the Line* (New York: Random House, 1996). See also the excellent documentaries *Jane: An Abortion Service*, by Kate Kirtz and Nell Lundy (Chicago: Juicy Productions, Inc. 1995), and *Leona's Sister Gerri*, by Jane Gillooly (Ho-Ho-Kus, NJ: New Day Films, 1994). In *Love with the Proper Stranger* (1963), Natalie Wood stars as the "good Italian girl" who finds herself pregnant after a one-night stand with costar Steve McQueen. The perils of abortion before the *Roe v. Wade* court decision are boldly rendered in this surprisingly political (for the era) Hollywood film.

114 "I felt there": O'Brien, *Interview*, p. 187.

114 "Suicide": AW, *Once*, p. 74.

115 "I pleaded with Alice": ECW phone interview with Ruth Walker Hood, April 21, 1997.

116 "I realized": AW, as quoted in O'Brien, *Interviews*, p. 188.

116 another classmate: ECW phone interview with Brooke Newman, December 27, 1999.

117 "We were just": ECW interview with Carole Darden, New York, NY, October 25, 1995.

118 "One day in": AW, "Once," in *Once*, p. 25.

119 "The Old Artist": AW, *Living by the Word: Selected Writings, 1973–1987* (New York: Harcourt, 1988), p. 339.

120 "After the ceremony": ECW phone interview with Julius Coles, May 5, 1999.

Chapter 15: New York

Information in this chapter is based on ECW interview with Diana Young, Oakland, CA, December 19, 1996.

121 "the borderland where": Kathleen Thompson and Hilary MacAustin, eds., *The Face of Our Past: Images of Black Women from Colonial America to the Present* (Bloomington: Indiana University Press, 1999), p. 177.

122 "tune in, turn on": Todd Gitlin, *The Sixties: Years of Hope, Days of Rage* (New York: Bantam, 1987), p. 206.

125 "She was jamming": ECW interview with Garland Jeffreys, New York, NY, October 22, 1997.

125 "extremely handsome": ECW phone interview with Joyce Engleson, March 4, 1996.

126 "I wouldn't be": ECW interview with Jan Heller Levi, New York, NY, June 13, 1999.

127 "The conventional wisdom": ECW phone interview with Mitch Douglas, September 28, 1999.

128 "kindred spirits": ECW interview with Jack Heyman, Oakland, CA., May 28, 1998.

129 "rooted kindredness": ECW interview with Robert Allen, Oakland, CA, April 24, 1996.

129 "I have been": AW letter to Muriel Rukeyser, June 4, 1966, AW personal files.

Chapter 16: Live or Die

133 "Niggers, Alligators": Gitlin, *Sixties*, p. 152.

134 "Mississippi was": ECW interview with Ruth Walker Hood, Atlanta, GA, October 3, 1995.

135 "I couldn't just": ECW interview with Mel Leventhal, New York, NY, October 26, 1995.

Chapter 17: In a Biblical Way

141 "Alice and I": ECW interview with Mel Leventhal, New York, NY, October 26, 1995.

142 "At about this time": Biographical Sketch, AW personal files.

145 "While Love Is Unfashionable": AW, *Revolutionary Petunias*, p. 68.

Chapter 18: Tulips

147 Johnnie Mae Chappell: "Martyr honored with Memorial Dedication," *SPLC Report*, January 2001 (published by Southern Poverty Law Center, 400 Washington Avenue, Montgomery, AL 36104; www.splcenter.org). The SPLC is also the site of the Civil Rights Memorial Plaza. Designed by the famed Vietnam Veterans Memorial architect-artist Maya Lin, the plaza honors the "ordinary people" who were slain during the civil rights movement.

148 "I was a nervous": ECW interview with Ruth Walker Hood, Atlanta, GA, September 23, 1995. All subsequent quotes from Hood in this chapter are from this interview.

148 "Alice introduced me": ECW interview with Mel Leventhal, New York, NY, October 26, 1995. All subsequent quotes from Leventhal in this chapter are from this interview.

151 "It was clear": ECW interview with Diana Young, Oakland, CA, December 19, 1996.

153 *What will happen*: James Baldwin, "The Fire Next Time,"

in *The Price of the Ticket* (New York: St. Martin's Press, 1985), p. 333.

153 Dr. King: "Letter from Birmingham City Jail (1963)," in James M. Washington, ed., *A Testament of Hope: The Essential Writings and Speeches of Martin Luther King, Jr.* (New York: HarperCollins, 1986), p. 289.

Chapter 19: Beyond Daily Bread

155 marriages between blacks: Interracial Married Couples: 1960 to Present, U.S. Bureau of the Census, Internet release date January 7, 1999, www.census.gov/population/socdemo/msla/tabms3 .txt.

156 "I didn't have": ECW phone interview with Bobby Walker, April 26, 1999.

156 "one of the sweetest": ECW interview with Carole Darden, New York, NY, October 25, 1995.

156 "What distinguished Mel": ECW phone interview with Marian Wright Edelman, March 20, 2000.

157 "steady on the television": ECW interview with James Graves, Clinton, MS, July 20, 1998.

157 "It's an absolute": Mississippi Department of Archives & History, Newsfilm Collection, Archives and Library Division, P.O. Box 571, Jackson, MS 39205.

158 "Don't breathe": AW letter to Muriel Rukeyser, August 8, 1967, AW personal files.

158 "the college butted": AW personal files.

159 "The stories were": AW, "Recording the Seasons," in *In Search*, p. 224.

Chapter 20: That *Alice?*

161 "The white American": ECW phone interview with Constance Nabwire, April 18, 2000.

161 "in blue suits": AW, as quoted in O'Brien, *Interviews*, p. 195.

161 Head Start teachers: For a discussion of the Mississippi battles over the education of black children during the civil rights era, see Constance Curry, *Silver Rights* (Chapel Hill: Algonquin Books, 1995).

162 "These were women": AW, " 'But Yet and Still the Cotton Gin Kept on Working . . . ,' " in *In Search*, pp. 27–28.

163 "In 1967, Monica": Hiram Haydn, *Words & Faces* (New York: Harcourt, 1974), pp. 242–243.

164   *Once* sold for $4.50: Signed first editions of the poetry volume would later command up to $1,800.

165   "The week after": AW, "Coretta King: Revisited," in *In Search*, p. 148.

165   "It was tough": ECW electronic correspondence with Mel Leventhal, April 22, 2000.

165   "Alice was a quiet": ECW interview with Carolyn Parker, Jackson, MS, July 21, 1998.

166   "The New York Times, For Some Reason": An excerpt of the poem reads as follows: "the new york times, never one to relay the facts exactly straight / The other day reported that senator kennedy / was a great success / in vietnam. . . . the senator's charm wore thin." *Activist*, March 1966, p. 5 (Activist Publishing Company, 27½ W. College, Oberlin, OH 44074).

167   "I am again": Lisel Mueller, "Versions of Reality," *Poetry*, February 1971, p. 328.

167   "At last": DeWitt Beall, *Chicago Daily News*, back jacket copy on *Revolutionary Petunias*, 1973.

167   "evoke a living": *Publisher's Weekly*, back jacket copy on *Revolutionary Petunias*, 1973.

168   "As a first": Langston Hughes, ed., *The Best Short Stories by Negro Writers* (Boston: Little, Brown, 1967), p. xii.

168   "Langston had nabbed Alice": ECW phone interview with John Henrik Clarke, 1998.

169   Hughes had titled: Langston Hughes, *Black Misery* (New York: Paul S. Eriksson, 1969).

169   Nor that lacking: For a masterful biography of Langston Hughes, see Arnold Rampersad, *The Life of Langston Hughes, Volume I: 1902–1941, I, Too, Sing America* (Oxford: Oxford University Press, 1986), and *Volume II: I Dream a World* (Oxford University Press, 1988).

169   "About two weeks": AW, *Langston Hughes: American Poet* (New York: Crowell, 1974) p. 34. Reissued in 2002 (New York: HarperCollins), with illustrations by Catherine Deeter.

Chapter 21: Nude

170   "all your titles": AW letter to Muriel Rukeyser, November 10, 1967, AW personal files.

170   "Muriel Rukeyser told me": ECW interview with Jerry Ward Jr., Orlando, FL, January 30, 1999.

171   "the mother of everyone": Jan Heller Levi, *A Muriel Rukeyser Reader* (New York: Norton, 1994), p. xvii.

171   "She talked about": Molly McQuade, ed., *By Herself:*

Women Reclaim Poetry (St. Paul: Graywolf Press, 2000), p. 345.

172   "From a Play": Rukeyser, *Collected Poems*, p. 518.

172   "a run-over shoe": AW, "Afterword," in *The Third Life of Grange Copeland* (New York: Pocket Books, 1988), p. 343.

172   "I had to look at": AW, *Third Life*, pp. 342, 344.

173   "As young men": David Bradley, "Alice Walker: Telling the Black Woman's Story," *New York Times Magazine*, January 8, 1984, p. 36.

173   "The way Daddy": ECW interview with Ruth Walker Hood, Atlanta, GA, September 23, 1995.

173   "My father picked up a lot": AW interview with Larry Bensky, Philo, CA, April 4, 1992, Larry Bensky personal files.

173   "The Democratic Order": AW, *Once*, p. 43.

174   "I arrived in Jackson": AW, "Choosing to Stay at Home," in *In Search*, p. 164.

175   "I met with the president": ECW phone interview with Margaret Walker, August 20, 1996.

175   "*come with a blast*": Langston Hughes, "When Sue Wears Red," in *Selected Poems* (New York: Vintage Books, 1974), p. 68.

175   "praying their prayers": Margaret Walker, "For My People," as quoted in Henry Louis Gates Jr. and Nellie Y. McKay, eds., *The Norton Anthology of African American Literature* (New York: Norton, 1997), p. 1572.

175   " 'Oh these older poets!' ": AW, "The Unglamorous but Worthwhile Duties of the Black Revolutionary Artist," in *In Search*, p. 134.

176   "entered the court": Gates and McKay, *Norton Anthology*, p. 1872.

176   "nigger can you kill": Nikki Giovanni, "The True Import of Present Dialogue, Black vs. Negro," in *Black Feeling, Black Talk, Black Judgement* (New York: William Morrow, 1970), p. 19.

177   "I don't want": Juan Williams, *Eyes on the Prize: America's Civil Rights Years, 1954–1965* (New York: Penguin Books, 1987), p. 244.

177   "The Girl Who Died": AW, *Revolutionary Petunias*, p. 45.

Chapter 22: Watered with Blood

180   In 2003: See Charles Johnson, "Essie Mae Williams (née Thurmond)," *Wall Street Journal*, December 23, 2003.

181   "They put that": ECW interview with Mel Leventhal, New York, NY, October 26, 1995.

182   "No one could believe": AW, *The Way Forward Is with a Broken Heart* (New York: Ballantine, 2000), p. 34.

184 "waiting for nurses": James Campbell, *Talking at the Gates: A Life of James Baldwin* (New York: Viking, 1991), p. 195.

184 "It finally dawned on me": AW, *My Life as Myself*, audiotape (Boulder, CO: Sounds True Audio Tape, 1995).

184 "It's very intimidating": Newspaper clipping, circa 1970, Ruth Walker Hood personal files.

Chapter 23: "Conformity is not Community"

188 "The novel, compacting": Victor A. Kramer, "Review of the Third Life," *Library Journal*, July 1970.

188 "Most poignant": Kay Bourne, "Alice Walker's First Novel Hits Home," *Bay State Banner*, August 13, 1970, p. 13.

188 "Black, but no polemics": Joseph Haas, "Black, but No Polemics," *Chicago Sun-Times*, undated, Ruth Walker Hood personal files.

188 "occasionally ponderous": Paul Theroux, "A Glimpse of Freedom," *Washington Post Book World*, September 13, 1970, p. 2.

188 Three other novels: The works were *When the Fire Reaches Us* by Barbara Tinker; *Snakes* by Al Young; and *The Beach Umbrella*, a collection of short stories by Cyrus Colter (1910–2002). An intriguing figure in African American letters, Colter was a lawyer who reassessed his life, at age fifty, and began to write. He went on to teach creative writing at Northwestern University.

189 "Can Josephine Hendin": AW personal files.

190 "It is imperative": AW personal files.

191 "It was for her:": AW, "Beyond the Peacock: The Reconstruction of Flannery O'Connor," in *In Search*, p. 52.

192 "My primary objection": AW personal files.

193 "My Daddy": ECW interview with Doris Reid, Decatur, GA, September 29, 1995.

195 "Must I still ask": AW, "The Diary of an African Nun," in *In Love & Trouble*, p. 113.

195 Hairston was among the few: Claudia Tate, ed., "Alice Walker," in *Black Women Writers at Work* (New York: Continuum, 1986), pp. 176–177.

196 "The Black Arts Movement": Larry Neal as quoted in Gates and McKay, *Norton Anthology*, p. 1960.

196 "two-thirds 'hate whitey's guts' ": AW, "Unglamorous but Worthwhile Duties," in *In Search*, p. 137.

197 "Dagger poems": Amiri Baraka, "Black Art," in Gates and McKay, *Norton Anthology*, pp. 1883–1884.

197 "It was the early 1970s": ECW interview with Sonia Sanchez, Oakland, CA, May 20, 1997.

198 "I'd read the novel": ECW interview with Nikki Giovanni, San Francisco, CA, November 8, 1997.

Chapter 24: The Children Grow in Love

199 "There was a huge uproar": ECW interview with June Jordan, Berkeley, CA, March 18, 1996. Subsequent quotes from Jordan in this chapter are from this interview.

199 "Alice and I almost always": Mel Leventhal electronic correspondence with ECW, May 28, 2002.

201 "Mel is the chief engineer": June Jordan, "Mississippi 'Black Home,' A Sweet and Bitter Bluesong," *New York Times Magazine*, October 11, 1970, p. 64.

202 "It was the first time": ECW interview with Clotie Graves, Clinton, MS, July 20, 1998.

203 "Dear Mr. Gibson": AW personal files.

203 Josephine Diaz Martin: Douglas Martin, "Josephine Martin, Healer of Rights Workers, Dues at 84," *New York Times*, July 23, 2000, p. 40.

205 "The dead": June Jordan, "Mississippi 'Black Home,' " *New York Times Magazine*, October 11, 1970, p. 64.

205 "The dead are remembered": In a memorial tribute to June Jordan, Alice Walker funded, in 2004, a poetry prize in her honor. Awards totaling $1,750 are presented annually, by Alice, to student poets in Oakland, California.

Chapter 25: A Kindred Lover of Beauty

206 "a college of books": AW, "The Unglamorous But Worthwhile Duties," in *In Search*, p. 131.

207 "These writers do not seem": O'Brien, *Interviews*, p. 200.

207 "I can't remember": AW, *Way Forward*, p. 201.

207 "It seemed like": ECW interview with Clotie Graves, Clinton, MS, July 20, 1998. Subsequent quotes from Graves in this chapter are from this interview.

208 "I want to explore": AW Radcliffe/Bunting Institute application, Bunting Institute files, Cambridge, MA.

209 "Alice was unhappy": ECW interview with Mel Leventhal, New York, NY, October 26, 1995.

209 "If Mel had sat": ECW interview with James Graves, Clinton, MS, July 20, 1998.

209 "I was really looking forward": ECW interview with

Henri Norris, San Francisco, CA, February 27, 1999.

210 "What is the value": Gates and McKay, *Norton Anthology*, p. 1518.

210 "What is striking": *Pound*, 1970 (Omega African Heritage Library Collection, Omega Boys Club, P.O. Box 884463, San Francisco, CA 94188).

211 *Atonement and Release*: The novel would also bear the working title *The Girl Who Forgave Everyone* before publication as *Meridian* (1976).

212 "Poems link, separate": Darwin T. Turner, "Introduction," in Jean Toomer, *Cane* (New York: Liveright, 1975 edition), p. xxii.

213 "She is stout": AW, "Lulls," in *In Search*, p. 195.

214 "By the time Rebecca": AW, "*One* Child of One's Own," in *In Search*, p. 369.

214 "Now I wanted a book": Toomer, *Cane* (1975 edition), p. xvi.

Chapter 26: A Kiss on Both Sides

217 "If you really examine": ECW interview with hattie gossett, Langley, WA, August 6, 1997.

217 "Alice Walker is one of the strongest": Jane Cooper reference letter, October 26, 1970, AW Radcliffe/Bunting Institute application, Bunting Institute files, Cambridge, MA.

218 assassination of Malcolm X: Robert Allen, "Malcolm X: 2/21/65," *Village Voice*, February 17, 1966, p. 3.

218 "as far as": ECW interview with Robert Allen, Oakland, CA, April 24, 1996.

218 "Mel wants to remain": AW letter to Diana Young, May 3, 1971, Diana Young personal files.

219 "[I] hate it": AW, "*One* Child," in *In Search*, p. 370.

220 protagonist Phoenix Jackson: Eudora Welty, "A Worn Path," in *Eudora Welty Stories, Essays, & Memoir* (New York: Library of America, 1998), p. 171.

220 In Welty's hands: For an impressive screen adaptation of the Welty story, see *A Worn Path* (1994). The thirty-minute release includes an interview with Welty conducted by Pulitzer Prize–winning playwright Beth Henley. Contact: Bruce R. Schwartz, Worn Path Productions, 5617 Denny Avenue, North Hollywood, CA 91601, Telephone (818) 505-1751.

221 "The more you think about it": Sally Fitzgerald, ed., *Flannery O'Connor: The Habit of Being* (New York: Farrar, Straus & Giroux, 1979), p. 537.

222 "Illness has always been": AW, *One* Child," in *In Search*, p. 370.

222 "As a biology major": ECW phone interview with Yakini Kemp, October 1, 1999. Subsequent quotes from Kemp in this chapter are from this interview.

223 "We now know": AW, "In Search of Our Mothers' Gardens," in *In Search*, p. 237.

223 "Black literature needed": ECW interview with Mary Helen Washington, Silver Spring, MD, March 22, 2000.

224 "Wheatley first had to write": Gates and McKay, *Norton Anthology*, p. 167.

Chapter 27: Love the Questions

225 "During the second year": AW letter to Alice K. Smith (dean of the Radcliffe Institute), January 6, 1971, Bunting Institute files, Cambridge, MA.

226 "I know how difficult": Alice K. Smith letter to AW, May 11, 1972, Bunting Institute files, Cambridge, MA.

226 "After five years": ECW interview with Mel Leventhal, New York, NY, October 26, 1995.

226 "I knew Wendy": ECW interview with June Jordan, Berkeley, CA, March 18, 1996.

228 "I was drawn to Alice": ECW phone interview with Julius Lester, February 19, 1998.

229 *Ms.* took its name: ECW interview with Gloria Steinem, New York, NY, July 18, 1995.

230 Harry Reasoner: Mary Thom, *Inside Ms.* (New York: Henry Holt, 1997), p. 43.

230 "I'd read Alice": ECW interview with Joanne Edgar, New York, NY, October 24, 1997.

231 "Somewhere in growing up": June Goodwin, "Book Briefings," *Christian Science Monitor*, September 19, 1973, p. 11.

233 "Everyday Use": For an excellent screen adaptation of the story, contact: Bruce R. Schwartz, Worn Path Productions.

234 "The Contrary Women of Alice Walker": Barbara Christian, *Black Feminist Criticism* (Elmsford, NY: Pergamon Press, 1985), pp. 33–34.

236 "What especially recommends": Jerry W. Ward, *College Language Association Journal*, September 1973, pp. 127–129.

236 "This is poetry": "Revolutionary Petunias," *Publishers Weekly*, December 18, 1972, p. 39.

236 had deemed "uneven": Susan Beth Pfeffer, "In Love and Trouble," *Library Journal*, August 1973.

236 tempered praise: "Books Noted," *Black World*, September 1973, pp. 51–52.

237   "It is a wonderful book": Jane Cooper letter to AW, October 7, 1973, AW personal files.

238   "Dear Alice Walker": AW, "Anais Nin 1903–1977," *Ms.*, April 1977, p. 46.

Chapter 28: Good Night, Willie Lee

239   "I couldn't understand": ECW interview with Jimmy Walker, Dorchester, MA, April 6, 1995.

240   "I was playing": ECW phone interview with Ruth Walker Hood, April 29, 2002.

241   "Whenever I talk": AW, "Father," in *Living by the Word*, p. 13.

241   "Like bulls, a man": AW, "Brothers and Sisters," in *In Search*, p. 328.

241   "I never wanted to be": AW, "Father," in *Living by the Word*, p. 11.

242   "I couldn't stand it": Gregory Jaynes, "Living by the Word," *Life*, May 1989.

242   "I wrote": Tate, *Black Women Writers at Work*, pp. 186–187.

243   "I am positive": AW, "Father," in *Living by the Word*, p. 9.

243   "I've never forgotten": Ibid., p. 12.

Chapter 29: We Are a People

246   "It . . . never died": AW, "From an Interview," in *In Search*, p. 268.

247   "The Revenge of Hannah Kemhuff": AW, *In Love & Trouble*, p. 60.

247   As Alice notes: AW, "Saving the Life That Is Your Own," in *In Search*, p. 3.

248   "What made me gravitate": ECW interview with Frankie Walton White, Jackson, MS, July 21, 1998.

249   "there is no book more important": AW, "Zora Neale Hurston: A Cautionary Tale and a Partisan View," in *In Search*, p. 86.

249   born January 7, 1891: In her 2003 biography, *Wrapped in Rainbows: The Life of Zora Neale Hurston* (New York: Scribner), Valerie Boyd notes that Hurston, at about age twenty-six, shaved ten years off her life to qualify for free schooling then available in Maryland to all black youths between six and twenty years old. Having successfully passed for a decade younger (Hurston gave

1901 as her birth date), she maintained the façade for the rest of her life.

249 "five lakes": Zora Neale Hurston, *Mules and Men* (Bloomington: Indiana University Press, 1978), p. 6.

250 "Here was this perfect book!": AW, "Zora Neale Hurston," in *In Search*, p. 84.

251 "Reading *Their Eyes*": AW, ed., *I Love Myself When I Am Laughing . . . And Then Again When I Am Looking Mean and Impressive: A Zora Neale Hurston Reader* (New York: Feminist Press, 1979), p. 2.

251 "a well nigh perfect story": Lucille Tompkins, untitled review, *New York Times Book Review*, September 26, 1937.

251 "minstrel technique": Richard Wright, "Between Laughter and Tears," *New Masses,* October 5, 1937.

251 "To me the most impressive": Richard Wright as quoted in Josyane Savigneau, *Carson McCullers: A Life* (Boston: Houghton Mifflin, 2001), p. 66.

252 According to Margaret Walker: Margaret Walker, *Richard Wright: Daemonic Genius* (New York: Amistad, 1988), p. 74.

252 "I have resolved to die": Robert E. Hemenway, *Zora Neale Hurston: A Literary Biography* (Urbana: University of Illinois Press, 1977), p. 322.

252 "[Hemenway] was the first": AW, "Zora Neale Hurston," in *In Search*, pp. 86–87.

253 "there's a circle": AW, "Looking for Zora," in *In Search*, p. 102.

256 "Alice was so encouraging": ECW phone interview with Robert Hemenway, September 12, 1996.

257 "the most widely taught": Henry Louis Gates Jr. and K. A. Appiah, eds., *Zora Neale Hurston: Critical Perspectives Past and Present* (New York: Amistad Press, 1993), p. xii.

257 "In placing the marker": ECW electronic correspondence with Valerie Boyd, January 15, 2001. In her 1983 book, *Frida: A Biography of Frida Kahlo,* art historian Hayden Herrera would help to raise to prominence another woman whose life and legacy, like Hurston's, had been relegated to the shadows.

258 "The novel of Toni": Julius Lester letter to AW, February 17, 1971, AW personal files.

258 "Dear Sir": AW letter to *New York Times Book Review*, December 28, 1973, AW personal files.

259 "Dear Alice Walker": Toni Morrison letter to AW, January 14, 1974, AW personal files.

Chapter 30: Changes

260 "We sat relaxing": AW, "Choosing to Stay at Home," in *In Search*, pp. 165–166.

261 "Go back to Mississippi": Washington, *Testament of Hope*, p. 219.

261 "attacked and murdered": AW, "Recording the Seasons," in *In Search*, p. 225.

261 "It was as if": AW, *Way Forward*, p. 8.

262 "One day Alice": ECW interview with Mel Leventhal, New York, NY, October 26, 1995.

262 "As a child": ECW interview with Rebecca Walker, Oakland, CA, November 10, 2000.

262 "Here it is": ECW interview with Clotie Graves, Clinton, MS, July 20, 1993.

263 "I was surprised": ECW phone interview with Margaret Walker, August 20, 1998.

264 " 'We really want you' ": *Alice Walker*, video (Los Angeles: Lannan Literary Videos, 1989).

265 "These chicks": Carolyn Heilbrun, *The Education of a Woman: The Life of Gloria Steinem* (New York: Dial Press, 1995), p. 268.

265 "I pitched": ECW electronic correspondence with Susan Margolis, June 24, 2002.

265 "I first fell": ECW interview with Gloria Steinem, New York, NY, July 18, 1995.

266 "We bought an old house": AW letter to Jane Cooper, February 6, 1974, Jane Cooper personal files.

Chapter 31: How Rare We Were

267 "I felt strongly": ECW interview with hattie gossett, Langley, WA, August 6, 1997.

268 "The fact that *Essence*": ECW interview with Esther Jackson, New York, NY, June 11, 1999.

269 "I was certainly a fan": ECW interview with Marcia Gillespie, New York, NY, June 11, 1999. Subsequent quotes from Gillespie in this chapter are from this interview.

270 "mix politics with poetry": Adrienne Rich letter to ECW, August 26, 1996.

271 "We together accept": Adrienne Rich acceptance speech, 1974 National Book Award, AW personal files.

272 "Dear Alice": Muriel Rukeyser letter to AW, May 1975, Library of Congress.

273   "Dear Muriel": AW letter to Muriel Rukeyser, May 19, 1975, Library of Congress.

274   "my wishes and love": Muriel Rukeyser letter to AW, undated, Library of Congress.

Chapter 32: We Were a Part of It

276   "No common failure": *Faithless*, videocassette, Ingmar Bergman (screenwriter), Liv Ullman (director), Swedish with English subtitles (Los Angeles, CA: First Look Home Entertainment, 2000).

276   "I thought Alice": ECW interview with John Leggett, San Francisco, CA, April 13, 1996.

278   "I am slowly": AW personal files.

278   "As a white woman": ECW interview with Fanny Howe, Berkeley, CA, February 2, 1997.

278   origins of the tarot: ECW interview with Karen Vogel, Oakland, CA, 2002.

279   "We had mustered": ECW interview with Mel Leventhal, New York, NY, October 26, 1995.

279   "open": ECW interview with Robert Allen, Oakland, CA, May 24, 1996. Subsequent quotes from Allen in this chapter are from this interview.

280   "I never saw": ECW interview with Rebecca Walker, Oakland, CA, November 10, 2000.

281   "I will tend": Hemschemeyer, *The Complete Poems of Anna Akhmatova*, p. 297.

281   "It really did seem": AW, *Way Forward*, p. 24.

Chapter 33: Meridian

285   "The black American": Baldwin, *Price of the Ticket*, p. xiv.

286   "*Meridian . . .* is": Jessica Harris, "An Interview with Alice Walker," *Essence*, July 1976, p. 33.

286   A brilliant tactician: For a superb biography of Ruby Doris Smith Robinson, see Cynthia Griggs Fleming, *Soon We Will Not Cry* (Lanham, MD: Rowman & Littlefield Publishers, 1998).

291   "His face was thrown back": For an incisive discussion of the career of B.B. King, see Bernard Weinraub, "Spinning Blues into Gold, the Rough Way," *New York Times,* March 2, 2003, p. A1.

291   "We are led": AW, Auburn Annual Lecture, Auburn Theological Seminary, New York, NY, April 25, 1995. See also AW, "The Only Reason You Want to Go to Heaven Is You've Been

Driven out of Your Mind," in *Anything We Love Can Be Saved: A Writer's Activism* (New York: Random House, 1997).

291 "I believe": Harris, "An Interview with Alice Walker," p. 33.

292 "I would give": Jean Toomer, "Blue Meridian," in Robert B. Jones and Margery Toomer Latimer, eds., *The Collected Poems of Jean Toomer* (Chapel Hill: University of North Carolina Press, 1988), p. 50.

292 "high-flown language": Greil Marcus, "Limits," *New Yorker*, June 7, 1976, pp. 133–136.

292 "But if *Meridian*": Gordon Burnside, "Books," *Common-weal*, April 29, 1977.

292 "as complicated": Margo Jefferson, "Across the Barricades," *Newsweek*, May 31, 1976, p. 71.

293 "Even with all the permutations": ECW interview with Tammy Sanders, Oakland, CA, 1998.

Chapter 34: Refuge

294 "I got physically ill": ECW interview with source who requested anonymity, New York, NY, October 1997.

295 "P. thinks Lynne": AW personal files.

296 "My parents": ECW interview with Rebecca Walker, Oakland, CA, November 10, 2000.

298 "I remember sitting": AW, "After 20 Years, Meditation Still Conquers Inner Space," *New York Times*, October 23, 2000, p. B1.

299 "I think about us": Toni Morrison, "A Knowing So Deep," in Wendy Martin, ed., *The Beacon Book of Essays by Contemporary American Women* (Boston: Beacon Press, 1996), p. 122.

300 "I never understood": ECW phone interview with Ntozake Shange, October 8, 1999.

300 even a cookbook: See Ntozake Shange, *If I Can Cook, You Know God Can* (Boston: Beacon Press, 1998).

Chapter 35: Correct Relationship

302 "My wife knew": ECW interview with Robert Allen, Oakland, CA, May 24, 1996.

303 "Mirror becomes a razor": Yoko Ono, *Grapefruit* (New York: Simon & Schuster, 1970).

303 "Janie Crawford": AW, *Good Night, Willie Lee, I'll See You in the Morning: Poems* (New York: Dial Press, 1979), p. 18.

304   *Cruelty*: See AW, "Like the Eye of a Horse," *Ms.*, June 1974, pp. 41–42.

304   "The book is so raw": AW letter to Jane Cooper, November 13, 1973, AW personal files.

305   "This bullshit": Frank Lamott Phillips, "Loving Her," *Black World*, September 1975, p. 89.

305   "who is a nice guy": AW letter to Ann Allen Shockley, October 8, 1974, Ann Allen Shockley personal files.

305   "I have had three fights": AW letter to Ann Allen Shockley, March 3, 1975, Ann Allen Shockley personal files.

305   "I was completely unknown": ECW electronic correspondence with Mary Gordon, August 19, 2002.

306   "There was blatant": ECW interview with Gloria Steinem, New York, NY, July 18, 1995.

307   "Well, last night": ECW interview with Diana Young, Oakland, CA, December 19, 1996.

Chapter 36: Country People

309   "the most impressive": Robert Towers, "Good Men Are Hard to Find," *New York Review of Books*, August 12, 1982, pp. 35–36.

310   "Alice had always": ECW interview with Joanne Edgar, New York, NY, October 24, 1997.

310   "They didn't like seeing," AW, "Writing *The Color Purple*," in *In Search*, p. 355.

311   Boontling: Charles C. Adams, *A Wee Deek on Boont Harpin's (A Brief Introduction to Boontling)* (Boonville, CA: Boontlingers Club, 1967).

312   "It's as if": ECW interview with Sue Sellars, Berkeley, CA, March 23, 1999.

312   "dared to create, agitate": Katherine Dieckman, "Photo Synthesist," *Village Voice Literary Supplement*, April–May 1999.

Chapter 37: An Ugly One at That

313   In it Wallace chronicled: See Michele Wallace, *Black Macho and the Myth of the Superwoman* (New York: Warner Books, 1978).

313   comedian Redd Foxx: Ibid., pp. 48–50.

314   "Black men often": Ibid., p. 23.

314   "conspired with": ECW interview with hattie gossett, Langley, WA, August 6, 1997.

316   "affirming themselves": See AW, "To *The Black Scholar*," in *In Search*, p. 320.

317　"The book was written": ECW phone interview with Michele Wallace, November 8, 1996.

317　"I think Michele": ECW electronic correspondence with Robin Morgan, March 25, 2002.

318　"It was a refuge": ECW electronic correspondence with Michele Wallace, March 28, 2002.

318　"I went from obscurity": See Michele Wallace, "To Hell and Back: On the Road with Black Feminism in the 1960s & 1970s," in Rachel Blau DuPlessis and Ann Snitow, eds., *The Feminist Memoir Project* (New York: Three Rivers Press, 1998), p. 426.

320　"Alice asked me": ECW interview with Mary Helen Washington, Silver Spring, MD, March 22, 2000.

320　"from unmerited oblivion": Randall Kennedy, "Looking for Zora," *New York Times Book Review*, December 30, 1979.

324　"forthright, spare": Genevieve Stuttaford, "PW Forecasts," *Publishers Weekly*, July 30, 1979, p. 61.

324　"theatrical": Alan Williamson, "In a Middle Style," *Poetry*, March 1980, pp. 348–354.

Chapter 38: A Room to Move Into

327　"Not to have seen it": Nora Ephron, "Deep Throat," in *Crazy Salad* (New York: Knopf, 1975), p. 62.

328　"legalized rape": See Linda Lovelace, *Ordeal* (New York: Berkley Books, 1980).

328　"With all the hype": ECW interview with Maryam Lowen, New York, NY, October 27, 1997.

329　"[Walker] is exceptionally brave": Alice Adams, "All about Women-Heroines and the Uneasy and Vulnerable," *San Francisco Chronicle and Examiner*, May 10, 1981, pp. F6–7.

329　"edge and sparkle": Katha Pollitt, "Stretching the Short Story," *New York Times Book Review*, May 24, 1981.

329　"ragged, often superficial": "You Can't Keep a Good Woman Down," *Kirkus Reviews*, March 1, 1981.

330　"The Diamonds on Liz's Bosom": AW, *Horses Make a Landscape*, p. 11.

332　"The Second Crucifixion": For discussion of the continuing Nat Turner controversy, see Molefi Kete Asante, "The Real Nat Turner," *Emerge*, March 2000. See also Tony Horwitz, "Untrue Confessions," *New Yorker*, December 13, 1999.

332　"Basically": Yvonne French, "The Confessions of William Styron," Library of Congress Information Bulletin, December 1998, www.loc.gov. Accessed March 1, 2003.

332 "suspended black woman": Mary Helen Washington, "An Essay on Alice Walker," in Roseann P. Bell, Bettye J. Parker, and Beverly Guy-Sheftall, eds., *Sturdy Black Bridges* (New York: Anchor Books, 1979), p. 133.

Chapter 39: Radically Brilliant

334 "country cook": ECW interview with Ruth Walker Hood, Atlanta, GA, October 9, 1995. Subsequent quotes from Hood in this chapter are from this interview.

336 "I carried my sister's comment": AW, "Writing *The Color Purple*," in *In Search*, pp. 355–356.

336 "Toward a Black Feminist Criticism": See Barbara Smith, *The Truth That Never Hurts* (Piscataway, NJ: Rutgers University Press, 1998).

336 "I read *The Color Purple*": ECW interview with Barbara Smith, Atlanta, GA, July 18, 1998.

337 "Dear God": AW, *The Color Purple* (New York, Harcourt, 1982), p. 1.

337 "I make myself": Ibid., p. 23.

338 "Dearest Alice": Gloria Steinem letter to AW, October 25, 1981, AW personal files.

Chapter 40: At a Double Remove

340 "Alice had taken": ECW interview with John Ferrone, New York, NY, July 30, 1996.

341 "The letter method": Sharon Wilson, "A Conversation with Alice Walker," in Henry Louis Gates Jr. and K. A. Appiah, eds., *Alice Walker: Critical Perspectives Past and Present* (New York: Amistad Press, 1993), p. 325.

341 "There was talk": ECW phone interview with Joyce Engleson, March 4, 1996.

342 "I had this": ECW interview with Gloria Steinem, New York, NY, July 18, 1995.

343 "At night in bed": See AW, "Beauty: When the Other Dancer Is the Self," in *In Search*, p. 384.

344 "It is square": AW letter to John Ferrone, November 10, 1981, John Ferrone personal files.

344 "Keep the house": AW letter to John Ferrone, December 1, 1981, John Ferrone personal files.

345 "It was a decided": AW letter to John Ferrone, August 9, 1981, John Ferrone personal files.

Chapter 41. God Love All Them Feelings

346   "Joel Chandler Harris": ECW interview with Ruth Walker Hood, Atlanta, GA, October 8, 1995. All subsequent quotes from Hood in this chapter are from this interview.

348   "permanent importance": Peter S. Prescott, "A Long Road to Liberation," *Newsweek*, June 21, 1982, p. 67.

348   "Language": Rita Mae Brown, "Learning to Escape the Emotional Tower of Babel," *San Francisco Chronicle-Examiner*, July 4, 1982.

348   "a lavishly gifted writer": Mel Watkins, "Some Letters Went to God," *New York Times Book Review*, July 25, 1982, p. 7.

349   "female bonding": Lucille Clifton, " 'The Color Purple' Tells Its Story in Letters," *Baltimore Sun*, July 18, 1992, p. D5.

349   "I bought the book": ECW phone interview with Norah Mellor, October 2002.

350   "Everywhere I went": ECW interview with Yumiko Yanagisawa, Tokyo, Japan, April 24, 1998,

350   "It is my happiest book": Ray Anello with Pamela Abramson, "Characters in Search of a Book," *Newsweek*, June 21, 1982, p. 67.

351   "Here's the thing": See AW, *Color Purple*, pp.199–204.

Chapter 42: The Balance Had Begun to Tilt

353   "My difficulty is with": Peter Prescott letter to Pulitzer administration, n.d., Peter Prescott personal files.

353   "books were talked about": ECW interview with Peter Prescott, New Canaan, CT, July 25, 1996.

354   "had trees in them": J. Douglas Bates, *The Pulitzer Prize* (New York: Birch Lane Press, 1991), p. 125.

354   "Why should I let": Peter Prescott personal files.

354   "but realized this cause": Ibid.

354   "It was a masterpiece": Peter Prescott personal files.

355   "A majority of the 1983": Peter Prescott personal files.

355   "Boys at the Beach": Midge Decter, *Commentary*, September 1980, pp. 35–48. In his essay "Pink Triangle and Yellow Star," Gore Vidal delivered a blistering response to Decter's article. See Vidal, *The Second American Revolution* (New York: Random House, 1982), p. 167.

356   "If you can honestly": Peter Prescott personal files.

356   "What a blend": Peter Prescott personal files.

356   "submitted by their": Midge Decter letter to ECW, September 18, 1997.

356   "couldn't possibly know": ECW interview with Peter Prescott, July 25, 1996.

Chapter 43: Some of Our Work

359   "I feel really happy": Michelle Ross, "Alice Walker Stunned over Pulitzer Prize," *Atlanta Journal-Constitution*, April 19, 1983.

359   "She was her usual": ECW interview with Belvie Rooks, Oakland, CA, February 27, 1997.

361   "an incredible moment": ECW interview with Gloria Steinem, New York, NY, July 18, 1995.

361   "I remembered Miss Minnie Lou": ECW interview with Birda Reynolds, Eatonton, GA, September 30, 1995.

Chapter 44: Through It All

362   "I'd had a huge": ECW interview with Susan Ginsburg, New York, NY, November 1, 1995.

363   Pulitzer festivities: The award prize has since been increased to $7,500.

363   "Alice is a real": ECW interview with Gwendolyn Brooks, Berkeley, CA, April 21, 1997.

364   thirty black children: For bracing examinations of the Atlanta Child Murders, see James Baldwin, *Evidence of Things Not Seen* (New York: Henry Holt, 1985), and Toni Cade Bambara, *Those Bones Are Not My Child* (New York: Pantheon, 1999).

364   "It was like a sentinel": ECW electronic correspondence with Ishmael Reed, July 2, 2001.

364   "Gloria Steinem was": Ibid.

365   "I am more cynical": AW personal files.

365   "Tillie was jealous": ECW phone interview with Susan Kirschner, December 22, 1998.

365   "lack of grace": ECW interview with Tillie Olsen, Berkeley, CA, December 16, 1998.

366   "When I got to her hotel": ECW phone interview with Mona Vold, December 17, 1997.

366   "An Unborn Poet": Muriel Rukeyser, "An Unborn Poet," *American Poetry Review*, November/December 1979, p. 11.

367   "Pagan": AW, *Her Blue Body Everything We Know: Earthling Poems, 1965–1990 Complete* (New York: Harcourt, 1991), p. 420.

368   "They are a kind": AW, "A Thousand Words," in *Living by the Word*, p. 101.

368   "She is short": Ibid., pp. 107–108.

369   "But Alice": Ibid., p. 109.
369   "Just what is it": AW, "My Father's Country Is the Poor," in *In Search*, p. 208.
369   "The more we insisted": Ibid., p. 211.
369   "How could I not": AW, "Hugging Fidel," in *Anything We Love*, p. 200.

Chapter 45: I Try to Make Sense

370   "This [book]": AW letter to John Ferrone, October 5, 1981, John Ferrone personal files.
371   "I have always": ECW electronic correspondence with Rebecca Walker, September 29, 2002.
371   "I am aware": AW letter to John Ferrone, January 26, 1982, John Ferrone personal files.
371   "For me, there": AW, "*One* Child," in *In Search*, pp. 362–364.
372   "It was a very": ECW electronic correspondence with Allison Sampson-Anthony, March 13, 2002.
374   Maria Stewart's 1831: For an excellent compendium of black feminist nonfiction analysis and thought, see Beverly Guy-Sheftall, ed., *Words of Fire* (New York: New Press, 1995). Also see Johnnetta B. Cole and Beverly Guy-Sheftall, eds., *Gender Talk* (New York: Ballantine, 2003).
376   "Alice Walker helped:" ECW phone interview with Rachel Clark, November 6, 2002.
376   "This womanist": Julian Bach, "In Search of Our Mother's [*sic*] Gardens: Womanist Prose," *Publishers Weekly*, September 2, 1983, p. 62.
376   "tough, enchanted": Lucretia B. Ward, "In Search of Our Mothers' Gardens," *Courier-Journal*, October 23, 1983, p. F6.
376   "This is one": Ben Okri, "Colouring Book," *New Statesman*, June 22, 1984, p. 24.
376   "disappointing": Patricia Vigderman, "From Rags to Rage to Art," *Nation*, December 17, 1983, p. 635.
378   "Traveling Watermelon": Ephron, *Crazy Salad*, p. 39.
378   " 'Womanist' ": ECW interview with Barbara Christian, Berkeley, CA, December 12, 1997.
378   "Alice Walker": See Barbara Christian, "Alice Walker: The Black Woman Artist as Wayward," in *Black Feminist Criticism*, p. 81. In the piece, Christian argues that the prevailing motifs in Alice's work are the black woman as creator and how the black woman's efforts to be whole impact the health of her community.
378   "Because Walker emphasizes": ECW electronic corre-

spondence with Rev. Irene Monroe, December 9, 1999.

379 "What we need": Georgette Mosbacher quoted in "I Am 'Womanist': Buy My Blush," *New York Times,* July 19, 1992.

379 Mosbacher . . . thanked Alice: October 5, 1992 letter from Georgette Mosbacher to Alice Walker, AW personal files.

379 "I like the word": Elizabeth Alexander, "Memory, Community, Voice," *Callaloo,* Summer 1994, Vol. 17, No. 2, p. 415.

380 "Oh, it was": ECW interview with Suzanne Murphy, Oakland, CA, May 2, 1998.

381 "By waging her": G. Kirkpatrick, Letters to the Editor, *New York Times Magazine*, February 12, 1984.

Chapter 46: The Glimpse of Life beyond the Words

383 "When I saw her": Sidney Brinkley, "Surviving Words," *Washington Blade*, January 3, 1997, p. 34.

384 "There has to be": Pearl Cleage, "There Has to Be a Chance for Love in a Middle Ground," *Atlanta Journal-Constitution*, September 26, 1982.

384 "Because of my politics": ECW interview with Sonia Sanchez, Oakland, CA, May 20, 1997.

384 "I always had": ECW interview with Mary Hoover, Oakland, CA, May 20, 1997.

384 "canonization": Trudier Harris, "On 'The Color Purple,' Stereotypes and Silence," *Black American Literature Forum*, Winter 1984, pp. 155–161.

385 Donna Green: Richard Colvin, "Mom Objects to Prize Novel for High School Reading List," *Oakland Tribune*, May 3, 1984.

385 "I wouldn't want my child": Colvin, "Mom Objects."

385 "If taken out of context": Ibid.

386 "cabbage patch": Cabbage Patch Kids-soft, chubby-cheeked dolls-took the American toy market by storm and, in 1983, became the "must have" holiday gift for children.

386 "what is said": Brett Martel, "School Board Bans Acclaimed Book," *Associated Press*, November 21, 1997. See also AW, *Alice Walker Banned* (San Francisco: Aunt Lute Books, 1996).

386 "a lie, a black": John Steinbeck, *The Grapes of Wrath* (New York: Penguin, 1992), p. xl.

386 a Boston teacher: See Jonathan Kozol, *Death at an Early Age* (Boston: Houghton Mifflin, 1967), pp. 193–202.

386 "Ballad of the Landlord": Langston Hughes, *Selected Poems*, p. 238.

387 "I am the darker": Langston Hughes, "I, Too," in *Selected Poems*, p. 275.

387 "Put on yo'": Langston Hughes, "Red Silk Stockings," in *Fine Clothes to the Jew* (New York: Knopf, 1927), p. 73.

387 "Let the blare": Langston Hughes, "The Negro Artist and the Racial Mountain," in Gates and McKay, *Norton Anthology*, p. 1267.

387 "Certain forms": AW, "The Glimpse of Life beyond the Words," in *Inside Borders*, Borders Bookstore Magazine, September 1998.

389 "Alice attended": ECW phone interview with J. California Cooper, February 3, 1998.

389 "When you remember": AW, "Mississippi Winter II," in *Horses Make a Landscape*, p. 20.

390 "When they torture": AW, "Torture," in *Horses Make a Landscape*, p. 63.

390 "In the tradition": Sonia Gernes, "Horses Make a Landscape Look More Beautiful," *America*, February 2, 1985, pp. 93–94.

390 "Whatever else": L. M. Rosenberg, "Largesse, Erudition, Wit and Sweetness," *New York Times Book Review*, April 7, 1985, p. 12.

Chapter 47: Something to Lift Spirits

392 *Jaws* became the first: Tom Powers, *Steven Spielberg* (Minneapolis: Lerner Publications, 2000), p. 38.

392 a reported $400 million: Susan Wloszczyna, "Spielberg, Reel to Real," *USA Today*, July 20, 1998, p. D1.

393 "the shortest book": ECW interview with Quincy Jones, Bel Air, CA, August 17, 1998.

393 "felt it was": ECW phone interview with Carole Isenberg, September 28, 1998.

394 "When she agreed": ECW phone interview with Peter Guber, September 16, 2001.

394 "It would be my first time out": ECW interview with Quincy Jones, Bel Air, CA, August 17, 1998.

395 The director would later: DVD release of *The Color Purple*, 2003.

395 "redefine how black women": ECW electronic correspondence with Julie Dash, March 2, 2000.

396 "Dear Julie Dash": AW letter to Julie Dash, May 7, 1980, Julie Dash personal files.

397   With yearly earnings: Shirley Temple Black, *Child Star* (New York: McGraw-Hill, 1988), p. 481.

398   "In order to get": ECW phone interview with Euzhan Palcy, September 4, 2001.

399   "audition": AW, *The Same River Twice: Honoring the Difficult: A Meditation of Life, Spirit, Art, and the Making of the Film,* The Color Purple, *Ten Years Later* (New York: Scribner, 1996), p. 137.

399   "Quincy had talked": AW, *Same River,* pp. 17–18.

Chapter 48: Guide and Protect

401   "From the moment": AW, *Same River*, pp. 24–25.

401   "I loved the way": Ibid., p. 25.

402   "It was Alice": ECW phone interview with Whoopi Goldberg, October 9, 1997. Subsequent quotes from Goldberg are from this interview.

402   "Dear Alice Walker": Whoopi Goldberg letter to Alice Walker, January 10, 1984, AW personal files.

403   "as a black man": ECW interview with Reuben Cannon, Beverly Hills, CA, September 1, 1998.

403   "There were at least": ECW phone interview with Desreta Jackson, October 7, 1998.

403   "either in a Spielberg": ECW interview with Akosua Busia, San Francisco, CA, October 9, 1996.

403   "I blacked out": ECW phone interview with Willard Pugh, August 8, 1998. Subsequent quotes from Pugh in this chapter are from this interview.

403   "there was so little": ECW interview with Margaret Avery, Hollywood, CA, February 17, 1997.

404   "Everybody was all": ECW interview with Quincy Jones, Bel Air, CA, August 17, 1998. Subsequent quotes from Jones in this chapter are from this interview.

404   "like holy water": ECW interview with Oprah Winfrey, Chicago, IL, April 29, 1997. Subsequent quotes from Winfrey in this chapter are from this interview.

405   "At the time": ECW phone interview with Menno Meyjes, March 13, 1998. Subsequent quotes from Meyjes are from this interview.

405   "I had completed": AW, *Same River*, p. 35.

405   Margaret Avery: In 1979, Avery appeared in a public television adaptation of *The Lathe of Heaven* by Ursula K. LeGuin. A remastered DVD edition of this science fiction classic was released

in 2002 by New Video, 126 Fifth Avenue, New York, NY 10011.
www.newvideo.com

406 *Close Encounters*: Powers, *Steven Spielberg*, p. 72.

406 First there was Goldberg's: AW, *Same River*, p. 150.

406 "the greatest movie": Ibid., p. 150.

407 "I was extremely precocious": ECW interview with Rebecca Walker, Oakland, CA, November 10, 2000.

407 "Growing up": Walker, *Black, White, and Jewish*, pp. 4–5.

408 "When my mother": Ibid., pp. 245–247.

408 "I don't really think": Ibid., pp. 248–249.

409 "sexually inattentive": AW, *Same River*, p. 27.

410 "I was very pleased": Elena Featherston, *Visions of the Spirit*, documentary (New York: Women Make Movies, 1989). See info@wmm.com and www.womenmakemovies.com.

410 "I am studying": AW, *Same River*, p. 28.

410 "sweetness, intelligence": Ibid., p. 27.

410 "homospiritual": See AW, "All the Bearded Irises of Life: Confessions of a Homospiritual," in *Living by the Word*, p. 163.

411 admiration of an Adrienne: *On Lies, Secrets, and Silence* also included "The Antifeminist Woman," Rich's ringing condemnation of *The New Chastity and Other Arguments against Women's Liberation* by Midge Decter.

411 "I keep feeling": AW letter to Tillie Olsen, July 14, 1980, Stanford University Library, Stanford, CA.

411 "I suppose I feel lesbianism": AW letter to Tillie Olsen, August 12, 1980, Stanford University Library.

411 "Really, *Doesn't* Crime Pay?": AW, *In Love & Trouble*, p. 10.

411 "Back then": ECW interview with Fannie Howe, Berkeley, CA, February 2, 1997.

411 "Alice was a lone voice": ECW interview with Ann Allen Shockley, Nashville, TN, February 12, 2003.

412 Alice began her review: See AW, "Breaking Chains and Encouraging Life," in *In Search*, p. 278.

413 "Alice was highly visible": ECW interview with Barbara Smith, Atlanta, GA, July 18, 1998.

414 "Any sister": Elaine Brown, panel discussion remarks, Yari Yari: An International Conference on Literature by Women of African Descent, New York University, NY, October 18, 1997.

414 "carefully packaged": Coalition Against Black Exploitation (CABE) letter to Warner Bros. Films, July 10, 1985, AW personal files.

414 "One must suspect": CABE "action bulletin," April 1985, AW personal files.

Chapter 49: More Than Many Hoped

416 December 18, 1985: The movie would also feature a nod to the April 18 date that Alice won the Pulitzer Prize. As written in the novel, none of the letters bear dates. However, the first letter that the character Celie reads out loud, in the movie, is dated April 18, 1935.

416 "There was major tension": ECW interview with Belvie Rooks, Oakland, CA, February 27, 1997.

416 "There was a whole": ECW interview with Robert Allen, Oakland, CA, May 24, 1996.

417 "The kiss on the lips": Philip Taylor, *Steven Spielberg* (New York: Continuum, 1999), pp. 115–116.

418 "a scenic drive": Peter Kobel, "Nabokov Won't Be Nailed Down," *New York Times,* April 22, 2001.

418 "I know Alice": See Toni Morrison, as quoted in *Massachusetts Review,*Vol. 36, No. 3., 1995, pp. 455–473.

419 "Without Quincy": ECW phone interview with Peter Guber, September 16, 2001.

420 "I was elated": ECW phone interview with Ruth Walker Hood, August 20, 1996.

420 "I think he": ECW electronic correspondence with Julie Dash, March 2, 2000.

420 "I see myself": Whoopi Goldberg quoted by Jeffrey Day, "If You Want to Understand, See Movie Then Read Book," *Macon Telegraph and News,* January 1986.

420 "*The Color Purple*": Ibid.

421 "Early on": David Ansen, "We Shall Overcome," *Newsweek,* December 30, 1985, p. 59.

421 "change-of-pace-movie": Judy Stone, "Many Shades of Purple," *San Francisco Chronicle,* December 20, 1985.

421 "a grand, multi-hanky": Janet Maslin, "Film: 'The Color Purple,' from Steven Spielberg," *New York Times,* December 18, 1985.

421 "too noble": Richard Corliss, "The Three Faces of Steve," *Time,* December 23, 1985.

421 "Mr. Reagan": Vernon Jarrett, as quoted in E. R. Shipp, "Blacks in Heated Debate over *The Color Purple*," *New York Times,* January 27, 1986.

422 "Our people's hunger": "Farrakhan on *The Color Purple*," videotape by Minister Louis Farrakhan (Chicago: AVC Records and Tapes, Circa 1986).

Chapter 50: She Liked Everything She Saw

423   "After I finished": ECW phone interview with Ruth Walker Hood, April 29, 2002. Subsequent quotes from Hood are from this interview.

424   receipts of nearly $200 million: AW, *Same River*, p. 266.

426   "If you missed out": Sloan Gregory, "Putnam Greets Pulitzer Prize Winner," *Eatonton Messenger*, January 23, 1986, p. 1.

427   "Talk about having a fit": ECW interview with Doris Reid, Decatur, GA, September 28, 1995.

Chapter 51: The World Is Held Together

428   "Most Dangerous Film": "Most Dangerous Film since 'Birth of a Nation,' " Ernece B. Kelley, *Guardian*, February 19, 1986.

428   "There'd always been": ECW interview with Daphne Muse, Oakland, CA, December 1, 1997.

429   "I will not read": ECW phone interview with Catherine McKinley, May 22, 1996.

429   "Alice had": ECW phone interview with Judy Dothard Simmons, July 15, 1996.

429   "In terms of": ECW phone interview with a source who requested anonymity, March 1996.

429   "She's a black woman": See "Davis, Angela," in Darlene Clark Hine, ed., *Black Women in America: An Historical Encyclopedia*, Vol. I (Brooklyn: Carlson Publishing, 1993), p. 306.

430   "*The Color Purple*": ECW interview with Angela Davis, Oakland, CA, October 9, 1997.

430   "do things crooked": ECW interview with Curtis Walker, Atlanta, GA, September 27, 1995.

431   "a white man's movie": See AW, *Same River*, pp. 223–225.

431   "I dislike the movie": Spike Lee, *Phil Donahue Show*, April 25, 1986.

431   "I thought that": Taylor, *Steven Spielberg*, pp. 118–119.

431   "Celie's story": ECW phone interview with Danny Glover, August 31, 1998.

432   "After a while": ECW interview with Reuben Cannon, Beverly Hills, CA, September 1, 1998.

432   "I was disappointed": ECW interview with Oprah Winfrey, Chicago, IL, April 29, 1997.

432   "creative producers": www.oscars.org/academyawards. Accessed January 19, 2004.

432   "As the person": ECW phone interview with Peter Guber, September 16, 2001.

433   "pissy political fight": ECW phone interview with Whoopi Goldberg, October 9, 1997. The Hollywood NAACP would again generate controversy when the organization nominated the movie *Barbershop* (2002) for its annual Image Awards. In the film, the black comic known as Cedric the Entertainer plays the role of a cantankerous barber. Taking aim at civil rights legends, Cedric's character asserts that other blacks had refused to give up their bus seats to whites in the segregated South, but that only Rosa Parks received credit. The character also makes "jokes" about the alleged promiscuity of Martin Luther King Jr. Invited to attend the awards ceremony because a film about her life, *The Rosa Parks Story* (starring Angela Bassett), was also slated for honors, Parks declined. "We with many others do not understand the endorsement the NAACP gave to the hurtful jokes in the movie *Barbershop*," Parks declared. Calling the uproar, "overblown," NAACP president Kwesi Mfume noted that "people have varied opinions on art."

433   "I'd never crossed a picket line": Black actor-activist Paul Robeson was also confronted with picket lines at the 1942 Los Angeles premiere of what would be his last film, *Tales of Manhattan*. An O. Henry–style saga told in a series of vignettes about the effect of a formal tailcoat on its various owners, Robeson played a sharecropper who gets a windfall when the coat, stuffed with $43,000, drops from an airplane. Deeming the cash a blessing from "de Lawd," Robeson and his wife (played by Ethel Waters) distribute the money throughout their impoverished community. The black press hated it, and Robeson, complaining that Hollywood had turned his character into a "plantation hallelujah shouter," pledged to join any future picket lines. Fed up, Robeson eventually called a press conference and announced his retirement from the film industry. With its depiction of the love, generosity, and unity of poor, rural blacks, *Tales of Manhattan* is not, to this viewer's mind, without redeeming qualities.

434   Willie Nelson: *Tonight Show*, March 25, 1986.

434   "there doesn't need to be any": *Phil Donahue Show*, April 25, 1986. Bill Cosby's remarks were made during a segment in which Donahue previewed the entertainer's appearance on a future show.

434   "I will not": Meghann Otinerv letter to AW, April 27, 1984, AW personal files.

434   "It was absolutely staggering": ECW interview with Joan Miura, Berkeley, CA, December 10, 1999.

435   "deep-down hater": AW, "In the Closet of the Soul," in *Living by the Word*, p. 78.

435   "There is a section": *Alice Walker*, Lannon video.

435   "A silent lake": AW, "African Images, Glimpses from a Tiger's Back," in *Once*, p. 6.

436   "He rather adored": ECW phone interview with Alexa Birdsong, October 25, 2002.

436   "With strength": Baldwin, "Sweet Lorraine," in *The Price of the Ticket*, p. 443.

437   "There will be bloody": James Baldwin, *No Name in the Street* (New York: Dial Press, 1972), p. 197.

437   "Knowing that": ECW phone interview with Gus Newport, November 2000.

437   "Black women writers": Hernton, *The Sexual Mountain and Black Women Writers* (New York: Anchor Books, 1987), p. xxi.

437   "Love has never been": *The Price of the Ticket*, documentary, Karen Thorsen (director). (Produced in association with American Masters and Maysles Films, 1990). See also Smith, "We Must Always Bury Our Dead Twice: A Tribute to James Baldwin," in *Truth That Never Hurts*, p. 75.

Chapter 52: They Saw the Airplane Coming

439   "abiding obsession": Judith Paterson, "The Abiding Spiritual Obsessions of Novelist Alice Walker," *Chicago Tribune*, July 17, 1988.

439   "In her fiction": Jill Nelson, "The World According to Alice Walker," *Washington Post Book World*, May 29, 1988, p. X3.

440   "Each was to the other": AW, "Turning into Love: Some Thoughts on Surviving and Meeting Langston Hughes," *Callaloo*, Autumn 1989, Vo. 4, No. 41, pp. 663–666.

441   "You can imagine": ECW interview with Beverly Guy-Sheftall, Palo Alto, CA, June 24, 1998.

441   "unveiling the complexity": ECW interview with Johnnetta Cole, Atlanta, GA, July 17, 1998.

442   "She caught me": See AW, *Same River*, p. 15.

442   "I told Alice": ECW phone interview with Elizabeth Ross, February 11, 1997.

442   "I had just started": ECW electronic correspondence with Jean Weisinger, February 7, 2002.

443   "two-spirited": AW, opening remarks, National Black

Gay and Lesbian Leadership Forum, Long Beach Hilton, Long Beach, CA, February 15, 1997.

443 "She could have": ECW interview with a man who requested anonymity, Long Beach, CA, February 16, 1997.

444 "I was vilified": ECW interview with Ani DiFranco, Oakland, CA, October 25, 2002.

444 "bitterly antibisexual": ECW interview with Ibrahim Farajaje-Jones, Berkeley, CA, April 18, 2002.

444 "sex outlaws": ECW electronic correspondence with Anastasia Higginbotham, February 25, 2002.

445 "I'm bisexual": "Alice's Wonderland," *Essence*, February 1996, p. 84. In her book, *Bisexuality and the Challenge to Lesbian Politics* (New York: New York University Press, 1995), Paula C. Rust poses the questions, "Does bisexuality really exist, or is it a phase one goes through while coming out as a lesbian? Is bisexuality a sign of political cowardice among those who are unwilling to give up heterosexual privilege, or is it the next step in sexual liberation?"

445 "They'd been given to me": Patricia Holt, "Walker Focuses on the Universal," *San Francisco Chronicle*, May 27, 1989

446 "When you love someone": AW, *The Temple of My Familiar* (New York: Harcourt, 1989), pp. 369–371.

446 "I wondered": Holt, "Walker Focuses."

447 "The richness": Ursula K. Le Guin, "All Those at the Banquet," *San Francisco Review of Books*, Summer 1989, p. 12.

447 "hootchie-cootchie dance": James Wolcott, "Party of Animals," *New Republic*, May 29, 1989, p. 28.

447 "catalogue of goofy": David Nicholson, "The Temple of My Familiar," *Washington Post Book World*, May 7, 1989.

447 "*The Temple* has": Christopher Lehmann-Haupt, "Alice Walker Stresses Man's Cruelty," *New York Times*, April 27, 1989.

447 "Cliché-ridden prose": J. M. Coetzee, "The Beginnings of (Wo)man in Africa," *New York Times*, April 30, 1989, p. 7.

447 "The Sunday *Book*": ECW electronic correspondence with Charles McGrath, December 3, 2002.

448 "If God ever listened": AW, *Color Purple*, p. 199.

448 "I think I'm being reviewed": Pamela Reynolds, "Alice Walker Walks Alone," *Boston Globe*, May 6, 1989.

448 "It is a formidable achievement": ECW electronic correspondence with Ishmael Reed, July 2, 2001.

449 "It's like any other thing": Reynolds, "Alice Walker Walks Alone."

450 "I was very moved": ECW phone interview with Len Riggio, July 26, 2002.

451   "We created a net": ECW electronic correspondence with Zelie Duvauchelle, December 11, 2001.

451   "reminds me always": AW, *Warrior Marks: Female Genital Mutilation and the Sexual Blinding of Women* (New York: Harcourt, 1993), p. 356.

451   "I don't think": ECW electronic correspondence with Chana Kai Lee, August 17, 2003. See Lee, *For Freedom's Sake* (Urbana: University of Illinois Press, 1999).

Epilogue: It's All Love

456   "In being transgressive": ECW phone interview with Thomas Glave, November 1, 2002.

456   "Alice Walker [was denounced]": Hernton, "Who's Afraid of Alice Walker?" in *Sexual Mountain*, pp. 6–7.

456   Michiko Kakutani: "If the River Is Dry, Can You Be All Wet?" *New York Times*, April 20, 2004, p. B7.

458   "I'd read Alice's": ECW phone interview with Judyann Elder, December 9, 2002.

458   "I wouldn't have": Craigh Barboza, "White Man's Burden," *Vibe*, February 1998.

458   "with tenderness and respect": Tina McElroy Ansa, *Los Angeles Times*, July 5, 1992.

459   "I wish Alice": ECW interview with a source who requested anonymity.

459   "As far as I'm concerned": Paula Giddings, "Alice Walker's Appeal," *Essence*, July 1992.

459   "Alice Walker planted": ECW phone interview with Stephanie Welsh, October 18, 1996.

460   "A culture that subjects": ECW interview with Fauziya Kassindja, Berkeley, CA, March 30, 1998.

460   "respect women's right": Michele Landsberg, "U.N. Recognizes Women Double Victims of AIDS," *Toronto Star*, July 1, 2001.

460   "We passed the hat": See "Alice Walker on Activism," *The Black Collegian*, 1st Semester Super Issue 1997. Also see Mumia Abu-Jamal, *All Things Censored* (New York: Seven Stories Press, 2000).

460   "She is righteous": ECW interview with Assata Shakur, Havana, Cuba, January 3, 1997. See also Assata Shakur, *Assata: An Autobiography* (Chicago: Lawrence Hill Books, 1987).

460   "visit the White House": AW, "A Letter to President

Clinton," *Anything We Love Can Be Saved* (New York: Random House, 1997), p. 215.

461   Supreme Court Justice: See Anita Hill, *Speaking Truth to Power* (New York: Doubleday, 1997).

461   "Given our friendship": ECW interview with Mary Helen Washington, Silver Spring, MD, March 22, 2000.

461   "We'd worked together": ECW phone interview with John Ferrone, circa 1999.

462   "Dear Ms. Walker": Ruth Walker Hood personal files.

462   "Whatever the word": AW personal files.

463   "Alice taught me": ECW interview with Wilma Mankiller, Navarro, CA, February 10, 1997.

463   "Love is big": Esther Iverem, "An Interview with Alice Walker," March 12, 2003, www.SeeingBlack.com. Accessed March 13, 2003.

Selected Bibliography

Adams, Charles C. *A Wee Deek on Boont Harpin's (A Brief Introduction to Boontling)*. Boonville, CA: Boontlingers Club.

Awiakta, Marilou. *Abiding Appalachia: Where Mountain and Atom Meet*. Memphis: St. Luke's Press, 1978.

Baldwin, James. *No Name in the Street*. New York: Dial Press, 1972.

———. *The Price of the Ticket*. New York: St. Martin's Press, 1985.

Bates, J. Douglas. *The Pulitzer Prize*. New York: Birch Lane Press, 1991.

Bell, Roseann P., Bettye J. Parker, and Beverly Guy-Sheftall, eds. *Sturdy Black Bridges*. New York: Anchor, 1979.

Bennett, Lerone, Jr. *Before the Mayflower*. New York: Penguin, 1986.

Black, Shirley Temple. *Child Star*. New York: McGraw-Hill, 1988.

Boyd, Valerie. *Wrapped in Rainbows: The Life of Zora Neale Hurston*. New York: Scribner, 2003.

Bridges, Robert, ed. *Poems of Gerard Manley Hopkins*. London: Oxford University Press, 1930.

Brooks, Gwendolyn. *Report from Part One*. Detroit: Broadside Press, 1972.

Cade, Toni, ed. *The Black Woman*. New York: New American Library, 1970.

Cagin, Seth, and Philip Dray. *We Are Not Afraid*. New York: Macmillan, 1988.

Campbell, James. *Talking at the Gates: A Life of James Baldwin*. New York: Viking, 1991.

Christian, Barbara. *Black Feminist Criticism*. Elmsford, NY: Pergamon Press, 1985.

Coleman, Kenneth, ed. *A History of Georgia*. Athens, GA: University of Georgia Press, 1977.

Cooper, Jane. *Scaffolding*. Gardiner, ME: Tilbury House Publishers, 1993.

Davis, Angela Y. *An Autobiography*. New York: Random House, 1974.

Dove, Rita. *The Poet's World*. Washington, D.C.: Library of Congress, 1995.

DuPlessis, Rachel Blau, and Ann Snitow, eds. *The Feminist Memoir Project*. New York: Three Rivers Press, 1998.

Ellison, Ralph. *Invisible Man*. New York: Random House, 1952.

Ephron, Nora. *Crazy Salad*. New York: Knopf, 1975.

Faulkner, William. *Go Down, Moses*. New York: Library of America Literary Classics, 1994. First published in 1942 by Random House.

Fitzgerald, Sally, ed. Flannery O'Connor: *The Habit of Being*. New York: Farrar, Straus & Giroux, 1979.

Franklin, John Hope. *From Slavery to Freedom*. New York: Knopf, 1980.

Freeman, Ronald L. *A Communion of Spirits: African American Quilters, Preservers and Their Stories*. Nashville: Rutledge Hill Press, 1996.

Friedan, Betty. *The Feminine Mystique*. New York: Norton, 1963.

Garrison, Webb. *Oglethorpe's Folly: The Birth of Georgia*. Lakemont, GA: Copple House Books, 1982.

Garrity, John A., and Peter Gay, eds. *The Columbia History of the World*. New York: Harper & Row, 1972.

Gates, Henry Louis, Jr., and K.A. Appiah, eds. *Alice Walker: Critical Perspectives Past and Present*. New York: Amistad Press, 1993.

———.Zora Neale Hurston: *Critical Perspectives Past and Present*. New York: Amistad Press, 1993.

Gates, Henry Louis, Jr., and Nellie Y. McKay, eds. *The Norton Anthology of African American Literature*. New York: Norton, 1997.

Giddings, Paula. *When and Where I Enter: The Impact of Black Women on Race and Sex in America*. New York: Bantam, 1984.

Giovanni, Nikki. *Black Feeling, Black Talk, Black Judgement*. New York: William Morrow, 1970.

Gitlin, Todd. *The Sixties: Years of Hope, Days of Rage*. New York: Bantam, 1987.

Goldschneider, Gary, and Joost Elffers. *The Secret Language of Birthdays*. New York: Penguin Studio, 1994.

Grant, Donald L. *The Way It Was in the South: The Black Experience in Georgia*. New York: Birch Lane Press, 1993.

Guy-Sheftall, Beverly, and Jo Moore Stewart. *Spelman: A Centennial Celebration*. Atlanta: Spelman College, 1981.

Haydn, Hiram. *Words & Faces*. New York: Harcourt, 1974.

Heilbrun, Carolyn. *The Education of A Woman: The Life of Gloria Steinem*. New York: Dial Press, 1995.

Hemenway, Robert E. *Zora Neale Hurston: A Literary Biography*. Urbana: University of Illinois Press, 1977.

Hemschemeyer, Judith, trans. *The Complete Poems of Anna Akhmatova*. Boston: Zephyr Press, 1992.

Hernton, Calvin C. *The Sexual Mountain and Black Women Writers*. New York: Anchor Books, 1987.

Hine, Darlene Clark, ed. *Black Women in America: An Historical Encyclopedia*. Brooklyn: Carlson Publishing, 1993.

Hughes, Langston. *The Best Short Stories by Negro Writers*. New York: Little, Brown, 1967.

———. *Black Misery*. New York: Paul S. Eriksson, 1969.

———. *Fine Clothes to the Jew*. New York: Knopf, 1927.

———. *Selected Poems. New York*: Vintage Books, 1974.

Hurston, Zora Neale. *Dust Tracks on a Road*. Urbana: University of Illinois Press, 1984. First published in 1942 by J. B. Lippincott.

———. *Mules and Men*. Bloomington: Indiana University Press, 1978. First published in 1935 by J. B. Lippincott.

———. *Their Eyes Were Watching God*. Urbana: University of Illinois Press, 1978. First published in 1937 by J. B. Lippincott.

Jones, LeRoi, and Larry Neal, eds. *Black Fire*. New York: William Morrow, 1968.

Jones, Robert B., and Margery Toomer Latimer, eds. *The Collected Poems of Jean Toomer*. Chapel Hill: University of North Carolina Press, 1988.

Kael, Pauline. *For Keeps: Thirty Years at the Movies*. New York: Dutton, 1994.

Kozol, Jonathan. *Death at an Early Age*. Boston: Houghton Mifflin, 1967.

Levi, Jan Heller, ed. *A Muriel Rukeyser Reader*. New York: Norton, 1994.

Lewis, John. *Walking With The Wind: A Memoir Of The*

Movement. New York: Simon & Schuster, 1989.

Lynd, Helen. *Field Work in College Education*. New York: Columbia University Press, 1945.

Martin, Wendy, ed. *The Beacon Book of Essays by Contemporary American Women*. Boston: Beacon Press, 1996.

McQuade, Molly, ed. *By Herself: Women Reclaim Poetry*. St. Paul, MN: Graywolf Press, 2000.

Merrill, Charles. *The Walled Garden: The Story of a School*. Boston: Rowan Tree Press, 1982.

Michener, James. *The Covenant*. New York: Fawcett Crest, 1980.

Morgan, Robin. *The Demon Lover*. New York: Norton, 1989.

Munro, Sheila. *Lives of Mothers & Daughters*. Toronto: McClelland & Stewart, 2001.

O'Brien, John, ed. *Interviews with Black Writers*. New York: Liveright, 1973.

Ono, Yoko. *Grapefruit*. New York: Simon & Schuster, 1970.

Powers, Tom. *Steven Spielberg*. Minneapolis: Lerner Publications, 2000.

Prenshaw, Peggy Whitman. *Conversations with Eudora Welty*. Jackson: University of Mississippi Press, 1984.

Rich, Adrienne. *On Lies, Secrets, and Silence: Selected Prose 1966–1978*. New York: Norton, 1979.

Roethke, Theodore. *The Collected Poems*. New York: Doubleday, 1966.

Rose, Phyllis. *Jazz Cleopatra: Josephine Baker in Her Time*. New York: Doubleday, 1989.

Rukeyser, Muriel. *The Collected Poems of Muriel Rukeyser*. New York: McGraw-Hill, 1978.

Savigneau, Josyane. *Carson McCullers: A Life*. Boston: Houghton Mifflin, 2001.

Smith, Barbara. *The Truth That Never Hurts*. Piscataway, NJ: Rutgers University Press, 1998. :

Steinbeck, John. *The Grapes of Wrath*. New York: Penguin, 1992. First published in 1939 by Viking Press.

Steinem, Gloria. *Outrageous Acts and Everyday Rebellions*. New York: New American Library, 1983.

Styron, William. *The Confessions of Nat Turner*. New York: Signet Books, 1968.

Tate, Claudia, ed. *Black Women Writers at Work*. New York: Continuum, 1986.

Taylor, Philip. *Steven Spielberg*. New York: Continuum, 1999.

Thom, Mary. *Inside Ms*. New York: Henry Holt, 1997.

Thompson, Kathleen, and Hilary MacAustin, eds. *The Face of Our Past: Images of Black Women from Colonial America to the*

Present. Bloomington: Indiana University Press, 1999.

Toomer, Jean. *Cane.* New York: Liveright, 1923.

University of Georgia Press. *The New Georgia Guide.* Athens: University of Georgia Press, 1996.

Walker, Alice. *Anything We Love Can Be Saved: A Writer's Activism.* New York: Random House, 1997.

————. *The Color Purple: A Novel.* New York: Harcourt, 1982.

————. *Good Night, Willie Lee, I'll See You in the Morning: Poems.* New York: Dial Press, 1979.

————.*Her Blue Body Everything We Know: Earthling Poems, 1965–1990 Complete.* New York: Harcourt, 1991.

————. *Horses Make a Landscape Look More Beautiful: Poems.* New York: Harcourt, 1984.

————. *In Love & Trouble: Stories of Black Women.* New York: Harcourt, 1973.

————. *In Search of Our Mothers' Gardens: Womanist Prose.* New York: Harcourt, 1983

————. *Langston Hughes, American Poet.* New York: Crowell, 1974

————. *Living by the Word: Selected Writings, 1973–1987.* New York: Harcourt, 1988.

————. *Meridian.* New York: Harcourt, 1976.

————. *Once; Poems.* New York: Harcourt, 1968.

————. *Revolutionary Petunias & Other Poems.* New York: Harcourt, 1973.

————. *The Same River Twice: Honoring the Difficult: A Meditation of Life, Spirit, Art, and the Making of the Film, The Color Purple, Ten Years Later.* New York: Scribner, 1996.

————. *The Temple of My Familiar.* New York: Harcourt, 1989.

————. *The Third Life of Grange Copeland.* New York: Pocket Books, 1988. First published in 1970 by Harcourt.

———— (with Pratibha Parmar). *Warrior Marks: Female Genital Mutilation and the Sexual Blinding of Women.* New York: Harcourt, 1993.

————. *The Way Forward Is with a Broken Heart.* New York: Ballantine, 2000.

————. *You Can't Keep A Good Woman Down: Stories.* New York: Harcourt, 1981.

Walker, Alice, ed. *I Love Myself When I Am Laughing . . . and Then Again When I Am Looking Mean and Impressive: A Zora Neale Hurston Reader.* New York: Feminist Press, 1979.Walker, Margaret. Richard Wright: *Daemonic Genius.* New York: Amistad Press, 1988.

Walker, Rebecca. *Black, White, and Jewish*. New York: Riverhead, 2001.

Wallace, Michele. *Black Macho and the Myth of the Superwoman*. New York: Warner Books, 1978.

Washington, James M., ed. *A Testament of Hope: The Essential Writings and Speeches of Martin Luther King, Jr*. New York: HarperCollins, 1986.

Welty, Eudora. *Eudora Welty Stories, Essays, & Memoir*. New York: Library of America, 1998.

Williams, Juan. *Eyes on the Prize: America's Civil Rights Years, 1954–1965*. New York: Penguin Books, 1987.

Zinn, Howard. *You Can't Be Neutral on a Moving Train: A Personal History of Our Times*. Boston: Beacon Press, 1994.

Permissions

Photo Credits

Grant and Walker with their children. Courtesy of Alice Walker.

Mary Poole. Courtesy of Alice Walker.

Curtis Walker. Photo by Larry Moore, 2003.

Minnie Lou and Willie Lee Walker. Courtesy of Alice Walker.

Alice and Bill Walker. Courtesy of Gaynell-Joyner Walker.

Alice, about age six Courtesy of Alice Walker.

Ophthalmologist Morriss Henry. Photo by author, 1995.

Birda Reynolds. Photo by author, 1995.

High school memory book, 1961. Courtesy of Alice Walker.

Alice Walker and David DeMoss. Courtesy of David DeMoss.

Alice Walker with Spelman College classmates. Courtesy of Alice Walker.

Alice Walker with Howard Zinn. Photo by Sean Connelly, 2002.

Alice and Muriel Rukeyser. Courtesy of Alice Walker.

Jane Cooper. Courtesy of Jane Cooper.

Carole Darden. Photo by author, 1995.

Alice Walker and Mel Leventhal, with pet dog Andrew. Courtesy of Alice Walker.

Alice, Mel, and their daughter Rebecca. Courtesy of Ruth Walker Hood.

Alice, Mel, and Rebecca, circa 1970. Courtesy of Ruth Walker Hood.

"The Problem We All Live With." A 1964 painting by Norman Rockwell. Reproduced by permision of the Norman Rockwell Family Agency, LLC. Collection of The Norman Rockwell Museum at Stockbridge, Massachussetts.

Mississippi police responding to group of freedom fighters. Photo by Danny Lyon, 1963, Magnum Photos.

The Sisterhood. Courtesy of Alice Walker.

The inscription Langston Hughes wrote to Alice. Courtesy of Alice Walker.

"The Shakespeare of Harlem." Courtesy of the book's illustrator, Catherine Deeter.

The June 1982 cover of Ms. magazine. Courtesy of Alice Walker.

Gloria Steinem and Alice Walker. Photo by Jen Siska, 2000.

Estella Perry. Courtesy of the Mildred Smith family.

Robert Allen, Alice Walker, and Rebecca Walker. Courtesy of Alice Walker.

Alice Walker and Robert Allen. Courtesy of Alice Walker.

Oprah Winfrey, Rebecca Walker, Alice Walker, and Quincy Jones. Courtesy of Alice Walker.

Alice and Rebecca Walker, early 1990s. Photo by Jean Weisinger.

Alice with her mother, Minnie Lou Walker. Courtesy of Alice Walker.

The headstone Alice placed on the unmarked grave of Zora Neale Hurston. Photo by Stephanie Welsh, 1998.

Alice Walker, Ding Ling, Paule Marshall, and Tillie Olsen. Courtesy of Alice Walker.

Alice Walker with portrait of Virginia Woolf. Photo by Tom Levy.

Alice Walker with Cuban president Fidel Castro. Photo by Gloria LaRiva, courtesy of Alice Walker.

Ruth Walker Hood and Mamie Walker. Photo by author, 1995.

Alice, Bill, and Gaye Walker. Photo by author, 1996.

Alice, Curtis, Jimmy, Fred, and Ruth Walker. Photo by author.

Family friend and Bobby Walker. Courtesy of Yeshi Neumann.

Temple Jook House with Luna Mahala goddess sculpture. Photo by author, 1995.

Admirers of Alice Walker. Photo by author, 1995.

Alice Walker with great-nephews, neice, Ruth Walker, and Jean Weisinger. Photo by Jean Weisinger, circa 1996.

Alice Walker and William Poy Lee. Courtesy of Alice Walker.

Tracy Chapman and Alice Walker. Courtesy of Alice Walker.

Tracy Chapman, Clarissa Pinkola Estes, Ruth Walker Hood, Gloria Steinem, Jean Shinola Bolen, Angela Davis, Carole Darden, Joan Miura, Wilma Mankiller, Belvie Rooks, Alice, Aneta Chapman, and June Jordan. Courtesy of Alice Walker.

James Baldwin. Photo by Phiz Mezey, 1964.

Alice Walker in velvet dress. Photo by Jean Weisinger.

Index